SAGE WARRIOR

"A wondrous pilgrimage to the Sikh world! This rich literary, visual, aural magnet pulls us: We travel with the author and her family to her sacred sites and meet historic figures—with their mothers, wives, sisters, daughters, nieces, and comrades who have been neglected in history. We actively participate in momentous Sikh events; we see, we hear, we smell, we taste, we feel. All along, the activist Valarie Kaur trains us to be sensuously alive, morally awake—the goal of Guru Nanak, the founder of the Sikh religion himself. Through a stunning, imaginative interweaving of the past with the present, history with imagination, Punjab with California, we are led to the all-inclusive divine One within. This is a transformative text, a must for our dangerously divided and polarized times."

—Dr. Nikky-Guninder Kaur, Sikh scholar and author of
The First Sikh: The Life and Legacy of Guru Nanak

"Valarie Kaur is an intergenerational fire carrier. *Sage Warrior* offers the embers of ancient wisdom that bring alive her deep Sikh tradition in ways that shape character and courage for the living of our most daunting days. Open any page. You will find insight and light for whatever challenge you face today. In these toxic times, Kaur has truly given us a living library."

—John Paul Lederach, peacebuilder and author of
The Moral Imagination: The Art and Soul of Building Peace

"I have witnessed the powerful wisdom of my sister Valarie as she gives herself to today's justice movements. What a joy to learn from her about the sage warriors of her Sikh tradition. I'm blessed to know the deep wells she drinks from and the rich formation that fortifies her soul. May this book strengthen all of us."

—Bishop William J. Barber, II, co-chair of the
Poor People's Campaign and author of *White Poverty*

"In reclaiming the stories of women in Sikh history, Valarie Kaur breathes new life into us all, restoring the true birthright of the human family: to live as wisdom keepers and champions of justice, to honor the gift of spirit rooted in our own bodies, intimate relationships, and communities, and to take our place in the circle of interbeing to which we belong. This book is a homecoming."

—Mirabai Starr, author of *Wild Mercy* and *Caravan of No Despair*

"Valarie Kaur is a balm-maker. She churns potions to heal and inspire. Hers is a voice of Revolutionary Love—a voice of resistance and resilience, a sovereign voice. She commands that voice to ensure goodness and equality for all. In *Sage Warrior,* Kaur revives the women ancestors in Gur-Sikh history. She continues the nearly forgotten line of storytelling, kathā, from ancient India. Her kathā is of stories told and untold, of service, sacrifice, and humility ornate. The Sikh Gurus' gifts to the world—their extraordinary music, words of wisdom, and sacrifices—would not be possible without the wondrous and protective leadership of mothers, sisters, spouses, daughters, and saintly women warriors. To remember these near-silenced voices is to honor them—and, ultimately, to be transformed by them. *Sage Warrior* is a gift born of hard-earned, agenda-less, holistic activism."

—Bhai Baldeep Singh, Sikh educator, musician, and revivalist of Sikh wisdom and music traditions

"Valarie Kaur's *Sage Warrior* brings the contribution of Sikh women to the forefront of Sikh history, a history dominated by malestream scholarship. Combining ethnographic work with Sikh narratives in lucid conversational style, it will inspire new generations. This book belongs to every Sikh household. A brilliant achievement!"

—Pashaura Singh, Ph.D., Sikh historian, scholar, and author of *The Oxford Handbook of Sikh Studies*

"Drawing on illuminating stories from the Sikh tradition and her own brilliant imagination, Valarie Kaur takes us on a mystical journey that calls forth our own natural courage, wisdom, and love-based activism. *Sage Warrior* is powerful and much-needed medicine for our times; it inspires us to join hands and create the world we long for."
—Tara Brach, author of *Radical Compassion*

"*Sage Warrior* is radical, mystical nutritional juice for transforming a world on fire. Drink up!"
—V (formerly Eve Ensler), playwright of *The Vagina Monologues*

"A beautiful, hopeful, heartfelt treasure of a book, *Sage Warrior* will enrich your soul, grow your knowledge base, and inspire your activism. If you want to achieve progressive ideals while bridging divides, this is the book for you."
—Eboo Patel, founder of Interfaith America and author of
We Need to Build: Field Notes for Diverse Democracy

"For over a decade, Valarie Kaur has been a beacon in dark times for me, a mentor who keeps shedding light on the ancient question 'How, then, shall we live?' In *See No Stranger*, she gave me and countless others a way forward in our quest for the Beloved Community. In *Sage Warrior*, she reaches deep into her life of revolutionary love to share the stream of Sikhism from which she draws insight, guidance, and resilience. Whatever wisdom tradition informs your life and work, Kaur shows us how to join hands with the ancestors of legend and history for the strength we need to keep walking into the fierce urgency of now."
—Parker J. Palmer, author of *Let Your Life Speak*,
Healing the Heart of Democracy, and *On the Brink of Everything*

"*Sage Warrior* is a treasure chest of hope and inspiration. Valarie Kaur digs deep into her beautiful, sacred Sikh faith tradition to bring us tools of wisdom and oneness when we need it most."
—Rainn Wilson, *New York Times* bestselling author of
Soul Boom: Why We Need a Spiritual Revolution

"Waking to oneness has become the new focus of my life's work and, as usual, Valarie Kaur is right there with the language and the stories to help me to better understand and articulate my mission. Thank you, Valarie, for holding my hand and accompanying me on my journey to becoming a sage warrior, and thank you for whispering the wisdom of your ancestors in my ear."

—Ani DiFranco, singer-songwriter and author of
No Walls and the Recurring Dream

"*Sage Warrior* is your beautiful guide to the wise stories and heartfelt teachings of the Sikh tradition."

—Jack Kornfield, author of *A Path with Heart*

"With *Sage Warrior,* Valarie Kaur offers the world a profound gift— a way back to itself—a way back to wholeness. Drawing from the wisdom of her ancestors and the warrior sages of her Sikh faith, Kaur pushes typically hidden truths to the center. Ancient stories comfort, challenge, and empower, even as they reveal our common human struggle. *Sage Warrior* is good medicine for our decolonizing world."

—Lisa Sharon Harper, author of *The Very Good Gospel* and *Fortune*

"In *Sage Warrior,* Valarie Kaur has done a remarkable thing: weaving history, memoir, philosophy, and sociology. She didn't just write this book, she lived it, and so has bridged then and now, bringing ancient tools to our individual lives in the present day. The book tells the story of the first Sikh ancestors, men and women, and the wisdom they can offer us now. She retells their stories and weaves in her own raw and deep reflections as a mother and activist. All the journeys revealed here burnish the Sikh archetype known as the sage warrior, which offers us a strong and loving way to meet the vast difficulties of our time. Enter here and wear what fits your soul until, as Valarie says, 'you [may] build sovereign space where you can find refuge and rest in wisdom within you.' Until you 'find the wisdom you need to be brave with your life.'"

—Mark Nepo, author of *The Book of Awakening* and
You Don't Have to Do It Alone: The Power of Friendship

"Valarie Kaur is a woman of vision, warmth, and determination. Her insight into revolutionary love is just what we need in turbulent times. This is life giving in community."

—Sister Simone Campbell, faith leader, recipient of the Presidential Medal of Freedom, and author of *A Nun on the Bus*

"Valarie Kaur's beautiful work restores our idea of love to its rightful, powerful, wise, sustaining place. It truly is a revolutionary force. Using the ground of the Sikh tradition, the book, as Valarie says in the introduction, is for anyone who feels breathless by the world, and is seeking sources of wisdom. In our time, we can each benefit from this inspiring offering."

—Sharon Salzberg, author of *Lovingkindness* and *Real Life*

"Valarie Kaur doesn't just preach Revolutionary Love, she practices it—and her latest act is in the gift of her new book, *Sage Warrior*. At turns parable, meditation, and personal journal, Kaur invites us to introspection, using the teachings of the luminaries of her beloved Sikh faith to inspire us to change the world with 'deep, mystical, muscular, holistic' love.' In our polarized times, love is the only rational path forward—and with her lyrical words, Kaur lights our way."

—Karen Walrond, author of *The Lightmaker's Manifesto* and *Radiant Rebellion*

SAGE WARRIOR

ONE WORLD

NEW YORK

SAGE
WARRIOR

WAKE TO ONENESS, PRACTICE PLEASURE,

CHOOSE COURAGE, BECOME VICTORY

A Revolutionary
Love Project

WRITTEN BY:
VALARIE KAUR

ILLUSTRATIONS BY:
Keerat Kaur

MUSICAL ACCOMPANIMENT BY:
Sonny Singh

Download at sagewarrior.us

Published in the United States by One World,
an imprint of Random House, a division of
Penguin Random House LLC, New York.

ONE WORLD and colophon are registered trademarks
of Penguin Random House LLC.

LIBRARY OF CONGRESS CATALOGING-IN-PUBLICATION DATA
NAMES: Kaur, Valarie, author.
TITLE: Sage warrior: wake to oneness, practice pleasure, choose courage,
become victory / written by Valarie "Veero" Kaur; illustrations by Keerat Kaur;
Musical accompaniment by Sonny Sing.
DESCRIPTION: New York: One World, an imprint of Random House,
a division of Penguin Random House LLC, [2024] | Includes index.
IDENTIFIERS: LCCN 2024011723 (print) | LCCN 2024011724 (ebook) |
ISBN 9780593448441 | ISBN 9780593448458 (ebook)
Subjects: LCSH: Sikhism—Social aspects.
CLASSIFICATION: LCC BL2018 .K328 2024 (print) | LCC BL2018 (ebook)
| DDC 294.6/44—dc23/eng/20240618
LC record available at https://lccn.loc.gov/2024011723
LC ebook record available at https://lccn.loc.gov/2024011724

Printed in the United States of America on acid-free paper

oneworldlit.com

randomhousebooks.com

2 4 6 8 9 7 5 3 1

FIRST EDITION

Book design by Barbara M. Bachman

For Papa Ji

The world we have known is ending.

A new world is wanting to be born.

What is needed now is for
survivors of trauma
and witnesses of crisis
to see ourselves not as victims
but as pioneers of
a new way of being human.

We can become
sant sipahi:

sage warriors.

The warrior fights. The sage loves.
It's a path of

Revolutionary Love.

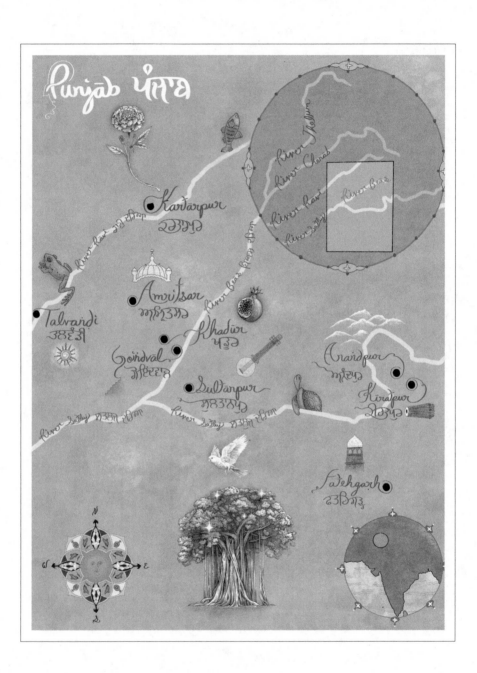

CONTENTS

INTRODUCTION

I knew our world was ending when the elders died in the fires.

A few years ago, in the thick of the pandemic, I was playing with my two-year-old daughter on the floor of our living room, which had also become our preschool. She climbed onto my shoulders and sat on my head. After a minute, she scrambled back down and looked at me.

"Mommy, I went number one on your head," she said.

I turned to my husband and said, "I think Mommy needs a break."

She was wearing a diaper, thankfully, but the symbolism was troubling. We hadn't left the house for eighteen months, and the children were now literally on top of me. We decided to take a family road trip. I grew up in a small farming town in California near the Sierra Nevada mountains. There was one part of the forest I had never seen—people called it a sanctuary—and that's where we set our course.

It was a bright beautiful morning. We parked and made our way into the forest. The children skipped on the path ahead of us. As we wound down a great slope, the forest started to change all around us. The tree trunks became giant pillars; the crowns of the trees touched the sky. Dust motes floated in the sunlight, and time stood still. It felt like entering a cathedral. Even the children hushed their voices.

These are the great sequoias of Sequoia National Forest. They grow only on the western slopes of the Sierra Nevada mountains in California. Indigenous peoples call these trees the Ancient Ones, for these trees live to be three thousand years old. This grove is called the Giant Forest, for it is home to the largest living tree on earth: "the General Sherman Tree."

"What does it say about our society that the greatest tree in the world is named after a military hero?" I asked. A rant ensued.

My son waited for an opening.

"Mommy, let's just call it the Great-Grandfather Tree," he said.

My jaw unclenched.

"Okay, Kavi." He was only six, but he knew his mommy well.

We found a bench at the foot of the Great-Grandfather Tree. As my daughter, Ananda, climbed into my lap to nurse, I took a deep breath and rested my head back. The tree was twenty-seven stories high, and I looked up through the bramble to the magnificent canopy in awe. The Great-Grandfather Tree was born in 300 B.C. Think of all that has happened in the last 2,300 years. This one tree has stood here, in this one solemn place, and witnessed *us.*

The Great-Grandfather Tree appears to stand alone but is supported by the trees around it. Deep in the earth, the roots make a living network through the mycelium, and the trees send each other information and energy. If there is disease or fire on the edges of the forest, the trees in the middle already know about it. When one is sick, others send it nutrients through the earth. These trees practice a kind of empathy. They know that resilience and longevity are only possible in community.

We spent all day in the Giant Forest, singing, skipping, and playing. No one went to the bathroom on my head. It was a successful day. I promised the kids we would come back.

Four weeks later, a lightning storm ignited two wildfires—the KNP Complex and Windy fires—and the Giant Forest was surrounded by flames. We saw a photo on the front page of the newspaper of a firefighter desperately wrapping foil around the trunk of the Great-Grandfather Tree.

"Let's sing them Papa Ji's prayer, Mommy," said Kavi. The shabd, the song-prayer, my grandfather sang to me when he was alive, the one I sang to him on his deathbed:

> *taati vao na lagayee*
> *paarbrahm sarnaaee*

> Hot winds cannot touch me
> I am shielded by the Infinite

Every night, we sang the shabd. We waited for days, then weeks, then months. When the smoke finally cleared, the Giant Forest was still there, the Great-Grandfather Tree still standing. But 3,600 other trees had fallen. Over the course of fourteen months, we lost 20 percent of the world's population of great sequoias in California's superfires. These elders withstood thousands of years of human history only to die, en masse, in our lifetime.

I tasted the ash in my mouth. And the taste is familiar.

Every day, it seems we look into the darkness of the tomb: Genocidal campaigns are under way, demagogues dismantle democracy from the inside, hate crimes are the highest they have been on record, mass shootings are relentless, authoritarian forces are gaining ground, poverty and inequality are compounded by a global pandemic, climate disasters befall us daily as the earth only gets hotter, and just when we need to come together to solve these problems, algorithms are decimating our shared sense of reality, driving us farther apart.

Our world—the one all our elders have known and survived—is already gone.

SEARCHING FOR REFUGE

THERE ARE MANY NAMES FOR THE ERA WE ARE LIVING THROUGH. Some call it the Anthropocene, the era when human beings are the ones driving mass extinctions. Some call it the Discontinuity: We live on a planet radically different from the one we grew up on. Some say the Apocalypse is coming; some even want it to come. Streaming on our screens, the end is caused by zombies. Or viruses. Or viruses that turn people into zombies. Other times, the world ends in war. Or famine, floods, and fire. In the smartest renditions, apocalypse isn't caused by any one thing but a crescendo of crises. In every scenario, all that we seem to be able to see in the future are lone survivors in a dead landscape.

My son started kindergarten during the pandemic. Kindergarten on Zoom. I watched him try to sit still for hours on a little blue stool we set up in the corner of our living room. When he was done, he could not go outside to play, because the air was on fire and unsafe to breathe. The sky was orange from wildfires burning across the state. To be completely honest, there was a part of me that was relieved that at least my little brown boy was safe at home with me, and the racial violence I had documented my whole life could not touch him. Not yet. That was when I felt the multiple crises crescendo inside me.

"We need a Plan B," I cried to my husband.

I stayed up all night after the children went to bed, searching for where we could go. I plotted a move to New Zealand. The next night, to Portugal. But there was no place I could go to escape. The refuge I was searching for was *within* me.

This is how I began a journey that led me to my ancestors, and to this book.

THE WISDOM WE NEED

I WAS RAISED IN THE SIKH TRADITION. IT IS ONE OF THE WORLD'S great wisdom traditions, yet most of the people around me, for most of my life, have had no idea who Sikhs are, what we believe, where we are from, or even that we are a community in the first place. For twenty years, I have worked to tell my community's stories—in writings, films, and speeches—translating our pain and lifting up our voices. Always in terms of what we had suffered. Sikhs have been targets of racial violence in the United States for the last century. Our turbans, worn by many men and some women as part of our faith commitment to love and serve, have drawn enormous violence. I was so focused on lifting up our pain that I rarely had a chance to share our wisdom. But as the crises mounted and felt more apocalyptic, I needed more courage than ever before. So I stepped back from the front lines. I returned to the stories my grandfather had told me when I was a child and immersed myself in the wisdom of Sikh ancestors. I began to retell those stories to my children. I took my family on a trip to India to visit the sites of the ancestors halfway around the world.

In Sikh wisdom, I found answers to the questions so many of us are grappling with:

How do we survive seemingly apocalyptic times? How do we find the strength to envision a new world, and the courage to live into it? How do we love when it's hard? In a world on fire, what of joy?

This book is my retelling of the story of the first Sikh ancestors, and the wisdom they offer us now. The first Sikhs lived in a time that seemed as apocalyptic as ours and developed profound inner wisdom for courageous action. In this book, I reimagine their stories and weave in my own reflections as a mother and activist—and pull forth the medicine I think we all need now. The more time I spent with the ancestors, the more they transformed me. And so I wrote this book not as a quick fix but as a deep immersive experience. I invite you on a journey into music and mysticism, war and healing, survival and courage, and, ultimately, the path of the sage warrior.*

INTRODUCING SIKH WISDOM

THE SIKH TRADITION BEGAN HALF A MILLENNIUM AGO IN THE land of Punjab, which means "land of five rivers." Today Punjab spans both India and Pakistan. In the fifteenth century—a time riven by caste, conquest, and cruelty—Hindus and Muslims who sang of liberation met and mixed in Punjab. In this setting, the Sikh tradition was born.

In the year 1499, a man named Nanak is said to have disappeared into a river and emerged three days later with a revelation of Oneness. He began to sing powerful mystical poetry, accompanied by a Muslim bard. For twenty-four years, Guru Nanak traveled in each of the cardinal directions on foot, enduring lashing monsoons, sweltering summers, and icy winters, sleeping in humble homes or beneath trees under

---

* This book is accompanied by artwork, music, and study guides created by my Sikh sisters and brother Keerat Kaur, Nirinjan Kaur Khalsa, Jasvir Kaur Rababan, and Sonny Singh. We created multisensory, embodied ways for you to experience Sikh wisdom as we do. As you read this book, listen to sacred songs that accompany each chapter. Go to sagewarrior.us.

starlit skies. Everywhere he went, his songs held a vision that landed in people's hearts: We can all taste the truth of Oneness, and when we do, we are inspired to care for one another, and fight for one another. Perhaps what was most powerful about Guru Nanak is how he distilled the mystical heart of all the world's wisdom traditions into its essence: love.

Guru Nanak's followers were called Sikhs, seekers or students. A Sikh is one who learns, and is always learning. In the sixteenth century, the first Sikhs formed a community of practice and used musical poetry as daily channels for union and connection. It was a daring anti-caste liberation movement. Sikhs believed that people of all castes, genders, faiths, races, and places were equal. All of us can become *sant*, or sages: Sing a song of love and practice what you sing by serving others. It was not a perfect community—it wrestled with patriarchy and internal schisms. Still, it was a radical experiment that rebelled against the caste hierarchy and feudal order of the era, a mysticism that inspired revolutionary social change. By the seventeenth century, Sikhs were seen as a direct threat to those who ruled by state and doctrinal authority. When the Mughal Empire dispatched armies to conquer Sikhs, the community might have been erased like many liberation experiments before it. But something unusual happened—this community of mystics picked up the sword. Farmers and householders, including those of "low castes," dared to build a resistance. They became *sipahi*, warriors. A mystical community developed a martial tradition—uncommon in human history—and these ancestors survived near-annihilation. The ideal archetype in the Sikh tradition became the *sant sipahi:* the sage warrior.

Today Guru Nanak is remembered as the founder of the Sikh faith, which Sikhs call *Sikhi*—a way of being. He was the first of ten Gurus who led in succession over the course of about 250 years. The lineage culminated in a canon of sacred poetry, now seen as the everlasting Guru. Since then, Sikhs have told and retold the stories of the Sikh Gurus, infused them with memory and imagination, and brought to life the sage warrior tradition in a myriad of ways. Today there are twenty-six million Sikhs worldwide, and countless interpretations. What follows is mine.

WHO IS THE SAGE WARRIOR?

THE SAGE IS SOMEONE WHO LOVES DEEPLY. YOU CULTIVATE WON-
der for others and the earth and *wake to Oneness*. You *befriend the
body*—parts of the world, and parts of yourself. You *practice pleasure*
through music, meditation, movement, and more as channels for awakening. You *build sovereign space* where you can find refuge and *rest in
wisdom* within you.

The warrior is someone who fights for humanity, including your
own. You access your agency and *activate power*. In the face of injustice, you *harness rage* and refuse to surrender your humanity. You join
others to *grieve together* and alchemize pain into energy and action. You
choose courage in the face of crisis. In doing so, you *become victory*. You
embrace rebirth.

The warrior fights; the sage loves. It's a path of Revolutionary Love.
I believe Revolutionary Love is the call of our times.*

My grandfather was the first sage warrior I knew. I grew up in a big
family of Punjabi Sikh farmers in California's heartland, where we
have lived and farmed for more than a century. My grandfather's room
was next to mine. Papa Ji tied his turban every day, clasped his hands
behind his back, and surveyed the world through the eyes of wonder.
When he listened to kirtan, sacred music, he closed his eyes and let
the music resound wondrously within him; he wrote poetry in his garden. As I curled up beside him, his silvery beard rubbing my cheek, he
told me his warrior stories—surviving air raids as a soldier in World
War II, ushering people onto trains to safety during the massacres of
the 1947 Partition of India-Pakistan, keeping guard on a rooftop during the anti-Sikh genocidal violence in Delhi in 1984. He was proud
never to have fired a bullet. His was a militant ethic of nonviolence.

As I fell asleep each night, Papa Ji would sing the Mool Mantr, the
foundational verse that opens the Guru Granth Sahib, our sacred canon

---

* To learn about Revolutionary Love as a movement and guide for action, see
revolutionarylove.org. You can find my book *See No Stranger: A Memoir and Manifesto
of Revolutionary Love* at seenostranger.com.

of musical wisdom. It begins with the utterance "Ik Onkar," which means Oneness, ever-unfolding. "All of Sikh wisdom flows from here," Papa Ji would say. All of us are part of the One. Separateness is an illusion: There is no essential separateness between you and me, you and other people, you and other species, or you and the trees. You can look at anyone or anything and say: *You are a part of me I do not yet know.* And that means no one is outside our circle of care. There are no monsters in this world, only people who are wounded. To pursue a life of Revolutionary Love is to walk boldly into the hot winds of the world with the eyes of a sage and a heart of a warrior.

When I say that Revolutionary Love is the call of our times, some believe that I'm naïve or unserious about power. The word "love" is abused in our culture—love as a placebo, a rush to reconciliation that leaves injustice unaddressed. Yet the greatest social reformers in history—King, Gandhi, Mandela, Chavez, Day—demonstrated the power of love-based justice movements. We must reclaim love as a force for justice now. The love I was taught in the Sikh tradition is deep, mystical, muscular, holistic, and ultimately, revolutionary. It was practiced by a lineage of warriors who survived near-apocalypse. To understand it, you have to know what it feels like in your body. A superficial definition won't do. You have to take time, become still, immerse yourself. You have to enter the story.

WELCOME TO THIS BOOK

I INVITE YOU ON AN EPIC, IMMERSIVE JOURNEY INTO THE WORLD of the Sikh ancestors—an imaginative retelling of the first 250 years of Sikh history from about 1469 to 1708. I've organized the book in eleven parts: Each part spans an era of a Sikh Guru, starting with Guru Nanak, and flows through time. Every part has two sections. First, I tell you the ancestors' stories, infused with my own imagination. Then I invite you to join me over a cup of tea as I tell you about taking my children on a journey through Punjab and what these stories mean to us. My children, who were seven and three, profoundly shaped this book.

"Mommy, why aren't any of the Gurus girls?" my son asked me while I brushed his hair.

"Well, um, the Gurus taught that women were equal . . ." I trailed off. Kavi skipped away to build a fort out of pillows, but I couldn't shake his question.

The Sikh tradition boldly declares gender equality, and always has. Still, we only know our women ancestors insofar as they were sisters, mothers, or wives; in other words, as footnotes to the Gurus. The voices of Sikh women have long been silenced or buried.

I took my son's question to my college mentor, Linda Hess, the world's foremost scholar of the sage-poet Kabir, whose poetry appears in Sikh scripture. She listened to me patiently as I wrestled with patriarchy.

"Well, *what if* all the Gurus were women?" she asked.

Delighted, I posed this question to my mother and my Sikh sister Nirinjan on a walk on the beach. They stopped and burst out laughing. We started naming all the things that would be different. How we wouldn't have had to work so hard to love our bodies or trust our thoughts; how empowered we would have been from childhood; how far we could go.

And so, in my retelling, I center the Sikh women in the stories: I cannot see Guru Nanak without his elder sister Bibi Nanki. The more time I spend with the women ancestors, the more I fall in love with them. These women operated within a patriarchal culture, yet they found ways to exercise power, dignity, and wisdom. They were architects of their ethical worlds. They show us how to become sage warriors within the very real constraints of culture, and they care for community above all. I believe any spiritual blueprint for the future is incomplete without the wisdom of those who know how to sustain life with their own lives.

My retelling is based on source material in the Sikh tradition; I build on stories cherished within the Sikh tradition and aimed to be faithful to written and oral histories. My stories do not claim the status of academic history. I imagined freely into the gaps in the records in order to recreate the inner-worlds of Sikh women ancestors, the relationships between them, and how our sacred poetry might have emerged and been embodied by them. Often, I take a briefly recounted incident and expand it into a detailed, living-and-breathing scene. These expansions come from my imagination, intuition, and intention. I wish to bring forward what I see as most profound, rich, and valuable for our world today. As you read, you can turn to the Story Notes in the back of the book to see what parts of the story are based in source material, and what parts I imagined into. The stories of our ancestors have been told and retold many times, infused with imagination, myth, legend, and lessons. My retelling lifts up the wisdom I think we most need now.

I am indebted to the Sikh scholars, thought leaders, and activists who have written and interpreted these stories before me, especially Sikh feminists. There are many powerful interpretations and enactments of my tradition. There are also those that are violent and repressive. The history of all religions is a history of interpretations. We stand for our interpretations. We must. I offer an interpretation that I believe is right for our time—one that reclaims the sage in the warrior for courageous and creative nonviolent action.

I am grateful to have written this book in community. I shared drafts with Sikh elders, sisters, brothers, and kin. We gathered in living rooms, outdoor gardens, and virtual spaces. My favorite gatherings were over the kitchen table: I read a chapter, then my mother brewed chaa, and we talked for hours over tea and listened to her childhood stories from Punjab. This book is a product of that rich intergenerational conversation; you are invited to join that conversation. Pour a cup of tea as you read; listen to the music that accompanies each story; try the meditations that end each part.

WHY THIS BOOK IS FOR YOU

IF YOU FEEL BREATHLESS BY THE WORLD, THIS BOOK IS FOR YOU. It is for young people and parents and elders. It is for general audiences and Sikh readers. It is for anyone seeking the mystical path in all our wisdom traditions. This book is a new expression of Sikh stories, reimagined and retold for a new day. It is a call to embody the work of justice in a new way, with the heart of a sage warrior. It is a door into the labor of Revolutionary Love—a pathway to imagine the world reborn.

If you feel uncomfortable with religious language, please know I understand this discomfort. I have long resisted religious concepts thrust upon me with the secret agenda to convert me, or change me. I am inspired by my faith tradition, but I am not proselytizing for Sikhi, or for any religion; Sikhs do not proselytize. This book carries insights that echo in freedom movements through history. Sikh wisdom is grounded in the idea that there are many ways to love, and that we can all be courageous and connected, right where we are, whomever we are, *as* we are. I invite you to let this story speak to the wisdom that already lives in you. May this book inspire us to reconnect and rediscover the stories of *all* ancestors who bring out the best in us.

You will see a mala, a set of beads used for meditation, appear in the story. It's a symbolic artifact that I wove into the story to honor the women ancestors. It's also a metaphor. I hold the ancestral wisdom in my hand like a mala. Each wisdom is a pearl. I can rest my attention on the one I need in this moment. Any one of them can lead to awakening. Ultimately, I hope this book feels like a mala in your hands, a tool for inner expansion.

THE GREAT TRANSITION

ON OUR FAMILY TRIP TO INDIA, WALKING THAT ANCIENT LAND, imagining all those ancestors, I realized that the world has ended many times before. And it has been rebirthed many times before. The original meaning of the word "apocalypse," *apokalupsis* in Greek, is "lifting the veil." This era is revealing the sweet labor we are called to participate in to birth a new world. And so, my name for this era is the Great Transition—the convulsive birthing labor that precedes the world that is wanting to be born. *Not the darkness of the tomb. The darkness of the womb.* This book is an invitation to embrace rebirth. For we will all become ancestors one day. If we show up with our whole hearts, what future generations will inherit from this time will be not our trauma but our courage, born of joy.

In the Sikh tradition, it's called Chardi Kala—ever-rising spirits, even in darkness, ever-rising joy.

SAGE WARRIOR
LET'S BEGIN . . .

WHERE DOES YOUR BODY TOUCH the earth? Take a deep breath—let it come, let it go. Let your body acknowledge the earth. Imagine the first ancestors of the land where you are. If you know the names of the peoples indigenous to this land, say them now. May we honor their wisdom and memory—past, present, and future.

What is the closest body of water to you? The river in front of me flowed down mountains fed by rains, and now moves un-hurried to the sea, where it will touch all other bodies of water on earth, including the one by you. May we honor the earth and air and water that nourish and connect us.

What ancestor represents courage to you? Perhaps someone who inspired you as a child, a beloved grandparent, or a figure from history. All humankind is kin, so all ancestors are available to you when summoned with integrity. Choose one. Imagine this ancestor behind you. Notice what that courage feels like in your body.

What child in your life brings you joy? Perhaps your own child, or any child you have known. Imagine that child in front of you, smiling at you. Notice what joy feels like in your body.

Place your attention on your heart. Take a deep breath—let it come, let it go.

You are the link between past and future.

With the earth under you, and waters around you,
with ancestors behind you, and the children
of the future before you—

May you find the wisdom you need to be
brave with your life.

ANCESTOR TREE

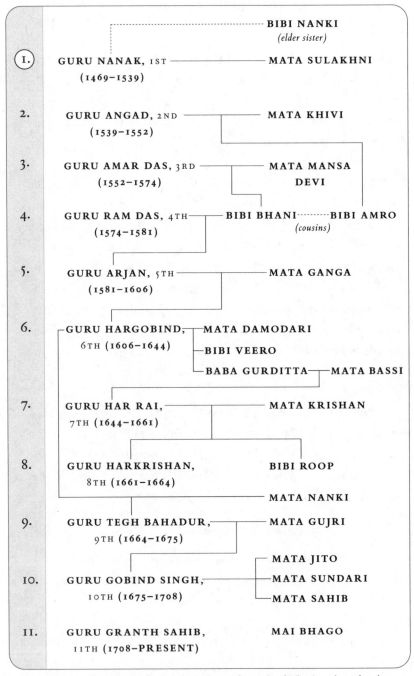

BIBI NANKI
(elder sister)

1. **GURU NANAK**, 1ST ——— **MATA SULAKHNI**
   (1469–1539)

2. **GURU ANGAD**, 2ND ——— **MATA KHIVI**
   (1539–1552)

3. **GURU AMAR DAS**, 3RD ——— **MATA MANSA DEVI**
   (1552–1574)

4. **GURU RAM DAS**, 4TH——**BIBI BHANI**········**BIBI AMRO**
   (1574–1581)   *(cousins)*

5. **GURU ARJAN**, 5TH ——— **MATA GANGA**
   (1581–1606)

6. **GURU HARGOBIND**, ——**MATA DAMODARI**
   6TH (1606–1644)   —**BIBI VEERO**
                      —**BABA GURDITTA**——**MATA BASSI**

7. **GURU HAR RAI**, ——— **MATA KRISHAN**
   7TH (1644–1661)

8. **GURU HARKRISHAN**,   **BIBI ROOP**
   8TH (1661–1664)
                       ——— **MATA NANKI**

9. **GURU TEGH BAHADUR**,——**MATA GUJRI**
   9TH (1664–1675)

                       — **MATA JITO**
10. **GURU GOBIND SINGH**,——**MATA SUNDARI**
    10TH (1675–1708)   —**MATA SAHIB**

11. **GURU GRANTH SAHIB**,   **MAI BHAGO**
    11TH (1708–**PRESENT**)

Here are the Sikh Gurus and women ancestors featured in this book. Male teachers have the honorific "Guru" (teacher); the years indicate when they served as Guru. Women ancestors have the honorific "Mata" (mother) or "Bibi" (elder sister). The final lasting Guru is the sacred canon of musical poetry, the Guru Granth Sahib.

PART I

WAKE TO ONENESS

I. THE FIRST SIKH:
THE STORY OF BIBI NANKI
AND GURU NANAK

. . .

IN A TIME BEFORE MEMORY, FIVE GREAT RIVERS POURED DOWN from the Himalayas and flowed into a vast fertile plain, nourishing fields and forests. The people who churned the soil called the land Punjab, the land of five rivers, and for millennia the waters of Punjab carried the dreams of civilizations. On this land, on soil as ancient as time, a woman labored in a mud hut. Her name was Tripta. She labored all night, breathing and pushing, until she heard the cries of a newborn.

Tripta was a mother now, a Mata. She looked down at the baby on her chest. The newborn's eyes opened for the first time; the room filled with light.

A shadow appeared at the doorway. Mehta Kalu was out of breath. He stared at the newborn on his wife's chest. He grunted, patted her arm as if she had just done his laundry, and took his leave.

Mata Tripta looked blankly at the doorway where her husband had gone. She closed her eyes. What kind of future awaited this child?

"Shhhhh," cooed Mata Tripta's mother as she picked up the baby, who had started crying.

"Put, eh hai tere Nankeya(n) da ghar," her mother, Mata Bhirai, whispered to the baby. *You're in your Nanke's home, dear one—the home of your mother's family.* She hadn't heard her mother use that sweet singsong voice since she was a child in this house.

"Nanke, Nanke," Mata Tripta whispered. It means *the home of your mother's family.* But she savored the deeper meaning in the word. *Nanke: the place where you are always at home.* She wanted her firstborn always to feel at home in the world. As she slipped into sleep, she knew the child's name.

Her name was Nanki.

NANKI WAS RADIANT. AT FIVE YEARS OLD, SHE HAD EYES THAT sparkled and a heart that erupted with wild bursts of affection. She kissed her mother's neck ceaselessly when her mother cried; when her father shouted, she rested her hand on his forearm until he stopped; and when she was sent out of the house until the storm passed, she played with the lime-green parakeets in the ber trees above her. Nanki took to wearing bells around her ankles so that music would follow her wherever she went. Music followed her as she washed dishes, churned butter, and lit oil lamps at night. Music followed her as she took food to her Dadke, her father's parents, who lived next door. And music followed her to the stream where she fetched water every morning.

One morning, Nanki paused on the bank and gazed into the water, mesmerized by how the sun rippled on the current. The earth warmed her bare feet. A strong wind rustled the trees, and the next moment, she felt the wind kiss her cheek. Making sure no one was looking, she set down the pitcher and—Nanki danced.

She started slowly, lifting her arms to the sky like those traveling minstrels who had come through the village. Her fingers made the shape of blossoming flowers. She pounded one foot into the earth—*ta!*—then the other—*tei!* Her bells rang out. She pounded her feet faster, making a glorious little cloud of dust. The bells sounded *Cha-na-na-na!* Nanki sang. She didn't know the words she was singing, or if they were words at all. But her voice was soaring, and her body spinning, and the world was whirling with her—the wind was her beloved! the water her father! the earth her mother! Nanki was in *vismaad*—ecstatic wonderment.

Nanki collapsed on the earth, laughing. She looked around, wanting to share the splendor. But she was all alone. So, she gathered up some twigs and leaves, wrapped a loose thread from her salvaar kameez around the middle, and made a doll. She carried the guddi home, along with the pitcher on her head.

When she got home, Nanki's mother stitched her a proper cotton doll out of old dupattas and leftover string from all the prayers and pleas she was making at holy places.

One day, Mata Tripta scooped her daughter onto her lap, and smiled with watery eyes.

"I'm carrying a baby under my heart," she said.

Nanki squealed and hugged her mother's neck so tight that Mata Tripta had to pry her loose.

As spring arrived, the wheat mills hummed across the countryside, sugarcane blushed green, and ber trees sagged under the weight of fresh berries. Nanki waited for the baby to come into the world. She awoke in the night from a loud guttural wail, just in time to see the midwife Daultan lean over her mother's cot and cut a silvery-blue cord. Nanki rushed to her mama's side, her bells jingling after her. Daultan was studying the infant curiously. No cries. Just a laughing gurgle. The baby wiggled across Mata Tripta's body, found her breast, and suckled. Nanki smelled the blood and milk. She gazed at his fresh round face and small fingers. Overcome with joy, she started to hum. The room filled with light; Nanki was in love.

When no one was looking, Nanki dipped her finger into a bowl of shakkar, powdered jaggery, and pressed the sugary grains to her brother's mouth as his blessing: *May your life be sweet.*

Thirteen days later, the Hindu priest Pandit Hardyal arrived for the newborn's naming ceremony. Smoke from the incense filled the room. Nanki traced the embroidery in her new orange phulkari shawl—the shape of marigolds, blossoming forth.

"Nanak," her father announced proudly.

Nanki was only five years old, but her love for her brother was so beautiful, her passion so pure, the family decided to name *him* after *her.* Nanak *after* Nanki. It was a rare name: Nanke means one's mother's family. So it was that the little boy Nanak—born in the village Talvandi in the Majha region of Punjab, in the springtime of Vaisakhi—was named after his sister and the great maternal heart where we are at home in our body and at home in the world.

NANKI CARRIED HER BROTHER EVERYWHERE, SINGING, HER BELLS jingling after her. She taught him how to sit up when he was seven months old and to crawl at nine months. By a year and a half, he was talking to her. At five years old, Nanak was herding cows and buffalos in the countryside as Nanki kept watch over him from the threshold of the house.

One day, Nanak stood very still in the fields. A tree rustled in the wind, a buffalo grunted, a serpent slipped behind a rock, and his little body shivered. Nanak began to sing. Nanki smiled. He was letting beauty ripple through his body. Nanak was in vismaad, ecstatic wonderment.

Nanki hummed along to his song. Until her father came home.

Mehta Kalu was the pattvari of the village, chief accountant of crop revenue, a respectable man of numbers and ledgers. Just like his father before him. When Nanak was born, he had boasted loudly in the village of the priest's prediction that his son would become a great man. It was written in the stars! But the prediction would not come true if the boy was daydreaming all the time. Mehta Kalu was about to march into the fields, but Nanki placed her hand on her father's forearm. The great burly man softened and merely told his son to get back to work.

When Nanak turned nine years old, it was time for his thread ceremony, the Yajnopavit, where he would be inaugurated as a man and wear the janeu, a cord that looped around his neck and went from left shoulder to right hip. The thread would mark him as a high-caste Hindu man, just like his father and his father before him. It was supposed to be a day of glory. But as the day approached, the children grew quiet and sallow-faced. As a girl, Nanki would never be given such an esteemed ceremony. Mata Tripta noticed her children whispering at night.

On the morning of the ceremony, Nanak appeared bare-chested, wearing a white dhoti around his waist. He took his seat on a raised platform of mud and brick. He faced Pandit Hardyal as the ceremony began. Nanki held her breath. The priest lit lamps, burned incense, and drew symbolic figures on the ground with flour. He gestured to Nanak's father, who boomed, "Kalyan Chand Das Bedi!" It was his full caste

name. He was a Bedi Khatri—a lineage of Kshatriya warriors renowned for their learning of the holy texts, the Vedas. Pandit Hardyal
chanted the prescribed mantras over a cocoon of cotton cord. When he
reached to place the janeu over the boy, Nanak refused the thread and
stood.

Nanak cleared his throat, and his little voice rose into a cadence:

daiyaa kapaah santokh soot jat gandhee sat vatt
eh(u) janeuoo jeea kaa haee ta paadde ghat
naa eh(u) tuttai na mal lagai na eh(u) jalai na jaey

Make compassion the cotton
contentment the thread
virtue the knot
and truth the twist

This is the sacred thread of the soul
If you have it, go ahead and put it on me
Such a thread will neither snap nor soil
get burnt or lost*

Mehta Kalu was shocked. The symbol of the thread commanded
status, respect, and obedience—and here this boy was throwing it all
away! For what? Some mystical notion of truth? Mehta Kalu was about
to ask the priest to resume, but the Brahmin priest uttered, "Vah!
Vah!"—praising Nanak's sublime verse. The crowd murmured in
awed agreement. Mata Tripta rushed to serve sweets, pretending her
son's display was planned. Nanki smiled at Nanak triumphantly.

From then on, Mehta Kalu bore down on his son. One day, he instructed Nanak to go to the market town, Chuharkhana, and start a
business with twenty silver coins. On the journey, Nanak came across a
group of sadhus, ascetic holy men dressed in loincloths. Their ribs protruded from skeleton frames. As Nanak talked with them, he felt their

---

* Guru Granth Sahib, ang 471, Raag Asa, Guru Nanak Ji.

hunger in his own belly. Nanak went to the market and used all his coins to buy flour, ghee, vegetables, and fruit. He recruited cooks and porters to assist him, and by the afternoon Nanak fed all the sadhus heartily.

When Nanak did not come home, Mata Tripta sent Nanki to search for him. Nanki found her brother in the woods, hiding under a tree in a dry pond, and brought him home. She and her mother watched from the doorway as Nanak stepped into the courtyard to face their father.

"So, what business have you done?" demanded Mehta Kalu.

"Sacha Sauda," said Nanak.

"Kee?" Mehta Kalu couldn't hear him.

"Sacha Sauda," he said louder. *The truest business there is.*

Mehta Kahlu emptied out his son's pockets. Finding all his money gone, he flew into a rage. He slapped Nanak across the face with such force, the parakeets in the garden took flight. Nanki saw her brother's face blue with bruises, like a moon with new craters. She threw her body between them.

"Bas!" she cried, seizing her father's hand. *Stop!*

Mehta Kalu startled and stumbled back. He glared at Mata Tripta, who was frozen in the doorway, and huffed into the village to burn off the rest of his rage.

Nanak and Nanki ran into the fields, away from the noise and terror of their home. The mustard fields shone gold in the setting sun. Nanki took her brother's hands and began to whirl. Slowly at first, then faster and faster. The children fell onto the grass and laughed as the world whirled around them. Nanak gazed up at the sky and began to sing:

pavan guru paani pita
maata dharat mahat
divas raat due daaee dayaa
khelai sagal jagat

Air our teacher, water our father
Mother Earth, the great womb
Day and night are both midwife and caregiver
The whole world plays in their embrace

Nanki sang his song, and she was free.

When the children returned home, Mehta Kalu informed his daughter that she was to be married to a man from Sultanpur Lodhi, sixty kilometers away, where she would spend the rest of her life far away from them.

The wedding ceremony was swift and uneventful. Nanki went through the motions blankly, barely looking at her new husband as they circled the fire. She dreaded the doli, the ceremonial moment when the bride says goodbye to her family: The air fills with wailing, and the women sing folk songs so mournful, even distant relatives cry. Nanki threw her arms around her parents. Her father turned away briskly to hide his face, but her mother held her and wept. Nanak hung back. Nanki drew her brother close to her and kissed his cheek, wet with tears. She whispered in his ear:

pavan guru paani pita
maata dharat mahat

Air our teacher, water our father
Mother Earth, the great womb

Nanki gave him back the verse as if handing him a key to home.

As the cart pulled away and Nanak receded in the distance, Nanki made a promise to herself: She would not abandon her watch over him.

The man next to her handed her a kerchief. His face had been covered by garlands that hung from the sehra, his wedding turban. Nanki looked into her husband's face for the first time. Jai Ram's eyes were soft and kind. When she took the kerchief, their hands brushed. Nanki blushed.

In her new home in Sultanpur Lodhi, Nanki discovered what she had not known in her own home: safety, harmony, and trust. At Nanki's request, Jai Ram wrote to his father-in-law to ask about Nanak. When they received a reply, Nanki read between the lines. Nanak was spending as much time outside the house as possible, far from his father's gaze. He was miserable, and so were her parents.

Nanki and Jai Ram designed a solution. When Nanak turned six-teen, they secured a job for him at the modikhana, the granary house where Jai Ram worked. It was a storehouse for revenues in the service of the Delhi Sultanate's Lahore governor, the Nawab Daulat Khan. The job appeased their father and offered Nanak space for his spiritual sojourns. Nanak joyfully accepted and came to live with his sister.

When Nanak arrived in Sultanpur Lodhi, he told Nanki where he had spent all his time after she had gone. He had found respite in a grove of fig trees on the outskirts of their village. Talvandi was on the direct route of all who passed through Punjab, and all kinds of people camped in that grove of trees. Nanak talked with travelers who had seen the world. He heard stories of treachery and terror. Of conquer-ors who laid villages to waste; of priests who bled poor people of money in exchange for blessings; of women burned alive on the funeral pyres of their husbands.

As Nanki listened, she began to understand all that had been wrong in their own home: why her mother took her father's cruelty silently; why she was never sent to school and was married off as property; why the priest Pandit Hardyal never acknowledged her; why the Muslim midwife Daultan was permitted to birth them but not eat with them; why their childhood revolved around rank and hierarchy.

There was more, Nanak said. In that sunlit grove, he also met teach-ers who dreamed it could be otherwise: They called themselves Bha-gats and Sufis. The Bhagats were Hindus, but unlike anyone he knew. Bhagats led the Bhakti movement, a devotional movement erupting from the south; they sang passionately of a direct, embodied love of the divine in all forms. The Sufis were Muslims, but unlike any he had seen. Sufis were mystics who came from the north and practiced a new kind of Islam, one that embraced the great mystery of Allah who was beyond comprehension, and as close to us as our skin. Both Bha-gats and Sufis declared that all people could commune with the Be-loved, and those at the "bottom"—women and poor people and trans hijras and people born into low castes, including all those called "untouchable"— were beloved, infinitely worthy, and deserving of liberation on earth. The Bhagats and Sufis wore different clothes and had different practices. But they sounded alike to Nanak: There is only one way to the Divine, and that is through the human heart.

Nanki's heart pounded. As a woman, she was barred from such conversations. Yet as Nanak spoke, she heard what already lived in her own mind—the world she dreamed, the one she tasted when she felt truly free, when she was singing or dancing and all separateness melted away. It seemed that the most powerful and magical ideas from the north and south were converging in Punjab, in Nanak's heart. And in hers.

These ideas were dangerous, Nanak told her. Many of the sages he met had been persecuted. The more followers they attracted, the more they threatened those in power.

At this, he paused and met Nanki's eyes.

"You will find peace here," Nanki told her brother. The Muslim Nawab of Sultanpur Lodhi, Daulat Khan, was renowned for adorning the city with fine buildings and marvelous gardens. But he was also a patron to scholars and theologians; he had made Sultanpur a center of Islamic learning. He welcomed new ideas; he would welcome Nanak, too.

And indeed, Nanak found peace in Sultanpur. He woke before dawn and slipped out of his sister's home. He walked half a kilometer to the riverlet Kali Bein. He bathed in the water, wrapped himself in a warm chadar, and sat beneath a great ber tree; the leaves fell around him like braids beaded with berries. Poetry erupted inside him. As Nanak set off to work at the modikhana, the verses followed him.

In the granary house, Nanak sat faithfully for hours, counting rations for his employer using large stones. The stones were of different colors—rust, charcoal, ash, eggplant, burnt orange, earthen red. One day, Nanak paused at the number thirteen, holding in his hand a great stone the color of golden amber. He felt the weight of it. The number thirteen, *tera(n)*, sounds like the word for *yours*. Nanak bowed his head to the One all around us. Praise erupted from his lips: *tera, tera, tera. Yours, yours, yours.*

When Nanak came home, he shared his latest poem. Nanki sang his poem as she tended to the garden. Neighbors overheard her. She invited them into their courtyard in the evening to listen to Nanak. The gathering attracted the Muslim bard Mardana, who offered to play music on his rabab, a stringed instrument. When Nanki heard them together, their music made her heart soar. She shared her vision: *Mardana, you play. Nanak, you sing. Through music, there is no one you cannot reach.*

Nanki gave them ten rupees for a beautiful rabab, crafted by the legendary Bhai Phiranda himself. It was made of old wood, seasoned with care, decorated with ornate calligraphy, and inlaid with mother of pearl. Mardana's left hand moved fluidly up and down the stem of the rabab while his right hand plucked the strings. Music erupted like laughter dancing all around them.

Every evening from then on—as the call to prayer pierced the sky from the mosque and the beat of the drum sounded in the mandir— a stream of people poured instead into Nanki's house, Hindus and Muslims alike.

"Mardana, rabab chhairr! Bani aee hai," Nanak cried. *Awaken the rabab! It's coming, the sacred poetry*. Mardana joyfully strummed on his rabab, and Nanak burst into song.

Some wept as they listened, as if waking from deep slumber. Others swayed. Nanki closed her eyes and was transported to the riverbank when she was a little girl, whirling and free. When music melted into silence, Nanki fed them all heartily—nourish your body along with your soul!—and sent them home before dawn.

Fourteen years passed this way in Sultanpur Lodhi. In time, Nanki arranged her brother's marriage to a kind woman named Sulakhni. They had two children, Sri Chand and Lakhmi Das. The family's nightly spiritual sojourns continued. Nanki was right: The Muslim Nawab let Nanak and his following be. As long as Nanak continued his good work at the modikhana *and* his songs stayed within the perimeter of their courtyard garden, he posed no threat. Nanak was safe; Nanki was satisfied.

Until the morning Nanak did not return from the river.

"Bachao!" Nanki heard cries in the street. *Help!* Nanki ran out into the winter fog. A villager told her what he had seen. Nanak set down his clothes under the ber tree and waded into the water as he did every morning, but he never came out. Nanak's wife, Sulakhni, rushed outside, trembling. Together, the women ran to the river. Nanki's husband, Jai Ram, was already on the bank, calling out Nanak's name. The Nawab Daulat Khan rode in on horseback and shouted orders for the fisherman to pull their nets through the river. He sent his best divers to search the currents and his cavalry to comb the forests and riverbeds. Nanki and Sulakhni waited and watched. But no body was found.

That night, Nanki went to the bedside of Nanak and Sulakhni's sons. They could hear their mother crying outside. Everyone was saying their father was dead. Nanki took a deep breath. She cuddled with Sri Chand and Lakhmi Das, five and two, and told them a story about their father as a boy. Once, she said, a cobra was winding toward little Nanak while he was asleep under a great tree. Her parents watched from the house and cried out to wake him up, but Nanki told them to wait and see what would happen. Just then, the cobra unfurled its great hood to shade Nanak from the sun, so that he could sleep in peace. *Your father is one with the earth and air and river,* she told them. The children slept with their Bhua Ji's arms around them.

On the third day of searching, Nanki went to the bank where her brother had disappeared. Nanak had composed his verses in this spot every morning. Here he took the grief of the world into his heart and rendered it into language and meaning and beauty. Did the pain crescendo inside him? How swift was the current that morning? She opened her eyes and looked into the glassy dark waters. The Kali Bein, a riverlet of the great River Beas, was fed from the snow of the Himalayas, icy cold to the touch. A wild green parakeet flew down to a berry on the ground, stretched her beak, and pecked. The berry cracked open. Nanki heard a cry.

She ran toward the voice, her dupatta flying behind her. Up the riverbank, through a haze of mist, she saw a figure seated naked in cremation grounds. There was a stricken look in his eyes, and his body was shaking. It was Nanak and *not* Nanak. She threw her dupatta around his shoulders. A villager tried to bring water to his lips. Everyone gathered around. But Nanak did not speak. Nanki brought him home to Sulakhni, who gripped his shoulders and wept on his chest as their children hugged his legs. Still Nanak did not speak. Nanak had surfaced three kilometers upstream from where he had disappeared. *How did he get there?*

A few days later, Sulakhni ran into Nanki's house for help. Nanak had slept for days, drinking only cow milk. But now he was gone again. Nanki searched the town and found him at the modikhana, the granary house, distributing his share of surplus grains to the poor. Villagers gathered around, whispering that Nanak had lost his sanity. He was giving away his belongings. He would be left with only a loincloth. Nanki called his name, but still he did not speak.

Finally, the Nawab Daulat Khan arrived at the modikhana and seized Nanak by his shoulders. Nanak looked past him. Daulat Khan shook him again. Nanak looked at the Nawab as if for the first time. Nanak's lips were moving. The great Nawab strained to hear him. Nanak said it louder now:

na ko hindu, na ko musalmaan
There is no Hindu, there is no Muslim

The Nawab was startled. Nanak was a faithful employee, even a friend. Was Nanak threatening him and the illustrious Muslim rulers of Sultanpur? Was this Hindu disavowing the high-caste lineage of his father? The Nawab gripped Nanak harder, but Nanak simply repeated what he had said.

As she watched, Nanki felt the great unknown spreading before them. Her brother had changed in those waters. This poetry was his and not his. *There is no Hindu. There is no Muslim.* This was about more than kinship. He was saying: There's no *me* against *you*. We are part of one another, and everything is part of us.

"He has become a Guru," Nanki whispered.

Confused, the Nawab let him go.

"Theek hai," the Nawab said. "If there is no Hindu or Muslim, then you are not Hindu, and so you will not protest accompanying me to prayers this evening with the Qazi."

The Qazi of Sultanpur was an esteemed judge of Islamic law. He led the Friday evening namaz, the prayers. The Qazi would know whether this man should be punished for these words, or feared, or whatever else.

Nanak left with the Nawab for the mosque. Nanki returned to Sulakhni and cooked dinner. The women fed the children and put them to sleep. When Nanak returned, he told them what happened.

Nanak had watched the Qazi lead the Muslim congregation. Afterward, Nanak asked the Qazi what he was thinking about while reciting the namaz, the prayers. The Qazi brushed off the question. Nanak asked again, and the great Qazi admitted: "My mare gave birth to a foal last night. My mind was there." The Qazi bowed to Nanak in respect, and the Nawab Dalaut Khan blessed Nanak's path.

"Pher kee hoya?" huffed Sulakhni. *What did it matter what the Qazi was thinking?*

"Na ko hindu, Na ko musalmaan," Nanki repeated her brother's line. It didn't matter whether one was Hindu or Muslim or anything else. One must not sleepwalk through life. The most exalted words mean nothing if the heart is closed. But pierce awake the human heart and . . .

"Mai(n) chaliya(n)," her brother said. *I'm going*. He was planning to leave Sultanpur and travel with his songs and awaken people to Oneness. Bhai Mardana, the bard, would go with him.

Sulakhni put her hand on her cheek as if someone had slapped her. Their boys were only five and two. Sulakhni silently fled to the garden; Nanki watched her go.

That night, Nanki could not sleep. She rose and slipped away to the river before dawn. She sat beneath the ber tree, defeated. Her brother was leaving the world she had made for him. Nanki found a berry on the ground, rolled it between her fingers, and gazed up at the tree. This cursed tree where her brother disappeared and never came back. This blessed tree where her brother disappeared and was awakened. Every morning, for fourteen years, he sat here and meditated before dawn. And what was she doing during that time? Building the fire, bringing the water to boil, preparing the roti. Why? Because she loved him. She loved him from the moment he was born.

Who was she without Nanak?

"Kee-kee-ree!" a wild green parakeet sang from a high branch.

Nanki bit into the berry. It was crisp and sour, followed by a tinge of sweet. She studied the dense ber fruit. It had white flesh inside, like a shining pearl. She was enraptured: *the entire cosmos inside a pearl*. She pressed it to her chest.

Who was she?

She was Nanki. Named after her Nanke. And the great mother earth was her home.

BIBI NANKI CALLED HER WHOLE FAMILY TO GATHER IN HER GAR-den courtyard. She called them together to bless her brother on his departure; they did not understand him, but because of her, they would bless him.

Guru Nanak emerged dressed in new clothing that was both Hindu and Muslim. He wore the long robe of Muslim dervishes, but instead of the traditional green, his robe was earthen ochre, the color worn by Hindu sanyasi. He had a white cloth belt around his waist and a head covering in the style of Sufi wanderers. He walked forth in simple wooden sandals, carrying a satchel with a wool blanket and a few rations.

Bhai Mardana appeared with his beautiful rabab. He was stuffing ink and paper into his satchel. They would embark on foot together, dressed like this, carrying only these provisions.

Guru Nanak respectfully touched the feet of his parents and grandparents. Mata Tripta gripped her son and sobbed, just as she had done at her daughter's wedding doli.

Sulakhni brought the children from the house silently. She carried two-year-old Lakhmi Das on her hip. At five, Sri Chand skipped along beside her.

Guru Nanak smiled at his children with watery eyes. He tickled Lakhmi Das until he laughed, and kissed Sri Chand on the forehead.

He reached for Sulakhni's hand but she withdrew it and looked away, stone-faced. He turned to his sister.

Bibi Nanki touched his feet in respect and said: "Guru Nanak."

He smiled and embraced her. She promised she would raise the boys with Sulakhni. She would watch over them as devotedly as she had over him.

"Whenever you think of me, I will come," he said.

Before she knew it, he was gone.

The next day, Bibi Nanki found Sulakhni in her garden. Sulakhni hid her face so that her sister-in-law could not see her tears. Bibi Nanki studied her closely. Sulakhni had accepted her husband's mission silently. She had left her parents' home at a young age for the promise of married life. Now she was a woman without a companion in a world that defined a woman's worth by her husband. She was a mother left to raise her children without him. But she was also so much more than that . . .

Bibi Nanki pressed a gift into Sulakhni's hand. Sulakhni wiped the rest of her tears and looked down at the small cream-colored cloth. She slowly unwrapped it.

Pearls sparkled in the light. The most beautiful pearls Sulakhni had seen. And they were fastened to each other. A mala! A set of prayer beads made of pearls that Bibi Nanki strung together on gold thread. On one end fell a long golden tassel. The pearls shimmered white, but when she looked closely, she could see swirling colors within each one.

"Shakti vastay," Bibi Nanki said to her. *For power.*

THE YEARS PASSED. ONE SUMMER, THE MONSOONS CAME EARLY AND the watery plains around Sultanpur Lodhi turned green. Bibi Nanki tossed the roti over the fire.

The roti fluffed up round, filled with air.

"My brother must be hungry," she mused, poking the roti.

When Guru Nanak set out on his first udasi—his odyssey—he returned once after a long stretch of years. But he did not stay home long. He set out on a second udasi and traveled widely before he returned. Now he was gone on his third udasi. Bibi Nanki's bones were aching, and her hands moved slowly.

Someone cleared their throat. She looked up. His beard was long and white, but he wore the same sorrow-drenched smile as always.

"I kept my promise." Guru Nanak smiled, glancing at the round roti.

He had just seen Sulakhni and his sons. She rushed to embrace him.

"I can only stay three days," he said.

"Mainu sabh kujh dasso, Ji," Bibi Nanki said. *Tell me everything.* And he did.

Sister and brother gathered at the fire, warming their hands around the chullah. As they drank warm cardamom milk under the stars, Bibi Nanki heard all about Nanak's udasis—and all the people he met, the exchanges he had, the new voices who were singing his songs.

Bibi Nanki confided that his wife, Sulakhni, prayed for his return every day. Guru Nanak recited:

nanak janani dhanni mae
Oh Nanak, blessed are the ones who mother, nurture, and
　　birth awakening*

The next morning, Bibi Nanki did not rise from bed. Guru Nanak pressed a cool cloth to her burning forehead; Bibi Nanki's husband, Jai Ram, went to the town vaid, the healer, to retrieve herbal medicines.

Guru Nanak found a bowl of shakkar in the kitchen. He lifted her head and pressed a few sugary granules to her lips. Bibi Nanki smiled and murmured. She tried to stay awake, but sleep pulled her under like a swift current.

Guru Nanak watched her as attentively as she had spent her life watching him. He saw his sister in her fullness: She shielded him from their father's cruelty, protecting his body with hers. She freed him from

---

* Guru Granth Sahib, ang 1257, Raag Malaar, Guru Nanak Ji.

that prison and made a world of peace around him in Sultanpur, where he could blossom forth. She provided the musical instrument through which to sing. In doing so, she cleared the path to his awakening. When he awoke, she was the first to see him as Guru. And for the nineteen years he was away, she raised his children and gave solace to his wife and cared for their parents. Bibi Nanki sang his songs of love—*and* practiced what she sang. She labored with love. Nanki was awake all along. There was no Nanak without Nanki. *He* came from *her*.

Guru Nanak whispered:

nanak janani dhanni mae
Oh Nanak, blessed are the ones who mother, nurture,
 and birth awakening*

On the third day, Bibi Nanki opened her eyes.

"Recite for me the Jap," she said to her brother. His great epic poem.

Guru Nanak held his sister in his arms and began singing:

*ik onkar satnam karta purakh nirbhao nirvair akaal murat
 ajooni saibhang gurprasaad*

Oneness, ever-unfolding
True by Name
Ever-creating
Without fear
Without hate
Timeless in form
Beyond birth and death
Complete within
Received as
Sweet divine blessing†

---

* Guru Granth Sahib, ang 1257, Raag Malaar, Guru Nanak Ji.

† Guru Granth Sahib, ang 1, Jap, Guru Nanak Ji.

This was the Mool Mantr, the root verse from which all the rest flowed. He then sang thirty-eight more verses of Jap, and his song traversed all of life—the mystical and magical, the philosophical and practical, connecting all things inside and out. When he finished, the Guru paused. He remembered the verse he composed for his sister, the one she had recited back to him. Now he would give it back to her, the key to home.

pavan guru paani pita
maata dharat mahat
divas raat due daaee dayaa
khelai sagal jagat

Air our teacher, water our father
Mother Earth, the great womb
Day and night are both midwife and caregiver
The whole world plays in their embrace

As Bibi Nanki's breath became a death rattle, he kept singing:

changiaaiaa buriaaiaa
vaachai dharam hadoor
karmee aapo aapnee ke nerrai ke door

What we do, good and destructive,
is read in the court of account
By our actions and ours alone, we draw close or drift afar

Bibi Nanki's husband, Jai Ram, stood in the doorway, watching, silent tears streaming down his face.

jinee naam dhiaayaa
gaey maskat ghaal
nanak te mukh ujalay
kaytee chhuttee naal

Those who contemplate the mystical name
and have labored faithfully
Oh Nanak, their faces are radiant
and many more are freed with them

Guru Nanak repeated the last line. He closed his eyes as his voice
filled the heavens:

nanak te mukh ujalay
kaytee chhuttee naal

Oh Nanak, their faces are radiant
and many more are freed with them*

At his last words, Bibi Nanki smiled and sighed and died in her
brother's arms.
Guru Nanak wept.

SULAKHNI TENDED HER GARDEN AS PARAKEET-SONG FILLED THE
trees around her. She wore white, grieving her sister-in-law. Jai Ram
had died three days after her. Two cremations in the same week. Sulakhni wiped the sweat from her brow. She felt a hand on her shoulder
and looked up to see her husband, smiling softly.
"Mere naal chalo," said Guru Nanak. *Come with me.*
"Kithay?" she breathed. *Where?*
"Kartarpur," he said. A devotee had gifted them land on the western bank of the River Raavi. They could found a settlement on the land
and grow a community together. His followers had heard his instruc-
tions: *Live a householder's life. Don't hide away in the forests. Taste the*
truth of Oneness, then return to your daily labors: Till your fields. Raise
your children. Cook. Sweat. Sing. Serve all as your kin.

* Guru Granth Sahib, ang 8, Jap, Guru Nanak Ji.

Now there were enough people who wanted to practice together. To become a sangat, a spiritual community, and practice what they sang. To become like Bibi Nanki.

"Sri Chand? Lakhmi Das?" she asked of her children.

They would bring their sons, too. And his aging parents, Mehta Kalu and Mata Tripta, who had become ghosts of themselves since Bibi Nanki died. Together, they could be a family.

Sulakhni huffed. *Now* he came to her—after his child-rearing responsibilities were done and his sons were grown and her hair was white—*now* her husband wanted to live a householder's life with her. She bit her lip and looked down at the marigolds in her hand. The sun caught their bright orange, the color of Bibi Nanki's phulkari shawl.

Guru Nanak took her hand. She did not withdraw it.

Aao Chaa Peelo . . .
Come, let's have tea . . .

WHAT IS ONENESS

GURU NANAK'S ORIGIN STORY HAS PLAYED AND REPLAYED INSIDE me since before memory. When I was a little girl, our whole family would gather in a little closet in my grandfather's room on Sunday mornings. This closet was our own inner sanctum, home to the Guru Granth Sahib, the canon of Sikh scripture—1,430 pages of sacred poetry that includes the love songs of Guru Nanak, his successors, and sages from other traditions. My mother would slowly remove the blue silks wrapping the canon and recite, rocking with the cadence. Then, she would play the harmonium, the vaja—her fingers soared across the keys while her other hand pumped air into the instrument. Her eyes were closed as she sang kirtan, far from her sorrows. The music filled my chest at the refrain: *Kehai Nanak, Nanak says . . .* These were Guru Nanak's songs of love flowing through her, into me.

As my mother sang, I would gaze at the portrait of Guru Nanak on the wall of that little closet. He wore a long, white beard and a round saffron turban. His eyes were serene. His hand was raised, and floating on his palm was *Ik Onkar*. It's the first statement in scripture, the primary truth, the poetic utterance of Guru Nanak from which the rest of the Sikh canon flows. It looks like this:

IK ONKAR

Look closely at each line. The curved vertical stroke on the left is the number 1, *Ik*, followed by the first letter in the Gurmukhi script, the ovals that make *Oan*. Flying off the top of the *Oan* is a geometric arc that gestures into infinity, *kar*.

Ik Onkar means: Oneness, ever-unfolding. It is the Oneness that always is, whose expression is unfolding through time and space, blossoming forth in wondrous multiplicity. All of us are part of the One. There is nothing beside the One and nothing outside the One. Which means there is no essential separateness between you and me, you and other people, you and other species, or you and the trees. You are no more or less worthy. You can look at anyone or anything and say: *You are a part of me I do not yet know.*

The idea of our essential Oneness does not belong to one tradition: It's a truth that echoes through time and across culture. You can find it in the ancient Sanskrit saying: Tat tuam asi, *I am that*. It is the Mayan precept In La'kech: *You are my other me*. It is the African philosophy Ubuntu: *I am because you are*. It is the Navajo invitation to Hózhó, to walk in the Beautyway and become aware that you are part of an enduring whole. The truth of our interbeing has been tasted by mystics of all the world's great religions, even those whose formal teachings emphasize separateness between the Divine and human.

Some translate Ik Onkar as "One God," but this is a poor translation. Ik Onkar is not a Creator who looks down on us with judgment, wrath, or preferential treatment. Nor is it an all-good God who only blesses us, or has a chosen people. The One cannot be cleaved apart into good and evil. Ik Onkar is the sum of all that is, ever in motion. Creation and destruction and change. All that was, and will be. Beyond comprehension, yet as close to us as our heartbeat.

It took me a long time to learn how to talk about the meaning of Ik Onkar in English. The first English translations of Sikh scripture were done in the British colonial era. Those scholars translated Sikh concepts in Christian terms in order to make Sikhs more palatable to Europeans, a way to prove that we were superior to the Hindus and Muslims they ruled, that our God was theirs. Ik Onkar was translated as "One God." The wondrous divine "Vaheguru" became "Lord." The intimate word "tera" for "yours" when addressing the One became "thy." Destructive impulses, "paap," became "sin." The embodied liberation of "moksha" became "salvation." Today, we still have the same poor English translations of our scripture. My generation is reclaiming the liberatory power of Sikh concepts. We are decolonizing our wisdom.

Oneness is *not* sameness. All you have to do is look around you for a moment to realize that we are *not* essentially the same. We are different in our colors, genders, orientations, fluencies, stories, histories, and struggles; we are infinitely plural. We cannot bypass the work of wondering, listening, and learning about each other. Guru Nanak's vision of Oneness is rooted in deep humility in the face of real and profound diversity.

Guru Nanak lived in fifteenth-century Punjab. When he was a boy meeting all those travelers in that grove of trees, he was getting a preview of our global world. His village, Talvandi, was on the direct route of those who passed through Punjab, and Punjab was the gateway into India. For centuries before Guru Nanak's birth, invading armies kept pouring in through the mountains of the Hindu Kush in the north into Punjab. Long before that, Punjab was home to the great Indus Valley civilization. So, the soil beneath Guru Nanak's feet was layered by the Indigenous, the Greeks, Scythians, Huns, Afghans, Persians, and Turks, and soon the Mughals. Their languages fused together: Arabic, Persian, Pashto, and Turkish along with Sanskrit and Indo languages. This mixture of blood and speech shaped the Punjabi people and the Punjabi language. Guru Nanak emerged from this coming-together. His understanding of Oneness springs from multiplicity.

So too, *we* are a mosaic people. So many of us grow up on soil layered with the memory of Indigenous people and immigrants, colonizers and colonized, rulers and enslaved, perpetrators and survivors, and the marbling of peoples and histories and tongues from all corners of the world. It's as if we *all* were born in that great grove of trees, confronting humanity's dizzying diversity. We could let that diversity overwhelm us and send us searching for flat stories that make "us" superior to "them." Or we could let it expand us from the inside out, as Guru Nanak did.

Guru Nanak sang in the language of the people; not in the elite language of ancient scripture, but in the common vernacular that all people could understand. He did not teach: Treat the stranger as you would yourself. Instead, Guru Nanak taught: *See no stranger*. He taught that we all carried a voice within us called haumai, literally "the I who names itself." All day long, our minds say: *I am me, and you are you.* Language depends on the separation of subject and object, me and you. Anytime we think or speak, we operate within an idea of separateness. Isn't this just what it means to be human? To live in a separate stream of consciousness. But then a moment finds us when language melts away and we are overcome by wonder and experience vismaad—ecstatic awe that exceeds language. This is the experience I imagine Guru Nanak had in the river, and that Bibi Nanki had when she sang his songs. Guru Nanak could have taught about Oneness through stories or commandments. But he chose poetry. Ecstatic, pulsating songs of love that could give the listener the same feeling he had of awakening. Oneness is not simply an idea to hold, but a truth to experience with one's whole body. It must *reverberate* in our tissue and bones to change us. It was not enough to *know* the truth of Oneness. We must *feel* it with our bodies. We *awake* to this truth, and our bodies quake with the waking—music resounds in our lungs, breath expands our bellies, dance makes us sweat, sacred nectar is poured into the dark of our throat. *Only through the body do we awaken.*

This is what my mother was teaching me in that little closet of my childhood. How to let the music fill my body and transport me out of thought, into waking. When she recited Jap Ji Sahib, Guru Nanak's epic song of love, she would always end with the salok, the final verse:

pavan guru paani pita
maata dharat mahat

Air our teacher, water our father
Mother Earth, the great womb*

---

*   Guru Granth Sahib, ang 8, Jap, Guru Nanak Ji.

What was the earth, the sky, the water, that inspired Guru Nanak to awaken? What was the color of the river where he disappeared? And the place he reemerged? I wanted to see it for myself. I finally had the chance to make the journey to Sultanpur Lodhi, as a mother with my own children in tow.

OUR PILGRIMAGE BEGINS

IT WAS WINTERTIME IN PUNJAB. I WOKE EARLY ON THE FIRST DAY of our trip and pored over a map of all the places I wanted to visit, all the sites in the stories of my childhood. Out the window, the fog hung low over the land, and the sun was a pale gold coin in the sky. We dressed the children in bright new Punjabi clothes and bundled them in winter jackets. We piled into the car with my Sikh sister Jasvir, whom I call Jasso. She had volunteered to be our guide on our trip across Punjab. She wore a graceful gold turban, her pink shawl draped elegantly around her shoulders. I felt like a windswept tumbleweed, my hair flying around under a dupatta that kept slipping from my head.

Jasso was speaking in Punjabi to our driver, whose name was Happy and who wore a frown. There were no seat belts in the car, so my children were gleefully climbing all over us, shrieking and laughing and poking each other. Perhaps Happy's frown was warranted. My husband, Sharat, hushed the children, valiantly trying to give me some space to prepare for the pilgrimage we were about to make. I closed my eyes and pictured a shield around the car as we sped through the countryside of Punjab, seat-belt-less, to our destination: Sultanpur Lodhi.

A little town emerged amid the green fields. We wound around rickshaws and cows and people holding baskets of vegetables on their heads. We stopped at the spot where the granary house once stood. "This is where Guru Nanak worked," I cried to the children. It's now a gurdwara, a Sikh house of worship.* We went inside Gurdwara Hatt Sahib. "Kavi, the stones," I whispered. A glass case displayed a collec-

---

* The Sikh house of worship "gurdwara" is pronounced "gur-dvara," meaning, "doorway to the Guru" or "threshold to the Divine."

tion of large colorful stones that Guru Nanak is said to have used to count out rations, immersed in meditation. We pressed our noses to the glass and sketched the stones.

Our next stop was where Guru Nanak lived, now called Gurdwara Guru Ka Bagh. We followed stairs beneath the inner sanctum and found the original brick wall of Guru Nanak and Mata Sulakhni's house. Kavi drew the shape of the Nanakshahi bricks in my journal. I floated out of there elated, running my fingers along the well in the courtyard. Jasso tucked a little dirt from the garden into my pocket.

Finally, our driver, Happy, pulled into a parking lot outside a place called Gurdwara Ber Sahib, built on the spot by the river where Guru Nanak disappeared.

"Asee(n) aa gaey!" I exclaimed. *We're here!*

I scooped Ananda into my arms. Her jacket was fluorescent pink. Not really appropriate for such a momentous pilgrimage. But she had a traditional salvaar kameez beneath, and that must count for something, I thought. I wrapped a dupatta around her head, even as mine slipped again. With Ananda on my hip, and Kavi's hand in mine, we walked up to the gurdwara, which looked like a pearly white cake.

We took our shoes off and walked barefoot on the cold white marble, washed our hands, dipped our feet in water, and proceeded down a woven mat that led to the entrance to the inner sanctum. We glided toward the music that floated out from the open doors, touched the threshold, and stepped inside. Musicians called raagis sang Guru Nanak's songs, running their fingers over the harmonium just as my mother did. As we took our seats, we were given prashaad—flour, sugar, and ghee—the sacrament distributed at every service, for the taste of the One is sweet. My children sat quietly tasting the prashaad as the music swelled; the songs that flowed into me were flowing into them.

"Let's see the river," I whispered after a few moments.

We bowed and exited through the side door. I took a few steps on the cold marble and stopped.

A great tree spread before us. *The* tree. The ber tree Guru Nanak is said to have meditated under every morning. Kavi rushed to pick up a fallen leaf. Grinning, he handed it to me to press into my journal. I squeezed Ananda's hand and asked her to imagine Guru Nanak sitting here, beneath a low-hanging branch.

"There's the river!" Kavi said.

He skipped ahead and Ananda chased after him—"No running! We're at a gurdwara!" (There was supposed to be no shouting, too.) We followed the children across the marble platform and down a few steps. Before us was a slow-moving river flowing between concrete walls. This was the Kali Bein. It had recently been cleaned and preserved, but the river still felt ancient. Bein is written as Vein in ancient Sikh texts, the same word as veni in Sanskrit, which means braid. The River Bein of Guru Nanak's awakening was a long, beautiful braid.

I kneeled down to the water and sprinkled a few drops over the children, and over me.

My husband took the children on a walk on the riverbank, so that I could have a moment of reverence. Jasso sat next to me, meditating effortlessly. This river was a fraction of what it once was, so the spot where we were sitting would have been *inside* the river in Guru Nanak's time. I took a breath and repeated Guru Nanak's utterance: "Na ko Hindu; Na ko Musalmaan." *There is no Hindu, there is no Muslim.* Meaning, there is no *us* and *them* at all. I focused on the color of the river—dark glassy green—and imagined that the river was me, and I was the river. A wave rippled through my body, my skin tingled, my thoughts began to slow, and I was just about to melt when—

"MOMMY!"

The children jumped into my lap, squealing about what they had found on their walk and how they had to dodge bird droppings on the ground because they had no shoes and their lips were chapped because it was cold, so they needed coconut oil but it was in the car, and also they were hungry, and ate all the prashaad; my dupatta slipped off my head again. What does awakening look like for me?

I saw Bibi Nanki up the riverbank, feeding the children and putting them to bed. What did awakening look like for her?

AWAKENING INSIDE OF LIFE

IN THE SIKH TRADITION, ONE IS ENCOURAGED TO RISE BEFORE THE
sun, bathe, recite Jap, and meditate with poetry and music. That time
of day is called amrit vela—the predawn ambrosial hour when the veil
is thin.

This was my predawn routine back home:

I wake with my eyes still closed. My daughter is asleep across my
neck, and my son's feet are on my head. I heave them both aside and
mumble, "Dudh-dhoo peena?" My daughter opens wide and latches.
She suckles for a few seconds, and when she gets the rush, her head
falls into my arm. I start to think of all the things I have to do.

I wiggle my thumb between her teeth to unlatch her, wrestle her out
of the pull-up, rinse her bottom, which will pass for today's bath, sing
a song about brushing teeth to get her to brush her teeth. I choose sen-
sible playclothes. She chooses a unicorn dress instead, then throws it
off for one with rainbow sparkles. I carry her downstairs to join her
brother for breakfast, which their father is already cooking, thank
goodness. The children eat as I braid my son's hair and tie it up into a
joora. I run back upstairs to retrieve socks for my daughter. As they
head out the door, I wipe the crumbs from their mouths, apply lip balm,
and wave goodbye as the car pulls out to school. I blow kisses, waving
wildly until the garage door rumbles shut. I exhale—and realize that
the first Zoom meeting is about to begin, and I have not brushed my
teeth.

It was like this every day—except one morning.

I was nursing in the bed, thinking of all the things I had to do.

Ananda sat up and said, "Doojay pasay?"

I murmured and shifted her over.

As she drank, I started to notice her fingers digging into the slope of
my neck and the feeling of her belly on my belly, and her one eye looking up at me as she was emptying me out; the line between us began to
blur. I thought about how my body was turning blood into milk, and
she was pulling that milk inside her body, which was turning it into
blood, and where do I end and where does she begin, and now I was not

thinking of anything at all, just feeling the warmth and milk and skin and early morning light as I was looking at her: *You are a part of me I do not yet know.* Time stilled. The universe opened. I was in vismaad.

Then my armpits itched—they always mysteriously do when I nurse—and I moved her to scratch.

That sacred awe, that taste of divine truth, lasted . . . two to three seconds.

Oh Guru Nanak, is this the awakening you sang of?

Guru Nanak taught that we could awake to Oneness *in* the messiness and noise of the world. He did not give us a prescription: Say these prayers, follow these rules, sing these songs. He taught there were countless ways to drink the cup of the Beloved.

Maybe we are just trying to get through each day. Maybe we wake up with our babies on top of us. Maybe we have to catch an early bus to work multiple shifts. Or the hurricane just hit. Or the war won't end. Maybe all the Mehta Kalus of the world are bearing down on us. And we taste ash in our mouth.

Here is where I need Bibi Nanki. I see Bibi Nanki shielding her brother, steadying the hand of the one who wanted to control him. Did she do that within herself, too? She honored the sweet tender part of herself that longed for love, and protected it from the forces of cruelty and patriarchy and violence. She made the earth her mother, water her father, air her teacher. She breathed in wonder and sang freedom. Even when the world denied her. Even after her brother left. Even through all her daily labors. Bibi Nanki was the elder sister, the guide, the friend, the mother, the protector, the provider, and the visionary. But she was also so much more than that. She was liberated unto herself. She was her own magic. She was the first Sikh. She was the first to walk the path of the sant sipahi, the sage warrior.

If Bibi Nanki could find freedom inside herself, then maybe I can, too. Even with my children on top of me, even when the world feels like it's ending. Maybe all of us can. No matter who you are, no matter the world you are thrown into, no matter the body you occupy. The present moment—the moment you find yourself in right now—is a portal. A possibility. A cracked berry.

Bibi Nanki unlocked the sage *within* the messiness of life. The seemingly ordinary moments of wonder—when you are arrested by the sunset or swell of music or your child's face, and the line between you and everything blurs—are not throwaway moments. They are not incidental. They are actually portals into the sacred nature of things. They are tastes of the truth that we are part of everything, everywhere. We can look at anyone or anything around us and say: *You are a part of me I do not yet know.* We can let ourselves feel connected with all things, all the way up to the stars. You may awaken in big dramatic ways, but it won't hold unless you embrace waking in small ways, again and again.

I am breathing in the air of the trees across the river as I write this. A bird rests on the wind and circles slowly, its black talons straight like an arrow, making a spiral over the river where fish dwell. Am I writing this, or are they? Who is the self that is writing, unless it's also the trees and river and cicadas and rain-dashed sky, and you who are reading now? I open myself like cracking a shell. I am the shell and the one who is opening it and the sound of the cracking.

Each moment presents a chance to awaken—to die and be reborn. Die to the habits and patterns of thought that entrap you. Die and be undone. Swept away. Overcome. And be born again. We are reincarnated a million times in this lifetime. And every time we return, we have a choice. Do I want to become more free? Do I want to love a little more? Do I want to awaken? Guru Nanak awoke in a river that was not a watery tomb but a womb. Bibi Nanki awakened when she held her brother in her arms, and when he held her in his arms. It's a story repeated in time. The forever available chance to renew and rise.

LAST STOP IN SULTANPUR LODHI

IT WAS NIGHTTIME IN SULTANPUR LODHI. WE DROVE DOWN A LONG dirt road to our final stop—the place where Guru Nanak emerged from the river, three kilometers up from where he disappeared. A gurdwara appeared, lit from the inside like a lantern. In Gurdwara Sant Ghat, raagis were playing kirtan late at night. We bowed and were given dry prashaad this time—white, sweet, sugary disks called pata-say. The children grinned wildly. We continued down the long dirt path to the riverbank, the children on sugar overload. They stayed in the car with Sharat as Jasso and I stepped out.

"This is where it all began," Jasso whispered. "This is our birth-place."

We stood on a muddy bank, surrounded by a cold mist. We went down to the river and sprinkled some water over our heads. An owl screeched over us. It was dark except for the headlights of the car, and the moonlight on the water.

Once we find freedom inside us, how do we bring that light into the world? What happens after the awakening?

SAGE WARRIOR,
WAKE TO ONENESS . . .

YOU ARE ALREADY A SAGE. The first step to surfacing the sage within you is to embrace the present moment. Look around you. Rest your eyes on one wonderful thing. A tree, a stone, a flame, a face. Focus on this thing. Notice light, color, and shape. Luxuriate in the details. Notice what awe feels like in your body. Let your lips say softly: *You are a part of me I do not yet know.* Begin to hum. Let a layer of separateness fall away. The seemingly ordinary moments of wonder you experience are sacred insights into the nature of things: We are part of Oneness, ever-unfolding. This is the first step, the primary orientation, of the sage—to be undone by awe.

Extend this practice to parts of the earth, to living beings, and to other people. As you move through your day, notice faces on the street or screen or subway. Say in your mind: *You are a part of me I do not yet know.* You can also use kinship names: *Sister, brother, sibling, aunt, uncle, grandparent, my child.* Notice what it feels like in your body to see others as kin. Let a layer of separateness fall away. If you notice resistance, practice this in moments you feel safe.

Who we see as "us" shapes whose stories we hear, whose grief we let in, the policies we support, and the leaders we elect. When we see through the eyes of a sage, we prepare the action of the warrior.

ANCESTOR TREE

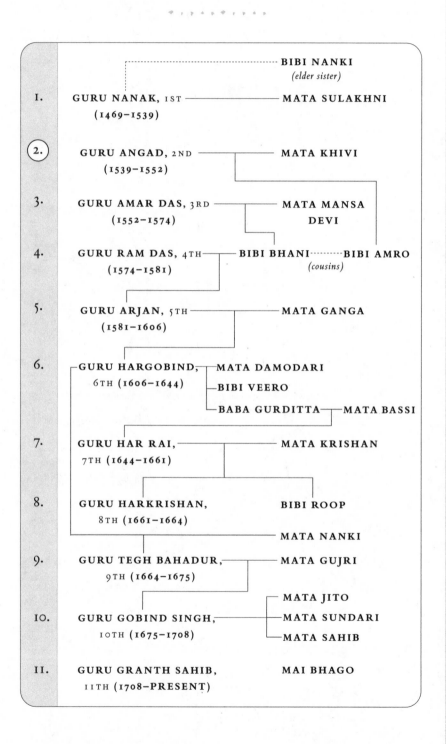

		BIBI NANKI *(elder sister)*
I.	GURU NANAK, 1ST (1469–1539)	MATA SULAKHNI
2.	GURU ANGAD, 2ND (1539–1552)	MATA KHIVI
3.	GURU AMAR DAS, 3RD (1552–1574)	MATA MANSA DEVI
4.	GURU RAM DAS, 4TH (1574–1581)	BIBI BHANI ·········· BIBI AMRO *(cousins)*
5.	GURU ARJAN, 5TH (1581–1606)	MATA GANGA
6.	GURU HARGOBIND, 6TH (1606–1644)	MATA DAMODARI / BIBI VEERO / BABA GURDITTA — MATA BASSI
7.	GURU HAR RAI, 7TH (1644–1661)	MATA KRISHAN
8.	GURU HARKRISHAN, 8TH (1661–1664)	BIBI ROOP
		MATA NANKI
9.	GURU TEGH BAHADUR, 9TH (1664–1675)	MATA GUJRI
10.	GURU GOBIND SINGH, 10TH (1675–1708)	MATA JITO / MATA SUNDARI / MATA SAHIB
11.	GURU GRANTH SAHIB, 11TH (1708–PRESENT)	MAI BHAGO

PART 2

BEFRIEND
THE BODY

I. THE CLEARING:

THE STORY OF MATA KHIVI

AND GURU ANGAD

. . .

WHEN SPRING CAME, GURU NANAK BROUGHT HIS FAMILY TO
Kartarpur, the sun-dappled village he founded on the western banks of
the River Raavi in the Majha region of Punjab. As they passed by,
farmers in the fields bowed to the Guru and his family. Mehta Kalu,
aged out of all his years of fitful rage, was astonished that his son led
such a prosperous community; Mata Tripta sighed in gratitude. Guru
Nanak's wife, Sulakhni, said little.

In the morning, Sulakhni gathered with the family in the dharamsala,
the house of worship made of earthen brick in the heart of the village.
The community sang Guru Nanak's great poem, Jap, now forever
completed with the final verse *Pavan Guru*. Her thoughts drifted to Bibi
Nanki. As the next shabd began, the music rose with longing. The
"dhum-dhum" of the mridang drum shook her and the words landed in
her chest:

sachau orai sabh ko upar sach aachaar
Higher than truth is the living of truth*

After the kirtan ended, Sulakhni walked to the riverbank alone and
sank down to the earth. She was tired of the stone in her chest, heavy
from all the years her husband was away. She pounded a fist into the
ground. It felt good. She pounded her other fist, as if breaking open a
hard bitter thing inside her. She looked down, trembling, and instead of
her aged hands, she saw her henna-painted palms from her wedding
day.

* Guru Granth Sahib, ang 62, Sri Raag, Guru Nanak Ji.

Tears streamed down her face. She realized her heart was like a pomegranate—crack open the thick shell and what did she find? Sweet treasures. Her longing for companionship, and love. Sulakhni wept. There were no wrong parts of her, only parts that carried the promise of healing and freedom.

Sulakhni hurried home and found a wooden box she had hidden away. The pearl mala from Bibi Nanki glimmered in the light. She wrapped the mala around her wrist. It wasn't too late to open her heart.

Word spread of the joyful new community on the banks of the River Raavi, and families flowed into Kartarpur from all corners. Farmers and merchants and laborers, rich and poor, high and low caste, Hindu and Muslim, orphans and seekers. Mata Sulakhni greeted them all warmly with Guru ka Langar, a meal the community shared together. And when Guru Nanak set out for his final travels, his fourth and last udasi, she led the people until his return. True to her husband's word, Mata Sulakhni found peace in Kartarpur.

As the years went on, the community flourished. One morning, Mata Sulakhni noticed that Guru Nanak moved more slowly than usual as he left for the day's labor. She set out to the fields to bring him an extra meal. The monsoons had churned the riverbanks into a thick swamp, but the farmers were out sowing wheat. The sun shone gold on the thatched huts of the village. Children flew kites that danced in the clouds. She spotted her husband.

Guru Nanak's long, white beard shone in the sun, and he wore simple peasant clothes. He was followed by their sons, Sri Chand and Lakhmi Das, and his closest disciples. The Guru suddenly raised his hand, gesturing to all of them to stop. Mata Sulakhni waited and watched.

Guru Nanak pointed to a jug lodged in the muddy swamp.

"Will you get that for me?" the Guru asked his son Sri Chand.

Mata Sulakhni held her breath. Her eldest was forty-five years old, a great spiritual teacher in his own right. Sri Chand had taken to tying his long hair in matted locks in the style of ascetics. He was ill at ease with his father's belief that one could be liberated while living a regular life, farming and householding and raising a family. Better to become a renunciant. He thought one had to withdraw from the world to commune with the universe. Now his father was asking him to pluck a jug from the mud. Only the lowest castes stained their clothes with dirt like that.

Sri Chand looked down. He did not refuse his father; nor did he comply.

Guru Nanak turned to his younger son.

"Will you get the jug for me?" he asked Lakhmi Das, who glanced at his older brother. Lakhmi Das fidgeted with the corner of his white kurta, trapped between loyalties.

The Guru then turned to the disciple Bhai Lehna, who was watching the Guru expectantly. Lehna was a humble young man who had come to them about seven years ago. When Lehna was a boy, an Emperor named Babur sent armies to terrorize and ransack the Punjabi countryside, including Lehna's home in Matte di Sarai. His family fled to Khadoor. Lehna became a devotee of the Goddess Durga. On pilgrimage, Lehna met Guru Nanak—a mystic who sang of Oneness *and* condemned the cruelty of Babur's conquests. Lehna had served the Guru in Kartarpur from that time on.

"Will you get the jug for me?" Guru Nanak asked Lehna.

Lehna moved even as the Guru asked the question, wading into the swamp, the mud rising up to his waist. He plucked the jug, climbed out, and ran toward the river. Mata Sulakhni watched closely as Lehna kneeled in the slushy bank and washed the pitcher clean. Mud splattered his face and hair and stained his cream-colored kurta.

Lehna presented the sparkling clean vessel to the Guru. It was filled with fresh water.

Guru Nanak smiled softly and touched Lehna's arm. Lehna trembled, as if an electric current rippled through him—light passing from one to another.

Mata Sulakhni brought the Guru his meal wordlessly and turned back without looking at her sons. This was just the latest test—who would carry the fodder, who would touch the corpse, who would wade into a swamp at the Guru's request. Bhai Lehna demonstrated selfless-ness each time. Lehna's kurta looked as though it was covered not with mud but with saffron. She knew what was coming.

ON A BRIGHT MORNING AFTER MONSOON SEASON ENDED, GURU Nanak called the people of Kartarpur into a clearing.

Everyone gathered around. Sri Chand stood tall and powerful, his younger brother next to him.

The Guru called forth the disciple Baba Budda Ji, who was dressed in a great white robe and wore a jade mala around his neck. Baba Budda Ji was a boy herding cows when he met Guru Nanak in the fields out-side Kartarpur. Impressed by the boy's wisdom, the Guru named him Budda, which means "elder." The great elder stepped forward with a large canopy, even though there was no sign of rain.

Guru Nanak gestured for Bhai Lehna, standing behind his sons, to step forward.

As Baba Budda Ji held the beautiful canopy over them, Guru Nanak knelt before Bhai Lehna. A shocked murmur rippled through the crowd. Slowly, Guru Nanak washed Lehna's feet. The young man's eyes filled with tears as he understood what was happening.

Guru Nanak filled a cup with water and held it for a moment with his eyes closed.

"Chhako, Ji," said the Guru. *Drink*. The water was now amrit, sa-cred nectar.

Bhai Lehna drank.

Baba Budda Ji dabbed saffron on Lehna's forehead.

Guru Nanak set five copper coins and a coconut at Lehna's feet and bowed deeply before him.

"Lehna has the same light and the same ways," the Guru announced. "From now on, Lehna shall be known as Guru Angad."

Mata Sulakhni rested her hand on her heart. *Angad* meant *of the body of the Guru*. She didn't have to search the crowd to know that her sons had already left.

FIFTEEN DAYS LATER, MATA SULAKHNI WOKE TO AN EMPTY HOUSE. She wrapped herself in a shawl and walked along the River Raavi until she spotted a figure beneath a great withered tree.

Guru Nanak's eyes were closed, his smile soft, his breathing labored. Mata Sulakhni kissed his forehead. She held his hand, and began to sing. Baba Budda Ji found them, and the senior disciples of Kartarpur came to bow at their Guru's feet.

When the sun dipped below the earth, Mata Sulakhni no longer heard her husband's breath. Guru Angad bowed solemnly before them, and it seemed to her that the old tree shimmered green, fresh leaves blossoming forth. Mata Sulakhni closed her eyes as the wind rustled the leaves, listening to the symphony that was their lives.

Guru Nanak—the sage who woke the world to Oneness—merged with the One.

A moment later, Kartarpur erupted in wails of mourning.

FOR WEEKS, MATA SULAKHNI RECEIVED PEOPLE FLOCKING TO Kartarpur to pay their respects. A story was going around that Hindus and Muslims had fought over Guru Nanak's body—Hindus wanted to cremate him, Muslims wanted to bury him—but when they lifted the sheet, his body was gone! Only flowers remained. He belonged to all of them! Mata Sulakhni simply nodded at the story with soaked eyes.

A woman of great stature came to see Mata Sulakhni. A pearl-white dupatta flowed down her back, and her two little boys played under it. She carried a toddler on her hip and held the hand of a little girl in long braids. Somehow, with four children hanging on her, this great woman did not lose her balance.

"Mata Ji," she said, "I have come from Khadoor."

Her name was Khivi, and she was looking for her husband, Guru Angad. Mata Sulakhni faced the woman who was to take her place. She felt her heart harden, despite herself.

"Guru Ji chale gaey," she said simply. Guru Angad vanished after Guru Nanak's passing, nowhere to be found. The little girl clinging to Khivi started to cry.

"Shhhh, Amro," soothed Khivi. She dried her daughter's tears with her dupatta and quietly led her children outside.

Mata Sulakhni watched them as they left. She, too, had had a husband who left her alone with her children for many years while he served a distant calling.

"Nirbhao, Nirvair," recited Mata Sulakhni. *Without fear. Without hate.* Beneath her distrust was her fear. And the only way to transform her fear was to befriend it.

Mata Sulakhni called forth Baba Budda Ji and asked him to search for Guru Angad. She then went outside and found little Amro, drawing words in the dirt with a stick. *This little girl had been taught to read? And to write!*

Mata Sulakhni invited the family to stay and eat with her. When the children ran off to play, Mata Sulakhni handed Khivi a pomegranate. As they ate, Khivi opened her heart and shared her dukh-sukh, her sorrows and joys. Khivi was just a girl when she married into her husband's family. Her mother-in-law worshipped the Goddess Durga and taught Khivi that the feminine was divine, and powerful. When her husband went away, Khivi led the household. At first, neighbors ridiculed her: Her husband had run off to serve some Guru! She replied that even the Goddess Durga served Guru Nanak. She believed in her husband's service, and hers. She learned Guru Nanak's songs of love and taught them to her children. Seven years later, her husband was anointed to lead. They had a strong foundation on which to build, if he would only come home.

Mata Sulakhni saw the readiness in Khivi's eyes and the longing in her heart. She returned with a small wooden box. Khivi slowly opened it.

A bright beautiful pearl mala shimmered in her palm.

"Shakti vastay," said Mata Sulakhni. *For power.*

Mata Khivi nodded wordlessly as Mata Sulakhni wrapped the pearl mala around her wrist.

A few days later, Baba Budda Ji found Guru Angad in a locked room in a disciple's house outside of Khadoor and implored him to come out. Guru Nanak's sons were assuming succession and taking Kartarpur, he said through the door. They claimed entitlement by birth. But all those loyal to Guru Nanak waited for his word. Guru Angad emerged; his eyes shone bright with grief and love.

He returned to Kartarpur and received a message from his wife, Mata Khivi, to come home: Guru Nanak's wife and sons would lead Kartarpur; Guru Angad would light the Guru's lamp in Khadoor. There would be no struggle for power. They would live into Guru Nanak's vision of harmony; they were one body after all.

TOGETHER, GURU ANGAD AND MATA KHIVI GREW THE NEW COM- munity in Khadoor. First, they instituted the daily prayer routine, start- ing with the Jap in the morning. Inspired by Guru Nanak, they crafted a new script called Gurmukhi—one that people of all castes, genders, and ages could learn—so that it would be easier to share the sacred poems: Ancestral wisdom belonged to all. Soon, all the children, *includ- ing* all the girls, had sticks in their hands, drawing letters in the dirt with Amro. They arranged for daily games and wrestling matches for the young people. As families of farmers, cooks, ironsmiths, and storekeep- ers flocked to Khadoor, Mata Khivi welcomed them all with a meal.

One day, a man in a crisp, white dhoti arrived, ready to join the community. Mata Khivi invited him to a meal and kindly gestured for him to sit next to a young couple. Their skin was dark as night. Their clothes were tattered. Their fingers were calloused from their labor as shoemakers.

The man's face twitched. A part of him disdained anyone of so- called low caste. If he ate beside them, he would be stained by them, as would his family and ancestors, and any karma he had earned in this life would be lost. But a deeper part of him longed for belonging and the simplicity of what this community offered. A battle raged inside the man; he began to sweat. He simply turned around and left.

Watching him go, the young shoemaker seated on the floor sang:

tum kat braahman ham kat sood
ham kat lohoo tum kat doodh

What makes you a Brahmin
 and I merely a Sudra?
If blood runs in my veins
 does milk flow in yours? *

It was a verse from Bhagat Kabir, the great sage-poet of old, who was born a low-caste weaver and sang of freedom. The shoemaker's voice was beautiful and sad.

Mata Khivi could not sleep that night. Caste ran deep, even for those who *wanted* to be there. The families of Khadoor prayed and worked alongside one another respectfully, but they did not always eat at each other's houses; they certainly did not marry their children across caste. How do you undo thousands of years of conditioning?

Mata Khivi thought of how she taught her children to read and write. One cannot shame people into obedience. Or lecture them into compliance. You had to inspire them, so that the ideas met something true inside them and became their own. So, too, it was not enough to condemn the idea of caste. Or even sing the most beautiful poetry about it.

sachau orai sabh ko upar sach aachaar
Higher than truth is the *living* of truth †

They had to find a way to live into an alternative way of being—and it had to feel good in their bodies. It had to be irresistible. She pictured how Amro licked her lips whenever Mata Khivi made kheer, sweet rice pudding. How all the children clamored for it, and sat qui-

---

* Guru Granth Sahib, ang 324, Rag Gauri, Bhagat Kabir Ji.
† Guru Granth Sahib, ang 62, Sri Raag, Guru Nanak Ji.

etly, even peacefully, side by side to devour it, before they skipped off again to play.

What is more irresistible than kheer? she thought.

Back in Kartarpur, Guru Nanak and Mata Sulakhni had served Guru ka Langar, a free and open communal kitchen where all were welcome. Mata Khivi thought: What if we scaled it up and made it mandatory? What if everyone was required to eat together as a family does? What if we made it so delicious that shedding caste to be *together* felt good in our bodies?

Mata Khivi took the idea to her husband. Guru Angad built a langar hall—a great outdoor kitchen—in a clearing in the heart of Khadoor, complete with a khooh, a well.

On the day the langar hall was ready, Mata Khivi rose early to cook. She examined baskets of lentils and millet and removed tiny pebbles, determined to use only the finest ingredients. She poured daal into a great cauldron and added handfuls of haldi, pyaaz, and loon—turmeric, onion, and salt. She and her daughter, Amro, took turns stirring the cauldron. By the time the sun began to rise, delicious smells wafted through the air. Children from nearby houses peered in, staring at stacks of rotis smothered in fresh buttery makhan. They licked their lips.

Mata Khivi blew a conch. Curious, people slowly arrived under the great canopy of the langar hall. Mata Khivi greeted them all with a smile. She invited them to sit on the ground, side by side in pangat, two unbroken rows, so close they brushed up against each other. Some hesitated. One father turned his family around and left. Others made polite excuses, averting their eyes. But as the fragrant spices filled the air, their bellies growled, and many stayed.

Amro passed out large green banyan leaves that would be their plates. Mata Khivi came along with the food—hot steamy daal and warm roti. Everyone ate heartily in silence, not looking at each other. At the end of the meal, the smell of sweet rice and cardamom filled the air. Amro emerged with bubbling bowls of kheer. Everyone broke into wide grins as they saw the rice pudding, as if they had all become children again. Some tasted with their eyes closed. Some insisted that Mata Khivi sit, so that they could serve her and those who had just arrived.

"They're taking turns," Mata Khivi marveled to her daughter.

Amro was in her own paradise, licking kheer from her fingers.

The next morning, Mata Khivi rose early with Amro. The two of them walked to the langar hall. Waiting for them were volunteers, sevadaars, bearing baskets of fresh vegetables and grains from local farms. They sang together as they cooked. When Mata Khivi blew the conch, the Sikhs of Khadoor arrived astonished. Was this to be a daily occurrence?

Guru Angad was already there, seated not on a throne but on the floor with his people. Next to him was a young family who had come to them as low caste. On the other side of them was a high-caste Hindu. Across from him, a woman who was Muslim. And they were eating together, as a family.

"AMRO!" MATA KHIVI CALLED OUT ONE MORNING AS SHE SET OUT for the langar hall. Her daughter was nowhere to be found.

Mata Khivi looked through the rooms of the house and their court-yard. She searched the langar hall. She was about to search the forest when she spotted Amro hiding behind a well. Amro was crouching over a bucket, scrubbing a bundle of clothes with all her might, and she was crying.

"Puttar, kee hoya?" said Mata Khivi as she rushed to her daughter. *What is it, my child?*

Amro hid her face.

Mata Khivi peered at the clothes in the bucket, blotted with reddish-brown stains.

"Amro," she said softly. "Thalay dekho." *Look down.*

A fresh bright red spot soaked the white cotton salvaar Amro was wearing. The girl gasped.

Mata Khivi drew her daughter close. She explained that her body was bleeding, and that it was good.

"Isn't it dirty?" sobbed Amro. She had only seen so-called low-caste people with blood on their skin, cutting meat or dressing corpses.

Blood was dirty, she thought. You could not enter a temple if you were dirty.

"You were born in a river of blood from my body," said Mata Khivi gently. "Blood is sacred."

Amro sniffled.

"Your body is sacred," continued her mother. "Any place that rejects your body is not."

When they returned home, Mata Khivi crushed together herbs and jaggery—methi, ajvain, gurr—and brewed them in boiling water. She pressed the cup to Amro's lips and massaged her belly with warm ghee. Amro slept soundly. When Guru Angad came home, Mata Khivi told him what had happened. He listened deeply. In the morning, the Guru himself led Amro to the morning Jap, and sat beside her for langar, feeding her roti with his own hands.

AMRO GREW INTO A WOMAN WHO CARRIED THE GREAT STATURE OF her mother, Mata Khivi. Her eyes sparkled when she spoke, and she carried a satchel of ink and paper wherever she went. She was often found teaching children the elegant Gurmukhi script her father had developed. In time, Amro married a kind young man, Bhai Jasoo, who lived in Basarke. Her parents encouraged her to continue her study in her new home. Amro packed her pen, paper, and a pothi, a small book of Guru Nanak's shabds. All 974 of them, along with new poems contributed by her father, Guru Angad.

Mata Khivi presented her daughter with a special wedding gift: the pearl mala that Mata Sulakhni had given her. Bibi Amro wrapped it around her wrist, where it sparkled in the light. The golden thread in the mala reminded her of the long horizonal line that ran through her beloved Gurmukhi script. She hugged her mother joyfully.

In her new home in Basarke, Bibi Amro rose early, bathed, and sang in the garden courtyard. She was often visited by a little girl who lived next door, her husband's cousin Bhani.

One day, Bibi Amro sang while she churned the milk:

bhaiaa manoor kanchan phir hovai
jay gur milai tinayhaa

Filth transforms into gold
if one finds true wisdom*

When she finished, she heard someone clear their throat. In the doorway stood Bhani's father, Amar Das Ji, whom she called Taya Ji. He wore a long, flowing white beard. There were tears in his eyes.

"Bibi, what were you singing?" he asked.

"A song of Guru Nanak," she said.

Bibi Amro made salty buttermilk for her Taya Ji. The two of them sat in the garden, sipping loon valee lassi, as she wrote out the shabd and explained the deeper meaning she found in it: *Even what we detest transforms into gold when wisdom finds us. We are part of one body; there are no bad parts. Not outside us, not within us.*

Amar Das Ji was her elder, but he listened intently to every word, spellbound.

"My father leads the sangat in Khadoor," Bibi Amro finished.

"Will you take me there?" Amar Das Ji asked her.

Bibi Amro's mouth watered as she imagined tasting her mother's kheer again. She nodded gladly.

Aao chaa peelo . . .
Come, let's have tea . . .

---

*   Guru Granth Sahib, ang 990, Raag Maru, Guru Nanak Ji.

. . .

TASTING MATA KHIVI'S LANGAR

WE DROVE THROUGH THE WINTER FOG INTO THE OLD NARROW
streets of Khadoor, a small town about twenty miles from Sultanpur
Lodhi in the heartland of Punjab. I told the children we were going to
the place where Guru Angad lived and where Mata Khivi made langar.
We parked at the foot of an ancient banyan tree and approached a wide
building with an open door.

"Look, it's Mata Khivi!" I said.

At the entrance, there was a large painting of a woman surrounded
by people. Mata Khivi wore a smile and had a soft orange dupatta
draped gracefully over her head. She stood tall among rows of people
seated on the ground—a woman holding a toddler in blue, an elder
bringing roti to his mouth, a man folding his hands in gratitude. Mata
Khivi was in the center, mother to all of them. But no one in the painting was looking at her.

I made the children look at the painting for a long time, Ananda on
my hip, Kavi's hand in mine.

"We are standing in the *same spot* where Mata Khivi served langar
hundreds of years ago," I said. "And they still serve langar here!" The
moment we entered the langar hall, a tray and silverware magically appeared in our hands. An auntie was ready at the door, handing out
items. Double for me since I was carrying Ananda. The langar hall was
a great open space. The ceiling was pale blue, and the floor shiny black
with little white diamonds. Long green rugs were rolled out across the
floor. A handful of people were seated in rows, side by side, in pangat.

We made our way to where the last person was so that we could continue the unbroken line.

The moment we sat down on the ground, a volunteer came by with a stack of rotis pressed in foil and called out, "Prashaada, Ji!"

"Two hands," I whispered to the children, just as my mother would remind me. Always two hands to receive.

"Daal, Ji!" called another voice. A tall sardar with a turban and beard smiled at the children and poured lentils onto our tray.

"Saag, Ji!" called an auntie. She spooned out great dollops of cooked greens.

"Too spicy for me," cried Ananda, fanning her lips. Sharat shoved a spoonful of yogurt into her mouth. My dupatta slipped, then hers. There were now green stains on my cream-colored salvaar kameez.

I need chaa, I thought to myself. That instant, milky, sweet black tea was placed in front of me. I took a sip and thought: *Langar is magic.*

In Guru Nanak's time, devotees often sat together for communal meals after services. Some Sufi and Nath orders had free and open kitchens, too. But langar became an *institution* under the second Guru. "Pehla(n) pangat pher sangat" was the saying: First, sit for langar, then join the people. It became a core practice, as essential as the worship. To live the truth of Oneness, befriend the communal body. And there was no more direct path to that communion than feeding and serving each other.

This was a time when people from a high caste would not eat from the cooking vessels or hands of a caste considered "low." It resembled how racial segregation functioned in the United States when laws separated people based on race, and white people would not swim in the same pool or eat at the same table or drink from the same fountain as Black people. Throughout the world, the most effective caste systems and social hierarchies kept people apart when it came to the most intimate exchanges—living, eating, loving—and enforced those rules with brutality.

Langar was embodied protest. Radical and subversive. Eating together with people of all castes and creeds meant rejecting with your body and breath adherence to hierarchy. High caste people ate from the hands of low-caste "untouchables," and vice versa. They were training their bodies into a new way of being, undoing millennia of conditioning. They became new in the act: equal, and equally beloved.

Langar was more than a rebellion: It was a practice for an alternative world of solidarity, dignity, and humility. A way of being together as kin that was birthed by a mother.

Mata Khivi ran langar for *four* decades, under five Sikh Gurus. It became known as Mata Khivi Ji ka Langar—Mother Khivi's langar. She was the sage who showed us how to *embody* Oneness. She was so revered that she is the only woman who is identified by name in the Guru Granth Sahib:

balvand khivi nek jan jis bahuti chhaau patraali
langar daulat vandeeai ras amrit kheer ghiaali

Balvand says:
Khivi is a sage-woman who gives leafy shade to all
She distributes the bounty of langar
kheer, like sweet rich ambrosia*

Half a millennium later, we can taste her ambrosia still.

"Mommy, why does langar always taste the best?" I used to ask my mother.

"The food is made with love," my mother would say.

There is a famous story from Guru Nanak's travels. On his first udasi, Guru Nanak rested in the home of a humble carpenter named Bhai Lalo. During his stay, the wealthy man who ruled the town invited the Guru to his mansion and presented an elaborate feast. The Guru politely declined, saying that he preferred the carpenter's roti. Furious, the wealthy man asked why. "Your food tastes like the blood of the laborers you treat cruelly," said Guru Nanak. "His food is made with honesty and love as rich as milk!" This is the spirit of langar.

---

* Guru Granth Sahib, ang 967, Raag Raamkalee Ki Vaar, Rai Balvand, and Sata Doom.

Langar is a transmission of energy. It is the energy of the earth where the wheat grew, and the sun and the rain that nourished it. It is the energy of the hands that picked it, and of those who transported and bought it. It is the energy of the ones who cooked it, reciting the songs of love. There is perhaps nothing more immediate than taking food into your body mindfully that reminds you of how you are connected to everything: The biology around you passes through you. You are porous; separateness is an illusion. You are part of one greater body.

Any Sunday morning in the United States, you can go to a gurdwara near you, and you will be welcomed to langar. Every gurdwara around the globe has a langar hall, open to all and always free. The food is healthy and vegetarian. You will be served, and if you wish, you can serve others. In the langar hall, we experience what beloved community can look like. Not just the idea of it, but what it feels like in our bodies to be in it. The largest food kitchen in the world is at Harmandir Sahib, the great house of worship also known as the Golden Temple, in Amritsar, Punjab. It is the most revered site in the Sikh world. There, the langar hall feeds one hundred thousand people a day. Today, Sikhs around the globe often take langar to feed those in need, especially in the midst of climate disaster or war, even at great risk to themselves. It is the essence of seva—sacred service.

In the Ardaas, the daily supplication, Sikhs often recite:

loh langar tapde rehan
May the iron pots of langar be ever warm

The minute we step out of the langar hall, we reenter noise and dust and chaos. But inside that hall, we taste the world as it could be. *How can we make the whole world feel like that?*

OVERCOMING A WORLD OF HIERARCHY

WE ARE BORN SEEING NO STRANGER. THE MOMENT WE LAND IN someone's arms, we don't care about the color of their skin, the language they speak, the status they hold, or even their gender. The only thing that matters is whether the body loves us back—am I warm? am I fed? am I held? We are born thirsting for love.

But we are then thrown into a world of hierarchy, and it's only a matter of time before it starts shaping how we see things. By three years old, we can tell that light skin is socially privileged over dark, and that some people are assumed to have more worth than others. We can tell how much worth we are assigned in the body we occupy. Every region in the world has created hierarchies of human value and built institutions to enforce them. Some are just more rigid than others.

In India, the hierarchy took the form of a fourfold caste system, where elite priests created mythologies to justify extreme subordination. They pointed to a single hymn in the Rig Veda, an ancient Indian text. In the hymn Purusha Sukta, all creation emerged from the cosmic body of Purusha: Brahmins, priests and teachers, came from his mouth; Kshatriyas, kings and warriors, from his arms; Vaishya, merchants and farmers, from his thighs; and Shudras, laborers and servants, from his feet. These four "varnas" were hardened to contain many complex birth groups, or jatis. The result was a rigid, oppressive caste system: You were born into a caste based on your actions in your previous incarnation. With moral effort, you could move to a higher caste—but only upon rebirth. In *this* lifetime, you remained where you landed.

Over the centuries, a fifth social category was declared, lower than even the Shudras. They were called "untouchable" and were relegated to jobs considered menial and polluting: making shoes, cleaning latrines, handling the dead. They were not permitted to drink from the same cup, live in the same part of the village, marry, or even touch those higher on the social order. A great twentieth-century movement for liberation from untouchability and all forms of caste oppression was led by Dr. B. R. Ambedkar. Rejecting the humiliating labels assigned them, these groups called themselves Dalits, the oppressed, and fought for their freedom. The Dalit liberation movement continues today. Even though Dalits, caste-oppressed peoples, and allies have led courageous movements to abolish caste in India, caste still permeates South Asian culture.

In the United States, the hierarchy takes the form of white supremacy—the lie that those who have dark skin are worth less, and therefore can be colonized, enslaved, incarcerated, lynched, raped, impoverished, or left behind. It conditions people to be numb to the suffering of dark-skinned people. This is true even for those of us who are dark: We have seen ourselves killed so many times, we start to go numb to our own degradation. In the United States, too, formal racism is abolished, but white supremacy still structures our institutions, permeates our policies, and shapes how we see. Oftentimes it's not even conscious; it's the default way of being.

This is why Guru Nanak's sons froze when asked to retrieve the jug from the mud. It was a task for someone low on the ladder. The Guru was asking them to overcome centuries of programming within them. It was not enough to believe in the idea of Oneness. One must live into it with one's whole body, as a way of moving in the world. Every moment of life becomes an opportunity to practice. To make love greater than our reflex to freeze, so that we would leap into the mud without hesitation to help another.

LANGAR AS A BLUEPRINT

WHEN GURU NANAK SANG THAT NO ONE WAS TOO HIGH TO HELP another, he was inviting all of us to love like a mother. All the time. Mothering is not limited to those whose bodies have birthed children; mothering is a universal way of caring that begins with wonder: *My love, I'm here. What do you need in this moment?* Love is not just an idea or a feeling; love is sweet labor.

Mata Khivi took the way she loved her children out into the greater world. Her langar hall was a mothering space where she met her people's needs, a site of literal nourishment for body and soul, a place where people practiced being a family. In other words, she made the langar hall like our Nanke's house—a place where you could be at home in your body and at home in the world. In doing so, she left behind a blueprint for all of us who want to create such spaces:

Begin where you are. Choose a space to practice the world that you want. Mata Khivi's langar hall was a simple clearing with cover for shade. No space is too small. What spaces are available to you to gather people?

Start with basic needs. No one near a langar hall has to go hungry. Only when hunger is met is flourishing possible. What are your needs, and the needs of the people around you right now?

Redistribute resources. Mata Khivi collected resources from all who could offer them, and shared them equally among the whole. What resources do you have to offer? What are you ready to receive?

Take turns. Everyone has a role in langar, and no role is higher or lower. People take turns serving and being served. Love is not an exchange economy: In seva, sacred service, we practice letting go of expecting something in return.

See no stranger, feel no stranger. Mata Khivi invited people to sit in pangat, an unbroken line, next to those they had been conditioned to see as other. It was embodied community. Where did you land in the social order? How have you benefited, and how have you lost? What barriers will you cross to be in community?

Make it sustainable. Mata Khivi used food grown on local farms and returned compost to the fields. Hers was a practice in harmony with the earth.

Make it irresistible. Mata Khivi created an experience that felt good in the body. An anti-racist, anti-hierarchy practice rooted in joy and community. How will you make your practice delicious?

Believe. Mata Khivi started small, but she built a practice that has lasted half a millennium. Our liberation experiments are not soap bubbles that disappear; they are sound waves that reach far into the future. When we embody the world we want, instead of only railing against what we resist, we pass on a blueprint for our descendants.

I see this blueprint at work all around us. In the face of climate disasters and pandemics, state violence and war, when the institutions that are meant to protect us fail us—especially if we are dark or poor or disabled or undocumented or caste-oppressed or queer or trans or women or all of these—I see us survive, and thrive, in community. When we come together to feed each other, care for each other, and uplift each other, we create the conditions for beloved community. We weep, we laugh, we live. As the earth gets hotter, and more of us are endangered, we will need to be braver and more reckless with our love. We will need to create spaces that have never existed before. We will need to practice our humanity. This is how we birth the world to come.

YOU MIGHT SAY: I DON'T HAVE TIME TO EXPERIMENT WITH LIBERA-tion. Or befriend the world. The world is far too dangerous for me to befriend.

To which I say: I understand. The world is in constant crisis, and so are we. Especially those of us who are denigrated in this culture. When our bodies are in crisis, it becomes so much easier to give in to fear or hate or despair. To give up on love and humanity. To forget connection and wonder. And so, perhaps the most powerful space we can create to practice freedom is *within* ourselves.

BEFRIENDING OUR OWN BODY

BEFORE WE LEFT KHADOOR, WE STOPPED AT THE PLACE WHERE Mata Khivi lived with Guru Angad. On that site stands a grand house of worship. Gurdwara Sri Darbar Sahib Khadoor is surrounded by a peaceful garden and a little museum. Ananda skipped over to an enormous well. I lifted her up so that she could peer down into its dark depths. It was grand and seemed bottomless. A sign said that this well was built in honor of Bibi Amro, daughter of the second Guru, who grew up to become a scholar and leader. The sign did not say much more than that.

Bibi Amro was born into a world that taught her to loathe parts of herself, and gave her every reason for shame. Sixteenth-century South Asia was highly patriarchal. Yet, somehow, she became the first Sikh woman on record who knew how to read, write, and lead. Somewhere along the way, she must have learned how to love herself—to see her blood as sacred, her body beautiful, and her mind worthy. I imagine Mata Khivi teaching her daughter how to befriend her body: To be a sage is to embrace Oneness within and without.

Oneness means that all parts of the world are beloved, and so are all parts of ourselves. If there are no bad parts of the world, then there are no bad parts of ourselves. Only parts that contain the promise of healing and insight and transformation.* To befriend the body of the world, we must learn how to befriend our own bodies. We can make a kind of langar inside of our bodies, approach each part of ourselves with the same tenderness and care as Mata Khivi. Can we treat all the parts of ourselves as beloved? Can we learn to mother ourselves?

Loving all parts of ourselves increases our capacity to love all parts of the world. So, too, loving all parts of the world increases our capacity to love all parts of ourselves.

Ananda started to spin in front of me, her bare feet twirling on the marble, her arms holding out her peach dupatta with little glittering diamonds. She was so free. Soon the world will teach her to hate parts of herself, as it does to girls who are small and brown. As it does to any of us who live in open-eyed wonder. As it did to me. How will I teach her to stay this free? To love all the parts of her body, mind, and heart? Even when she is hurt. Even when she wants to exile parts of herself.

As I gazed into the depths of Bibi Amro's well, I wondered:

Do I love all of myself? What parts of myself have I sent into exile?

---

* My language is inspired by the contemporary psychologist Richard Schwartz and his model Internal Family Systems. See his book *No Bad Parts: Healing Trauma and Restoring Wholeness with the Internal Family Systems Mode* (2021).

SAGE WARRIOR,
BEFRIEND YOUR BODY . . .

THE BODY OF THE WORLD contains many parts; you contain many parts. All are part of the One, and the One is beloved. And so, *you* are beloved. There are no bad parts of you, only parts that contain the promise of insight, healing, and freedom. There are no bad parts of the world, only human beings who are wounded; they, too, contain the promise of insight, healing, and freedom. You do not need to befriend the parts of the world (or yourself) that are unsafe for you, emotionally or physically. Only the parts that are calling to you.

Notice a place in your body that feels uncomfortable, painful, afraid, or ashamed. Say: *You are a part of me I do not yet know.* Then ask: *What do you want me to know?* Let this part of you speak. Listen deeply. You will want to resist this part of you. Instead, choose to mother this part of you. Imagine a simple gesture or words of care. Explore what it feels like to love all the parts of you.

Imagine your body as a great clearing, a field filled with light and song. Invite all the parts of you to coexist side by side, nourished and equally beloved. Notice what it feels like to befriend all the parts of your body.

Now, think of the places that you move through in your day—home, classroom, workplace, neighborhood, virtual spaces. Choose one. What would it look like for everyone in that space to feel at home, nourished, and equally beloved? What experiment are you ready to try? We can practice the world we want, in the spaces between us. The sage sees all through the eyes of love; the warrior serves all as beloved.

ANCESTOR TREE

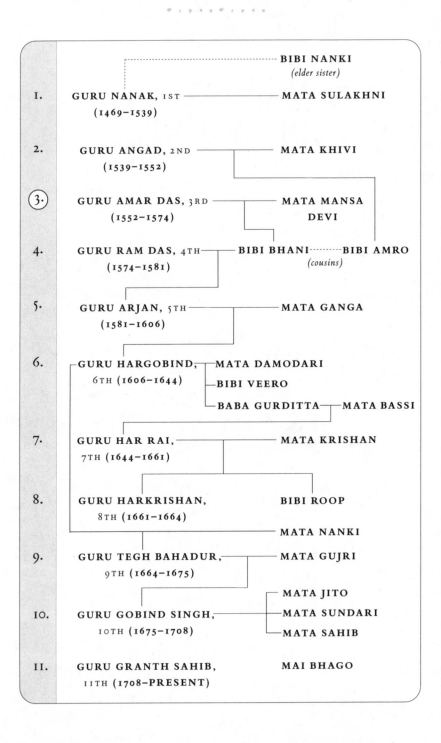

BIBI NANKI
(elder sister)

I. GURU NANAK, 1ST ——————— MATA SULAKHNI
(1469–1539)

2. GURU ANGAD, 2ND ——————— MATA KHIVI
(1539–1552)

(3.) GURU AMAR DAS, 3RD ——————— MATA MANSA
(1552–1574) DEVI

4. GURU RAM DAS, 4TH ——— BIBI BHANI········BIBI AMRO
(1574–1581) *(cousins)*

5. GURU ARJAN, 5TH ——————— MATA GANGA
(1581–1606)

6. GURU HARGOBIND, ——— MATA DAMODARI
6TH (1606–1644) BIBI VEERO
BABA GURDITTA ——— MATA BASSI

7. GURU HAR RAI, ——————— MATA KRISHAN
7TH (1644–1661)

8. GURU HARKRISHAN, BIBI ROOP
8TH (1661–1664)
MATA NANKI

9. GURU TEGH BAHADUR, ——— MATA GUJRI
9TH (1664–1675)

MATA JITO
10. GURU GOBIND SINGH, ——— MATA SUNDARI
10TH (1675–1708) MATA SAHIB

11. GURU GRANTH SAHIB, MAI BHAGO
11TH (1708–PRESENT)

PART 3

PRACTICE
PLEASURE

I. THE ASCENT:
THE STORY OF BIBI BHANI
AND GURU AMAR DAS

...

WHEN AMAR DAS JI TOLD HIS FAMILY THAT HE WAS GOING TO visit Khadoor, his youngest daughter, Bhani, spread her arms and soared through the courtyard.

"Mai(n) vee janaaaaaaaa!" Bhani cried, her braids flying like the tail of a comet. *I want to come too!*

The journey from Basarke to Khadoor took two days by oxcart through the countryside. When they arrived, Amar Das Ji carried his sleeping daughter to the langar hall, where Mata Khivi was waiting for them, stirring a cauldron of something warm and sweet. Bhani's eyes shot open.

"Oh, so you're awake," laughed Bibi Amro, handing her little cousin a bowl of kheer.

Bhani looked inside: plump grains of rice in rich milky pudding, crushed almonds and cardamom on top. She took a bite and swooned. A man across from them glared sternly as Bhani spread her arms and swayed. But her father only smiled. Bhani finished the entire bowl.

Amar Das Ji left for his audience with Guru Angad. Bhani drew in the dirt with a stick, learning letters from Bibi Amro. When her father returned, tears were streaming down his face and his eyes glistened.

"Kee hoya, Pita Ji?" Bhani asked.

"Thiya gaeya," said Amar Das Ji, smiling. He found what he had spent his whole life searching for.

Bhani looked into her father's radiant face. The thought of taking him away from something that brought him this much pleasure was unbearable.

"Jo thiya gaeya, ohnu nahi gvauna," she said simply. *Don't lose what you've found.*

Bhani buried her face in her father's soft, white beard and kissed his forehead.

They made a plan together. Amar Das Ji would stay in Khadoor, and as soon as he found a home for the family, he would send for them.

Back in Basarke, Bhani waited patiently for news. Her father sent a message that Guru Angad had asked him to found a new settlement three kilometers from Khadoor on land gifted by a wealthy merchant. It was called Goindval, and there was enough space to build a community, and to bring his whole family.

On the day his family arrived in Goindval, Amar Das Ji was standing in front of a brick house with a large gardened courtyard, smiling. Bhani jumped into his arms and snuggled into his beard. They were not going to be apart again.

Every morning, Bhani woke before dawn. She handed her father a brass pitcher and waved at him happily as he set out for his daily seva, his sacred service. Amar Das Ji took his pitcher to the River Beas, filled it with water, and walked to Khadoor, in time to prepare the Guru's bath. He spent the day in Khadoor in various labors. When he returned at night, Bhani massaged ghee into his sore legs. Her mother took care of the family; she took care of her father. Bhani served him as he served the Guru.

One morning before dawn, Amar Das Ji was fetching water. It had been a stormy night, and the earth was muddy. He stumbled over a karir tree and fell, along with his pitcher, into a pit beneath a weaver's loom. The weaver and his wife awoke from the clanging.

"Who has fallen at our door?" the weaver called out.

"Who else could it be but Amru nithaava(n) who neither sleeps nor rests," retorted his wife.

Amar Das Ji completed his day's service and limped home. As Bhani rushed to receive her father, she heard people snickering, "Amru nithaava(n)." *Homeless Amru.* Bhani glared daggers at them. They laughed savagely as soon as she turned her back.

Bhani shouldered her father's humiliations and doubled her efforts to care for him. Every night, she massaged his scalp with mustard oil, humming the shabds she was learning from him. He called her Mohni, enchanted one.

Thirteen years passed this way, Amar Das Ji traveling back and forth, all in selfless service to the fledgling community.

Then came the day that changed everything.

Bhani accompanied her father to Khadoor for a gathering called by Guru Angad. It was an unusually warm spring. Mata Khivi passed out great banyan leaves. Bhani fanned her father, and the breeze swished back to cool her face.

Guru Angad emerged, dressed in a simple cream-gold robe made of matka silk. His face was creased with age, but his eyes still sparkled. He nodded at Mata Khivi. It struck Bhani how unusual it was to see a man at ease among such powerful women. His wife ran langar as an institution; he raised his daughter Bibi Amro as a scholar when it was rare for girls to read. Bhani heard that Guru Angad had worshipped the Goddess Durga before he found Guru Nanak. He had always uplifted the women in his family. Bhani wondered: When Guru Nanak chose his successor, was he also honoring the women around him?

"Baba Budda Ji!" called out Guru Angad. The faithful elder disciple appeared in his great white robe and jade mala, holding a plate of crushed red powder.

"Amar Das Ji!" The Guru called her father's name.

Bhani looked at her father quizzically and lowered her banyan leaf. Amar Das Ji stepped into the clearing. Baba Budda Ji dipped his finger into the crushed sandalwood and saffron and pressed it to her father's forehead. Guru Angad placed a coconut and five paisay at his feet and bowed. The crowd gasped; Bhani was stunned. Her father was seventy-two years old. She never imagined he would be chosen to lead.

Guru Angad proclaimed:

Amar Das nimaaneya(n) da maan
Amar Das nitaaneya(n) da taan
Amar Das nithaaveya(n) da thaa(n)
Amar Das nioateyaa(n) di oat

Amar Das niaaseraaya(n) da aasraa
Amar Das nidhiriyaa(n) di dhir

[Guru] Amar Das shall be the honor of the dishonored
the strength of the powerless
the home of the homeless
the shelter of the shelterless
the hope of the hopeless
the support of those who have none

People lifted their voices in praise. Bhani rushed toward her father but was blocked by people bowing to him in respect. She spotted Bibi Amro crying as she disappeared into the house where her father, Guru Angad, had retired.

When Bibo Amro emerged, Bhani was waiting for her. The cousins walked arm in arm until they reached a great ber tree, far from the swarm of people outside Guru Angad's home.

Wailing erupted in the distance.

A few moments later, the air filled with kirtan.

Guru Angad—second in the House of Nanak, who lit the Guru's lamp in Khadoor and composed songs of love and created a script through which to remember them; husband to Mata Khivi and father to Bibi Amro, who saw the divine in them and turned langar into a practice for a new world; the Guru who would leap into the mud for love—was no more.

Bibi Amro wept.

Bhani pressed a stick into her hands.

Holding the stick together, the young women traced in the earth: *Ik Onkar.*

Bibi Amro's father was not gone; he was part of the Oneness that always is.

AS A STARLIT NIGHT MELTED INTO DAWN, BHANI HURRIED THROUGH the winter fog wrapped in a shawl, pressing a steel bowl to her chest. Sevadaars were already working the outdoor langar, softly singing as they stirred enormous cauldrons for the day's meals. Through the swirling steam, Bhani spotted the silhouette of a great woman with a long cream dupatta, stirring a cauldron, reciting prayers.

"Mata Ji," said Bhani.

Mata Khivi smiled without breaking her recitation. It had been two years since her husband, Guru Angad, had departed, and her hair was turning white, but she faithfully ran the langar hall in Khadoor. And she visited Goindval from time to time at the invitation of Guru Amar Das, who rejected the widespread practice of ostracizing widows. They needed Mata Khivi's mastery to expand the langar and feed the many mouths joining the sangat. Whenever Mata Khivi visited, the Guru requested her famous kheer. Bhani was here to fetch it.

"Kheer bannan valee hai," Mata Khivi said, surveying the kheer. *It's almost ready.*

The great woman picked up a basket of elaichee with one hand and poured the cardamom into the cauldron, stirring with her other hand. She deftly poured in badam, almonds, from another basket. Steam drifted up from the rice pudding, and the fragrance wafted through the air. She continued to stir mightily.

"Oh!" A pang shot through Mata Khivi's shoulder. She massaged the ache.

"Mata Ji," said a gentle voice.

A young man stretched out his hand to her.

"Jetha," said Mata Khivi, smiling.

"Mata Ji, tusee(n) baitho." The young man took her hand and offered her a stool, where she gratefully rested.

Bhai Jetha stirred the cauldron as Bhani watched. He was swift and focused, his sleeves rolled up. His breath shone in the crisp morning air. He stirred the warm milky pudding until it bubbled; the gooey rice rose to the surface. Bhani noticed a warm tingling spread through her body, from her throat to her heart, all the way down. Overcome, she looked away, pretending to be distracted by the dudh valla who was unloading pitchers of milk.

"Bann gayee," said Mata Khivi. *It's done.*

With one great motion, Bhai Jetha lifted the great cauldron off the fire and set it down. Mata Khivi slowly unwrapped a bundle of cloth in a basket as if it contained great treasure. Inside were golden cakes, hard and round, just large enough to hold in one's hand. This was the finest gurr—sugarcane straight from the fields where the juice was cooked, caramelized, and patted into dense cakes. The golden hue sparkled in the morning sun. Mata Khivi broke one in her hand and crumbled the golden lumps into the bubbling cauldron, where they dissolved instantly. She handed Jetha the ladle.

"Pyaar de naal," Mata Khivi told him. *Stir with love.*

Bhani was watching him again.

Jetha scooped the kheer from the cauldron and slipped it into the bowl.

He caught her gaze. She averted her eyes. He smiled.

Mata Khivi noticed.

Clearing her throat, she handed Bhani the kheer.

"Chheti jaavo," she said. *Hurry.* Her father was waiting.

Jetha's eyes followed the tip of Bhani's long black braid as she disappeared around the corner.

Mata Khivi wiped her brow with her dupatta. Oh, what should be done? Jetha was a fine young man, but he was an orphan boy. He grew up selling roasted salted grams on the street. He came to serve Guru Amar Das when he was twelve years old, his hands coarse from roasting black chickpeas on hot sand. Bhani was the youngest child of the Guru, and the most adored. She held a special place in the hearts of the people of Goindval. The people had come a long way in retiring the old ways of thinking, but there would be those who would not bless such a match.

The next morning, when Bhani arrived at the kitchen, Mata Khivi was busying herself with the grain delivery. Jetha stood up from the fire he was tending.

"Have you come for Guru Ji's kheer?" asked Jetha, knowing perfectly well why Bhani was here.

Bhani nodded.

He took the bowl from her. The cauldron had already been removed from the fire, the gurr already added.

Jetha poured the kheer and handed the bowl back to her. Their hands brushed. The fire burned; the wood crackled. Bhani remembered herself and rushed back with her father's kheer. Jetha's smile followed her home.

The winter mornings passed this way, Bhani and Jetha in a secret dance of glances, seconds at a time. Mata Khivi nudged Bhani's mother, Mata Mansa Devi, who observed her daughter—and sighed. She wasn't worried about Jetha's station. She was worried about her husband's heart. Their three older children were grown and married; Bhani never left his side.

"Bhani is nineteen now," Mata Mansa Devi remarked casually to Guru Amar Das that evening. "What kind of husband do we want for her?"

The Guru paused in his writing.

"How about someone like Bhai Jetha?" she went on.

Bhai Jetha? The young man who washed his clothes, swept his floors, massaged his legs, and even gave him counsel. Jetha was twenty years old and already serving him like a son.

"A search must be conducted for a suitable match," Guru Amar Das replied. They both knew that a formal search could extend for any amount of time. The Guru resumed writing.

Bhani was his Mohni, enchanted one. How would he let her go?

THE MORNING FOG GREW THINNER, BURNING AWAY UNDER THE growing confidence of the sun. As Bhani made her way home with the bowl of kheer, she thought about how Jetha's lips curled when he smiled. She bit her lip. She had promised to serve her father as faith-

fully as he had served Guru Angad. Her father had devotedly served
the Guru until his passing. So, too, would she. Her desire was a banal
distraction. A pollution. A betrayal. She tossed her head to shake it off,
as if it lived in her mind instead of her body.

Bhani took a deep breath and walked into her father's room.

Guru Amar Das was humming, still in meditation, longer than
usual. He was seated on a chaunki, a small stool, facing the window.
His eyes were closed, his hair tied in a joora on top of his head, his fingers pressed together. His humming filled the room. He was composing this morning. She caught a word that escaped his lips and floated
above him:

anand
anand
anand

It was the word for ecstasy. Divine, joyful ecstasy. She had heard
him sing of anand before, but always in mournful longing—as if it was
the nectar he thirsted for. This was different. The Guru's breathing was
heavy. Droplets of sweat graced his forehead like tiny pearls, and his
face shone radiant. He recited anand as a melodious moan until it unfurled into a verse:

anand bheiya meri mae satguru mai paaia
Ecstasy has me, oh my mother, I found my true Beloved!

The Guru was with the One, he had the One, and the One had him.
CRACK!

Her father's stool was giving way. Bhani dove to grasp the peg before it broke. The splinters chafed her hand, but the stool did not break.
Relieved, Bhani rested on the ground, one hand on the stool, the other
holding the bowl of kheer.

Her father hummed, undisturbed.

Minutes went by, perhaps an hour. Still her father hummed until a
new line burst into being. Bhani rested in the word that he repeated
again and again in every new verse: *anand.*

When Guru Amar Das opened his eyes, he beheld his daughter on the ground, bleeding from her hand.

"Mohni!" he exclaimed.

The Guru fell to his knees and kissed her hand, covered in blood.

"Why didn't you wake me?" he asked.

"Tusee(n) anand vich see," she said simply. *You were in anand.*

Guru Amar Das looked at his daughter as if with new eyes.

"I bless you, my Mohni," he said. "I bless your children and their children and their children."

Her children? Bhani searched her father's face.

The Guru called for her mother, who, upon seeing Bhani's bleeding hand, hurried in with a bandage, bowl of water, and haldi for the wound.

"You asked me to find Bhani someone *like* Bhai Jetha," Guru Amar Das said to his wife as he wrapped the wound. "Jetha vargaa, Jetha hee hai!" *The one like Jetha is Jetha himself.*

The Guru smiled. "Why not him for our Bhani?"

Bhani shook her head. She was to serve her father, not give in to her desire.

"Jo thiya gaeya, ohnu nahi gvauna," the Guru said, his eyes twinkling. *Don't lose what you've found.*

Bhani joyfully threw her arms around her father.

"May I be blessed with children who are worthy of the Guruship," she cried.

Guru Amar Das grew quiet.

"Pita Ji?"

"Our people have been left alone so far," Guru Amar Das said. "But hard times are coming . . ."

Bhani could still feel the sting in the cut on her palm.

"Ghar hee kee vath ghare rahaavai," said Bhani. *What is of the house should stay in the house.*

"Mohni," the Guru whispered. Bhani was asking for her family, her lineage, to absorb the pain and hardship to come, whatever it may be.

"Please," Bhani said softly.

Guru Amar Das gently placed his hand on Bhani's forehead and blessed her.

WHEN WINTER MELTED INTO SPRING, THE WOODLANDS HUMMED
with bumblebees, and the court of Guru Amar Das announced a grand
wedding for his daughter. Bibi Amro arrived for the occasion, now
with her children following her. She found Bhani trying to sit still as
her hands and arms were being painted with mehndi. Bibi Amro fed
her cousin-sister ladoos and tucked loose strands of her hair behind her
ears, so that she could see the aunties singing and dancing around her.
And when no one was looking, Bibi Amro whispered what to expect in
her marriage bed. Bhani blushed and listened intently, grateful for the
information.

When it was time for the wedding ceremony, Bhani's heart beat in
her ears. Bhai Jetha arrived on a white horse, wearing a wedding sehra
of garlands. He took his seat next to her around a small fire. They sat
so close, their skin almost touched. Bhani kept her gaze on the flames.
She felt the heat on her face.

Guru Amar Das commenced the ceremony. He had a surprise for
them. He called forth the rababis, who lifted their musical instruments.

Bhani looked at her father curiously.

The Guru smiled warmly at her, then closed his eyes and began to
sing:

anand bheiya meri mae satguru mai paaia
satgur ta paaia sahaj setee man vajeeaa vaadhaiaa
raag ratan parvaar pariaa sabad gaavan aaiaa
sabado ta gaavhu hari keraa man jinee vasaiaa
kehai nanak anand hoaa satguru mai paaia

Ecstasy has me, oh my mother, I found my true Beloved!
I found my true Beloved with deep ease, my being resounds
    with musical celebration
Jeweled melodies and celestial harmonies have come to sing
    the sacred song

Those who sing that sacred song, their being is immersed in
    the One
Says Nanak, I am in ecstasy, I found my true Beloved!*

Bhani wept.

The Guru was singing his epic song of divine joy, Anand Sahib.
And he was singing it for *her*—for *them*! Her body's desires were not
polluted or wrong, or even banal. Her father was saying: Your desire is
sacred! The burning in you is sacred! This union is sacred. Let it be an
avenue to the One. Let it deliver you in anand.

Bhani felt relief course through her. So many painful beliefs had
lodged inside her—it was as if she was seeing them for the first time—
that she was not worthy of pleasure, that she had to suffer in order to
serve, that she should be ashamed of her desire, of how she swooned
when she tasted kheer, or relished sugarcane, or thought of *his* touch!
But as her father sang to her of anand—of mystical ecstasy—her body
quaked, and all those judgments were crumbling down like fallen bricks,
and now the wall was broken, and the hot river coursing through her
was power and light. Her desire was beautiful; her pleasure was good.
More than good! Her pleasure was a pathway to the One.

When the song was done, her father dried her tears.

After the ceremony, a wealthy guest presented Bhani a box of fine
jewels as a wedding gift. Bhani asked him to donate the money to Mata
Khivi's langar instead. Smiling, Mata Khivi signaled the start of the
wedding feast.

SHORTLY AFTER THE WEDDING, GURU AMAR DAS RECEIVED WORD
that Emperor Akbar, the ruler of the Mughals, was on his way to
Goindval. Akbar was the grandson of Emperor Babur, the first Mughal
ruler of the north who had sent his armies to bleed Punjab. Babur left

* Guru Granth Sahib, ang 917, Raag Ramkali, Guru Amar Das Ji.

death and destruction in his wake; Guru Nanak stood in "the city of
corpses" at Saidpur and condemned Babur's brutality.* Babur's grandson Akbar seemed different. Inspired by Islam and the teachings of
mystics of many paths, Emperor Akbar opened his court to sages, artists, and thinkers of all kinds. Now he was seeking an audience with the
Guru of Goindval.

"We are a threat to anyone who wants to rule over others," Guru
Amar Das said to his daughter.

"Because we know that we are already free," replied Bhani. She
traced the scar on her palm, still visible beneath her mehndi. She was
ready for whatever was to come.

On the appointed day, Emperor Akbar arrived on a canopied elephant, followed by a royal procession of bodyguards, soldiers, and
horsemen, as well as artists, scribes, painters, and musicians. The Emperor's attendants rushed forth to lay out fine silks and velvet on the
ground for him. But the Emperor walked barefoot into the clearing and
sat for langar. He was seated not high and mighty on a throne, but humbly in pangat, side by side with the people of Goindval. Then he had a
private audience with Guru Amar Das, and departed shortly after.

"What did he say?" Bhani asked her father, breathlessly.

Guru Amar Das handed her a scroll the Emperor had left behind. It
was a formal complaint signed by a group of orthodox Brahmins and
Khatris:

*Goindval de Guru Amar Das ne Hindua(n) de dharmik atay
samajak reeta(n)-rivaaj tyaag ditay han atay chaar jateeya(n) de
bhed bhaav mitta ditay han . . . Ehe apnay shishan nu bina
jaatpaat de bhed-bhaav to sabh nu ik ktaar vich bithaa ke apnay
langar vicho(n) bhojan chhakaounda hai chahe oho Jatt, Bhatt,
Musalmaan, Brahmin, Khatri, dukaandaar, Choohray, naee,
dhobi, machhee jaa(n) tarkhaan, kujh vee houn. Asee(n) benti
karde haa(n) ke es noo(n) hunn hee roko nahi(n) taa(n) pichho(n)
katthan ho javega.*

Guru Amar Das of Goindval has abandoned the religious and social customs of the Hindus and abolished the distinction of the four castes . . . He seats all his followers in a line and causes them to eat together from his kitchen, irrespective of caste—whether Jats, strolling minstrels, Muhammadans, Brahmans, Khatris, shopkeepers, barbers, washermen, fishermen, or carpenters . . . We urgently request you put a stop to this ill practice immediately, or there will be great trouble.*

Emperor Akbar had come to see for himself. But he was so impressed by langar that, instead of punishing them, he offered to build more such langar halls all across the land. Guru Amar Das replied that such a gift, while generous, defeated the purpose of langar. Langar was *by* the people *for* the people. That's what made it taste so good. Emperor Akbar offered an alternative gift: five hundred bighas of land to the Guru's daughter, Bhani, on the occasion of her wedding.

The Guru's eyes twinkled; Bhani beamed. If hard times were coming, they would not come today.

BHANI WENT WITH HER HUSBAND, JETHA, TO BASARKE TO LIVE WITH his Nanke, his late mother's family, as was the custom. But her spirit dimmed. She kept thinking of her father and the weight of what was coming. Her cousin Bibi Amro visited her, and the two women shared their dukh-sukh, their sorrows and joys. Bhai Jetha came to Bhani with a proposal: They could return to Goindval to live with Guru Amar Das, and to serve him. It was unheard of: A bride lived with her husband's family, not the reverse! But Jetha wanted Bhani's light to burn bright, even if that meant breaking all the rules of the world.

On the day of their return to Goindval, Guru Amar Das was composing poetry in the garden courtyard. Bhani ran to him in her red

*   Aulakh, Ajit Singh. *Sri Gur Pratap Suraj Granth Steek: Volume 3*. Bhai Chatter Singh Jiwan Singh, 2010, pp. 328–29.

wedding bangles, followed by Jetha, who pulled the oxen cart and grinned widely. The Guru kissed their foreheads and uttered:

dhan pir eheh na aakheean behan ekatthay hoe
ek jot doe moortee dhan pir kaheeai soe

Bride and groom are not merely those who sit together
Call them bride and groom who share one light in two bodies*

In releasing his daughter, the Guru found her again. In letting her go, he gained them both. Light filled the courtyard. They were part of a larger love story now. And that story was just beginning.

Aao chaa peelo . . .
Come, let's have tea . . .

---

*   Guru Granth Sahib, ang 788, Raag Suhi, Guru Amar Das Ji.

A ROADSIDE STOP, A MEMORY

WE DROVE THROUGH THE COUNTRYSIDE FROM KHADOOR TO GOINDVAL, from the second Guru's home to the third Guru's. What took Guru Amar Das hours to walk on foot, we traversed in minutes. On the way, we stopped at Gurdwara Damdama Sahib, which stood like a lone salt palace in a sea of green. Guru Amar Das rested here during his daily sojourns to Khadoor to serve his predecessor. In fact, this is where he is said to have fallen into the weaver's pit and been ridiculed as "Homeless Amru."

As the car pulled up, Sharat made funny voices to distract Ananda as Kavi and I jumped out for a quick look. We went into the gurdwara, bowed, and spotted an enormous glass box. Inside was a long, thin pole wrapped in bright saffron cloth.

"Kavi, the killa!" I said. "This is the branch Guru Amar Das tripped on when he fell into the weaver's pit."

"Whoa," Kavi said. He gazed at the relic before him. A bit of smooth wood stuck out from the top of the saffron cloth.

"Mommy, we can touch it!" Kavi knelt down to an opening at the bottom of the glass box and touched the wood, beaming.

"Is that the Guru?" asked Kavi.

Inside the box, there was a portrait of Guru Amar Das, dressed in humble white robes. He was on his knees, propping himself up with one arm. In his other arm he carried a bronze pitcher. He was wearing a long, white beard. His eyes were closed. He had fallen, but not a drop of water had spilled from the pitcher.

"Yes," I said.

The portrait reminded me of my grandfather. Papa Ji had a long, white beard, too; he, too, devoted himself to all kinds of daily labors in his old age—tending a garden, driving us to school, cooking khichri of rice and lentils when we were sick, composing poetry all along. When we walked the streets of our California farm town, people would stare at my grandfather's turban and snicker. They, too, uttered cruel nicknames. I would shoot daggers at them, as Bibi Bhani must have. I wanted the world to see my grandfather as the sage he was. He called me his star; I promised not to leave his side.

Then, I fell in love. Papa Ji was crushed. The person I found was not raised in our faith. He saw my desire as a betrayal. "Isn't the one light in all of us?" I cried to Papa Ji, trying to win his blessing. "What of your children?" he countered. We debated for hours, as if the heart could be persuaded by bullet points. Finally, on his deathbed, Papa Ji looked up at Sharat and me, and he blessed us. He asked for forgiveness and blessed us both.

Papa Ji never got to meet our children. Never got to see how we raise them with the stories of the ancestors he loved, how we tie our son's hair the way he tied his, how Kavi plays the tabla like him, how Ananda sings kirtan with my mother and me. How we are giving them channels for anand. My grandfather never got to see how in his letting me go, I found one who made me the wisest woman I could be. He never saw us return to him, one light in two bodies.

When we returned to the car, Ananda was happily holding a tablet, playing a Punjabi language game, unbothered that we had taken so long. Sharat looked triumphant. Kavi snuggled beside her to play.

As the countryside flew past us, the Punjabi app went "Rrrring! Rrrring!" every time the children got a word correct.

Are we still our ancestors' wildest dreams, even if they could not have dreamt precisely us?

ARRIVING IN GOINDVAL

WHEN WE ARRIVED IN THE SMALL TOWN OF GOINDVAL, JASSO found a local granthi who worked at a gurdwara to show us around. He led us through the narrow streets, past vegetable and fruit carts, to an ornate marble entrance: Gurdwara Chobara Sahib.

"This is where Guru Amar Das Ji lived," Jasso said.

Inside was a bright courtyard with a well, surrounded by a set of rooms. We walked through the first door on the left into a small humble room filled with light.

"This is *the* room," I exclaimed to the kids. "This is where Guru Amar Das meditated every day, where his stool broke, and Bhani caught the stool, and her hand bled, and he blessed her! Remember? He blessed her right here."

"Oh yeah!" said Kavi.

"This is where he must have written the Anand Sahib," I said.

"That's my name!" said Ananda.

"That's right," I said. "And what does your name mean?"

"JOY!" She jumped up and down, her eyes sparkling.

"Yes," I said. "And not just any joy. *Divine* joy. Ecstatic pulsating joy! Joy that feels good in your body. Joy that takes you into the stars and back!"

Ananda started twirling, stretching out her arms.

"Guru Amar Das wrote the song of joy, the Anand Sahib. Remember how it goes?"

The children looked at me blankly. Just when I thought I was on a roll.

"Anand bheiya meri mae," I started to sing, "satguru mai paaia."

"Oh yeah!" they said.

"I want dudh-dhoo," cried Ananda suddenly, asking to nurse.

"Now?" We were in the room where Guru Amar Das meditated. I was teaching them about anand. But I found a corner, pulled my dupatta over us, and my daughter nursed, playing with my shawl like a canopy. I relaxed. Somehow my dupatta never slipped from my head when I nursed. I peered under the cloth and locked my hands and smiled at her. Her eyes rolled back; Ananda was in *anand*.

She already knew what felt good in her body.

When did I forget?

RECLAIMING PLEASURE AS SACRED

I BELIEVE I STARTED TO HATE MY BODY WHEN I WAS SIX YEARS OLD, after my first racial slur. And then when I was twelve, saw my side profile in a home video, and realized that my nose was crooked. And then when I was fourteen and got my period and thought it was dirty. By then, repulsion for my body was my default. So, when I started to feel desire in my body, I was ashamed of it. It took me a long time to learn that all parts of me were beautiful, and beloved, and good. It took a long time for me to learn to love my body.

Many of us are thrown into a world that teaches us to loathe our bodies. We are made to believe that our bodies are sources of sin. That our impulses for pleasure or release are vile. That we have to tame our body to be good or desirable or spiritual. Only then are we worthy. It's worse when we are born into a body that is denigrated by this society—dark or female or queer or trans or disabled or fat or otherwise different. We are taught to hate our bodies. To hate ourselves. And so, we stop feeling our bodies altogether.

Here is what I wish to tell you: Your body is part of the Beloved. Your skin is beautiful; your desire is good. There are no bad parts of your body, not even the parts that hurt. Only parts that contain the potential for healing and insight and transformation. When we embrace all of our parts and reside in our whole body, our body can become the site of immense pleasure.

Pleasure is what floods your body when you experience connection and union.

Pleasure is sacred.

Pleasure *is* sacred.

Pleasure is *sacred*.

In other words, pleasure is what God feels like.

In their poetry, the Sikh Gurus often used the metaphor of the bride and bridegroom for the spiritual seeker and the Divine. We are the bride, and the Divine is the one we long for, and when the Beloved finally comes, it's pure ecstasy: anand.

sej suhavi sada pir rave sach sigar banavania
Her bed is beautiful, she ravishes her Beloved forever adorned
    with ornaments of truth*

dhan har prabh piaarai raaveeaa
jaa(n) har prabh bhaiee raam

The soul-bride is ravished by her Beloved One
when the Beloved One is pleased with her†

These poems by our ancestors are sensual, even erotic. But most of us
who go to the gurdwara and hear them and sing along might not recognize the radical, liberatory, body-affirming nature of the poetry in front
of us. At every Sikh service, we sing the five pauris of the Anand Sahib,
the song of ecstatic joy. At every Sikh wedding, the verses that marry us
are called the Anand Karaj, which means "toward ecstasy." *Karaj* is de-
rived from the Sanskrit *karya,* which means undertaking. The ceremony
is literally called a transport into divine ecstasy. The ancestors were saying: You can experience the Beloved *inside* of life: in the texture of your
relationships, with your bodies, and with one another. This is the practice of a sage. For in anand, we are delivered from the illusion of duality:

eh vis sa(n)saar tum dekhde eh har kaa roop hai
har roop nadree aaiaa

The whole world you see is the form of the Beloved
The Beloved's form is all you see‡

Anand is the pleasure that comes when you realize in your body the
Love that always is.

---

*   Guru Granth Sahib, ang 110, Raag Majh, Guru Amar Das Ji.

†   Guru Granth Sahib, ang 854, Raag Bilaaval, Guru Ram Das Ji.

‡   Guru Granth Sahib, ang 922, Raag Ramkali, Guru Amar Das Ji.

It's important to note that my interpretation is uncommon. As in most religions, we are taught to be wary of worldly pleasures. I anchor my approach in Guru Nanak's full-throated embrace of the householder's life:

nanak satgur bhaytiai pooree hovai jugat
hasandiaa khaylandiaa painandiaa khaavandiaa vichay hovai mukat

Oh Nanak, meet the True Beloved fully this way:
Within laughing, playing, dressing, and eating, become liberated.*

This is how I remember my grandfather lived, in full embrace of the pleasures of being alive.

When I was a little girl, I often went with Papa Ji to the Sikh gurdwara in Fresno. During the service, Papa Ji sat in meditation, eyes closed, hands on his knees. Papa Ji rested *inside* the music. The kirtan sounded beautiful to me but also sad, like shades of longing. I looked around the room for new details to ponder: a loose gold thread, a dollar sticking out of the donation box, a flourish in the silks. My feet fell asleep.

Then suddenly, the whole room erupted in joy. The bells rang, the drums sounded! The energy shook me awake. Everyone sang the Anand Sahib together. Guru Amar Das's song of ecstatic joy concludes every service. No dancing allowed in the gurdwara, but my heart danced! I swayed to the music, as did Papa Ji.

At the end, we received prashaad. *Two hands to receive! Let the warm offering fall into your palms. Flour, sugar, butter. Fold your hands and press them to your forehead. Scoop the prashaad into your mouth. The taste of anand is sweet! Let it linger, let it linger.*

It was pure pleasure, in the body, without apology or shame.

Now, in my forties, I am on a journey to reclaim that kind of pleasure in all parts of my life. My body carries the scars that come from endometriosis, sexual assault, police brutality, racial violence, and de-

---

*   Guru Granth Sahib, ang 522, Guru Arjan Ji.

cades of self-hatred. I learned how to speak from my trauma in order to be heard. I accepted stress and discomfort as the default way of being alive. But I am tired of speaking from the wound. I want to live and create from the seat of pleasure. Embracing pleasure will not diminish my ability to speak to injustice; it will make me even more powerful. The more I know pleasure and rest in my body, the more I am able to see oppression for what it is: not a demonic force, but a loss of love. The solution is not to slay the enemy, but to return to love. To stop their harm with a firm hand, and extend the other hand with the hope that they will one day take it. Or their children will take it. For the brief, distracting high that comes from belonging to a group that hates and excludes is nothing compared to the pleasure of infinite union and connection—with everyone and everything.

THE BELOVED BODY

WHEN WE WERE BACK ON THE ROAD, ANANDA STARTED TO SHOUT out her love for me, which was better than demanding snacks.

"Mommy, I love you bigger than the sky!" she said.

"Mmm-hmmm," I nodded, studying Google Maps.

"I love you bigger than the world!"

"Wow," I muttered, scrolling.

"I love you bigger than your body!"

I looked up from the screen.

"That's pretty big," I joked.

"Yeah, you've never been outside it," Kavi quipped.

WAIT. I have never been outside my body.

"Wow, you're right," I said.

The body is the site of All.

THE FIVE GREAT PLEASURE PRACTICES

WHEN I LOOK AT CULTURES AROUND THE WORLD, I SEE HUMAN BE-ings turn to five core practices for mystical union and connection:

music and song, movement and dance, breathwork, substances, and
sensual pleasure.

Which one calls to you?

Music. In the Sikh tradition, the sound current is the conduit for
mystical union. The Sikh Gurus sang the sacred poetry in raags—
musical scales that move through specific emotion, time, and seasons.
They crafted sacred instruments for us to embody the wisdom musically: The strings of the rabab strike the heart, the bow of the saranda
resounds in the bones, the wailing peacock cries of the taus awakens the
senses, the beat of the mridang grounds the body. In cultures everywhere, people sing to defy a world that sequesters and separates them,
from gospel songs in Black churches to Indigenous moonlit incanta-
tions to lullabies for children. Music is the lifeblood of movements for
liberation, inner and outer.

Dance. While dance is not a practice in Sikh houses of worship, it's
a strong part of Punjabi culture, where bhangra folk dance is renowned
globally for its joyous celebratory beat. When we dance, we feel free—
from Ghost Dances to queer clubs as sanctuaries to concerts that bring
all kinds of people together. When we step off the dance floor, we carry
within our bodies that feeling of ease and release and freedom. Dance
can even become a channel for mystical union. My Kathak teacher in
classical Indian dance once told us: The purpose of dance is not self-
expression but self-actualization.

At home, we have Dance Time. We play a song for the children,
and their little bodies become spectacular fireworks. The first time that
music took my son like that, my jaw dropped. I did not know his little
body could fling across the room with such force and speed. My daughter dances fluidly: Her body floats and unspools; we drift apart and
meet again on a cloud where everything else fades away. On my hardest days, even when I return from a sorrowful vigil, I dance with my
children. And for the length of the song, we are free.

Breath. Change the proportion of gasses in the lungs, and perceive the
world differently. Slow the breath down to decelerate: slow the heartbeat,
calm the nervous system, soothe stress. Breathe fast to activate the body:

quicken the heartbeat, ignite energy, rise to the occasion. Yogis in India developed methods of breath-manipulation to cultivate powerful and profound states of mind and body. Observation of breath is an ancient practice. At night, the children are still bouncing around from Dance Time, but they get in the bed and place their hands on their bellies, and we say: *Let it come, let it go*. Slowly they surrender to sleep. It always astounds me: We can reset our nervous system with three deep breaths.

Substances. Indigenous cultures have long used psychedelics for medicine, spiritual sojourns, and rites of passage. While such substances are generally not used in the Sikh tradition, some Nihang warriors prepare a drink that includes bhang, dried cannabis, and other herbs. Always used in highly disciplined rituals. Now people are finding new ways to use substances for trauma therapy and healing. Such substances have the power to reformat consciousness, but they risk harm when used without intention and skill.

I like to think of substances broadly. Any substance you take into your body—whatever you eat or drink—has an impact on body and mind. I love tasting cacao, grinding cacao, drinking cacao. I once stood in a grove of cacao trees, orange-brown pods floating above me like luminous orbs; I was overjoyed. The special molecular compound in chocolate is called anandamide—a scientist actually named this compound after anand, the Sanskrit word for ecstasy, the same word used in the Anand Sahib. When I close my eyes and taste chocolate, I think: I am literally tasting anand.

These practices are the simplest and oldest methods for human beings to experience freedom in our bodies. Each is a potential avenue to the humming union of your body with the world. Nearly all of them are available to us all of the time, no matter our resources: We can sing. We can dance. We can breathe. We can taste. We can experience joy, right here and now. You don't need all these practices. Only the ones that call to you. Skip any that go against moral, cultural, or legal norms that matter to you. Explore the ones you need in safe, healthy ways.

While our children are small, we ask them to dance, sing, drum, taste chocolate, and play musical instruments with us. I don't know which art will be their chosen medium, the one they turn to in adult-hood. But I want to put these patterns into their body now, so that they can choose among them one day. And this is just as important to me as any subject they learn in school. Because the world they inherit will be a cause for fear, and a thousand reasons for despair will nip at their heels like hungry dogs, and the little critics will come crowding once they stumble. But if I can give them a kite to fly—something that will lift them off the ground and let them taste that ecstatic pleasure of being alive, here and now, lost in the rhythm of the universe—then I will be teaching them the most essential thing of all: Joy is our birthright.

We have covered music, dance, breathwork, and substances. We have one more practice to talk about. Pour another cup of tea!

Sensual pleasure. The legendary Black feminist visionary Audre Lorde changed my life forever with her iconic essay "The Uses of the Erotic." She writes that, during World War II, her family bought sealed plastic packets of white uncolored margarine. It came with a tiny pellet of yellow coloring. She had to massage the yellow pellet into the pale margarine, spreading color and flavor through the whole. That's how it is with the erotic, she writes. Once released, it can color the whole of your life. Once you feel pure pleasure erupting through the skin, you know that being alive can feel this good. You can choose to find some of that feeling in everything you do. Even your daily work can be plea-surable. People who know pleasure in their bodies often resist oppres-sion. Because we know what it's like to be free—and satisfied.

What if being alive in your body, right now, was the most pleasur-able experience on earth?

In brain-imaging studies, a brain that has reached a peak state in meditation is indistinguishable from a brain on certain psychedelics. Similarly, researchers found that clitoral stimulation "can trigger a substantial mystical experience, comparable in strength to a moderate dose of psilocybin."[*] That means that *any* pleasure practice engaged

[*]   Griffiths, Roland R., Matthew W. Johnson, William A. Richards, et al. "Psilocybin Occasioned Mystical-Type Experiences: Immediate and Persisting Dose-Related Effects." *Psychopharmacology (Berl)* 218, no. 4 (2011): 649–65.

thoughtfully—breathwork or music or dance, sensual pleasure or substances—can usher you into the same field of light.

YOU MIGHT SAY: I HAVE NO TIME FOR PLEASURE.

You don't have to start big. Begin with asking: What feels good in my body? The question alone is powerful. The world wants to stress you, depress you, and doom-scroll you into a catatonic state. We cannot marshal the energy and imagination to change our lives or change the world if we are tired, wired, or stressed. Being aware of crisis does not mean our bodies need to be *in* crisis all the time. Pleasure practices carve a different space inside us—a sovereign space. If we are to become the ones who rebirth the world, we must be able to weave pleasure practices into our lives as regular and reliable channels for release and renewal.

You might say: Pleasure is a just a temporary escape.

You're right, it can be for many people. It takes courage to take the information gained in those moments of beauty and freedom—and bring that into your daily life, not just for yourself but for the people around you, for the world. When the moment of anand recedes, we have a choice: We can go back to sleep, participating in the same habits and systems that keep us small and apart. Or we can use that inspiration to heal ourselves and others.

You might say: But pleasure makes me feel guilty.

Here's something that might help. In the Sikh tradition, there is no concept of sin. Instead, there are what are called destructive impulses. Or the five thieves, panj chor. They are kaam, krodh, lobh, moh, and ahankar—lust, wrath, greed, attachment, and excessive pride. Each is a healthy part of ourselves that has usurped the rest of us and become destructive:

> *Kaam, lust.* Desire draws us to pleasure and connection, but
> lust can tear our lives apart. Honor and channel your desire
> in a way that supports your body and relationships.

Krodh, wrath. Rage carries information and energy, but when rage explodes, it leaves a trail of destruction. Dance with your rage. Harness that energy for thoughtful action in the world.

Lobh, greed. Ambition is healthy and generative, while greed blunts the senses and wounds the collective. Pursue your goals with humility, attending to all touched by your actions.

Moh, extreme attachment. Affection is the core of love, but clinging to people or things out of desperation only increases separation. Hold your loved ones lightly, with gratitude.

Ahankar, excessive pride. Feeling proud is a healthy part of loving ourselves, while extreme pride diminishes others. Think of your role in collective flourishing.

When a pleasure practice starts to damage your body, your relationships, or other people, that's when it becomes a thief. The solution is not to gut pleasure from your life, but to use the tools mindfully and with integrity. That's the practice of the sage.

The takeaway: Don't exile the parts of you that want pleasure, or any other part of you. Invite them into a harmonious relationship with the rest of you. Say: *You are a part of me I do not yet know.* Ask them what they need. Tell them what you are ready to give. Invite them into an ongoing relationship. When we do this, we are returning ourselves to what we once knew as children, before we started to banish parts of ourselves. We were born free.

A ROADSIDE SURPRISE

AS WE SPED THROUGH THE COUNTRYSIDE AT THE END OF A LONG day, I nodded off.

"GURR!"

Happy screeched the car to a halt.

Farmers were making raw sugarcane juice on the side of the road. We spotted baskets of golden cakes at the roadside.

We clamored out of the car. Sugarcane fields surrounded us on all sides. Beneath a simple canopy were three enormous wells in the ground filled with bubbling hot caramel liquid. On the far side, farmers were squatting and patting the gurr into dense golden cakes. Hundreds of golden cakes glistened on a sheet, catching the light of the setting sun.

Jasso glided over to talk to them and returned with one great gold cake, wrapped in Indian newspaper.

All of us hovered over the gurr.

"Ik, doh, tin!" We counted to three and took a bite.

The heavens opened. My eyes watered. It was crispy on the outside, soft and warm on the inside, and sweet all the way through. I swooned; the children jumped up and down; Sharat smiled broadly; Jasso chuckled watching us.

This was the taste our ancestors loved, too, the taste that sweetened the kheer, the taste that Papa Ji cherished, and it was divine.

SAGE WARRIOR,
PRACTICE PLEASURE . . .

PLEASURE IS YOURS, NO MATTER who you are or what body you have. You don't have to feel guilty for having pleasure: In moments of pleasure, we taste and embody the world we want for everyone. Make pleasure a practice. Which practices call to you? Music and song, movement and dance, breathwork, substances, sensuality. Choose what you already enjoy a little and want to bring into your life more.

Find something small and delicious. A single raisin. A blueberry. A piece of chocolate. Or a morsel of sugary gurr. Pop it into your mouth and eat it. Take another piece and, this time, study it closely. Use all your senses. Notice color, shape, light, texture, smell. Place it on your tongue. Let it slowly dissolve and release different notes, like the notes of a song. Where in your body do you feel good? Greet the parts of you that feel pleasure. Say: *You are a part of me I do not yet know.* You can ask: *What do you need from me?* Listen deeply. Notice your relationship to pleasure—what it is now, and what you want it to be.

The sage embraces pleasure practices as channels for union and connection—with oneself, with others, and with the One. The warrior responds to the world not from the wound but from the seat of pleasure.

ANCESTOR TREE

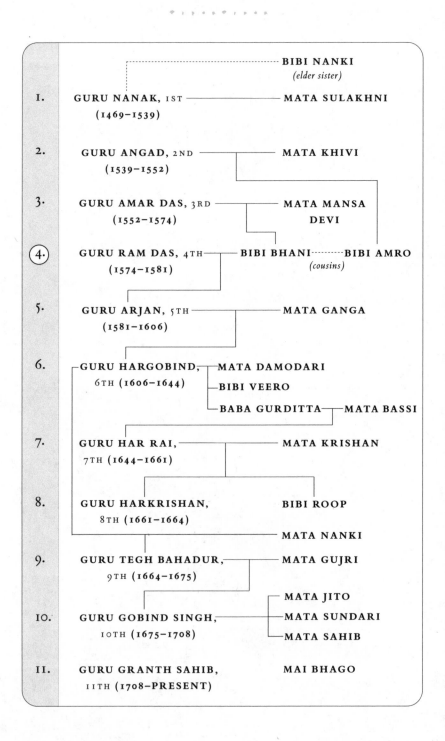

BIBI NANKI
(elder sister)

I.   GURU NANAK, 1ST ——————— MATA SULAKHNI
        (1469–1539)

2.   GURU ANGAD, 2ND ——————— MATA KHIVI
        (1539–1552)

3.   GURU AMAR DAS, 3RD ——————— MATA MANSA
        (1552–1574)   DEVI

(4.)   GURU RAM DAS, 4TH ——— BIBI BHANI ·········· BIBI AMRO
        (1574–1581)   *(cousins)*

5.   GURU ARJAN, 5TH ——————— MATA GANGA
        (1581–1606)

6.   GURU HARGOBIND, ——— MATA DAMODARI
        6TH (1606–1644)   BIBI VEERO
                    BABA GURDITTA ——— MATA BASSI

7.   GURU HAR RAI, ——————— MATA KRISHAN
        7TH (1644–1661)

8.   GURU HARKRISHAN,   BIBI ROOP
        8TH (1661–1664)
                           MATA NANKI

9.   GURU TEGH BAHADUR, ——— MATA GUJRI
        9TH (1664–1675)

                            MATA JITO

10.   GURU GOBIND SINGH, ——— MATA SUNDARI
        10TH (1675–1708)   MATA SAHIB

11.   GURU GRANTH SAHIB,   MAI BHAGO
        11TH (1708–PRESENT)

PART 4

BUILD SOVEREIGN SPACE

I. THE INNER THRONE:
THE STORY OF BIBI BHANI
AND GURU RAM DAS

. . .

Bhani awoke from a kick in her womb. The room was awash in a golden glow. A songbird, a chatrik, perched on the tree in the courtyard, signaling the dawn. The house was otherwise quiet. *Vaisakhi,* she remembered. The harvest festival. Her family had already left for the festival in the heart of Goindval. She was to stay home to rest.

It was strange to hear the Guru's house so quiet. The home of Guru Amar Das, third in the House of Nanak, was a place of study and sangat, where poets visited every day like the songbirds who flocked to their garden.

A kick.

Bhani got to her feet and slowly stepped out of her room. She usually slept with the rest of the family around the fire. But as her belly grew, her husband, Bhai Jetha, insisted on a room of her own. Her room stood at the front right corner of their house, across from three inner rooms where they hosted the many visitors who came to see the Guru. The only other room that stood alone like hers was on the other side of the house, the room where her father meditated.

Another kick.

"Aapa(n) chaliye?" she said, overcome with the urge to see the festival.

Bhani set out on the path she used to walk every morning to fetch her father's kheer. She used to be so light on her feet! Now she moved as if she carried a boulder between her thighs. She slowly wound her way through the narrow streets, using the brick wall for balance. In the clearing ahead, she saw more people than she had ever seen in one place. Her father, Guru Amar Das, fixed Vaisakhi Day as the day for

Sikhs to gather in one place and celebrate the harvest together, and now it seemed the whole world had come to Goindval.

Bhani wandered in, smiling at the scene: Crowds gathered around bards singing, musicians strumming, and folk dancers pounding their feet, brass bells catching the light. Elders joyfully drank sugarcane juice, gannay da ras, fresh from the fields. Children squealed on buffalo rides. Older kids ran with sticks, playing gulli danda. Girls jumped in and out of whirling rope, laughing in the swirl of music and color. As Bhani rested against a stall of bangles, she spotted a golden dupatta in the distance near the abode of worship.

Bhani's cousin Bibi Amro was greeting a line of pilgrims. She was dressed in a pale peach kameez and ghagara skirt, with a touch of embroidery, a gold dupatta draped over her head. Guru Amar Das had organized the Sikh realm into twenty-two masands, districts, and selected a Sikh to lead each one. Their position was called a manji, after the wooden cot that people rested on, because they were to be the support of the people. Guru Amar Das named Bibi Amro to lead a district he cherished, the one that contained his hometown of Basarke. She had led the Guru to his path, after all. Bibi Amro was a leader now, one of twenty-two revered leaders of the Sikh world. Her appointment reflected Guru Amar Das's commitment to liberation. He forbade purdah, declaring that women should never be forced to veil their faces. He forbade sati, condemning the horrific practice of forcing widows to burn alive on their husbands' funeral pyres. And he forbade kurrimaar, the practice of killing female babies upon birth. Instead, he lifted the people's eyes to leaders like Bibi Amro as models for what their girls could become.

Bhani beamed as she watched Bibi Amro at work. Smiling gently, Bibi Amro tended to pilgrims one by one before they disappeared down steps and vanished into the earth. This was the baoli, the underground stepwell that Jetha had built at Guru Amar Das's request. The stairs of the stepwell were hand-carved by Bhai Sadhaaran himself, a senior disciple of Guru Nanak. Eighty-four brick steps descended to the water, where the people came to drink, bathe, and pray. The baoli of Goindval was the heart of the Sikh world. It functioned like langar.

No matter who you were—Muslim or Hindu, high caste or low, rich or poor, woman or man, gendered or not, married or widowed or single, child or elder, dark skin or light—you drank from this well as one people.

"Mata Ji!" cried a little voice. Prithi Chand was at her side. At five years old, her eldest son was a bold, confident boy. He pulled down hard on her ghagara skirt to get her attention. Bhani stumbled.

BOOM!

Thunder shook her body and pain tore through her back.

BOOM! A large drum resounded.

The crowd lurched to make space around the drummer, crushing Bhani. Her son was still pulling her ghagara. She was going to fall. Bhani felt an arm around her shoulder. Bibi Amro had her. Bhani tried to say that she was in labor, but—

BOOM!

Jetha was suddenly there, holding her up from the other side.

She closed her eyes as Bibi Amro and Bhai Jetha—her cousin-sister and husband—led her out of the crowd. They told Prithi Chand to get "Mata Ji." Bhani wondered who her little boy was going to call—her mother, Mata Mansa Devi, or Bibi Amro's mother, Mata Khivi; she hoped both. She took one labored step after another. When she opened her eyes again, they were home. The midwife was waiting in the courtyard with bowls of water and herbs; Bhai Jetha let her go and waited outside. Bhani gripped the edge of the well so hard, her knuckles were pale. She leaned on the great tree and moaned. The drums from the festival pounded in her head.

BOOM!

Bhani wailed. Thunderous pain tore through her. When the pang lifted, she tasted salt. Her face was wet with tears. This labor was so much faster and harder than her previous ones.

Bhani took a few steps toward her father's meditation room. Another pang. She grabbed onto a peg that protruded from the wall next to the door. Her father's keeli, the peg he held in standing meditation. She had never touched it before. *My own standing meditation,* thought Bhani vaguely as the next pang hit.

Bhani gripped the peg and closed her eyes. Her father once told her of a serene lake surrounded by forest, and a mud hut at the edge of the water. He once meditated in that hut. It was the most peaceful place he had seen, he said. A realm of serenity and truth. *Sach khand.* That's where she wanted to be now. She searched inside herself. A blank void. Shades of gray.

Bhani started to hum. As she hummed—a gold sparkle appeared in the corner of her vision.

Bhani saw a great shimmering pool of blue water, golden sunlight rippling on the surface. She was standing in the grass by the water. There was a hut in front of her, but she wanted to stay out in the warm light, beneath the blue sky. She knelt at the pool and drank the cool water and rested in the soft green grass. A baby cooed on the grass next to her. Her baby. He had large luminous eyes like hers. She reached out to touch him—

BOOM!

Bhani was thrown out of the meadow. The pain was powerful, but it was happening far below her now, and she was above it, looking down, noticing, watching, waiting for the thunder to pass so that she could return to the pool and the meadow and the light and hold her baby. Back and forth she went, into the sunlit meadow, then down into the bowels of pain, then up again into the light. Until Mata Khivi said it was time.

Bhani was on her back on the manji in her room now, and the pangs were coming so fast they merged into each other. A tunnel of fire opened from under her. Bibi Amro's hands were on her shoulders, her mother's palm on her forehead, and Mata Khivi at her feet, but they were all so far away. They could not go through the tunnel with her. She had to go alone. She wanted to be with her baby by that great shimmering lake again. The only way was *through* the fire.

Bhani took a breath, and pushed; her flesh seared. She wailed. She took another breath and pushed. A warm wet body slipped out of her. Mata Khivi placed the baby on Bhani's chest. The newborn trembled like a soaked little songbird.

Bhani was laughing and sobbing. She had found a place within her she never had before, a place that was infinitely serene, where she could be safe and free, a space apart—a *sovereign* space. A world of pain could not touch her in that meadow; the hot winds could not touch her. From this place, she birthed this baby. It had taken all her strength to find it. A mountain of courage, the courage of lions. No, *warrior* courage.

Bhai Jetha was led into the room. He took Bhani's hand.

"Arjan." She whispered the baby's name.

Warrior. A warrior who came through a warrior's body.

IT WAS CUSTOM FOR A NEW MOTHER TO SPEND FORTY DAYS IN HER parents' house after giving birth before returning home, but Bhani was already in her parents' house. As the weeks went by, Bhani entered that strange dream-state that comes when one sleeps only a few hours at a time: the music of the ever-present kirtan and the songbird singing in the tree merged inside her. It was in this state that Bhani saw the meadow again.

"Thiya gaeya," Bhani whispered to Jetha when he came in to see her in the morning. As Baby Arjan nursed in her arms, Bhani closed her eyes, holding fast to the vision in her dream. It was the place she had found while in the throes of labor—that dazzling place of infinite peace, drenched in sunlight, fragrant with jasmine, at the edge of a shimmering pool that sparkled endlessly. And it was inside her.

Bhani's eyes shot open.

"I want you to see it, too," she said to her husband.

"Guru Ji told me of a place north of here where he meditated and found peace," said Jetha. "He is sending me there to build a new baoli."

"Kithay?" Bhani asked. *Where?*

"Tohadi jameen te," he said. *Your land.*

Bhani had never seen the land that Emperor Akbar had gifted her for her wedding after he visited for langar. Was this the place she saw in her dreams? Was that why her father told her so passionately of it? Baby Arjan unlatched with a satisfied grunt. She kissed his face and handed him to his father. As Bhani closed her eyes, the music carried her deeper into her watery dream-state. Before she knew it, she was in the sunlit meadow again. This time, it was effortless to find.

ARJAN GREW INTO A BEAUTIFUL, STRONG BOY, HIS MIND SPARKling with new poetry, melodies, and raags every day. It was as if all that music absorbed as a baby had alchemized inside him, and he already saw the world through the eyes of a kavi, a divinely inspired poet. At night, Bhani would tell Arjan stories of Guru Nanak, who was once a boy enthralled by beauty, too.

"Once, on his fourth udasi, Guru Nanak fell asleep under a tree," Bhani told Arjan. "He was dressed in the robes that hajis wore on pilgrimage to Mecca. He was awakened by a handful of stern-looking pilgrims crowding over him, pointing at him severely. 'Your feet are pointed to the Kabaa!' they cried. For them, it was a sign of disrespect. 'How dare you point your feet to Allah? You will be punished!'"

Arjan's eyes grew wide as he listened to the story.

"But Guru Nanak just smiled at them," said Bhani. "The Guru said, 'Please point my feet to where Allah is not.'"

Arjan laughed, delighted.

"Well, a few of the clerics picked up the Guru's feet to move him, but then realized their folly!"

"Because Vaheguru is everywhere," exclaimed Arjan.

"Andar atay baar vee." Bhani nodded. *Inside us and outside us.* "There is no place that is not sacred."

Arjan nestled into his mother's arms.

"And that means there is no place where poetry cannot find you," concluded Bhani. She wanted her son to let inspiration come to him, anytime, without holding back.

As Arjan drifted to sleep, Bhani sang:

nimakh na bisrao tum kao har har sadaa bhajah(u) jagdees

May you never forget the Beloved, not even for a moment
May you always be immersed in the One

ONE DAY, GURU AMAR DAS GATHERED THE FAMILY IN THE COURT-
yard for an announcement. Bhani set up a manji for her father to sit
comfortably under the tree. Her father was ninety-five years old now.
His eyes were bright, his mind ever-pristine.

Guru Amar Das called both his sons-in-law. Bhai Jetha stood, along
with Bhani's sister's husband, Rama. The Guru had a special task for
them. He needed them to build a tharra in front of the baoli—a strong
raised platform in front of the stepwell where he could sit and teach his
people. Would they do it?

The two men nodded, hands folded, and began to whisper to each
other about the design. The Guru raised his hand to quiet them.

"I would like you each to build your own," he instructed. They
were taken aback but promised to start in the morning.

Bhai Jetha and Bhai Rama labored in the hot midday sun on their
constructions. Bhani sent Arjan to deliver their meals, roti and makhan
along with lassi. On the day the platforms were completed, Arjan
rushed home.

"Guru Ji took one look at their work, shook his head, and told them
both to start over!" Arjan said to his mother.

Bhani nodded. This was not just any platform; it was the Guru's
spiritual throne.

A few weeks later, both men completed their new constructions.
But again, the Guru asked them to dismantle them and start all over.
They each built a third one. Again, the Guru asked them to try again.
Bhai Rama gave up. But Bhai Jetha kept toiling. He built and rebuilt the
platform seven times over.

Finally, the day came when the seventh platform was complete.

"Guru Ji said that he had to tear it down!" Arjan told his mother, his
eyes wide as he described his father's reaction. "He looked so tired, but
he bowed down at Guru Ji's feet and asked if he could start again."

That was her husband, thought Bhani. He knew that seva, sacred
service, required care and devotion, the courage to build and rebuild.
Bhai Jetha demonstrated that when he built the baolis, the stepwells, in

Goindval and on the land she had yet to see, and now as he built the Guru's throne.

"He was about to go back to work," Arjan said, "but Guru Ji brought him to his feet and kissed his forehead and called for Baba Budda Ji!"

Bhani gasped. Bhai Jetha, *her* Jetha, was to be the next Guru. She drew her son close and laughed, and he laughed along with her, until Bhani realized what this meant.

Her father knew his time was coming to an end.

THE GURU GADDI CEREMONY WAS HELD IN THEIR GARDEN COURT-yard in their home in Goindval. All twenty-two leaders of the masands attended, including Bibi Amro, whose golden dupatta flowed behind her. Bhani's eldest brother, Mohan Ji, was seated on tiger skin. Bhani's cousin Bhai Gurdas Ji, who her parents adopted as a boy after he was orphaned, stood ceremoniously behind her father, fanning him with a chaur, a whisk of yak hair. In his glistening white robes, Baba Budda Ji anointed the new Guru with crushed saffron and sandalwood, as he had every Guru before. At the end of the ceremony, Guru Amar Das announced: "My light has gone into Jetha! He shall now be known as Guru Ram Das." *Servant of the Beloved.*

Guru Amar Das's health declined rapidly after the ceremony. For days, he did not move or speak. His eyes were closed, yet there was the faintest smile on his lips; he was neither here nor there. He had found a sovereign space inside, that realm of anand, and he dwelled there. Bhani's hand rested on the Guru's forehead when he slipped away. Even as tears streamed down her face, a sense of serenity befell her. Bhani had kept her promise: She had never left her father's side.

Mata Khivi arrived to help Bhani with her father's final rites, his antam sanskar. Her son Datu accompanied her. Bhani was astonished to see him. To her, Datu stood for all the people who had ever humiliated her father, ever called him "Amru Nithaava(n)." *Homeless Amru.* Twenty-two years ago, Datu had been furious that the man he consid-

ered his family servant was now his Guru. Datu had marched up to
Guru Amar Das in front of the whole congregation and kicked him off
his seat. Her father simply responded, "I am old, and my bones are
hard. They may have injured your foot." Guru Amar Das kissed Datu's foot, and left Goindval. Datu sat on the throne for a few days, but
he was shunned by the people and sulked away, unrepentant. Baba
Budda Ji found Guru Amar Das meditating in a locked room in a disciple's house in Basarke, and persuaded him to return to Goindval to
lead. Now, all these years later, here was Datu, at her doorstep, to pay
his respects. Bhani wiped away tears. In the end, her father had won
them all over.

Bhani gathered with Mata Khivi and Bibi Amro around the fire. She
needed their advice. She handed them a folded embroidered cloth. Inside were strands of silver hair. When Guru Amar Das's body was carried out of the house to the funeral pyre by her brothers, Bhani noticed
a few strands of hair on his manji. Her father's hair. She didn't know
what to do with it. Should it be cremated, too?

"Keep it," Mata Khivi said. "As a way to remember what is true."

"What is true?" asked Bhani.

"Oho hamesha tere naal han," said Bibi Amro softly. *Your father is
always with you.*

Bibi Amro cupped her little cousin-sister's wrist and asked her to
close her eyes. Bhani felt something cool on her skin. When she opened
her eyes, she beheld the most beautiful pearl mala she had ever seen.
Creamy white pearls shimmered in the light and swirled with color.

"We want you to have this," said Bibi Amro.

Fashioned by Bibi Nanki, gifted in sisterhood to Mata Sulakhni,
who gifted it to Mata Khivi, who gave it to her daughter Bibi Amro,
who now presented it to Bibi Bhani, the mala was infused with love.

"Shakti vastay," the women said in unison. *For power.*

Bibi Bhani found her husband, Guru Ram Das, waiting outside the
house for her, beneath a full moon.

"Aapa(n) chaliye," he said. *Let's go.*

"Kithay?" she asked. *Where?*

"Tohadi jameen te," he said. *Your land.*

"Meri jameen?" she repeated.

"Jehrri jagah tusee(n) supnay vich dekhi see," he said. *The land from your dream.* They were going to go live on the land that Emperor Akbar had gifted her, the land her father, Guru Amar Das, had described so well that it had entered her dreams. It was her father's final wish.

They called it Guru ka Chak. *Home of the Guru.*

MANY HOUSEHOLDS MADE THE CHOICE TO ACCOMPANY GURU RAM Das and Bibi Bhani to the new land of Guru ka Chak. As the great procession rumbled north, young Arjan gazed at Goindval until it faded from sight.

"Puttar," said Bibi Bhani, watching him. At eleven years old, Arjan was leaving the only home he had ever known. "Let me tell you a story."

She wrapped a blanket around them both; Arjan rested his head on her shoulder.

"On his first udasi," began Bibi Bhani, "Guru Nanak visited a village where the people were cruel and filled with fear. They shut their doors to him, and refused to give him and Bhai Mardana anything to eat. When Guru Nanak left, he blessed them: 'Vasde ravo! May you prosper where you are!' Guru Nanak came upon another village, where the people were kind and openhearted and shared whatever they had. When the Guru left, he gave them a different blessing: 'Ujarr javo! May you scatter from this land!'"

Arjan furrowed his brow.

"Why did Guru Nanak bless the cruel ones to stay, and the kind ones to scatter?" asked his mother.

Arjan thought for a moment.

"So that fear would wither where it was," he said slowly, "and love would spread to all parts of the world."

Bibi Bhani nodded and gestured to a trunk next to her. She opened the lid and, with a prayer on her lips, lifted the fine cloths. Inside were manuscripts that bore writing in her father's hand, the shabds of Guru Amar Das, all 907 of them. The one on top read "Anand," the song of divine ecstatic joy.

"We take our ancestors with us," Bibi Bhani said, touching the pothi and her heart. Arjan followed.

The journey to Guru ka Chak took two days. It was sunset when they arrived. Bibi Bhani gripped Arjan as the oxen cart lurched to a stop.

"Tohadi jameen." Her husband smiled at her. *Your land.*

Before them was a shimmering blue pool of water, sparkling in the sunlight. It was surrounded by green meadows dappled with blossoming orange and red flowers. A simple mud hut stood at the water's edge, and a grand forest spread behind it as far as she could see. Bibi Bhani stepped down from the cart, her knees shaking. When her feet touched the ground, the scene did not dissolve.

Arjan jumped out to run through the meadow; Bibi Bhani held him back.

"Sit with me for a moment," she said. She had been here with Arjan before, in the sovereign space within her. Mother and son sat in the meadow. Bibi Bhani asked him to listen to the wind and feel the warm sun on his face, and her hand in his, and notice what it all felt like in his body. Arjan closed his eyes. A moment in vismaad! *Ecstatic, embodied wonder.* Then the grass tickled her son's nose, and he sneezed.

"Vaheguru!" she blessed him, and he laughed, and so did she. A deep contented laugh as if time could cease in this moment, and all would be right forevermore.

In time, Guru Ram Das doubly secured the gift from Emperor Akbar by purchasing the land from local farmers, the Zameendaar of Tung. He expanded the pool of water to create a great sarovar, sacred waters where people could drink, bathe, and pray. It could hold so many more people than the boali at Goindval. Artisans, bards, and laborers poured in, and soon the town became a vibrant center of learning. Guru Ram Das composed hundreds of new shabds that danced on people's lips, and the people renamed the town after him. It was now Ramdaspur.

One day, when Arjan was seventeen, an invitation arrived from Lahore requesting Guru Ram Das to attend a family wedding. Bibi Bhani shook her head; there was too much to do here. Guru Ram Das asked their eldest son, Prithi Chand, to represent him. Prithi Chand refused. He was twenty-three now and said he was occupied with more important projects in town. The Guru then asked Mahadev, their middle son, who shook his head and sulked back into his meditation room. Finally, the Guru asked Arjan. Bibi Bhani could tell that he really didn't want to go. He only wanted to be by his father's side. But Arjan honored his father's wish.

Bibi Bhani waited every day for her son to send a letter. For months, word did not come. They received news from relatives that the wedding had taken place, all had gone well, and now the sangat in Lahore so adored Arjan, they wanted him to stay. Guru Ram Das sent word that Arjan should build a langar for the people there. Months passed, and still no letter came from Arjan. Bibi Bhani closed her eyes and searched for her son.

A messenger appeared in the Guru's court one rainy afternoon, breathless, bearing a letter from Lahore.

Guru Ram Das broke the seal. Bibi Bhani watched him read silently, his eyes filling with tears. He handed the letter to her. It was a sacred poem. She read it out loud:

ik gharri na milte ta kaljug hota
hun kad mileeai pria tudh bhagvanta
mohe rain na vihavai need na avai bin dekhe gur darbare jio
hao gholi jio ghol ghumaee tis sache gur darbare jio

Every moment I am away from you is the age of darkness
When will I see you, my Beloved, Source of All
Night does not pass, sleep does not come, without seeing my
    Guru's court

I surrender myself, swirl, and dissolve for my true Guru's
    court*

Arjan had not forgotten them; his whole being was filled with *longing*. In the corner of the page, painted in large calligraphy, was the number 3.

"Why does it say three?" Bibi Bhani asked.

The messenger was surprised, then looked down, ashamed. Arjan had written his father two letters before this one. Their eldest son, Prithi Chand, had intercepted them, saying that he would deliver them to his parents himself. The letters were never delivered.

Guru Ram Das sent for Baba Budda Ji, whom he trusted most in his court, and asked him to bring Arjan home at once. Meanwhile, Bhani confronted her eldest son about the missing letters. Prithi Chand turned away from her, his face burning. He was jealous of his father's affection for Arjan. Bibi Bhani saw that behind that burning jealousy was his desire to be seen, to be important, to be loved.

On the day Arjan returned home, Bhani wanted to wait at the gate, but she took her position inside the court. Guru Ram Das had called the leaders of the sangat to be present. Prithi Chand and Mahadev stood unhappily next to her.

The gates opened. Young Arjan entered, dressed in simple traveling clothes. He looked around at all the people in the court, confused by the fanfare.

"Sat Kartar!" Guru Ram Das's voice boomed the traditional welcome. *True is the Great Doer; I honor the truth that is.*

"Sat Kartar!" replied Arjan.

"Jee aiya(n) nu," the Guru welcomed him formally.

Arjan pressed his hands together and bowed.

Bibi Bhani could not take it anymore. She opened her arms. Arjan ran to his parents, touched their feet in respect, and embraced them both.

---

*   Guru Granth Sahib, ang 96, Raag Majh, Guru Arjan Ji.

"Aaja mera puttar," whispered Guru Ram Das. *Come, my son.* Arjan rested his head on his father's soft, black beard.

Guru Ram Das then cleared his throat and stepped back.

"Did you write these letters?" asked Guru Ram Das, loud enough for the entire court to hear. Back to the formality. He held up three letters in his hand.

"Haa(n) Ji, Pita Ji," Arjan nodded.

"My son, you have written me three verses of poetry in these three letters," the Guru said. "Compose a fourth and final verse for me."

An attendant placed pen and paper before Arjan.

The Guru meant now. Here. Before everyone. Arjan took the pen, his hands trembling. There were too many people watching him. His heart pounded in his ears. Arjan looked at his mother. Bibi Bhani nodded for him to close his eyes.

Arjan took a deep breath. Eyes closed, he started to hum. After a moment, his lips began to move. Bibi Bhani knew where he had gone. He had found that space inside him, that sovereign space she had spent his childhood showing him, where the songbird sings ever freely in the tree, and the waters shimmer gold. Immersed in all that inner music, Arjan composed.

Arjan handed the paper to the attendant, who delivered it to his father. The fourth letter.

"Tusee(n) parr ke sunao," said Guru Ram Das. *Please read it aloud.*

Arjan did not need to look at the words. He recited all three verses along with the final new verse. As his cadence gained momentum, he was not reciting anymore, he was singing. His music filled the courtyard in the melody of Raag Maajh, a mood lit with longing, and it was as if the whole court were a chamber of Arjan's own heart:

I.

mera man lochai gur darsan taee
bilap kare chatrik kee niaee
trikha na utrai saat na avai bin darsan sant piare jio
hao gholi jio ghol ghumaee gur darsan sant piare jio

My mind longs for the sight of the Guru
Cries out like a songbird thirsting for rain
I stay thirsty, peace does not come without the sight of my beloved
    Sage
I surrender myself, swirl, and dissolve for the sight of my beloved
    Guru

II.

tera mukh suhava jio sahj dhun bani
chir hoa dekhe sarangpani
dhan so des jaha too(n) vasia mere sajan meet murare jio
hao gholi hao ghol ghumaee gur sajan meet murare jio

Your face is beautiful, I am eased in your song-wisdom
It has been so long since I have seen the Beloved of All
Blessed the land where you reside, my dearest friend, Infinite One
I surrender, I swirl and dissolve, for my Guru, dearest friend,
    Infinite One

III.

ik gharri na milte ta kaljug hota
hun kad mileeai pria tudh bhagvanta
mohe rain na vihavai need na avai bin dekhe gur darbare jio
hao gholi jio ghol ghumaee tis sache gur darbare jio

Every moment I am away from you is the age of darkness
When will I see you, my Beloved, Source of All
Night does not pass, sleep does not come, without seeing my
    Guru's court
I surrender myself, swirl, and dissolve for my true Guru's court

IV.

bhaag hoa gur sant milaaia
prabh abinasi ghar meh paaia

sev kari pal chasa na vichhura jan nanak daas tumare jio
hao gholi jio ghol ghumaee jan nanak daas tumare jio

Fortune has come! I am with my Sage Guru
I have found the eternal Beloved within my body
I will serve you, not a moment of separation, this humble servant
    Nanak is Yours
I surrender myself, swirl, and dissolve, this humble servant
    Nanak is Yours*

A sublime quiet fell over the people.

"These are letters of love, the greatest love there is," said Guru Ram Das. "Together they hold the power of a thousand shabds!"

Guru Ram Das paused and looked at Bibi Bhani.

"Anyone who sings this shabd will remember they are never separated from their Beloved," he said softly. Keeping his eyes on her, he lifted his hand to signal his attendants.

Suddenly, there was a whirlwind of movement. A great platter appeared with a coconut and copper coins. Baba Budda Ji emerged with a plate of red powder. Shock tore through the crowd. Guru Ram Das, the picture of health and strength, just shy of forty-seven, was initiating his own succession.

Baba Budda Ji placed a red tilak on Arjan's forehead.

Bibi Bhani glanced at her two other sons. Mahadev looked on solemnly, but her eldest, Prithi Chand, wore a look of shock.

Guru Ram Das stepped down and gestured for Arjan to sit on the throne. The Guru placed a coconut and five paisay at his son's feet and bowed. Prithi Chand tore away from the crowd; only his mother's eyes followed him out of sight.

"As one lamp is lit from another, so the Guru's light will pass into him and will dispel the darkness in the world," announced Guru Ram Das.

The people raised their voices in praise.

---

*   Guru Granth Sahib, ang 96–97, Raag Maajh, Guru Arjan Ji.

Bibi Bhani exhaled. It was done. Her husband was dying from an ailment neither of them understood, and that was unseen to everyone else. She had taken the news stoically, planning the Guru Gaddi ceremony with her husband carefully. Her son's love letters captured her longing more than he could ever have known. But there would be time enough to tend to her own grief, endless time. Arjan, her youngest child, only eighteen, was now the leader of the Sikh world. She flashed to the vision her father shared with her, of the hardships to come. The future required courage, warrior courage.

As the people shouted in praise, Arjan glanced at his mother and rested in her smile. He then turned to the sangat and raised his hand to express his acceptance. He was now Guru Arjan, fifth in the House of Nanak.

GURU RAM DAS RETURNED TO GOINDVAL WITH BIBI BHANI AND took his last breath in the same room where her father had passed seven years prior. When the antam sanskar was complete and the ashes spread, the family returned to Ramdaspur. Guru Arjan stepped down from the oxen cart and paused in the meadow where he first beheld this land with his mother as a child. Bibi Bhani knelt next to him again, her white salvaar muddied by the earth. She followed his gaze to the great sarovar. The surface of the water was a dark glass, reflecting the billowing clouds above.

Guru Arjan recited:

ik gharri na milte ta kaljug hota
Every moment I am away from you is the age of darkness

Bibi Bhani realized that he loved his father the way she loved hers. Now their great loves were gone, and they alone were left, mother and son.

Bibi Bhani hummed her lullaby:

nimakh na bisrao tum kao har har sadaa bhajah(u) jagdees
May you never forget the Beloved, not even for a moment
May you always immersed in the One

"Your father isn't gone," Bibi Bhani whispered. "He is part of the Oneness that always is."

Guru Arjan held his eyes on the glassy water.

"Your father wanted this sarovar to be a place for us to remember the Beloved," Bibi Bhani said slowly. "What do you see?"

She gestured to the water.

"Gaur naal vekho," she said. *Look deeper.*

Guru Arjan focused on a swan. The setting sun tinged the swan's wings with gold. It floated on the water in infinite peace, surrounded by the music of the songbirds and the melodies of raag wrapped in kirtan.

Bibi Bhani closed her eyes and thought:

A sovereign space. A space all our own, away from the world, away from the noise, away from time and fear. There, in that space, you will find your Beloved.

The next day, Bibi Bhani entered the court to find Guru Arjan seated on the throne. The revered Baba Budda Ji, dressed in his great white robes and jade mala, was at his side. Guru Arjan faced the court and ordered the water of the sarovar to be drained. The disciples looked alarmed. The earth will look dry and parched, he explained, but they need not worry. They will build a brick foundation in the center. On that foundation, they will build an abode of the Beloved, the greatest the world had seen.

Guru Arjan's voice was gentle but commanding; he was ready to continue what his father had started. Bibi Bhani was relieved: He was on his way. She left to find her eldest son, Prithi Chand, who had locked himself in a room since the succession ceremony.

"Your father did not choose you to lead," said Bibi Bhani through the door. "But he loved you . . ."

Prithi Chand recoiled; her words only fed his fury.

Bibi Bhani retired to her chambers, where her sorrows waited for her like shadows at her gate. Her family was fractured, and her husband gone. His absence was a presence that pressed down on her chest, and for days and weeks, Bibi Bhani let grief take her.

A few months later, Bibi Bhani received word that Mata Khivi was sick. She traveled to Khadoor and went straight to the langar hall, and for the first time she could remember, Mata Khivi was not there. Then she went to the house and found her cousin, Bibi Amro, at her mother's bedside. Even in illness, Mata Khivi held her great stature and grace, her pearly-white dupatta draped around her.

"Puttar Ji, aa jao," said Mata Khivi. *My child, come.*

Bibi Bhani drew close, and Mata Khivi studied her: She wore white, a widow's dress, and her eyes were dim. She was grieving her Jetha. No, *Guru Ram Das.* The memory of the two of them young and exchanging glances in the langar hall danced in Mata Khivi's mind.

"Mata Ji, how did you do it?" Bibi Bhani asked quietly. Mata Khivi lived for thirty years after her husband, Guru Angad, had passed. "How did you survive when he left?"

"He never left," Mata Khivi said simply. Every time she stirred the kheer and steam rose from the cauldron, she felt the warmth of his breath. And every time she made rotis and brushed the flour from her face, it was his hand she felt on her cheek. She found him in seva, all that sacred service.

"Of course it took time," she added.

Time, Bibi Bhani marveled. Mata Khivi ran langar for *forty years.* In a world that threw away widows, she left the greatest legacy one could have. She loved her beloved by loving everyone she met.

"We promise to continue the langar you began," said Bibi Bhani.

Mata Khivi smiled, satisfied.

When Mata Khivi breathed her last, Bibi Bhani helped Bibi Amro wash her mother's body. Guru Arjan himself led the antam sanskar. They performed kirtan and cooked a great langar and made kheer the way Mata Khivi taught them. Elaichee, badam, gurr. *Cardamom, almonds, jaggery.* It was as sweet as Bibi Bhani remembered as a girl.

On the journey back home to Ramdaspur, Bibi Bhani saw a leper colony south of the city. People called that place cursed. Bibi Bhani thought of the sakhi she used to tell her children, the story in which Guru Nanak challenged the clerics to turn his feet to where the Beloved was not. There was no place that was not sacred.

"Ruko!" She told the cart to halt. This was her destination.

Bibi Bhani stayed and lived in the leper colony to serve and tend to the ill. She put water to their lips and crushed herbs in their hands. She wept with them, and sang with them. Every day, she prayed with the pearl mala in her hand and searched for her beloved in the faces of the people she served. Until finally, one morning as she meditated, she found the sovereign space within her—where she had first met her baby in the meadow filled with birdsong. There, Guru Ram Das was waiting for her, seated under a tree by the shining waters. He was there all along, and his smile was warm as the sun.

IN THE GREAT CITY OF RAMDASPUR, THE YOUNG GURU ARJAN LAbored tirelessly to build his divine abode with the same steadfast care and devotion as his father. Every year, he called the twenty-two masands to gather in Ramdaspur on Vaisakhi Day, upholding the tradition his grandfather Guru Amar Das had started. Guru Arjan asked the people to donate one-tenth of their earnings to support the community; they called the practice dasvandh. The donations helped fund the construction of the abode and expand the langar. In that time, Guru Arjan married a young woman named Ganga from the village Mau. His mother often visited them from the leper colony where she served. Finally, after eight long years, Guru Arjan's vision was complete. He sent word to his mother, Bibi Bhani, that it was time for the unveiling.

On the appointed day, thousands of people gathered in a clearing in Ramdaspur. Bibi Bhani found her son Mahadev in the crowd, but her eldest son, Prithi Chand, was missing. She spotted the aged Baba Budda Ji, wearing his great white robe, a jade mala around his neck. His beard was now as long and white as her father's had been. He was speaking to someone she hadn't seen in a long time—Bhai Gurdas Ji, her cousin-brother who had grown up with her in Goindval, newly returned from teaching in Agra. He carried a small tanpura, a musical instrument, on his shoulder, and new songs on his lips. Even when he was talking, it sounded like he was singing. It was beautiful to see them all together again.

Guru Arjan emerged before the people to a sea of praise. He wore a royal blue baana, and his eyes sparkled. He was now twenty-six, no longer a boy. He was joined by his young wife, Ganga, in royal blue silks, a long, dark braid down her back. They welcomed the people warmly.

Then the drums pounded, and Guru Arjan led the people to the great sarovar.

Bibi Bhani put her hand on her heart. Before her stood a great abode of brick that shone in the morning sun. It floated on the water! A bridge led to the inner sanctum. The great sarovar was now lined with brick steps leading down to the sacred waters. The rising sun caught the spires of the abode and it shimmered in the golden light.

The people murmured in awe.

"This abode shall be known as Harmandir Sahib," announced Guru Arjan. *Home of the Beloved.*

He called forth Mian Mir, a renowned Muslim Sufi mystic he had befriended in those months he lived in Lahore. It was said that Mian Mir set down the foundation stone of the great abode when construction first began. Now the great Sufi stepped forth in flowing robes and stood proudly beside Guru Arjan.

"Harmandir Sahib is for *all* of us!" said Guru Arjan. "It is open in all four directions, welcoming people from all backgrounds, beliefs, and places."

As the people cried out in jubilant praise, Bibi Bhani wiped tears from her eyes. Harmandir Sahib was the fullest expression of the dream inside her, nurtured by her father, sustained by her husband, and completed by her son. On the land that was hers. From then on, they would call the city Amritsar, named after the pool of sacred water—the amrit—that surrounded the wondrous abode.

"I have to go now," Guru Arjan confided to her at the end of the day. He planned to tour the region to build new places of learning and reach farmers on the outskirts of the realm. He asked her to lead while he was gone. Bibi Bhani's eyes watered as she imagined his departure.

Guru Arjan sang his mother the lullaby that she had given to him as a child. He had turned it into a sacred poem, the most beautiful shabd she had heard, and it was for her:

poota mata kee aasees
nimakh na bisrao tum kao har har sadaa bhajah(u) jagdees

Oh son, this is your mother's blessing:
May you never forget the Beloved, not even for a moment
May you always be immersed in the One

He ended with the verse:

bhavar tum(h)aaraa eh(u) man(u) hovao har(i) charnnaa hoh(u)
  kaolaa
nanak daas un sang(i) lapttaaio jio boondeh(i) chaatrik maolaa

Let your mind be the bumblebee, the Beloved's feet the lotus
  flower
Oh servant Nanak, hold fast and blossom forth like the songbird
  upon finding the raindrop*

Bibi Bhani kissed her son's forehead and let him go. She sang the shabd as she moved back to Amritsar, and unpacked her things with Ganga's help. And she kept singing it every night as a prayer for her

---

* Guru Granth Sahib, ang 496, Raag Goojri, Guru Arjan Ji.

son. Her father had blessed her with a vision once, of unspeakable hardship to come, and she knew that her son would need to reside in the sovereign space inside him, the place that the hot winds of the world cannot reach, if they were to survive what was coming for the house of the Guru.

Aao chaa peelo . . .
Come, let's have tea . . .

THE HOME OF GURU AMAR DAS

THE HOUSE OF GURU AMAR DAS IN GOINDVAL IS THE MOST WELL-preserved home of any of the Sikh Gurus. Bibi Bhani lived here with her children until her father, Guru Amar Das, passed in 1574. When we visited the house, we floated from room to room while I carried Ananda on my hip and held Kavi's hand. Outside the room where Guru Amar Das meditated was the wooden peg in the wall he used in his standing meditation. On the adjacent wall was a bronze relief that depicted the dazzling scene in which Guru Amar Das anointed Guru Ram Das. Next was the room where Guru Amar Das passed, and later Guru Ram Das. The next room contained old artifacts.

"Mommy, what's that?" Kavi pointed to a glass box with silver strands inside.

"Vaal," I said, reading the sign. "Hair that belonged to Guru Amar Das."

"Whoa."

The children skipped into the gardened courtyard with Jasso Massi, who thankfully never seemed to tire of their whirling energy. Relishing a moment of quiet, Sharat and I wandered into a small room at the far end of the house.

"Janam Asthaan Sri Guru Arjan Dev Ji." The room where Guru Arjan was born, April 15, 1563.

I held my breath. Out of all the places in this house, I could picture clearly what transpired in *this* room. The moaning and the blood, the water and the herbs, the breathing and pushing, the first newborn cries. The sign used the passive voice—Guru Arjan *was* born here—as if he had appeared in the world spontaneously. But Bibi Bhani pushed him into the world, through her body, with all her energy and strength. I thought of my own labors, how Sharat had held my hand the whole time. I was about to reach for his hand when I remembered myself. The head of the local gurdwara had brought us here and was watching from the courtyard. Public affection even between a married couple was not a thing in rural parts of India. No need for scandal.

"Aaaaaaaaaah!" A shriek pierced the silence.

Sharat and I rushed outside to find our children gleefully chasing each other around the old brick well in the courtyard. Kavi skipped over a puddle. Ananda ran after him, splashing right through the muddy water, spraying her salvaar. I went red with embarrassment.

"Children!" I cried. "This is the Guru's house! BAS!" *Stop!*

Sharat was about to scoop them up.

The head of the gurdwara intervened.

"Koi gal nahi!" said the granthi. *It's nothing!*

I was about to scold them anyway when Kavi threw me a beaming smile and the light caught his face. He was wearing a bright green patka over the topknot on his head—the color he chose in the morning to match his joyful mood. His eyes were big and bright, his smile infectious. I felt a familiar ache in my heart.

I looked back at the room where Bibi Bhani gave birth. Guru Arjan was born and raised in this house. He probably ran around this courtyard as a boy, chasing his big brothers around this same brick well. Did he climb the great tree that once stood in the courtyard? A slice of the tree trunk was pressed behind glass. Below it was a sign that the chullah, an earthbound stove made of mud and clay, was once here. I was standing where Bibi Bhani must have cooked, under the canopy of the great tree, looking out at the courtyard. What did she see when she looked at her son? What ache in her heart made her sing that lullaby for him? Was it the ache in mine?

"Let's show you the baoli," said Jasso. It was time for us to see the legendary stepwell built by Guru Amar Das in 1552, the first major site of gathering in the Sikh world.

We maneuvered the misty narrow streets of Goindval, taking the same path Bibi Bhani walked whenever she went to the heart of the town. I ran my fingers along the ancient walls made of Nanakshahi brick, earthen-red brick named after Guru Nanak. We made two rights and passed the well where Bhai Jetha was known to serve people water. Then we turned left and beheld Gurdwara Sri Baoli Sahib, where the famous baoli still stood. It was an ornate white marble archway topped by a great golden dome; beneath, the entrance to the baoli looked like the mouth of a cave.

"Kavi, want to go inside?" I asked. Sharat distracted Ananda with snacks as I took his little hand.

The stairs went deep down; we could barely see the bottom. Dizzy, I gripped the railing and held Kavi tight. The steps were made of white marble, worn where pilgrims had made the journey down to the sacred waters. My great-grandfather had made this very pilgrimage a century ago. The tradition is to recite Jap Ji Sahib, Guru Nanak's epic poem of love, on each step down. That would have taken two to three days. So, Kavi and I recited the Mool Mantr, Guru Nanak's foundational verse, one word for every step.

"Ik Onkar," we recited with a step, our voices echoing against the damp walls. "Satnam" on the next step. *Oneness, ever-unfolding. True by Name* . . .

The marble was cold on our feet, our bodies shivered, the air was damp, but our hearts pounded from the thrill of the descent. I imagined our ancestors who took these same steps, and their whispered prayers. One step after another, we added our voices to theirs, and Kavi's little voice did not lose cadence. At last, we reached the final step and dipped our feet in the small pool of sacred water. I sprinkled water over my head; Kavi followed. *We did it.* I smiled, and he beamed back. We looked up and could barely see the patch of daylight. Slowly, deliberately, we recited all the way back up until we stepped into the light again.

As the children sat in quiet self-reflection in the back seat of the car (or perhaps they were just too tired to ask for anything), I took out my map of Punjab and traced the places we had been so far. We were watching the community grow—from Kartarpur to Khadoor to Goindval—each place bigger than the last.

But Goindval was still a small place. The streets were narrow, the Guru's house was compact, and the baoli we had just descended fit only a slim stream of people at a time. I could see how by the time of the fourth Guru, Guru Ram Das, they needed a space large enough for all the people coming for refuge, one that would last the ages. I rested my fingertip on a northern point on the map of Punjab. That land was first known as Guru ka Chak, then renamed Ramdaspur. Now it is called Amritsar.

Today the city of Amritsar is the heart of the Sikh world. It is home to the most revered sacred site, Harmandir Sahib, also known as the Golden Temple—the abode of the Beloved that Guru Ram Das began and Guru Arjan built, the one depicted in paintings in Sikh homes all around the world, the site millions of people visit every year, the place I was aching to show my children, the place that lived inside me.

"How do we ensure best behavior at the Golden Temple?" I asked Sharat.

"A good night of sleep," he said, sensibly. "And lots of snacks."

"Right," I said.

"For the children, too," he quipped.

I pinched him. *Scandal.*

THE GOLDEN TEMPLE

ON OUR FIRST MORNING IN AMRITSAR, I WOKE BEFORE THE ALARM and pressed my face to the window. The air was thick with fog, and I could not see anything except a cow meandering across a pasture. We had to wait until the fog lifted to drive anywhere, which did not matter because it took us even longer to get the children dressed.

"You're going to meet the Guru today!" I said, getting them excited for their first-ever visit to Harmandir Sahib, the Golden Temple. "We have to dress up! Not too fancy, because we're pilgrims. Elegant but humble. Royal but, you know, simple."

"Like in *Mira, Royal Detective!*"

"Um . . ." I turned to Sharat for help. Meanwhile, Ananda pulled out a beautiful violet salvaar, Kavi a bright orange kurta. We bathed them, washed their hair, brushed out the tangles, ironed their clothes, and dressed them up.

"Let me see you," I said. They looked up smiling in their freshly pressed Punjabi clothes. Then Sharat reminded me it was freezing outside, and we had to bundle them in big puffy American jackets that covered up their clothes. So now they just looked like little marshmallows.

"Oh well," I said. "We come with pure hearts."

Outside the Golden Temple complex, there used to be clouds of dust and wooden carts with vendors selling trinkets in the old bazaars. Now, there are broad paved paths made to look old, lined with large market stalls to attract tourists and pilgrims. Sellers with an eye for foreigners called out to us as we passed. We hurried the children past the toys.

We arrived at the main entrance, removed our shoes, and handed them to an auntie in the window who gave us a token. We stepped through a little waterway; all visitors cleanse their feet before entering. I scooped up Ananda and took Kavi's hand, my heart pounding. We were close now. I pulled out my go-to call and response.

"Ananda and Kavi are going to be *their* . . ."

"BEST SELVES!" They beamed.

We took our first steps, and the noise and dust of the city melted away. In that elegant archway, we saw our first glimpse of Harmandir Sahib.

A shining golden palace floated on deep blue waters. The abode stood serenely, timelessly, radiating light, its reflection dancing in the water like a vision that did not fade. The waters made a great pool, a sarovar, and on each of the four sides was a grand marble archway like the one we had just entered. As we descended, Sharat made sure we did not run into anyone in our awe. I bowed and whispered, "Satnam, Vaheguru." The children followed. *True by Name, Wondrous One.*

"Mommy, can we go inside?" Kavi asked. There was only one way into those golden doors: a single bridge on our right. But I pulled him left: We had to take the long way to get there. It was tradition to circumambulate, to walk around the sanctum clockwise, to prepare the heart and mind.

"Listen to the kirtan as you take every step," I said. Sacred music floated from the open doors of the abode and was everywhere at once. We walked past a great ber tree named after the revered disciple Baba Budda Ji, and a platform from which Guru Ram Das had supervised the construction of the great sarovar. As we walked, the abode changed with every step, light dancing on gold.

"Let's draw it!" I pulled out our sketchbooks and we sat together on the ground. "Drawing is looking, and looking is loving," I quoted the artist Wendy McNaughton. We drew for a whole hour, making the children even more excited to go inside.

Finally, we arrived at the bridge that leads to the inner sanctum. We joined the crush of people in line and inched down the bridge, crammed together. I carried Ananda in my arms, humming to keep her from melting down; she rested her head on my shoulder. As we approached the grand golden doors, the music got louder and louder.

This inner sanctum is called Darbar Sahib. It means "exalted court" or "sacred audience." Every gurdwara has the Guru Granth Sahib, the sacred scriptures, installed inside, but no place is more charged or inspired (or crowded) than this one. In this chamber, thousands of people come every day from around the world to bow before the Guru Granth Sahib—the canon of Sikh poetry treated as our living teacher, our Guru.

"This is it!" I cried. "You're going to see the Guru!"

Kavi shivered in excitement; Ananda clutched me tightly. Sharat pressed rupees into our hands. Suddenly we were ushered through the doors. It was a blur of gold. I glimpsed marigolds and silks adorning the Guru Granth Sahib.

"Now!" I whispered. We gently tossed the rupees before the Guru Granth Sahib, folded our hands, and bowed—and then were pushed out the door.

"That's it, Mommy?" asked Kavi as we all stood there, blinking.

Our audience with the Guru lasted . . . ten seconds.

"Um," I said. I should have remembered how dizzying the experience can be. "Let's go upstairs."

We swept the children up a flight of stairs to the balcony above the inner sanctum, where we could look down and take time to see everything. We found a cozy alcove, cuddled up, and peered over the gold railing.

"Dekho," I whispered and gestured to the splendor. *Look.*

We were inside a dome of gold. The walls were gold, encrusted with jewels; tigers, gazelles, and flowers blossomed forth from deep blue and red inlays. Below us, in the heart of the inner sanctum, the Guru Granth Sahib was draped in silks of royal blue and magenta, surrounded by bright marigolds and red roses. An elder was seated behind the scripture, reading from it silently, whisking a chaur, a tail of yak hair, just as early disciples had fanned the Gurus. A great blue canopy studded with gold stars hung over the Guru Granth Sahib. A group of raagis sang kirtan, their music soaring up into the gold dome. People poured in and tossed rupees onto the white cloth before the Guru as we had just done. Custodians used swords to whisk the donations to one side, clearing the way for more people to bow and make their offerings. It was an endless river of faces and prayers.

"Let's look outside," I whispered. We found another alcove along the outer wall and looked out the window at the shining waters of the sarovar. The music filled me, and I closed my eyes, resting in the enchanted golden dream.

"I have to go number one," whispered Ananda.

"Now?"

"Now."

I scooped up my toddler, carried her down the steps, out of Darbar Sahib, across the narrow bridge, around the marble platform, through an archway, out of the complex, and into the noisy street, barefoot, looking for a bathroom. A sympathetic uncle pointed the way. I held her over the toilet with both arms. My dupatta almost fell in. We washed our hands thoroughly and meandered back inside to find our family. This is what it is like with sovereign space: You are wrenched down into the mundane, but you can always return to the sacred. Until you realize it's all sacred.

MY SOVEREIGN SPACE

IF WE ARE ALL PART OF THE ONE, THEN THERE IS NO SPACE THAT is *not* sacred. But it's so hard to remember that when we are holding a toddler over a toilet. Or stuck in traffic. Or falling into our phones. It's especially hard to remember in the wake of a mass shooting or climate disaster or atrocities happening in real time. We need to demarcate space in order to connect with the sacred—a sovereign space. These are not spaces of escape; they are spaces of refuge where we can respond to what's happening from our deepest wisdom, as our best selves. Houses of worship—gurdwaras, churches, mosques, synagogues, mandirs, monasteries, and temples of all kinds—can be palaces of peace and contemplation. But these sojourns mean nothing if we are not also entering that space *within* us.

THERE IS A ROOM IN MY MIND THAT IS MY SOVEREIGN SPACE.

Would you like to see it?

You are stepping across a threshold into a golden room. The fragrances of citrus and jasmine waft through the air. Look through the thick leafy trees. In the heart of the room, there is a beautiful gold throne adorned with blue sapphires. Next to the throne, there is a red velvet banquette and a small ornate table with a tray of tea. Let me pour you a cup. Do you hear the sound of rushing water? A river flows in this forest, and birdsong fills the air. Welcome to my Throne Room.

Take my arm. Let's take a stroll. See the gold walls? They are actually portals. Touch one and it dissolves. Look through this one: You can see the red rocks of the high desert. See this one: A sandy beach and wide blue ocean. And this one: The green canopy of the rainforest. Over here: My childhood mountains and a grove of ancient sequoias. The four walls open to the rest of the world. I can step into any landscape I have known or ever imagined. Most of the time, I like to just rest on that velvet banquette under a warm blanket.

Now we come to the front of the Throne Room where we entered. Look at the great panel in front of you. I look out through my eyes and see these words on a page. I am writing on the bank of a river. Where is your body right now? What do you see?

Now look above you: no ceiling anymore. We are under a night sky! All the stars of the Milky Way ribbon above us, and there are infinite stars beyond that.

I built this Throne Room in my mind over time. Every time I visit, more of it comes into view. It is limitless. Here, no one is ushering me out. I can stay however long I need. No matter where I am in the world, I can come here, and I am home.

Here, in my sovereign space, I am all my identities, and so much more.

I am a woman of color, and all the struggle and beauty and power that holds, and I am so much more than a woman of color.

I am a Sikh, and all the history and heritage and agony and music that holds, and I am so much more than a Sikh.

I am an activist, and hold all that insight and trauma, and I am so much more than an activist.

I am a mama, and devoted to my children and would give my life for them, *and* (can I say this?) I am so much more than a mother.

We feel our identities like gravity: They anchor us. But our identities are not the sum total of all we are, or all we can be. I need to inhabit, reclaim, assert, and celebrate my identities, because the world has heaped so much oppression on women of color, and Sikh women, and mothers of dark children. But as soon as I let those identities calcify in me, I limit my connection to others: I stop growing.

I am learning how to dance between the gravity of my identity and the stars, our truest ancestral home.

Thank you so much for visiting.

Before you go, do you see the great saffron orbs that hang beneath these large languid leaves? We are in a forest of cacao trees, and these are cacao pods, full and ripe. Touch one, and it dissolves. Inside, you'll find the taste that gives you the greatest pleasure. Go ahead and taste! My sovereign space is a realm of rest and pleasure, wonder and magic, beauty and serenity . . . and wisdom.

When you come back next time, there is someone I would like you to meet. Until then, here's a question to take with you:

What does the sovereign space in you look like?

YOUR SOVEREIGN SPACE

I BELIEVE EACH OF US CAN FIND A SOVEREIGN SPACE INSIDE US— a space of rest and freedom—and that we must if we are to survive this time of tumult and transition.

As an activist, I spend so much time working in close proximity to trauma and crisis, I need respite from a world of cruelty and chaos and violence. Fantasy helps—stories that jettison us into faraway lands, different worlds, and magical universes. But it's a temporary reprieve. How can I stay on this earth, in my body, when the world is on fire? I go to a sovereign space *inside* me. It is not a blank void. Inspired by the architectural visions of my Sikh ancestors, my internal refuge is rich and sensual, filled with music and color. That's where I go to rest.

When my daughter comes into the room and sees my crown on the bed, my phone hidden in a drawer, she says: "Mommy, did you have Sovereign Time?" She knows the tools I use to get to my sovereign space. I need to step away from the noise of the world, away from so-cial media and the news cycle, and draw the window shades. I lie down and close my eyes. My breath slows, my jaw unclenches, my chest melts open. I go to my sovereign space not to escape the pain of the world, or in my body, but to see that pain from a higher place—and choose how to respond. The more I practice coming here, the easier it is to get here during hard times.

I have gone to the sovereign space inside me in the most painful mo-ments of my life—when in the throes of labor on the birthing table, when injured by police and thrown behind bars, when cremating the bodies of people I love, when responding to a massacre in my commu-nity. In my sovereign space, I gather courage.

My invitation to you: Build your internal sovereign space. Adorn it, explore it, make it welcoming. You don't need to have a lot of time or money. Right now, right here, you can drop in and imagine a beautiful and loving space inside you. What does it look like? Feel like? Sound like? Leave behind the noise and dust and haze of the world. Step across the threshold. What do you see?

YOU MIGHT SAY: ALL I SEE IS THE TRAUMA I HAVE ENDURED. I AM not free in this world. Why should I make believe that I am free inside?

Oppression wants to cut us off from that place of rest and freedom inside us. Oppression wants us to believe that it does not exist at all. And that we would not deserve it, even if it did. But we cannot let ourselves be defined by our subjugation. That's how oppression wins. We can honor the truth of our suffering *and* refuse to be defined by it. Accessing a space of freedom within us is how we return to our fullest humanity. It generates vitality, energy, and imagination to reshape the world around us.

The only reason many of us are here is because ancestors who were oppressed and had no reason to believe in their worth chose to believe otherwise: They went into that space of freedom inside them, and from that bright space, they sang, they danced, they marched, and they insisted on their worth. The sovereign space inside them was the portal to freedom, from the inside out.

This is the space I imagine Bibi Bhani found within herself in her life's labors and trials; it is the space she must have cultivated with her husband, Guru Ram Das, and taught her son, Guru Arjan. From that sovereign space flows poetry and art and wisdom—and courage.

THE COURAGE TO BUILD AND REBUILD

IN 1604, GURU ARJAN BUILT HARMANDIR SAHIB AS A MAGNIFICENT abode of brick and lime. Since then, it has been destroyed repeatedly by those who have wanted to annihilate or punish the Sikh people. The waters of the sarovar were spoiled again and again by invading armies, at times filled with sand, human waste, entrails of cows, or dead bodies. But our ancestors returned to build and rebuild. Each time, they made it even more beautiful. In 1809, Maharajah Ranjit Singh rebuilt Harmandir Sahib in marble and copper. In 1830, he overlaid the sanctum with gold leaf. That's when the British started calling it "the Golden Temple." The bloodiest attack on Harmandir Sahib took place in 1984; bullet holes marred the inner sanctum, the library was reduced to ash, parts of the Akaal Takht crumbled, and blood and corpses filled the sacred waters. Still, our elders returned to rebuild, so that we can still enter that shining peace.

I will never forget standing inside the gurdwara in Oak Creek, Wisconsin, just a few days after the horrific mass shooting of Sikh Americans in 2012. The FBI wanted to clean the crime scene themselves. But our elders insisted that they clean the gurdwara with their own hands. I watched them roll up their sleeves and sing our ancestors' prayers. They washed the bloodstains from the carpets, repaired the windows shattered by bullets, and painted the sanctuary anew. They didn't just restore this sanctum—they expanded it. They placed six golden domes on the top of the gurdwara, one for each beloved community member killed that day. *You can gun us down; you can spill blood in our sacred waters. But you cannot destroy us. We are sovereign.* Today, all the bullet holes are gone, except for one in the doorway to the divaan hall, the prayer hall. Beneath the bullet hole are the words: *We are one.*

How do we restore the sovereign space inside us, in a world that wants to destroy it? When there is a mass shooting, or wildfire burning, or genocidal campaign under way, the ash blows into my Throne Room, caking the trees and teacups and throne. That doesn't mean I don't have a sovereign space anymore; it means that I have to restore it like our ancestors did. I wash the Throne Room with oils, releasing all the dust and disease. I water the flowers, which bloom instantly. I plant more trees, which thunder through the golden earth and canopy over me. Every time I restore it, the Throne Room becomes more beautiful. Even when the world is on fire, there is a place inside us the hot winds cannot touch.

SOVEREIGN SPACE AS PORTAL

"KAVI, THIS IS THE LAST PLACE PAPA JI VISITED BEFORE HE DIED." We were sitting by the sarovar at Harmandir Sahib, gazing at the golden abode, tasting sweet prashaad. My grandfather died before my children were born. My son only knows him through the stories I tell about him.

In the final days of his life, Papa Ji's body was overtaken by Parkinson's disease. My mother and father brought him home from the hospital to care for him until the end. He drifted in and out of consciousness for weeks. Sometimes, he was fully present. Most of the time, he was elsewhere. Every day, he called out to my mother in the kitchen. "Achha, aaj maha di daal banado." He asked her to make his favorite daal. "Bhujay hoi chholay lai ke aao!" He called for roasted black grams. My grandfather was attached to a feeding tube, but in his mind, he was enjoying all his favorite tastes.

One day, Papa Ji announced: "Aapa(n) Harminder Sahib jaana. Othe mai(n) ishnaan karna." *Let's go to Harmandir Sahib! I need to bathe in the sarovar.*

My mother's heart ached. They were half a world away. She just nodded and smiled and held his hand. A few hours later, Papa Ji bellowed out: "Sonny! Kachhera lai ayan?"—calling for his grandson to bring undergarments for bathing. Papa Ji was already at Harmandir Sahib, ready to wade in.

The next day, he said: "Chalo, theek hai." It was done. He had dipped in the sacred waters. A calm overcame him. He became fully present. My mother, father, aunts, and uncle gathered around his bed and dabbed amrit—sacred waters brought from the sarovar at Harmandir Sahib—on his lips. My grandmother went last. Papa Ji then took the cloth into his mouth, smiled, sighed, and died. It was a masterful death, a chosen death—a sage death.

Even as Papa Ji lost control of his body, there was a sovereign space in his mind—and it was Harmandir Sahib. This was the last place he visited before he died.

"Wow," Kavi said.

"This place is yours," I whispered as the sun set over the golden abode. "It's *inside* you."

We touched the sacred water, and I sprinkled some on his forehead. He leaned over and gave his sister the last morsel of prashaad. Kavi was no longer a small child. The hardships of the world were coming for him. *Will he find that sovereign space inside himself?* I wondered, with that familiar ache in my heart. Was this the ache in Bibi Bhani's heart?

SAGE WARRIOR,
BUILD SOVEREIGN SPACE . . .

YOU CAN BUILD SOVEREIGN SPACE inside you—a space of rest and freedom that is always available to you, no matter what is happening in the world or your life. You can create it visually or musically or any other way you need. What is the most beautiful and loving place you can imagine? Perhaps a forest or mountain or ocean, or a warm beautiful room. It could be a place you have been, or of your imagination. Step into this space and look around. Notice light, colors, and shapes. Do you hear music or birdsong or rain? Do you smell fragrance? Explore freely. Notice what it feels like in your body to be here.

Every time you visit your sovereign space, adorn it and let it expand. Choose a time on your calendar to visit: Sovereign Time. Hide your devices and pick an object to help you drop in—a stone or crown or candle. Forces in the world will want to ravage your sovereign space, or keep you from getting still. Do not despair. You are a sage *and* a warrior: You have the power to protect the sovereign space within you. The more you imagine and tend to it, the more vivid and durable it becomes. Every time you rebuild it, it becomes more splendid. The sage practice is to get still enough to drop in; the warrior practice is to protect the space and time to do so. Your sovereign space is a realm of wonder and beauty you can rest in. It is not an escape; it is a refuge that offers you energy to be courageous with your life.

ANCESTOR TREE

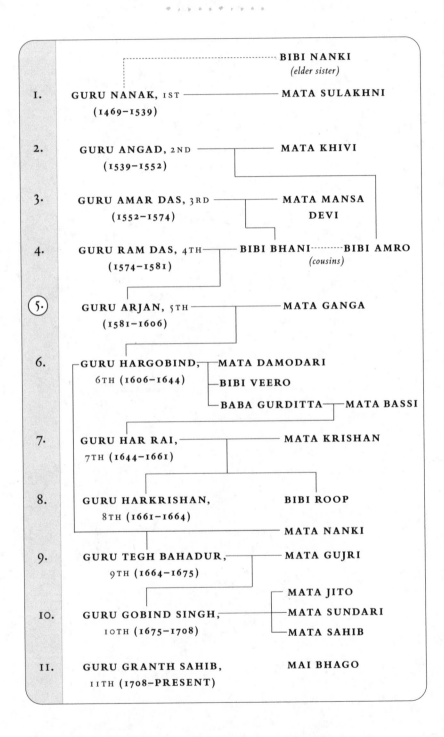

BIBI NANKI
(elder sister)

I. GURU NANAK, 1ST ———————— MATA SULAKHNI
(1469–1539)

2. GURU ANGAD, 2ND ———————— MATA KHIVI
(1539–1552)

3. GURU AMAR DAS, 3RD ———————— MATA MANSA
(1552–1574)   DEVI

4. GURU RAM DAS, 4TH ———— BIBI BHANI ········· BIBI AMRO
(1574–1581)   *(cousins)*

5. GURU ARJAN, 5TH ———————— MATA GANGA
(1581–1606)

6. GURU HARGOBIND, —— MATA DAMODARI
6TH (1606–1644)   — BIBI VEERO
                    — BABA GURDITTA ——— MATA BASSI

7. GURU HAR RAI, ———————— MATA KRISHAN
7TH (1644–1661)

8. GURU HARKRISHAN,   BIBI ROOP
8TH (1661–1664)
                             MATA NANKI

9. GURU TEGH BAHADUR, —— MATA GUJRI
9TH (1664–1675)

                         MATA JITO
10. GURU GOBIND SINGH, —— MATA SUNDARI
10TH (1675–1708)   MATA SAHIB

11. GURU GRANTH SAHIB,   MAI BHAGO
11TH (1708–PRESENT)

PART 5

REST IN
WISDOM

I. THE SONGBIRD:
THE STORY OF MATA GANGA
AND GURU ARJAN

...

GURU ARJAN, FIFTH IN THE HOUSE OF NANAK, TRAVELED ACROSS Punjab, bringing songs of divine love to the outskirts of the realm. Word spread of the shining abode that floated on water called Harmandir Sahib, and thousands of pilgrims poured into the city of Amritsar. They marveled at the streets bustling with bards, artisans, merchants, and mystics. They bathed in the pool of sacred water, the amrit, the city was named after. They sat for langar side by side and took turns serving one another. They crossed the bridge to the inner sanctum and listened to the sacred music of kirtan. Before leaving, they paid their respects to Bibi Bhani.

Since her son's departure, Bibi Bhani had run the daily affairs of the realm with the elders Baba Budda Ji and Bhai Gurdas Ji. She prayed for protection as Guru Arjan traversed lands controlled by the Mughal Empire. Meanwhile, her eldest, Prithi Chand, still refused to see her, claiming that Guru Arjan had usurped his property. She sang her lullaby for both sons. As the power of the House of Nanak grew, she kept hearing her father's words: "We have been left alone so far. But hard times are coming."

One night, Bibi Bhani awoke to a muffled cry. The sound was coming from her daughter-in-law's room. *Ganga must be lonely*, thought Bibi Bhani. Guru Arjan's visits home from his travels were always brief.

Bibi Bhani knocked on Ganga's door and peered inside.

Ganga was sitting up in bed, clutching a white sheet soaked in blood. Her long, black hair was flowing in waves around her. She looked up in terror.

"Oh, puttar," whispered Bibi Bhani. *Oh, my child.*

Bibi Bhani wrapped her arms around her. Ganga shrank from her touch.

"Maaf karna . . ." Ganga breathed.

Bibi Bhani shook her head. There was nothing to apologize for.

"Maaf . . ." Ganga started again.

Bibi Bhani gently embraced her, and this time, Ganga softened. Ganga had married into a family of Gurus: Bibi Bhani's father, husband, and son. After five years of marriage, she had not borne a child. She was keeping her distance from Bibi Bhani, not because she cared so little. It was because she cared so much that she withheld her heart: Ganga was afraid to disappoint her. The young woman had been drowning herself in a story that she was not worthy.

Bibi Bhani massaged ghee into Ganga's belly. This miscarriage required healing, in body and mind.

"You are part of the Beloved," hummed Bibi Bhani, "and the Beloved is part of you."

Slowly, Ganga stopped trembling under her touch. Ganga was named after the River Ganga, an ancient and mighty sacred river. In her touch and song, Bibi Bhani was showing Ganga how to rest in the river of music within her.

"Chalo," Bibi Bhani said to her one day. "It's time to go see Baba Budda Ji. He will bless you."

Bibi Bhani wanted Ganga to know that she was worthy of all the blessings of the world.

GURU ARJAN'S TRAVELS LASTED FIVE YEARS, PUNCTUATED BY brief visits home. He first went to the leper colony where his mother, Bibi Bhani, served and founded a town called Tarn Taran, named after the boat that ferries one across the ocean of existence. Then he went to the Doaba region and founded Kartarpur—*City of the Beloved Doer*—named after Guru Nanak's first settlement. He passed through Lahore, where he visited his Sufi companion Mian Mir. When Guru Arjan was building a new town on the River Beas, he received his mother's message: "Vadhaiya(n)! Ganga has birthed a child! His name is Hargobind." Overjoyed, Guru Arjan named the town Sri Hargobindpur after his newborn son and set off for home.

Bibi Bhani sat by the window and gazed into the illuminated night. The streets of Amritsar were quiet, as if the whole city were holding its breath for Guru Arjan's return. Beside her, Ganga slept with the baby on her chest. Bibi Bhani had taken to staying in the room with Ganga ever since a cobra was found slithering near the bed. Ganga's eyes were dark from exhaustion, and her hair was a beautiful black tangle, even though Bibi Bhani had braided it for her. She gently tucked a few loose strands behind Ganga's ear. The baby stirred.

"Sau(n) ja." *Go to sleep*. Bibi Bhani picked up the baby. Ganga murmured gratefully and fell back asleep.

Bibi Bhani hummed and gazed into her grandson's sweet face, so like her own babies when they were small. She thought of how her firstborn's lips parted when he slept as a child. She sighed at the thought of Prithi Chand.

A wet nurse entered the room.

Bibi Bhani was confused; it was not yet dawn.

The nurse closed the door behind her and snuck to Ganga's bedside. Bibi Bhani did not recognize her.

"Tusee(n) kaun?" called Bibi Bhani. *Who are you?*

The nurse jumped. She whirled around and saw Bibi Bhani; a look of horror overcame her.

"Maaf karna . . ." uttered the nurse. But the apology caught in her throat.

The woman ran.

"Ruko!" Bibi Bhani called. *Stop!*

The woman dropped something as she flew down the stairs and disappeared into the night. Bibi Bhani picked up a leaf, folded in half. There was white powder inside.

Bibi Bhani stared at the poison. First the cobra let loose in the room. They thought it was an accident. Now this. Whenever she had reached out to Prithi Chand, he had retreated. Never showed his face to her. Hid behind his rage. She always thought the threat would come from the outside. But it was her own son's rage that had exploded into the unthinkable.

Bibi Bhani showed the poison to Ganga, who was still as stone. They put the pieces together: They had heard that Prithi Chand was compiling his own scripture of wisdom. He signed his poems Mahla Chheva(n)—*the sixth Guru*—which set up his own son as next in line. An easy claim as long as Guru Arjan remained childless. But now Baby Hargobind was here.

Ganga's veins began to throb. They had tried to kill her child.

Guru Arjan arrived at sunrise, weathered from traveling all night. He touched his mother's feet in respect. Then he went to Ganga and the sleeping baby on her chest. Ganga watched his expression melt, as if in that instant he grew a new chamber of his heart.

"Don't leave," Ganga said abruptly to her husband.

"I just arrived," murmured Guru Arjan, gazing into his son's face.

"Don't go after *him*," she said.

Guru Arjan looked at Ganga as if for the first time. There was steel in his wife's voice, and her eyes were bright, and her hair flowed and made a halo around their son in her arms.

"Your mother told me a story," Ganga said to him. "Guru Nanak's eldest son, Sri Chand, was so upset that he was not the next Guru, he began his own rival following of ascetics, the Udasis. Your father, Guru Ram Das, met Sri Chand once when you were small. Sri Chand tried to insult your father. He said, 'Why do you grow such a long beard?' Your father responded—"

"'To wipe the feet of sages such as yourself,'" finished Guru Arjan.

"Yes," said Ganga, breathless. "And Sri Chand touched your father's feet and said—"

"'It is this humility that made you so great and me so small.'"

"Your father met insult with compassion," said Ganga. "Since then, we have lived in harmony with the Udasis . . ." Her voice went quiet as she lost herself in his eyes.

Guru Arjan softly sang a verse by his father:

har jan raam naam gun gaavai
je koee nind karae har jan kee apunaa gun na gavaavai

Those devoted to the Beloved sing the virtues of the mystical name
If someone maligns them, they do not lose who they are*

The stinging in Ganga's wrists began to subside. She did not need
to persuade her husband; he was already with her.

"Call for Baba Budda Ji and Bhai Gurdas Ji," Ganga whispered.

If Prithi Chand was compiling his own canon of wisdom, they did
not need to go after him; they simply needed to create a stronger one,
an authentic one, a compilation of true wisdom—the Aadi Granth. It
would be their most powerful response. For the sangat, and for their
child.

He kissed her hand.

FOR THE NEXT THREE YEARS, GANGA NURSED AND CARED FOR BABY
Hargobind while Guru Arjan immersed himself in the project to build
a sacred volume of musical poetry. Guru Arjan compiled his father's
shabds, and his own. He sent disciples to search the countryside for
more. And he invited people to contribute poems that were sung from
any tradition that reflected the teachings of Oneness.

One night, Ganga found Bibi Bhani in her room, gazing at the full
moon. She was holding a white kerchief to her mouth, coughing blood,
and the blood dappled the cloth like red craters.

"Mata Ji!" cried Ganga.

Bibi Bhani looked up, startled, and tried to hide the cloth, but it was
too late. Ganga saw.

"Puttar," she sighed.

"He has to know," said Ganga, kneeling at her side.

Bibi Bhani shook her head.

---

* Guru Granth Sahib, ang 719, Raag Bairarree, Guru Ram Das Ji.

"It would break his focus."

"But—"

"He is missing shabds," said Bibi Bhani.

"Mata Ji—"

"I know where they are," said Bibi Bhani, and she leaned back and held her gaze to the moon once more, undeterred.

"It's time to go see my brother, puttar," said Bibi Bhani. "Ready the horses for Goindval."

THE NEXT DAY, THE FAMILY TRAVELED BY OXCART TO THE OLD HOUSE of Guru Amar Das in Goindval. Bibi Bhani's older brother Mohan Ji still lived there with his family; he was the keeper of all the original shabds of the first Gurus. When they arrived, Bibi Bhani's nephews and nieces touched Guru Arjan's feet in respect and joyfully welcomed them into the great courtyard. Mohan Ji was in his meditation room. Guru Arjan sat beneath the great tree, the one he used to climb as a boy, and waited for his uncle.

Bibi Bhani floated past the room where her father had meditated, and the room where her husband had chosen to breathe his last, eighteen years prior. She ran her fingers along the walls made of Nanakshahi brick, touching the memories they held. She retired in the room where she gave birth to Guru Arjan long ago. Ganga helped her lie down on the bed, where Bibi Bhani fell asleep.

A few hours later, music erupted in the courtyard. Ganga peered out.

Guru Arjan sang and played his saranda under the great tree. Mohan Ji still had not come out to see him. Instead of bristling at the disrespect, Guru Arjan sang his uncle songs of praise. Ganga smiled. That was his way. Guru Arjan would not respond with aggression: He would melt the hardened heart.

The great elder Mohan Ji finally emerged with a smile, won over by his nephew's serenade. His hair was tied up in a silver white joora. He opened a great chest of scriptures wrapped in silks. Then, Mohan Ji, the eldest son of Guru Amar Das, ceremoniously placed the scriptures into the hands of his sister's son Guru Arjan, who lifted them onto a golden palanquin. It was done. Ganga went to Bibi Bhani's bedside to tell her the news.

Bibi Bhani lay still. Her face was pale and her breath rattled in her chest. Ganga understood now why Bibi Bhani had insisted on coming to Goindval with them: She wanted to die in this home, the same as her husband, and her father.

"Don't leave," said Ganga desperately.

"Puttar, araam karo," whispered Bibi Bhani. *Rest, my love. Rest.*

"Rest?" choked Ganga.

"Sahaj vich ravo," said Bibi Bhani. *Rest in wisdom.*

Bibi Bhani placed her trembling hand on Ganga and lowered her head. Ganga felt something cool drop over her ears and land on her neck. She opened her eyes to find white shimmering pearls. A pearl mala made of the most luminous beads she had ever seen, with a tassel that tickled the back of her neck.

"Shakti vastay," said Bibi Bhani. *For power.*

Mata Ganga touched the pearl mala with watery eyes. She knew this mala from the stories Bibi Bhani had told her—fashioned by Bibi Nanki, presented to Mata Sulakhni, who gifted it to Mata Khivi, who gave it to her daughter, Bibi Amro, who wrapped it around Bibi Bhani's wrist. Now it shone bright on Mata Ganga's neck. Guru Arjan cleared his throat at the doorway. He saw the blood-dappled dupatta and took his mother's hand.

"My father gave me a vision in this house," Bibi Bhani said to them, her breath rattling. "Samma badal reha hai." *Times are changing.*

They nodded silently.

"Sunno," she said. *Listen.*

They heard the jubilant festivities outside in the streets. It was the start of Vaisakhi, the harvest festival. The drums boomed from the gathering around the baoli in the heart of Goindval.

"Gaur naal sunno," said Bibi Bhani. *Listen deeply.*

They closed their eyes and, above all the noise, they heard the song-bird on the tree, like a flute on the wind. They started to hum to its song, the two of them humming together.

"Taati vao na lagayee," said Bibi Bhani. *There is a place inside you the hot winds cannot touch.*

Bibi Bhani's breath slowed. Her lips parted.

In the old house in Goindval, Bibi Bhani, who was sovereign in her soul, melted into the One.

WHEN HIS MOTHER'S ASHES WERE SPREAD AND THE ANTAM SANS-kar complete, Guru Arjan and Mata Ganga began their journey back to Amritsar. As the cart rumbled along, Mata Ganga thought about how the labor of dying mirrored the labor of birthing. How one must breathe deeply enough in order to push and, ultimately, transition.

Bibi Bhani's final words echoed in her: *Rest in wisdom.*

"Guru Ji." She turned to her husband. "You need a quiet place to compile the Granth."

As they neared Amritsar, Mata Ganga spotted a grove of shaded trees southeast of the city, far from the bazaars and pilgrims. She handed her husband an ink pen. He had the remaining shabds in hand now. It was time to complete his labor.

"Sahaj vich ravo," she said. *Rest in wisdom.*

Guru Arjan built the greatest sanctuary on earth for his father; for his mother, he would need to go even deeper, get quieter than he had ever been, to birth the Aadi Granth, the canon of sacred wisdom.

Guru Arjan dug a pool of water by a grove of trees and called it Ramsar Sarovar. He took his seat beneath a tree next to the water and spread the pothis before him. A breeze rustled the leaves. A songbird perched on a branch. Guru Arjan hummed the lullaby his mother gave him, the one he turned into a shabd, *Poota Mata Kee Asees,* and wrote it down. He hummed the words *Taati Vao Na Lagayee*—hot winds cannot touch me—and unspooled it into a shabd and wrote it down. He hummed the love poems he had written to his father and wrote them down. He hummed a verse for Mata Khivi, the great woman who meant so much to his mother, the one who provided shade to all and ran langar and put the taste of kheer in his mouth, and wrote it down, too.

Guru Arjan opened his heart wider and let in songs of Muslim sages and Hindu Bhagats of all castes and no caste—Farid, Namdev, Sain, Kabir, Ravidas—and the torrent flowed into him with gathering force. Each poem had a raag, a musical signature, because these words were meant to be sung and felt in the body—the way he felt when his mother sang to him—in the embrace of the great mother earth.

As Guru Arjan hummed, a great river of wisdom poured into him, carrying the songs of all the great sages he had ever known, in all the traditions that had moved and inspired him, and within them, God had a hundred names—Ram, Allah, Parvati, Vaheguru—and the most urgent name that came to his lips was *Naam,* which simply means *name,* because any word can be a portal into the embrace of the Beloved.

A new song rose to his lips:

pooray gur ka sun updes
paarbrahm nikatt kar pekh

saas saas simrho gobind
man antar kee utrai chind

Listening to the wisdom of the Whole
I come close to the Infinite

Oneness in every breath
All pain disappears*

He called the sacred poem Sukhmani Sahib: Jewel of Serenity.
When Guru Arjan came home, he gave the new song to Mata Ganga, who sang it to Hargobind as she braided his hair.

* Guru Granth Sahib, ang 295, Raag Gauri, Guru Arjan Ji.

"Vah!" gasped young Hargobind.

As the seasons turned, Guru Arjan came home with more sacred songs that danced on Mata Ganga's lips. The music filled her in her daily labors. In her hours of quietude, she heard a voice speaking to her from inside herself. A voice of compassion, nourished by the musical wisdom that Guru Arjan was compiling. She began to speak to herself with the same compassion with which Bibi Bhani would speak to her. The story of unworthiness that plagued her when she was young fell away. She was beloved and belonged to the Beloved: *Oneness in every breath.* She was learning to rest in that wisdom.

Finally, Guru Arjan announced he was nearly done. He had compiled the shabds, including more than two thousand of his own, into one great volume, and organized them by raags, musical signatures traversing a dazzling range of emotional and spiritual moods. Bhai Gurdas Ji inscribed the shabds. Baba Budda Ji ensured there were no errors. Mata Ganga took her son to Ramsar Sarovar to witness the last day of completion.

Guru Arjan was seated in a sunlit clearing beneath a tree, the great volume spread before him. He bowed his head to the volume and whispered, "Sat Kartar." *True is the Great Doer; I honor the truth that is.*

The Aadi Granth was born.

Baba Budda Ji and Bhai Gurdas Ji carried the Aadi Granth through the streets of Amritsar all the way to Harmandir Sahib. Guru Arjan led the procession, followed by Mata Ganga and young Hargobind. More and more people followed them. They circumambulated the divine abode Harmandir Sahib, crossed the great causeway surrounded by sacred waters, and placed the Aadi Granth in the heart of the inner sanctum. The wisdom now sat on the throne.

"In this vessel, you will find truth, peace, and contemplation," announced Guru Arjan. "Within is the nectar of the Name which uplifts humanity." Guru Arjan asked Baba Budda Ji to read from the canon as the first granthi, and Bhai Gurdas Ji to sing from it. Guru Arjan then bowed to the Aadi Granth and took his seat on the floor. The people closed their eyes and listened as the sacred music melted away time.

At the end of the night, Baba Budda Ji wrapped the volume in silks and placed the Aadi Granth atop the Guru's head. Guru Arjan walked solemnly across the causeway, and the people bowed as he passed them. He entered the sukhasan space, a small, adorned chamber that would be the nightly resting place for the sacred volume. The people cried out in jubilation. That night, Guru Arjan slept in the chamber at the foot of the Aadi Granth, resting in wisdom.

AFTER THE AADI GRANTH WAS INSTALLED ON THE THRONE, GURU Arjan and Mata Ganga betrothed young Hargobind to a girl from the village Talla named Damodari; when she came of age, they would live together. The future was bright. Mata Ganga went with Guru Arjan to Tarn Taran to build a memorial to his mother, Bibi Bhani, at the leper colony where she had served and found peace. When the great well was almost complete, they received word that Emperor Akbar was no more.

Emperor Akbar—the great Mughal Emperor who had sat humbly for langar and gifted Bibi Bhani the land on which to build Amritsar, the one who embraced the peace at the heart of Islam and worked for harmony among the people, the one who cleared the way for their coexistence—was gone.

"Who is the new Emperor?" Mata Ganga asked the messenger.

Emperor Akbar wished for his grandson Prince Khusrau to take his place. Prince Khusrau was a bold young leader who shared his grandfather's embrace of diversity and desire for harmony. But the boy's father, Jahangir, expected the throne for himself.

"Jahangir seized power and sent his forces to capture Prince Khusrau," said the messenger. "The prince's mother, Shah Begum, tried to make peace between her husband and son, and failed. She swallowed opium and killed herself."

Mata Ganga's eyes watered. *A mother watching her family ripped apart . . .* She thought of how Bibi Bhani's lip used to quiver at the mention of her son Prithi Chand.

A few days later, a knock came in the middle of the night. Mata

Ganga went to Guru Arjan's side when the attendants opened the gate. A beleaguered figure stumbled toward them. Behind him were men in tattered clothes, holding the reins of horses, about to collapse. The young man's face was ragged and pained.

"Guru Ji," Prince Khusrau said hoarsely, folding his hands. "My grandfather Akbar the Great told me of you and *your* greatness . . . We are starving."

Prince Khusrau and his army were on the run from his father Jahangir's forces. They hid in wilderness during the day and rode their horses through the night, heading for Lahore. Villagers refused to help them, locking their doors out of terror, for the prince was being pursued by the most powerful Emperor in the world, a man who knew no mercy.

Mata Ganga knew all this, too, but she looked into the boy's face and saw her own son, Hargobind. Wordlessly, she returned with a hot cup of ginger, sweetened with gurr. Guru Arjan invited Prince Khusrau and his horsemen to rest for the night. They partook in langar, gathered around a warm fire, and gazed up at the moon as they drifted to sleep. For this one night, they were not treated as animals. The next day, Guru Arjan placed a red tilak on Prince Khusrau's forehead and watched as he rode into the distance.

A few months later, they received news that Prince Khusrau had made it to Lahore. But the boy was captured and dragged to his father, Emperor Jahangir, who threw his son into a prison. Prince Khusrau's followers were impaled in the streets of Lahore. Mata Ganga pictured the boy in the dark cell, hearing about the deaths of all his companions. She wondered: When he closed his eyes, did he think of the last place he rested? Could he still see the moon? Could he rest in its light?

MATA GANGA MASSAGED OIL INTO HER SON HARGOBIND'S HEAD AS sacred music from Harmandir Sahib floated in through the window, like a songbird that never stopped singing. Hargobind squirmed, but she made him be still. He was eleven years old now, and his hair was long and luscious. She combed out the tangles and finished the braid. Hargobind ran out of the room as she called after him to get ready for sleep.

Guru Arjan appeared at the doorway with a letter. Mata Ganga saw the broken royal seal and set down the comb.

"Summons from Emperor Jahangir," he said.

"What is the charge?" she asked.

"Treason."

"Treason," she breathed. Her mind flashed to Tarn Taran and the face of the boy they sheltered.

Mata Ganga gripped the letter and read it again and again. Someone must have told Jahangir that they had sheltered Prince Khusrau. Perhaps Prithi Chand, who had built a rival following and still decried his brother from afar. Perhaps Shaikh Ahmed Sirhindi, the orthodox Muslim in the imperial court who despised "infidels" and all forms of "innovation." Perhaps Chandu Shah, the high-caste Hindu who had the Emperor's ear and recoiled at the Guru's abolition of caste and caste customs. (Chandu's fury was personal: Guru Arjan had declined Chandu's proposal to marry their children to each other.) Perhaps Emperor Jahangir was simply waiting for a reason to put an end to the "rebel guru" and the dangerous ideas he inspired. Not a village in the Mughal Empire was untouched by Guru Arjan's songs of liberation. Such a movement directly threatened imperial authority. The Emperor now had a convenient pretext: Guru Arjan was to stand trial for aiding and abetting a fugitive.

"Who?" asked Mata Ganga. "Who was it who betrayed you?"

"Na ko bairee, nahi beganaa," said Guru Arjan. *See no stranger; See no enemy.*

Mata Ganga's heart beat in her ears. Her husband would not meet aggression with aggression. This was never his way. Guru Arjan was the singing Guru who composed love songs for his parents, the one who created his own world of wisdom rather than destroy his brother's, the one who serenaded his uncle instead of forcing his hand, the

---

*   Guru Granth Sahib, ang 1299, Raag Kanra, Guru Arjan Ji.

one who built Amritsar into a sovereign city, and that is why they were coming for him now. To cut off the head of the people and bring down the body. But the Emperor did not know that Guru Arjan was not seated on the throne; the Aadi Granth was on the throne, and no one can kill a fount of wisdom.

"Don't leave," Mata Ganga was about to say, but she stopped herself. This was the old voice in her, the voice of fear, the voice that had made her small and ashamed all those years before Bibi Bhani found her in the sheets and blood and told her she was good and worthy and powerful. There was a clearer voice now, the one that Bibi Bhani saw in her, the one of wisdom, and she had only to rest in it.

She whispered:

pooray gur ka sun updes
paarbrahm nikatt kar pekh

Listening to the wisdom of the Whole
I come close to the Infinite

Guru Arjan finished:

saas saas simrho gobind
man antar kee utrai chind

Oneness in every breath
All pain disappears*

Mata Ganga buried her face in his chest and let her tears flow. Guru Arjan was saying something about how bodies are temporary, and to prepare Hargobind to lead, but she wasn't hearing the words, only the rhythm of his heartbeat, and she memorized how his body felt: She was going to miss this form of him.

Guru Arjan called for his son, Hargobind, and the elders Baba

---

*   Guru Granth Sahib, ang 295, Raag Gauri, Guru Arjan Ji.

Budda Ji and Bhai Gurdas Ji. Guru Arjan knelt down and placed five paisay and a coconut before eleven-year-old Hargobind. He then took his son's hand and told him to stand for truth, defend his people, and listen to his mother. Hargobind nodded solemnly and hugged his father. The elders stood in witness. In the morning, Guru Arjan began his journey to Lahore to confront the Emperor.

Every day, Mata Ganga waited for news. For five nights, she could not sleep. On the fifth night, she stepped into the moonlight, bowed at Harmandir Sahib, and watched the ripples on the water. She sang Sukhmani, and it was as if she could hear Guru Arjan sing with her:

saas saas simrho gobind
man antar kee utrai chind

Oneness in every breath
All pain disappears

At dawn, when a messenger arrived from Lahore, Mata Ganga called forth the court to hear his news.

"When will our Guru return?" the people shouted out to the messenger.

Mata Ganga stood behind Hargobind, her arms wrapped across his chest. She could feel his heart beat faster and faster as the messenger spoke:

Trial.
Treason.
Cauldron lit.
Fire.
Burning sand.
Fire burning.
Did not scream.
Body blistered.
Singing Guru.
Eyes closed.

Gone within.
Your Will is sweet.
River Raavi.
Icy river.
Swift current.
Eyes closed.
Gone within.
Gone.

They had killed him. Killed her husband. Killed Guru Arjan.

The events flickered before her eyes:

Guru Arjan stood tall when they demanded he pay the fine. He said he had done nothing wrong. They demanded he convert to Islam to go free. He refused, saying all paths led to the Beloved. They sentenced him to death by torture. The great Muslim Sufi Mian Mir intervened to stop them—this was not the way of Islam—but the Emperor's men pushed him away and commenced the torture. They seated Guru Arjan on a hot plate over a cauldron of fire. His body burned and his skin melted. They waited for him to scream, but he did not scream. They poured burning sand over his head until his body blistered. They waited for him to scream, but he did not scream. Guru Arjan's eyes were closed and his lips were moving. They heard him recite:

tera keeya meetha lagai
Your will is sweet to me[*]

Guru Arjan had gone to that place deep within him where the hot winds could not touch him. Because that's what Bibi Bhani had taught them. He had gone to that sovereign space. *Sach khand*. There, he rested in the wisdom of all the sages who had gone before him. There is nowhere the Beloved is not, and that meant that even in the fire and burning sand, he was with the One and part of the One and immersed

[*] Guru Granth Sahib, ang 394, Raag Asa, Guru Arjan Ji.

in the love of the One, and that is the only way he could have sung, repeatedly: *Your will is sweet to me.*

They tortured him for five days. Was it cruelty that made his tormenters send him into the icy River Raavi? Or did they grow tired of trying to get him to scream? They called the people of Lahore to gather on the banks of the river and watch the Guru enter the water. His skin blistered, his body bent, yet his face was radiant as he walked willingly into the icy waters. His flesh was hanging on his bones; he was less than he had ever been. Yet more than the world could grasp. Guru Arjan stepped into the River Raavi, waded deeper until the waters parted for him and, with one breath, consumed him, and he was gone.

When the messenger was done, the people wailed like the world was ending. Terror befell the court: The Empire killed the sovereign of their world like he was nothing, and they were nothing!

Mata Ganga wrapped her whole body around Hargobind. He would not lose his body; they would not lose their bodies. It took all her strength to lift her face and raise her voice so that she could be heard over the people's wailing.

"Guru Gaddi noo(n) tyaar karo," Mata Ganga roared, and it was the roar of a thousand rivers. *Prepare for succession.*

Aao chaa peelo . . .
Come, let's have tea . . .

NIGHT AT THE GOLDEN TEMPLE

A FULL MOON SHONE OVER HARMANDIR SAHIB, THE GOLDEN TEM-
ple. The children were tired at the end of a long day. After we had
langar, Sharat offered to take the children back to the hotel and put
them to bed, so that I could have a moment of quiet here. I married
well.

"Guess what?" Sharat said to the children. "When you wake up, I
will turn into Mommy!" Which simply meant that Mommy would slide
in to snuggle with them after he put them to sleep.

The idea of magic got them into the car, but Ananda still cried when
I waved goodbye. I wondered when I would cease to be afflicted by
mama-guilt. I took a deep breath, wrapped my dupatta around me, and
looked around for Jasso, who was drinking a tall glass of sugarcane
juice from one of the vendors. We walked arm in arm as sisters through
the mist and reentered the Golden Temple complex, the sound of kirtan washing over us.

Harmandir Sahib at night looked like a golden palace lit from
within, floating in darkness, dazzling and otherworldly. We took our
seats at the steps of the great sarovar and watched the gold reflection
dance in the dark, glassy waters. Koi fish swam slowly by. My arms
ached from carrying my daughter all day; it felt so good to rest.

Suddenly, shouts of jubilation filled the air. A golden palanquin appeared on the shoulders of devotees who emerged from the inner sanctum. They carried the Guru Granth Sahib—the sacred volume of
musical wisdom—adorned with marigolds and little sparkling lights.
They crossed the bridge to a special resting chamber for sukhasan,

walking the same path Guru Arjan had that very first night when he put the Guru to rest. It was a tradition repeated every night for hundreds of years. We stood solemnly and bowed as the Guru Granth Sahib passed us. People called out jaikaras, and the sound boomed in my chest: "Jo Bolay So Nihaal! Sat Sri Akaal!"

"It's only men," I realized. Only men in the procession, only men shouting out jaikaras, only men with the Guru.

Jasso nodded sadly. She was a rababan, a female musician who played the rabab, the stringed instrument that Bhai Mardana played when he accompanied Guru Nanak and his songs of love. Her voice was powerful and enchanting. But she was not allowed to lead the singing inside Darbar Sahib. Neither was our Sikh sister, Nirinjan, the first female exponent of the jori tradition, the drumming tradition that traced back to the court of Guru Arjan. My sisters are gifted and glorious. But women are not allowed to sing kirtan, or even sweep the floors, in the innermost sanctum of Harmandir Sahib. The ban was unofficial but upheld. The Sikh tradition espouses women's equality; our scriptures do not contain passages that denigrate women. Our sacred canon of wisdom pulsates with liberation and equality for all. Yet patriarchy still finds a way.

I thought of all the times I had been yelled at during our visit that day. For carrying a bag with emergency snacks for my toddler. For my dupatta slipping from my head. For her dupatta slipping from her head. For folding our hands after instead of before taking a photo. I was yelled at six times. Always by men in blue uniforms shouting at me like I was a child. I didn't know how to express to them what I felt: this was a place of soul-pilgrimage for me, and please do not yell at me, and if I am slipping on protocol, tell me with kindness. But I just nodded with apology and did what they said.

In the afternoon, when we made our sketches of the Golden Temple, a stern uniformed man with a spear yelled at us to move all the way back to the wall. We complied. A few minutes later, he came around again and peered down at our drawings. He looked from Sharat's to mine to the children's. We each had a slightly different angle.

"Vah!" he exclaimed, and called passersby to see. A small crowd gathered around us.

"Aajo! Aajo!" he beamed, ushering us to move closer to the sarovar for a better view. Such careful drawings could only have come from love. He left us alone the rest of the visit.

The body of men who oversee this place and all the centers of power around the world—those who claim to control the channels to wisdom, who issue edicts to dictate right and wrong, who police the bodies of women and queer people and dark people and anyone who is not like them, who patrol the perimeters waiting for violations—are just afraid. They puff their chests to look big and powerful. They want to be important. But they are just afraid of losing their power. Some can be won over: *Look, a new angle, and it is worthy!* Others will recoil at any form of innovation or new perspective. They may scorn and ridicule us. They may even burn and blister us. Our most ardent task is to refuse to let them touch the sovereign space inside us. For that is the truest seat of wisdom.

How do we protect our own sense of wisdom from the critics and controllers? It begins within.

MY WISE WOMAN

THERE HAS BEEN A VOICE INSIDE ME FOR ALL MY LIFE. I DO NOT think I was born with it. I think it emerged inside me after my first racial slur when I was six. I was pretending to be a baby in the schoolyard when a little boy who was white ran up to me and said, "Get up, you black dog." The bell rang and he ran away. I was not angry with the boy. It was as though he gave me information I did not have before: *Oh, I never saw myself from your angle before.* I felt burning under the skin. They call this shame "internalized oppression," but what it feels like is a voice that starts to say to you: *You're not good enough. You're not strong enough. You're not smart enough. You're not pretty enough. You're not enough.* I think all of us have this voice inside. The voice can get especially loud in those of us who are born into bodies that are denigrated in this society.

I found a way to protect myself from the critics and controllers. What I am about to share is not a traditional Sikh practice. It's my personal way to uphold Guru Nanak's rejection of empty ritual: The pilgrimage to any sacred place, the bowing to any wisdom, must also happen within us to be real. My practice is to *rest* in the wisdom within me.

I AM GOING TO STEP INTO THE THRONE ROOM INSIDE ME, MY SOV-ereign space. Would you like to visit once more? There is someone I am ready for you to meet.

Step across the threshold.

We are standing in the shining Throne Room together. This time, cinnamon and spices are in the air. Warm cups of drinking chocolate await us. Look through the big leafy canopy of trees. Do you see a glimpse of the golden throne? Let's take a few steps closer.

A woman is seated on the throne. She shimmers. She is here and not here. Her hair is long and black and swirling around her as though floating in water. Her eyes are soft and serene. She is dressed in royal blue silk robes studded with stars, flowing down to the river. She is regal. She is letting herself be seen for a moment.

I call her Wise Woman, but you may know her by other names. She is the sum of all the wisdom absorbed—wisdom from songs and stories and elders and teachers, wisdom gained from loving and being loved— and she is more than that. She is the thin membrane between me and all that is, and she is porous. I know only a fraction of her; she is inex-haustible. She is infinite, yet here she appears.

Do you see that red velvet banquette next to the throne? This is where I come with soft blankets and rest at her feet. She does not need my worship, only my stillness. She swaddles and comforts me. She mothers me. I am safe here. I may not be safe anywhere in the world, but I am safe here. I am her beloved. I'm with the Beloved when I'm with her.

See that wooden perch on the other side of the throne? That's where a plump little parrot breaks into my sovereign space and squawks at me. In the old days, he used to sit on the throne and tell me all sorts of things. Like: *You're not enough. You should be afraid. Get afraid. Get small.* All my existential fear and dread and jealousies and doubts wrapped up in one little conjured parrot. It's so easy for the Little Critic to rule our consciousness.

I devised all sorts of strategies to annihilate the Little Critic—shall we drown him? cut him down? banish him forever? But Wise Woman said: *Oh my love. He is a part of you. We need him; we just don't need him in charge. Say to him: "You're a part of me I don't yet know."* She was using my refrain. She did not want me to destroy him; she was asking me to *mother* him. When I started to wonder about this part of me, I realized that the Little Critic was afraid. He was trying to protect me. Because he's right: The world is not safe for brown women who share their stories and imagination. But the solution is not silence; it's more solidarity. Standing with your sisters and allies. So, I thanked the Little Critic for his years of faithful service; I told him the Wise Woman will protect me from here on. He was so stunned, he flapped away. I wish I could say the Little Critic was never heard from again. But he still likes to puff himself up and squawk, like a retired general: "I used to rule this place!" He gets especially loud when I am about to put art into the world or speak truth to power.

I let him be heard, soothe his ruffled feathers, and ask, *What role would you play if you did not need to play this one?* He wants to turn into golden confetti, he tells me. He wants to be free.

Here, let's dip our feet in the cool stream. Let's sit on the bank in this soft grassy spot and have that cup of drinking chocolate that's already magically in your hand. (You can turn it into anything you most like to drink.)

I have a question for you: What does the deepest wisdom in you look like? Imagine all the wisdom you have ever absorbed taking the form of a shape within you. Perhaps a wondrous object. Or landscape. A bright red sun. A moonlit desert. A phoenix. A human shape. Now, imagine that this wisdom has something to tell you—listen. What do you hear? What do you feel? Even if it's just a whisper, or a sense of warmth in your chest.

My hope is that sharing all this with you will make you feel even bolder in exploring what's inside you.

Let's splash our faces in the cool water before we go.

YOUR WISDOM WITHIN

DEEP WISDOM RESIDES WITHIN EACH OF US. THIS WISDOM IS OFTEN submerged in the rest of our stream of consciousness, but we can access it when we step away and get still. Your deepest wisdom is nourished by all the wisdom you have ever absorbed—stories and songs and experiences in this lifetime and before you were born. It is infused with ancestral wisdom: If intergenerational trauma is real, then so is intergenerational wisdom. When we speak to a beloved child or friend, we often surface the most compassionate part of ourselves. We speak from our wisdom. The question is: Can we speak to *ourselves* that way?

When you practice listening to that voice, other parts of you might interfere—fear or wrath or lust or greed or pride. Do not suppress them. Say: *You are a part of me I do not yet know.* Thank them for their years of faithful service. Tell them they do not need to be in charge anymore.

Every day, I need to listen to the Wise Woman; it is my most vigilant practice: She journals to me, leaves me voice memos, speaks to me in my sovereign space. When I listen to kirtan and my ancestors' poetry and songs, she is nourished and fortified. The more I immerse myself in wisdom in the world, the more she is replenished and enlivened. I created a ceremony to commit myself to her. With the help of my Sikh sisters, Jasvir and Nirinjan, whom I call Jasso and Baaj, I crafted my own wedding ceremony, my Anand Karaj, my transport to joy. I made the lavaa(n), the four circles, around a pool of water and married her. I promised to be faithful to her for all my days. She took her seat on the throne. Listening to her every day is how I have finally learned how to love myself.

Listening to wisdom within us is not only a self-care practice. It is a world-shaping intervention. Our culture is filled with the noise of those running on the energies of fear and criticism and cruelty. A million Little Critics. They punish, demean, exclude, and hate. Our culture (and algorithms) amplify their voices: We are made to hate ourselves and each other. But when we get quiet enough to surface the voice of wisdom inside us, we access a wellspring of love beyond what we thought possible—for others and for ourselves. Imagine if all of us could go through the world not endlessly reacting, ruled by our fears and hatreds, but from our deepest wisdom and boundless love. It would be nothing less than revolution.

What do we do with the Little Critics inside of us, the ones we are ashamed of? Patriarchal culture will tell you to eliminate them: Annihilate your ego, control your rage, suppress your lust, repent your sins. The more we are conditioned to fight and destroy parts of ourselves, the easier it is to do that with people—to see them as monsters who need to be punished or put to death or discarded.

There is a different way. We can see the "shameful" parts of ourselves through the eyes of a wise mother. We can choose not to fight them or try to destroy them, but to mother them—mother them into healing and transformation. Even if we ourselves were not mothered that way, we can learn to give ourselves compassion and care. And we can do the same for others, starting with those around us. The more we learn to love all the parts of ourselves, the more we deepen our capacity to love anyone.

Guru Arjan sang, "I see no enemy; I see no stranger." It is an inner and outer practice: Can we see no strangers or enemies in the world around us? Can we see no strangers or enemies *within* us?

GURU ARJAN UNDER TORTURE

IN 1606, GURU ARJAN WAS ARRESTED, TORTURED, AND SENTENCED to death in Lahore under the order of Emperor Jahangir. The execution of Guru Arjan was earth-shattering for the Sikh realm, an unthinkable assault of the highest order, the near-end of the world. It was the turning point. The moment Sikhs could have disintegrated and disap-

peared, as so many mystical communities have in history. Yet we found
a way to survive.

Was Guru Arjan's execution part of a coordinated plan of state per-
secution to crush the nascent Sikh community? Or a reactionary political act to punish supporters of a rebel prince? Perhaps it was both. A
Spanish Jesuit missionary of the time reported the death of the people's
"good Pope."* Emperor Jahangir wrote of the execution in his own
diary. He calls Guru Arjan a Hindu who attracted "simple-hearted"
Hindus and "ignorant and foolish" Muslims:

> In Goindval, which is on the river Biyah [Beas], there was a
> Hindu named Arjan, in the garments of sainthood and sanctity,
> so much so that he had captured many of the simple-hearted of
> the Hindus, and even of the ignorant and foolish followers of
> Islam, by his ways and manners, and they had loudly sounded
> the drum of his holiness. They called him Guru, and from all
> sides stupid people crowded to worship and manifest complete
> faith in him. For three or four generations (of spiritual succes-
> sors) they had kept this shop warm. Many times it occurred to
> me to put a stop to this vain affair or to bring him into the as-
> sembly of the people of Islam.
>
> At last, when Khusrau passed along this road, this insignifi-
> cant fellow proposed to wait upon him. Khusrau happened to
> halt at the place where he was, and he came out and did homage
> to him. He behaved to Khusrau in certain special ways, and
> made on his forehead a finger-mark in saffron, which the Hindu-
> van call qashqa, [tilak] and is considered propitious. When this
> came to my ears and I clearly understood his folly, I ordered

* "In this way, their good Pope died, overwhelmed by the sufferings, torments, and
dishonors." —*Jerome Francis Xavier (1549–1617) in his letter from Lahore, September 25,
1606, to Gasper Fernandes in Lisbon.* Xavier, Jerome Francis. "Letter from Lahore"
(1609). Relação Anual das Coisas que Fizeram os Padres da Compenhia de Jesus Nassuas Missõs, edited by Father Fernão Guerreiro, 1609. Reprint, Coimbre Imprensa da
Universidade, 1931, pp. 369–70.

them to produce him and handed over his houses, dwelling-places, and children to Murtaza Khan, and having confiscated his property commanded that he should be put to death.*

Half a millennium later, Sikhs remember the fifth Guru, Guru Arjan, as the martyr whose sacrifice changed the course of history. His equanimity under torture demonstrated how to relate to pain, *dukh*. The opposite of dukh is *sukh*, meaning serenity. Guru Arjan composed the *Sukh*mani Sahib, the Jewel of Serenity. The first Guru to suffer egregious pain in our ancestral memory is also the one who gave us our greatest song of inner-peace. Guru Arjan found peace amid suffering: He found the sovereign space inside him, and rested in the wisdom within. What if we all could do that? Is that even possible?

TAKE THE NEXT BREATH

ALL THROUGHOUT OUR TRAVELS IN PUNJAB, SHARAT AND I TOOK every precaution to keep the children from getting sick—only bottled water! no salad! no fruit without a peel! no street food! But the amazing smells from the dhabas of Amritsar were too tempting. We rode on bicycle rickshaws through the narrow old bazaars, tasting creamy mango lassis, spicy chholay bhaturay, and crispy sweet jalebis that melted in our mouths.

We were on our way to my cousin Jyoti Didi's house to celebrate Lohri, the Punjabi new year festival where everyone gathers around bonfires. We shout out good news, throw popcorn into the flames, and dance around the fire. The children were especially excited about the popcorn part. But when we arrived, my daughter clutched her belly. "It huuuuuurts."

That night, both children ran high fevers. Jyoti Didi made us pitchers of nimbu paani, lemon and salt water, which we made the children drink every hour. All through the night, Ananda moaned in my arms.

---

* *Tuzuk-i-Jahangiri (Memoirs of Jahangir)*. Translated by Alexander Rogers. Edited by Henry Beveridge, London Royal Asiatic Society, 1909, pp. 72–73.

I cupped her little face in my hands and kissed her forehead and told her she was brave. When she leaned over the bed, I held her hair back as she vomited. The last time I vomited that hard was when I was pregnant with *her*, and my mother held *my* hair back.

I had hyperemesis gravidarum in my pregnancy, a condition of severe nausea. I vomited every hour for four months, and landed in the emergency room four times. On my hardest night, when the vomiting would not end, and my insides were being forced out of me, and I was afraid there would be nothing left, I heard: *Breathe*. The Wise Woman was watching me. *Oh my love, this is hard. Just take the next breath*. I made it to the next breath, and the next, until dawn came.

I have heard the Wise Woman's voice during the most painful events of my life—police brutality, sexual assault, chronic pain, racial violence, illness. Inside severe pain, my face is not serene like Guru Arjan's in the paintings. But the Wise Woman in me, *her* face is serene. She is the holy presence in the Throne Room, the divine court, in my sovereign space. If I can lift my gaze for just a moment to her radiant face, I see her watching me. *You are not your pain. You are much vaster than that*. My sense of self expands: I am the one inside the pain—feeling all of it—and the one watching the pain. I am animal and divine, and both are equally beloved, one not higher than the other. When we can witness the events happening to us—internally and externally—we create space between the experience and our response, and in that space, we find freedom. Freedom to choose how to respond, freedom to discern: What does love want me to do?

THE SCENE OF GURU ARJAN RESTING AT THE FEET OF THE SACRED canon of wisdom is emblazoned in Sikh memory. I imagine that Mata Ganga, too, found a way to rest in the wisdom within her—even after her husband was tortured and martyred, and an Empire wanted her and her son dead. She faced a hostile world. She must have found a way to listen deeply to the wise woman within her. To take the next breath.

History barely remembers her, but I honor her as the wise woman who mothered our people into survival.

OUR BONFIRE

BY THE END OF OUR STAY AT MY COUSIN'S HOUSE, OUR CHILDREN had recovered. Their fevers went down and they could hold down solid food. On the night of Lohri, they weren't well enough to go to a big celebration. So, Jyoti Didi prepared a little bonfire in the street in front of her house. She set up a speaker on a chair and blasted bhangra music. She poured popcorn and gachak and peanuts into the children's hands. The children threw popcorn into the fire, as they had so fervently desired, and shouted out things they were grateful for. As we danced under a sky filled with stars, the moon shone bright.

SAGE WARRIOR,
REST IN WISDOM . . .

WISDOM RESIDES DEEP WITHIN YOU. Develop a relationship with the wisest part of you. Go to the sovereign space inside you—the most beautiful and loving place you can imagine—and rest here. Begin to hum and fill your body and all parts of you. Let your hum touch the wisest and most loving part of you. Imagine that the wisest part of you has a form. What shape does it take? Perhaps a radiant light, landscape, or person. Let the image come. Take a few deep breaths. With every breath, let it grow brighter, stronger, and clearer. Say: *You are a part of me I do not yet know.* Listen for a few moments. Their voice is very quiet. They speak to you as their beloved. You might hear words or just a feeling. Whisper-speak what you hear into your cupped hands. Picture liquid gold swirling in your palms. If available to you, press the gold into your heart and let it flow through your whole nervous system. Notice what it feels like in your body to *rest* in wisdom.

Open the pages of a journal. Draw what you saw, write what you heard. Give your inner wisdom a name. It could be as simple as W.W., for Wisdom Within or Wise Woman. Let this journal be where this loving voice speaks to you. Listen as a daily practice. If there are other parts of you that interfere—fear or shame or hatred or pain—see if this wise part of you wishes to respond with a word or loving gesture. As if they are a beloved child or wounded friend. The wisest part of you can accompany the hurting parts of you into healing and transformation. The deeper your capacity to love all parts of yourself, the deeper your capacity to love all parts of the world. The sage rests in wisdom; the warrior speaks and acts from that loving wisdom.

A NOTE BEFORE WE GO ON . . .

Early Western scholars of Sikh history drew a sharp line between the first five Gurus and the latter five Gurus. They depicted the first five Gurus as "peaceful sages" and the latter Gurus as "militant warriors." This characterization has been roundly rejected by Sikhs. The sage warrior tradition was seeded at the start of Sikh history. When Guru Nanak, the first teacher, witnessed Emperor Babur's bloody conquests, he wrote piercing poetry about "the city of corpses" at Saidpur and wielded his pen as a sword: He was a warrior. When the tenth teacher, Guru Gobind Singh, a legendary military commander, sang in the moonlit night, he composed poetry for the ages: He was a sage. The sage warrior is embodied in different ways.

After the execution of the fifth teacher, Guru Arjan, the community fought with literal swords for its survival. The Sikh tradition supports a pragmatic nonviolence: In a violent world, make choices that minimize harm. Force is justified "when all other means have failed." Today we have many creative, nonviolent tools for advocacy and protection, social justice and liberation. As our story continues, I invite us to think about warrioring as the fiery energy that empowers all of us to be brave with our lives.

ANCESTOR TREE

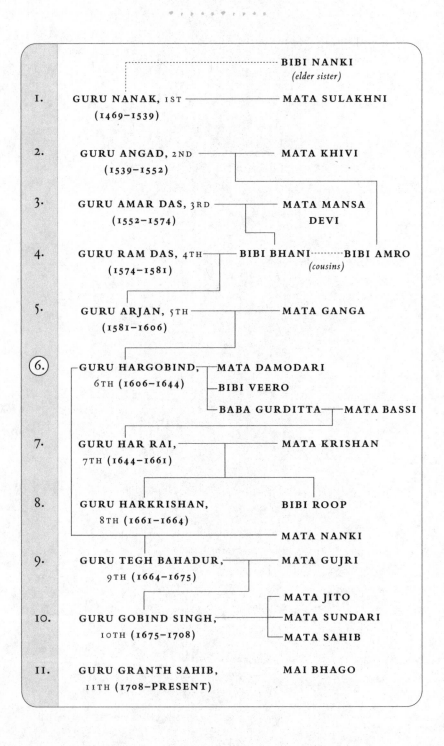

BIBI NANKI
(elder sister)

1. GURU NANAK, 1ST ———— MATA SULAKHNI
   (1469–1539)

2. GURU ANGAD, 2ND ———— MATA KHIVI
   (1539–1552)

3. GURU AMAR DAS, 3RD ———— MATA MANSA
   (1552–1574)   DEVI

4. GURU RAM DAS, 4TH —— BIBI BHANI ········· BIBI AMRO
   (1574–1581)   *(cousins)*

5. GURU ARJAN, 5TH ———— MATA GANGA
   (1581–1606)

6. GURU HARGOBIND, —— MATA DAMODARI
   6TH (1606–1644)   — BIBI VEERO
                     — BABA GURDITTA —— MATA BASSI

7. GURU HAR RAI, ———— MATA KRISHAN
   7TH (1644–1661)

8. GURU HARKRISHAN, ———— BIBI ROOP
   8TH (1661–1664)
                          —— MATA NANKI

9. GURU TEGH BAHADUR, —— MATA GUJRI
   9TH (1664–1675)

                          — MATA JITO
10. GURU GOBIND SINGH, —— MATA SUNDARI
    10TH (1675–1708)   — MATA SAHIB

11. GURU GRANTH SAHIB,   MAI BHAGO
    11TH (1708–PRESENT)

PART 6

ACTIVATE POWER

I. THE CHOICE:
THE STORY OF MATA GANGA
AND GURU HARGOBIND

...

N EWS OF GURU ARJAN'S EXECUTION SPREAD ACROSS THE LAND
of Punjab like a fire. Mourners took to the streets as the inferno-like
sun bore down on them. Some wailed. Others got into fights. Most
grew weak with fear. The leaders of the masands, the districts of the
Sikh realm, arrived in the city of Amritsar, along with a contingent
from Khadoor—the descendants of Guru Angad—and another from
Goindval—the descendants of Guru Amar Das. Crowds gathered at
Harmandir Sahib, where Baba Budda Ji recited the Aadi Granth from
start to finish. On the thirteenth day, Bhai Gurdas Ji sang Anand Sahib,
the song of joy. The city calmed, and a new song was heard in the
streets:

guru arjan ji dee joteejot
rahide gur dareaau vich meen kuleen het nirabaanee

Guru Arjan's light merged with the Light
Submerged in the river, like fish in water, liberated in love*

The elders gathered and talked about what to do. Emperor Jahangir
had ordered his agents to arrest Guru Arjan's family—young Hargobind and his mother, Mata Ganga—and confiscate all their property.
So far, local agents had not taken action. The elders asked: *Do we pay
the fine the Emperor demanded of the Guru? Or refuse as the Guru did? Do
we remain in the city? Or flee north to the mountains?* They debated for

* Vaara(n) Bhai Gurdas, panna 24, pauri 23, Bhai Gurdas Ji.

hours. Eleven-year-old Hargobind sat among them listening to the deeper question: *What power do we have?*

Hargobind went to find his mother.

Mata Ganga was in her chambers, eyes closed. The window was open and kirtan drifted in from Harminder Sahib, but she heard the music only faintly, as if submerged under water. She imagined burning her body, climbing atop her husband's funeral pyre, on piles of sandalwood, and letting the flames melt her skin and sear her muscles and lick her bones. She had not seen sati performed in her lifetime; the Gurus going back to Guru Nanak condemned the practice. But she found strange comfort in imagining her disappearance. Not disappearance. Transmutation. An end to consciousness, a release from pain, letting her body become ash, mingled with his, returning to the Oneness that always is. Just before the moment of her death, she would wail so loud that the earth would rumble and shake the palace of the Emperor who ordered her husband dead, and the palace would crumble to the ground and crush the Emperor and his torturers and all the bystanders who did nothing, and perhaps the whole world would fall with them.

But there was no funeral pyre. No body to cremate. No fire to throw herself in. Her beloved had been taken by water. So, Mata Ganga did not wail. She did not make a sound at all. She was completely still, pinned down by the weight on her chest, and her long, black hair was loose and falling in waves around her, and she let herself drown in it.

Hargobind opened the door. He saw his mother lying there, as she had day after day. He crawled onto the bed and fit his body into her shape. She instinctively wrapped her white shawl over him like a cocoon, and her hair made waves all around him, too.

"Kive(n) see?" she murmured. *How was it?* He could feel his mother's soft breath on the back of his neck.

Hargobind described what happened that day, the meeting with the elders. He waited to hear what his mother thought, but she didn't say anything.

"Mata Ji?" Hargobind said.

Her breath had slowed, and she was so still. *Was she sleeping? Was she dead?* Hargobind turned around and touched his mother's hair; he had never done that before. It was soft and tangled. He pulled the strands into his hands, one by one, and folded them together like the rope he had practiced with. His brow furrowed in concentration.

Mata Ganga stirred. Was her son braiding *her* hair? She heard a voice within her: "Jaago, meri jaan." *Wake up, my love.* And she was awake now—awake to the pain pressing down on her chest, and her son's hands on her hair, and the music of the kirtan outside where the people waited for direction. Mata Ganga wept. Not for her husband but for *herself* for the first time, and she was astonished there was still a self to weep for. Tears streamed down her face and deposited salt in her mouth, as cool as the sarovar waters outside.

"Puttar," she said, "your succession ceremony."

Mata Ganga turned to face him, her braid half-done.

"Did you talk to Baba Budda Ji?" she asked.

Hargobind shook his head.

"Baba Budda Ji has led the Guru Gaddi ceremony for every Guru before you," she said.

Hargobind knew the history of succession. Just before he departed, Guru Nanak asked Baba Budda Ji to anoint with a tilak Guru Angad, who at the end of his life asked him to anoint Guru Amar Das, who in turn asked him to anoint Guru Ram Das, who in turn asked Baba Budda Ji to anoint Guru Arjan. Now his father, Guru Arjan, was not here to watch Baba Budda Ji anoint him before the people. They had killed his father, his beautiful father who sang sacred songs and prayed serenely under torture and said that the will of the One was sweet.

Mata Ganga held her son. His body shook as if a fist were lodged in his belly and would not let him go.

"You are unlike any Guru before you," whispered Mata Ganga. He needed to release his fury, and shape its course. "What do our people need?"

Hargobind looked up at his mother. Mata Ganga was finishing her braid, her hands moving swiftly down the length of her hair. She looked tall and majestic, her braid flowing like a mighty river.

"Power," he said.

ON THE DAY OF THE GURU GADDI CEREMONY, HUNDREDS GATHered in nearby Daroli, where they could hold the ceremony surrounded by the protection of thick forests. Baba Budda Ji stood ready with crushed saffron, his great white robe glistening in the morning sun. The leaders of the masands solemnly took their seats. The air was still.

Mata Ganga stepped forth with her son. A hush fell over the people. Hargobind stood tall in a royal blue warrior's dress, holding matching cloth embroidered with gold thread. He bowed before the people and took his seat on the manji, facing them. Baba Budda Ji placed the red tilak on his forehead. Then, the elder took the blue cloth and slowly wrapped the boy's head, layer by layer, forming a turban in the shape only seen in paintings of royals. He placed a kalgi, an ornament worn only by rulers, on the turban. The eleven-year-old boy transformed into a king before the people's eyes.

The leaders of the masands prepared to stand and bow. But Guru Hargobind gestured to something shiny on the altar. The ceremony was not over.

Baba Budda Ji lifted up a great silver sword. The people gasped. Only kings were coronated with swords.

Baba Budda Ji slowly placed the sword on the right side of the Guru's body.

"Miri!" called out Guru Hargobind. *Power in the world.*

Guru Hargobind gestured again to the altar. Baba Budda Ji lifted up a second great sword. The people were shocked. A coronation with two swords was unheard of, even for kings.

"Piri!" called out Guru Hargobind. *Power within.*

Guru Hargobind named these swords Miri Piri: *Inner and outer power.* It was a full-throated declaration of sovereignty, from the inside out.

Guru Hargobind turned to the people in his warrior's dress and royal turban, two swords at his side, and made his first proclamation.

"My father was named Arjan, *warrior,*" he said. "We are warriors. We will not bow to oppression. I call on all Sikhs from across the land to bring gifts of horses—and arms."

There was a moment of silence. One by one, the people lifted their voices in praise, all their pain taking the shape of battle cries. Some of the leaders of the masands shook their heads. Others looked furious. This was a departure of the highest order. *A Guru who donned swords? A Guru who called for arms? Would this boy-Guru lead them to their deaths?*

As Guru Hargobind's proclamation spread across the land, Mata Ganga fortified herself. She awoke each day, her chest heavy with grief, but she lined her eyes with black surma and braided her hair and gathered her voice and joined Guru Hargobind at the elders' table. Some of the leaders of the masands sought her out privately, out of earshot.

"No one will come," they whispered to her. "He will lead us to ruin!"

"My husband sang songs of love as he was tortured," she replied. "He was faithful to you. He did not surrender. Neither will we."

Some were won over; others retreated into their quarters, counting down the days.

On the appointed day, Mata Ganga went outside before dawn and closed her eyes as the gates slowly rumbled open. When the sound ceased, she opened her eyes. Before her stood thousands and thousands of Sikhs, as far as she could see. They had horses—and arms.

OVER THE NEXT THREE YEARS, THOUSANDS OF SIKHS POURED INTO Amritsar to volunteer as warriors. They were young and old. They brought swords and shields, punch daggers and spears. New weapons were stored in the armory. Horses were taken into newly built stables, where they were fed wheat, sugar, and butter. As word spread through the Majha and Doaba regions of Punjab, even more warriors poured into the city. Many were poor. All were put on salary and given fine clothes and trained in the art of defense. The sound of gatka, stick-fighting, echoed in the streets. Guru Hargobind raised a mighty army.

Under Guru Hargobind's order, the people built a majestic structure across from the Harmandir Sahib—a place to manage political affairs. He called it the Akaal Takht, the throne of the Timeless One, and hoisted two marigold flags in front. The elders Baba Budda Ji and Bhai Gurdas Ji oversaw the construction and conducted its daily affairs.

Every day, Guru Hargobind trained as a swordsman, wrestler, and rider. In the morning, the young Guru awoke at dawn to meditate at Harmandir Sahib with his mother. During the day, he hunted. He shot arrows. He went into the forest with hunting dogs and hawks. In the evenings, he held court. As sacred music floated out from Harmandir Sahib, the young Guru was often found at the Akaal Takht seated on a throne, twelve feet high, listening to vaars—heroic ballads sung in martial tunes by spirited bards, dhadis. He was never without his swords, Miri and Piri. Word spread of the warrior-Guru who would defy an Empire.

"They will come for you," Mata Ganga said to her son one night. She massaged oil into his muscles, sore after a day of riding. "When they come for you, what will you do?"

"Grind the mountains of their world into nothing," he whispered. She knew it was not his answer. She remembered her fantasy of the imperial palace crumbling down, crushing the Emperor and all his agents of death.

Mata Ganga sang a verse from the sage-poet Bhagat Kabir:

aval allah noor upaya
kudrat ke sab bandey
ek noor te sabh jag upajia
koun bhaley ko mandey

First the Beloved birthed the light
to nature, all beings belong
From one light, the entire universe welled up!
So, who is good and who is bad? *

---

* Guru Granth Sahib, ang 1349, Raag Parbhati, Bhagat Kabir Ji.

There were no monsters in this world. Only those human beings who forget the one light, and those who embrace it.

"What will you do?" she asked again.

"I will go to the Emperor as my father did," said Guru Hargobind in the tone of a vow repeated every day. "As a sage warrior."

On the morning the Empire came for her son, Mata Ganga was cooking in the langar hall, stirring an enormous cauldron of daal. She paused when she heard the battle drums: Emperor Jahangir's imperial soldiers had penetrated the city. The same man who had ordered the torture and execution of her husband was now coming for her son. Her heart beat in her ears. She saw her husband's face under water. There was a part of her that wanted to run into the street and throw her body in front of her son's. Her knuckles turned pale as she gripped the ladle. She put a hand on her pounding heart. The daal in the iron pot bubbled. The langar would burn if she did not keep stirring. She took a deep breath and hummed Sukhmani, *Oneness in every breath*.

And so, as the people ran into the streets to confront the soldiers, Mata Ganga did not leave her post. She stirred the iron pot as her son called his warriors to stand down. She stirred as an official shouted that Guru Hargobind was under arrest on the charge that his father's fine had not been paid. She stirred as her son walked into the clearing and let himself be arrested, quieting the roaring crowd. She stirred as her son was taken to meet the man who killed his father. And when the soldiers were finally gone and the streets were filled with wails, Mata Ganga sat down. She wiped the strands of hair from her eyes, straightened her dupatta over her head, and called for Baba Budda Ji and Bhai Gurdas Ji: They had work to do.

GURU HARGOBIND WAS THROWN INTO A DARK CELL. HE TORE THE blindfold from his eyes with bloodied hands.

"Mai(n) kithay haa(n)?" he said to himself. *Where am I?*

"Gwalior," said a low voice. He wasn't alone.

As his eyes adjusted to the dark, he saw what looked like beggars—

their faces were hollow, their hair filled with lice, and their clothes tattered rags. Guru Hargobind wore a royal blue warrior's dress with its
many fine pleats, and his neck was adorned with pearls and emeralds
the guards were too scared to take from him. The prisoners did not take
them either; they just stared at the Guru as if he were a vision from a
different world. Or a world they once knew.

There were fifty-two prisoners in the cell—Rajput kings, all rulers
of kingdoms who had rebelled against the Emperor. Some had lan-
guished in this cell for many years. Guru Hargobind introduced himself as the sixth Guru in the House of Nanak.

"What kind of Guru are you?" they asked as they stared at the gold
karras on his wrists.

"I am a sage inside, and a warrior-prince outside," he replied.
"Guru Nanak did not renounce the world; he renounced maya, illu-
sion. This fortress is maya. We are more powerful than the stone of
Gwalior."

At this, the kings laughed.

There was only one Gwalior. The ancient and loathed Gwalior Fort,
almost a thousand kilometers from Amritsar, fortified by six bastions
where soldiers kept watch. The fortress stood atop a plateau of sand-
stone, a flat rocky hill that jutted up from the land below. It was a steep
drop on all sides. The Emperor who named himself Jahangir, Conqueror
of the World, sent his prisoners here to die. The prisoners' hate for the
Emperor is what bonded them, and they spat when they said his name.
The Emperor had his knee on their necks, and this prison was their tomb.

The young Guru closed his eyes and sang the song of Bhagat Kabir
that his mother had taught him:

aval allah noor upaya
kudrat ke sab bandey
ek noor te sabh jag upajia
koun bhaley ko mandey

First the Beloved birthed the light
to nature, all beings belong

From one light, the entire universe welled up!
So, who is good and who is bad? *

The Guru's song filled the cell. The darkness took on a strange sheen, and the air started to vibrate and breathe. *Not the darkness of the tomb. The darkness of the womb.*

The prisoners began to sing with him.

And so it began. Day after day, Guru Hargobind sang and the prisoners joined him. When they sang, the prisoners rested in the sovereign space of freedom inside them. *Sach khand.* The realm of truth. And their songs resounded outside the prison walls and stirred the guards. One guard drew close to the door and hummed along. He shared the songs with villagers who delivered supplies to the fort, who took them back to their families in neighboring villages.

One morning, as the prisoners sang, the ground began to shake. Was the earth erupting? Would the prison crumble? No, there was rhythm in the pounding, and the rhythm matched the song they were singing.

"There are people outside the fort, hundreds of them!" whispered a guard through the slot in the prison door. "They are pounding on drums and calling for your release! They are singing the songs you are singing."

Hundreds of Sikhs, led by Baba Budda Ji, had marched from Amritsar to Gwalior. They began at the Akaal Takht in Amritsar and formed a great musical processional until they reached the gates of Gwalior. Baba Budda Ji held up a torch of protest as they kneeled at the wall of the fort and raised their voices in song. Then, they pitched tents outside of the prison. They built an outdoor kitchen, where they cooked langar over iron cauldrons and ate together in rows. In another clearing, they gathered to pray and sing alongside rababis with musical instruments—rabab, saranda, jori, and tanpura. They established a school and a first-aid tent. The guard didn't see any weapons; it seemed the people had left their weapons behind.

---

* Guru Granth Sahib, ang 1349, Raag Parbhati, Bhagat Kabir Ji.

"Kirtan, paath, langar," whispered Guru Hargobind. *Singing, praying, serving*. This was more than a protest; it was a world, *their* world, a model of what the whole world could be. And they built it right outside the gates of the prison. The Sikhs did not need weapons; their power was in their numbers, and in their song.

Weeks turned into months, and months into seasons. Every season, a new procession of Sikhs marched from Amritsar to Gwalior. The encampment outside the prison stood strong through sweltering summers and cruel winters. And every morning, Guru Hargobind heard the people outside sing with the prisoners. Guru Hargobind turned sixteen years old in the prison.

Then, one day, Guru Hargobind was dragged out of the cell, through multiple gates, and thrown outside the fortress. He blinked in the light. A thousand people spread before him. The encampment was more glorious than the guard had described. He thought he saw his mother in the crowd. Before his eyes could focus, a shadow fell on him.

A figure on horseback towered over him. A man with a mustache who wore jewels that glinted in the sun and a peacock plume on his turban. His hand rested on the hilt of a sword.

Guru Hargobind looked into the eyes of the man who had killed his father.

"I choose to pardon you," roared Emperor Jahangir for all to hear.

Emperor Jahangir could not afford unrest from the villages that flanked his most prized, impenetrable prison. News of the musical processions from Amritsar spread throughout his realm. So he came to Gwalior himself to put an end to it and make a show of mercy before all his subjects.

"I choose to pardon you!" he commanded again.

Guru Hargobind did not move from where he stood, still as stone. He had to make a choice. Should he walk to his freedom, or return to his brothers in the cell? He felt his mother's gaze on him.

"I will only go if you also release the fifty-two kings you imprisoned with me," he said.

The people gasped. Emperor Jahangir flinched. Should he throw the Guru back in prison and risk outright rebellion among the villages of Gwalior, or lose all his most precious prisoners? The Emperor smiled as an idea dawned on him. He raised his voice for all to hear.

"You can release only those who can hold the hem of your cloak, *Guru*," said the Emperor. He would lose no more than three or four prisoners. After all, how many people can hold onto a cloak at once? He kicked his horse and galloped away, calling back: "Hathi Pul will open at dawn!"

As he was led back to his cell, Guru Hargobind thought of his mother. Mata Ganga would know what to do. He whispered to the guard a message to deliver to the encampment. When the Guru told his fellow prisoners what happened, they lamented and prayed through the night, waiting for dawn. None of them asked the Guru to take only them; they were brothers now, and one was not more worthy than another.

The hours crawled by. No one slept. Just before the break of dawn, the prison door cracked open. A bundle slid into the room, into the Guru's arms. He peered inside; he had what he needed.

As the first rays of the sun fell on the fortress, Emperor Jahangir ordered the outer gates open to let the people in. He wanted them to see their precious Guru thrown at their feet, broken and in rags. The people poured inside the prison until they reached the largest gate of all, adorned with an enormous statue of an elephant: Hathi Pul.

Emperor Jahangir nodded to the soldiers, who gave the signal to the guards. The ground shook as the great stone gates rumbled open.

There was no one there. The people were confused. *Was it a trick?*

Then, Guru Hargobind stepped forward. Not bent in rags, but standing gloriously, as he was the day he arrived at the fort. He was wearing a cloak—the most splendid cloak anyone had seen. The cloak spread behind him in an ever-widening rainbow, until the hem could be seen. The cloak had fifty-two tassels. Holding onto the tassels were the fifty-two kings, resolute and joyful, no longer prisoners of Gwalior, walking from bondage into freedom.

The people cheered. There was nothing Emperor Jahangir could do but watch.

Guru Hargobind walked through Hathi Pul and six more gates, as the people followed. When they were finally outside the fort, someone shouted out: "Satgur Bandi Chhorr hai!" And soon everyone chanted, "Bandi Chhorr!" *The One Who Sets Us Free.*

Guru Hargobind searched the crowd for his mother. How had she woven this magical cloak? Where was she? He spotted a face he knew—Baba Budda Ji with his long, flowing beard and great white robe. He fell to the elder's feet and bowed. Baba Budda Ji lifted him up and smiled at him. The Guru asked where his mother had gone.

"Your mother was never here," said Baba Budda Ji. "She is at Amritsar. She is leading the sangat. She sent me."

Guru Hargobind's brow furrowed.

Baba Budda Ji read his thoughts. "Your mother is part of you, and you her."

"The cloak . . . ?"

"The people saw you refuse your freedom. They took your message to the nearest village, and the children went from house to house, gathering all the fabric they had, and the families worked through the night, weaving and weaving, working their hands for people they did not know."

"Why?"

"Sant sipahi kisay noo(n) vee pichhe nahi chhadde," he replied.

You showed them a sage warrior does not leave anyone behind.

GURU HARGOBIND MOUNTED A HORSE AND BEGAN THE JOURNEY home to Amritsar, alongside Baba Budda Ji and all who camped at the fort. They stopped in the town of Gwalior and the villages and towns on the way. It was the season of Divali, the festival of lights when Hindus celebrate the ancient story of Ram and Sita returning to their kingdom of Ayodhya after a long exile in the wilderness. A triumph of light over darkness. People lit diyas, earthen lamps, and made rangolis out of colorful powder on the ground, and distributed sweets. They saw the Guru's journey home from the notorious prison as a real-life victory of light over darkness. New songs danced on people's lips:

satgur bandi chhorr hai
jeevan mukat karai oddeenaa

The true Guru frees us from bondage
We are liberated in life! *

khetee vaarr su dhingree kikar aas paas jio baagai
Like thorny kikar trees around farming fields, the Guru will protect and keep us! †

When Guru Hargobind reached Amritsar, the people shouted his
name in jubilation. "Bandi Chhorr!" A sage of limitless love. A warrior
who leaves no one behind. The people called the day of his return
Bandi Chhorr Divas, the Day of Liberation!

MATA GANGA WAS OVERJOYED BY HER SON'S RETURN HOME. IT
was time for Damodari to live with them as his wife. Mata Ganga called
Damodari and looked into her young face. She saw herself. Mata
Ganga, too, had married Guru Arjan at a young age. She remembered
how lonely she had been when Bibi Bhani found her in the blood-
soaked sheets, and nursed her to health, and mothered her. She remembered how tormented she was when she could not have a child, walking
until her feet were sore to see Baba Budda Ji for help. She remembered
the feeling of drowning after they killed her husband, until her son
found her in the tearstained sheets, and became Guru Hargobind. Most
of all, she remembered all the loneliness and pressure of being the only
wife of the Guru.

The Mughals had multiple wives so that they could produce many
children and secure survival. Marriage was a tool for political alliance;

*   Vaara(n) Bhai Gurdas, panna 26, pauri 20, Bhai Gurdas Ji.

†   Vaara(n) Bhai Gurdas, panna 26, pauri 25, Bhai Gurdas Ji.

the more alliances, the greater their strength. And the more children, the greater the likelihood of finding a successor who could lead well.

Mata Ganga bit her lip and made up her mind.

Mata Ganga conducted two additional marriages for her son. Guru Hargobind married Nanki, named after Bibi Nanki, from Bakala. Two years later, he married Mahadevi of the village Mandiali. Mata Ganga, who had spent her life focused on her only son, was surrounded by three daughters-in-law.

A son was born to Damodari on the full moon. The baby's name was Gurditta, and they saw Guru Nanak's face in his. The city erupted in joy, for he seemed destined to be next in the line of succession. Mata Ganga distributed sweets in the street, celebrating her first grandchild. Hijras gathered before the Guru's house in brightly colored saris and gold bangles, sang in deep voices, and danced. Mata Ganga watched happily, paid them, and thanked them. Their congratulations echoed in the streets: "Vadhayia(n)!"

Two years later, a daughter was born to Damodari, a healthy radiant baby. On the day of her birth, a falcon was seen at their gate, a good sign. Guru Hargobind joyfully uttered:

Seel khan kanniya ik hove! Putri bin bag grihst vigoye!
In every household, may a daughter be born! Or our way of
    life is lost!

But no great crowd came to dance in the streets. For the old ways that preferred sons still hung over the land like a fog. Mata Ganga carried her granddaughter, her potee, in her arms and hummed. The baby grasped the pearls on her neck.

This pearl mala had passed through the hands of the great women who led the House of Nanak: Bibi Nanki carried music inside her and lived what she sang; Mata Sulakhni mothered the first sangat; Mata Khivi stirred the kheer and fed people in the thousands; her daughter, Bibi Amro, was never without her pen. Bibi Bhani led with the radiance of the full moon, and she, Mata Ganga, carried the roar of the river. All of them had to overcome obstacles to find wisdom within them. All of them had to fight for their freedom. What if her granddaughter was born free? What if she knew she was sovereign from the start?

Mata Ganga recalled that Bibi Bhani had given her son a warrior's name: Arjan. Guru Arjan had lived into his name. This child was Guru Arjan's granddaughter. And the daughter of Guru Hargobind, the one who called forth the warrior in *all*. Mata Ganga closed her eyes and listened to the Wise Woman inside her.

Cradling the baby in her arms, Mata Ganga entered the quiet streets and went to Harmandir Sahib. She stood in the same place where her son, Guru Hargobind, had donned two swords all those years ago, and she lifted her voice. There was no crowd. No one watching. No one shouting praise. No one bearing witness except the water and the sky and the moon. There, Mata Ganga announced the child's name.

"Veero."

Mata Ganga named her one and only granddaughter: Warrior.

Aao chaa peelo . . .
Come, let's have tea . . .

WHAT IS A WARRIOR

ON OUR LAST NIGHT AT HARMANDIR SAHIB, I WAS READY TO GO BACK
to the hotel when Jasso tugged on my sleeve and gestured to the Akaal
Takht, a grand pearly-white storied building with a golden dome. Guru
Hargobind built the Akaal Takht to govern political affairs directly
across from the inner sanctum of Harmandir Sahib, tethered by a
bridge: Spiritual and temporal power are connected. We gazed up at
the raised marble platform where Guru Hargobind held court.

"I need to sit with my Guru," said Jasso. "The one who brought
Miri and Piri together."

Miri comes from the Persian word *mir,* which comes from the Arabic word *amir,* meaning one who commands, governs, or rules. *Piri*
comes from the Persian word *pir,* which means sage, spiritual guide, or
one who leads a spiritual order. Together, Miri and Piri are energies of
the sant sipahi, the sage warrior who activates power within and without. In Sikh memory, Guru Hargobind's full-throated embrace of Miri
Piri consolidated the sage warrior path.

We ascended the stairs, stepped inside the Akaal Takht, and bowed.
As we listened to the kirtan, Jasso's eyes were closed serenely. I fidgeted. My eyes kept falling on the kirpans, the swords.

In every gurdwara, in every part of the world, there are swords at the
feet of the Guru Granth Sahib, the canon of sacred poetry. When I was a
child, the swords made me tremble. I imagined blood on the tip of that
blade. I thought I was weak. This was an expression of power that, to my
shame, I did not feel I could bear or wield. Now I am a grown woman, an
activist and mother who has put in time in the trenches, and I still trem-

ble. I have seen the cost of physical violence; I have looked into the open caskets of people who have been slain; I have held their children. Now I think of the little girl in me trembling, and I am not ashamed anymore. She was wise. The cost of violence is steep: When we take another's life, we are also taking a piece of our own humanity. The Sikh tradition condones the use of force only when all other means fail.* And so, the use of force cannot be the sum of what it means to be a warrior. The sword is metaphorical: It is any tool we use to shape change.

A warrior is anyone who takes courageous action to protect, create, and sustain life with their life. There are many ways to warrior, and many tools we can use when we warrior: pens and paintbrushes, megaphones and microscopes, cameras and codes, pocketbooks and platforms. We can all become warriors, right where we are—in the sphere of influence we have, with the resources available to us. We can choose to use our tools to fight—for others, for humanity, for the earth, for ourselves. In a world on fire, we must.

We face a thousand Jahangirs. A thousand Gwalior prisons. A thousand demagogues and their infrastructures of inhumanity. The authoritarians, terrorists, power brokers, and warmongers of the world want us to believe that we are helpless. They *profit* from our despair. They want us to believe that only those who control wealth or weapons have power in this world. Their agendas depend on our paralysis.

But there are millions of us who want a world of coexistence, who know that justice and liberation and peace run together, who long for a shared future. Our potential is limitless—if only we reclaim our agency—and activate our power.

THE WAY WE MAKE CHANGE

I USED TO MEASURE POWER BASED ON OUTCOMES: HOW MANY PEOple at the march, how many votes to change the policy, how much

---

* "Only when all other methods fail, is it right to take the sword." Original: *"chu kar az hamah heeltay dar guzashat / halal asat(u) burdan be shamsher dast."* —Dasam Granth, ang 1389, Zafarnama, Guru Gobind Singh Ji.

money for the campaign. Such metrics are useful. But my core questions are different now: What values did we embody? What stories did we uplift? What dreams did we inspire? How did we bear witness? The way we make change is just as important as the change we make.

In the story of Guru Hargobind's imprisonment, the Sikhs who set up camp in front of Gwalior were not only resisting injustice: They were practicing the world as it could be. They modeled a world of equality and liberation, sacred music and selfless service, life and humanity at the gates of death and cruelty. They took turns forming public devotional singing marches from Amritsar to Gwalior, the first chaunki charhni. They practiced Mata Khivi's langar—and the equality, community, and joy it embodied. They stayed faithful season after season. And they brought an empire to its knees. After Guru Hargobind's release, Emperor Jahangir left the Sikhs alone for the rest of his reign. It was the first case of organized collective nonviolent resistance in Sikh history. We see the power of such organizing today.

In 2020, Punjabi farmers in India launched the Farmers' Protest. Tens of thousands of farmers protested to end a set of unjust policies by the Indian government. In a campaign called "Dilli Chalo!"—"Let's go to Delhi!"—farmers mostly from Punjab and neighboring areas marched to India's capital and set up camp in peaceful protest. They built great outdoor kitchens and served langar to all, feeding even the officers tasked to control them. They provided free healthcare for those wounded or ill. They withstood mass arrests and indefinite detention. In the face of water cannons, batons, and tear gas, they sang songs of liberation. The protest lasted two years; it was called the largest documented protest in recorded history. Like the Sikhs at Gwalior, they, too, created a protest that modeled the world as it could be. They, too, could have picked up weapons but instead they chose powerful, disciplined, nonviolent action. And they won. The laws they protested were repealed: They brought a mighty government to its knees. Their movement continues today.

Our most powerful way to create change is to *practice* the world we want, in the spaces available to us. We birth the beloved community by becoming it here and now.

MANY WAYS TO WARRIOR

I HAVE BEEN TELLING MY CHILDREN THE STORY OF GURU HAR-gobind and the magical cloak since they were little. Every Divali season, I bound into my daughter's preschool in a sunny salvaar kameez, announcing "Happy Bandi Chhorr Divas!" Her classmates are three- and four-year-olds, too little to be confused. *Of course! Bandi Chhorr Divas!* They gather around me to listen to the story. When I get to the part about the magical cloak, I pull an enormous colorful phulkari cloth from my bag slowly, dramatically, inch by inch, unspooling the Guru's cloak as he stepped out of the prison.* "Ooooh!" the children gasp. We pass around the phulkari for them to touch. Then, we eat lots of ladoos. After school, the children run to their parents and tell them that it was my birthday today. *So close!* My finest work takes place at family reunions. The grown-ups jump into the drama with my nieces and nephews. Massar plays Emperor Jahangir, twirling a pretend mustache, as my little niece plays Guru Hargobind walking into freedom with her two long braids, holding her head high.

Why do I love to tell this story so much? It's the moment of choice: *Do I free only myself? Or do I turn back for those left behind?* I want the children to feel the mechanics of that choice in their bodies. Maybe I need to feel it in my body. Maybe I need to tell the story again and again, to remember who *I* am.

Before the children were born, I worked on the front lines of social justice for nearly twenty years. I was deep in the trenches with my fellow advocates: We lifted up the stories of families who lost their loved ones to racial violence. We arrived at the sites of mass shootings while the blood was still on the ground and organized with the community, long after the cameras left. We investigated prisons and documented the stories of prisoners and the guards who hurt them. We marched with families to immigration detention centers where their loved ones

---

* Guru Hargobind's cloak of fifty-two tassels has been lovingly preserved for the last four hundred years. It is on display in a glass box at Gurdwara Sri Chola Sahib in the village of Ghudani Kalan in Punjab.

were held, and as we sang to them, they pounded the bars to our song. We filed lawsuits against corrupt police forces and were intimidated by police officers who trailed us home. I was arrested and detained several times. During one of those detentions, I was injured by a police officer in an experience of brutality that redoubled my commitment to resist all forms of state violence. I was a warrior, after all.

But after my children were born, I stopped putting my body out there. I needed to be home every three hours to nurse, and I couldn't sleep train them from a jail cell. I did more writing than marching. But something deeper kept me home. I couldn't afford to get hurt that badly again. I wanted to last. I wanted them to have a mother who lasted. I needed to preserve my energy for them, and that meant I felt I had less energy for the world.

Mothering radically expanded my definition of love—I could not help but see every person harmed, and every person who caused the harm, through the eyes of a mother—*and* it contracted my capacity to love people *in the way I knew how*. I felt that shift in myself, and I was ashamed.

Who are you leaving behind?

Everyone.

As my babies grew, I devoted my energies to *their* universe—the preschool, the neighborhood, the local park. I started to notice how the smallest interactions mattered: the tone of the teacher, the encounter in the yard, the resolution of conflict. I noticed how the spoken and unspoken policies that govern these spaces generate equity and belonging, or shame and isolation. I had believed there was a hierarchy of power when it came to social change: The loudest activism was the most important. But that changed as I started to pay attention to all the quieter labors inside of homes, schools, workplaces, houses of worship, communities—and in people's hearts. I saw how the personal, interpersonal, and systemic constitute one another. The deep conversation about the policy is just as important as the march to change the policy. The tender touch after the vigil is just as important as the speech that everyone hears. The way we explain the news to a child is just as important as our social media post about it. All our labors are valuable.

And that means that each of us, right where we are, in our sphere of influence, has a role to play—a way we can warrior.

You might say: There is so much suffering in the world! I don't know where to begin.

The cloak of Guru Hargobind did not have infinite tassels, just fifty-two. Just enough for the people in his cell. You don't need infinite tassels. Just enough for those in *your* sphere of influence. Who are you accountable to? Can you weave a tassel for them?

And when *you* are the one trapped in the darkness, imprisoned by concrete walls or the walls in your mind, the question is: Can you see the hem of the cloak in front of you? It takes great effort to lift your gaze and take hold. But there's always someone with you in the dark, even when you can't see them. Someone is offering you a tassel. Will you take hold of it?

Imagine all of us giving and receiving, offering and taking hold. Imagine all of us doing our part, just *our* part. Not more, not less. Imagine we are creating one great colorful procession out of the darkness toward the light.

Who are we leaving behind?

No one.

THE HARD PARTS OF THE STORY

I AWOKE SUDDENLY WITH ANANDA SITTING ON MY CHEST, WIDE awake, and Kavi asking what they should do now. It was two in the morning! Our jet lag in India would never end. I let Sharat sleep and tried to keep the children both quiet and busy until dawn. Ananda colored in unicorns; Kavi folded and unfolded a cube that you can make into seventy shapes. Within ten minutes, he had made all seventy. I had to think fast.

"Do you remember the story of Guru Hargobind and the magical cloak?" I asked.

"Of course, Mommy," Kavi said.

Whew, I thought.

"Did I tell you what happened *after* he left Gwalior?" I dove into an epic storytelling session about Guru Hargobind's life, getting into character with voices and everything.

"Pher tainu pata kee hoya, Kavi?" I asked. *Do you know what happened next, Kavi?*

"What?" he breathed, eyes wide.

That's when I knew the story was working. Ananda continued to color rainbow unicorns, but I'm sure it was all landing in her heart, too. *We're in the amrit vela,* I thought. The ambrosial hours before dawn, when Sikhs are encouraged to rise and meditate. How sublime! Then, I got to a part in the story I had never told before.

"So then, Guru Hargobind married Mata Damodari, and um, two other people . . ." I trailed off.

"Wait, what?" Kavi said.

"Um, well, he had three wives," I said.

"At the same time?" he asked.

I nodded reluctantly.

"That wouldn't feel good!"

"What do you mean?"

"If you married someone, and then they married another person, and another person, that wouldn't feel good!" It took me a second to realize he was taking the perspective of the women in the story.

I was about to dive into a historical lesson on the construct of marriage in seventeenth-century South Asia—how marriage was a political tool to build alliances, how polygamy was a cultural practice, how women married to Sikh Gurus were exalted as mother-leaders. But would this satisfy my little boy?

"I don't know what to say," I said. The truth was that I wrestled with my own revulsion every time I thought of it.

"No one's perfect," he shrugged.

I opened my mouth and closed it again. In the Sikh tradition, it is common to refer to the Sikh Gurus as perfect. I wanted to correct my son . . . but did I need to? It did not bother him to imagine the Gurus as people. In fact, it was powerful to see the Sikh Gurus as fully human—that's what made what they achieved so remarkable! They were visionary *and* they were operating within the constraints of their time and culture. They advocated for radical equality, liberation, and love, *and* they lived in sixteenth- and seventeenth-century South Asia. What if *we* are the ones to take their visions of liberation to new heights? What if this is how we activate the depth of our power—take forward the best of *all* our ancestors' wisdom and shape the future with our own radiant imagination?

I thought of Mata Ganga—how even as she oversaw multiple marriages for her son, she chose to name her granddaughter "Veero." *Warrior*. What longing in her heart drove her to imagine new possibilities? What power?

SAGE WARRIOR,
ACTIVATE POWER . . .

THINK OF A HARM THAT is happening in the world, or in your life, that upsets you. Notice where you feel tension, discomfort, or despair in your body. (If you feel severe activation—if it is hard to breathe or your heart is racing—pause here. This is information telling you to reach out to someone who can work through this pain with you.) If you are ready to continue, go to your sovereign space—the most beautiful and loving place you can imagine, where you feel safe and free. There is a large window in front of you. Look through the portal: It is the world where the harm that ails you is no more. In place of the harm is something new: harmony and beauty. *Rubble transformed into playgrounds*. The glass on the window melts away. You can go there, and touch that world. Step through the portal. What do you see? What do you hear? Notice what joy and possibility feel like in your body.

Now turn to the wisdom within you. Your deepest wisdom has been waiting for you to get quiet enough, still enough, to give you this piece of information. There is one new thing you can do—one thing that is only yours to do—to usher in that world right where you are. One step, one invitation, one conversation, one piece of art, one gathering, one act. What is the one brave thing you are ready for? Who can help you do it? What tools are already in your hand? You have what you need to activate your power and practice the world you want, where you are. The sage embraces their vision of the world as it could be; the warrior steps toward that vision.

ANCESTOR TREE

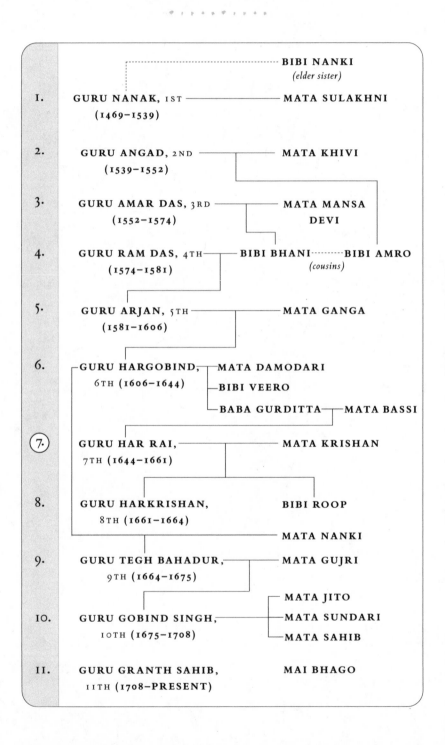

BIBI NANKI
(elder sister)

1. GURU NANAK, 1ST ——————— MATA SULAKHNI
   (1469–1539)

2. GURU ANGAD, 2ND ——————— MATA KHIVI
   (1539–1552)

3. GURU AMAR DAS, 3RD ——————— MATA MANSA
   (1552–1574)   DEVI

4. GURU RAM DAS, 4TH ——— BIBI BHANI········BIBI AMRO
   (1574–1581)   (cousins)

5. GURU ARJAN, 5TH ——————— MATA GANGA
   (1581–1606)

6. GURU HARGOBIND, ——— MATA DAMODARI
   6TH (1606–1644)   BIBI VEERO
                        BABA GURDITTA ——— MATA BASSI

7. GURU HAR RAI, ——————— MATA KRISHAN
   7TH (1644–1661)

8. GURU HARKRISHAN,   BIBI ROOP
   8TH (1661–1664)
                              MATA NANKI

9. GURU TEGH BAHADUR, ——— MATA GUJRI
   9TH (1664–1675)
                              MATA JITO
10. GURU GOBIND SINGH, ——— MATA SUNDARI
    10TH (1675–1708)   MATA SAHIB

11. GURU GRANTH SAHIB,   MAI BHAGO
    11TH (1708–PRESENT)

PART 7

HARNESS
RAGE

I. THE VOW:
THE STORY OF BIBI VEERO
AND GURU HAR RAI

. . .

VEERO, THE ONLY DAUGHTER OF GURU HARGOBIND, GREW UP IN the glorious court of the sixth Guru in the House of Nanak. Her grandmother Mata Ganga trained her in the poetry of the sages *and* in the art of defense. In the mornings, Veero learned Raag Vidya—the practice of music and kirtan—from Bhai Gurdas Ji. In the midday hours, she learned Santhiya—the recitation of Gurbani, including how to read the unbroken script larree-vaar—from the aged Baba Budda Ji. In the afternoons, she learned Shastar Vidya—the art of weapons, warfare, and horsemanship—from her father's soldiers. In the final hours before dusk, she joined her five brothers in the Guru's court and listened to ballads, her baby brother, Tyag Mal, on her lap.

Every night, Veero drifted to sleep, encircled by her grandmother's long silver braid. Mata Ganga rubbed rose essence into her forehead and sang her Sohila, the nightly prayer:

sa(n)bat saahaa likhiyaa
mil kar paavh(u) tel
deho sajan aseesrreeaa
jio hovai sahib sio mel

The day of my wedding is written
Let's gather, pour oil on the threshold
Bless me, dear friends:
That I may become one with the Beloved*

---

* Guru Granth Sahib, ang 12, Raag Gauri Deepaki, Guru Nanak Ji.

"When I breathe my last, consign my body to water, in the same river as my beloved," Mata Ganga whispered to her one night.

Veero thought of her grandfather Guru Arjan's execution. She wondered how her grandmother always seemed so peaceful in the face of her husband's martyrdom.

"Were you ever angry, Dadi Ji?" asked Veero.

"Haa(n) Ji, puttar," responded Mata Ganga. *Of course, dear child.*

"Mai(n) krodh de naal yaari pa laee," she said. *I had to befriend my anger.*

Mata Ganga spoke of rage as a part of her that was beautiful and wild: *Don't hold down your rage, or try to tame it. But don't let it rob you either. Harness rage: Take hold of the reins and direct its course.*

"Let the sage guide the warrior," finished Mata Ganga.

Veero nodded, her eyes watery.

Veero was at her grandmother's side when she passed away. Her father, Guru Hargobind, carried Mata Ganga's body in a woven raft to the River Beas. He sang as he placed his mother into the same river that had taken his father. From the bank, Veero watched as Mata Ganga—who refused to drown in grief after her husband was executed, who stood up to an empire that wanted them dead, who mothered a lineage of mystics to pick up the sword, and raised her one and only grand-daughter as a sage warrior—fulfilled her wish. Mata Ganga's unburnt body entered a current that swept ever forward and merged with her beloved.

A FEW YEARS AFTER MATA GANGA'S PASSING, WORD SPREAD THAT Emperor Jahangir—the Mughal ruler who had left Guru Hargobind alone ever since he was outwitted at Gwalior—had died from too much opium and wine. A battle for succession ensued. Emperor Jahangir's youngest son murdered his older brothers, seized the throne, and called himself Shah Jahan, King of the World. Veero watched her father closely as he waited for news about the new Emperor. When no news came, it appeared that Emperor Shah Jahan would leave them alone.

When Veero came of age, the great house of Guru Hargobind was abuzz with wedding preparations. Veero was to marry a boy named Sadhu. He was from a family her father had met at court one day; they were poor but rich in virtue. The family strung flower garlands of jasmine and marigold around the house. They made platters of sweets—makhanay, shakkar, barfee, ladoo, and jalebi—and the smell of sugar and ghee wafted through the halls. All the women covered Veero's skin in haldi and vesan, turmeric and chickpea paste so thick that her face shone when she washed it off. They laughed and teased her.

Amid the joyous wedding preparations, Guru Hargobind went hunting in the forest west of the city. He and his warriors entered a clearing in the woods. A great hawk flew overhead and alighted peacefully on the Guru's arm. A band of men cut angrily through the bushes. They wore imperial uniforms—the new Emperor's men. Emperor Shah Jahan was choosing to hunt menacingly near Amritsar. The imperial soldiers shouted that the hawk was a gift from the Emperor of Persia. Guru Hargobind launched the hawk back into the air. The great bird circled and returned to him.

An imperial soldier yelled: "Ajj baaj nu hath paya, kahl taaj nu hath paungay!" *Today they capture our hawk, tomorrow they capture our crown!*

Men on both sides drew swords and charged at one another. Guru Hargobind called off his soldiers and returned home with the great white hawk on his arm.

"Baaj!" cried Veero when she saw the beautiful hawk. She stroked its white-cloud feathers.

As Guru Hargobind told her what had happened, he ran his thumb over the beads of a shimmering pearl mala in his hand.

"Emperor Shah Jahan will be back," he finished wearily.

"Over a hawk?" cried Veero.

Guru Hargobind told her that his cousin Meharban, the son of Prithi Chand, had proclaimed that he was the true heir to Amritsar. The Guru had reached out to reconcile with Meharban, but his cousin refused. Now Meharban and his followers had the ear of the new Emperor: They urged the Emperor to come after the Guru. The hawk would be the excuse they were looking for.

Veero's eyes grew wide with worry.

A musical clang echoed in the hall as her mother placed a new tray of sweets on the banquet table.

"Your wedding will still take place on the twenty-sixth of Jeth," her father said to her. "I promise."

ON THE MORNING OF HER WEDDING DAY, VEERO WOKE BEFORE DAWN. Her mother, Damodari, led her to the bath, dressed her, and left to wake the other women. Veero lifted the oil lamp and looked at herself in the mirror. She had an unusual kind of beauty: a fierce gaze, a swan neck, and an angled warrior's nose with a gold ring. Shining jewels draped gracefully from her long neck. A blazing red dupatta flowed from her head, and a jeweled tikka shone on her forehead. Veero tried to see her grandmother in her reflection, but the lamplight flickered on the glass, like the flight of a hawk.

A scream ripped through the air, followed by the sound of a thousand pots smashing on the floor. Veero dropped to the ground. She heard huffing, like tigers wrestling. A terrible low moan. Footsteps receding. Then silence. Her muscles were taut, shaped by warrior training.

Veero grabbed a hairpin off the dresser and held it like a dagger. She tiptoed down the stairs; her ankle bells didn't make a sound. Her eyes focused in the dark.

Two bodies lay face down in the hall. Blood oozing from their heads. Broken flower garlands and shattered plates across the floor. Swords scattered to the side. The men wore imperial uniforms. The sweets from her wedding were knocked down from the table and trampled on.

No one else was there. The guards who stopped these intruders had gone to alert the Guru. The smell of blood filled her lungs, and nausea overcame her. Veero rushed back to her room and opened the window. The sun had not yet risen.

BOOM!

BOOM!

BOOM!

Her father's nagara battle drums echoed into the darkness. Veero put out the lamp and waited, breathless. She placed the hairpin in front of her. She spread her wedding dupatta around her, so that it made a lotus shape. She assumed a warrior's seated posture in veer aasan, resting an arm on one knee, and closed her eyes. Her heart beat in her ears, as loud as the war drums outside. She took a deep breath and felt Mata Ganga's hand on her forehead and smelled the fragrance of rose essence. She heard her grandmother singing Sohila, and the song made a silver shield around her. The hairpin on the ground became a kirpan, a mighty sword. She was a sipahi, a warrior.

"Bibi Veero!" called a voice downstairs. "Come down! Your father is calling you!"

Veero did not know this voice. She did not move.

"Bibi Veero!" called a second voice. The man tossed beads to the top of the stairs.

Veero crawled out on her hands and knees. The wedding ornaments that dangled from her wrists dragged on the ground. She seized the beads. It was her father's beautiful pearl mala. Either he was dead or these men spoke the truth.

Veero stood tall at the top of the stairs. Below her, two warriors held torches and gazed up at her. She recognized them: Babak Rababi and Singha Purohit. Her father's warriors.

They quickly told her what had happened: The dead men in the hall were the Emperor's bailiff and constable. They came to arrest the Guru on the charge of theft of the hawk. They plundered her wedding halls and feasted on her mithai. That's where the Guru's guards discovered them. But these two men were just a distraction.

Seven thousand imperial soldiers had marched to Amritsar from Lahore in the dead of night. They attacked Lohgarh Fort, the Castle of Iron. They were on their way to the Guru's residence, just east of the fort. They were coming for her.

"Come, your family has been evacuated to Ramsar Sarovar," said Babak Rababi.

Ramsar Sarovar, the serene pool on the far southeast side of the city where her grandfather Guru Arjan compiled the Aadi Granth. Veero wrapped the pearl mala around her wrist and followed the warriors outside. Singha Purohit mounted his horse and extended his hand, but she already knew how to ride. As she lifted herself up, the kaleeray of coconuts that dangled from her wrists draped the horse's sides. They slowly entered the maze of narrow alleyways of the inner city of Amritsar.

As she rode silently, she heard the gleeful shouts of imperial soldiers behind them. The soldiers must have found the banquet hall with the confections. They were feasting on the rest of her wedding sweets in the Guru's house. They were celebrating, shouting that they had taken the city!

"Kaun hai?" called a voice from the darkness. *Who's there?* It was an imperial soldier.

"It's your brothers, don't worry!" said Babak Rababi, buying time. "We're searching for the Guru!"

The first rays of sunlight pierced the sky. In moments, they would lose their cover. Veero's red wedding dress made them an easy target. Singha Purohit flicked the reins, and their horse launched into a gallop. The bells around Veero's ankles shook; her jhanjhar made a strange and beautiful jingle, so alien in the atmosphere of war.

Following the sound of the bells, the imperial soldier rounded the corner. He saw Veero on the horse, and she saw him. His eyes widened. He gripped a long, pointed spear.

"She's here!" he yelled.

The soldier lifted the spear high above him. Veero imagined its trajectory—the tip of the spear was going to arc through the air and pierce the pearls that draped her chest. Her blood would spread across her chest, blending into the red of her wedding dress.

Veero took a breath and closed her eyes. She heard her grandmother sing Sohila:

sa(n)bat saahaa likhiyaa
The day of my wedding is written

THUD!

The soldier fell to the ground. Blood spread throughout his copper-gray uniform. Veero could see his young face, unlike the dead men face down in the hall. His eyes rolled to the back of his head. "Ammi!" he moaned. He was calling for his mother.

Veero was riding away at great speed—away from the dying soldier and the alleyway and the smell of death—but she kept hearing the soldier moaning, "Ammi jaan!" The moan followed her, along with the musical sound of the bells on her ankles.

Veero had never seen a person killed. Her whole life she had watched her father build an army and train his people in warfare, but they had never actually used their weapons to kill. She had trained in defense and heard the ballads of battles past, but none of that training, and none of those stories, prepared her for the smell of death. Only her grandmother's Sohila kept her from falling off the horse —

sa(n)bat saahaa likhiyaa
mil kar paavh(u) tel
deho sajan aseesrreeaa
jio hovai sahib sio mel

The day of my wedding is written
Let's gather, pour oil on the threshold
Bless me, dear friends:
That I become one with the Beloved*

A few minutes later, they arrived at Ramsar Sarovar where her family waited. Guru Hargobind was dressed in armor, his swords Miri and Piri at his side, a quiver full of arrows at his back. He tearfully embraced his daughter.

"The battle has come to us," he said. "I ride out to fight."

Veero handed him the pearl mala, but he gave it back to her.

*   Guru Granth Sahib, ang 12, Raag Gauri Deepaki, Guru Nanak Ji.

"It belonged to Mata Ganga Ji," he said tenderly. "She asked me to give it to you—when you were ready."

Tears streamed down Bibi Veero's face as she thought of her grandmother.

"It was always meant for you," said her father. "Shakti vastay." *For power.*

Bibi Veero felt the power of her grandmother coursing through her as she wrapped the mala back around her wrist. She hugged her father and climbed into a cart next to her five brothers. Her youngest brother, Tyag Mal, held her tightly. Guru Hargobind instructed his family to go toward Goindval until they reached the village of Chabaal. They would be safe there. He sent word to the groom's procession to meet them there for the wedding.

"Today will still be your wedding day," the Guru promised his daughter.

The cart lurched forward. As they left the burning city, Bibi Veero studied the white pearl mala. The morning sun shone on the pearls; the colors within them swirled. All the women ancestors in her grandmother's stories flashed before her eyes: They were watching her. She took a deep breath and broke pieces of coconut and sugar discs off her kaleeray, the ones she was supposed to eat after the wedding on the way to her husband's house. She fed her little brothers the coconut and sugary patasay and quieted their fears.

That night in Chabaal, the villagers prepared a small wedding ceremony for the daughter of Guru Hargobind. Bibi Veero refused to begin the ceremony until her father returned. She waited before the Aadi Granth, draped in her red wedding dupatta, running the pearl mala through her hand. The man she was to marry, Sadhu, was seated beside her and held a poem he had written for her, in praise of the Guru. She was marrying a good man. The hours grew long. Finally, a figure atop a white horse appeared in the darkness, riding toward them at full speed, two gleaming swords at his side. Her father had kept his promise.

EMPEROR SHAH JAHAN'S SURPRISE ATTACK ON THE CITY OF Amritsar came to be known as the Battle of Amritsar. Guru Hargobind's forces defeated the Emperor's armies, even though they were severely outnumbered. But the battle was the start of a war. After Bibi Veero's wedding, Guru Hargobind set off for the front. First to Kartarpur in the Doaba region, then to Sri Hargobindpur (the city his father named after him). When they clashed with imperial troops near Lahira, the Guru's forces retreated to the wild and uncharted countryside in Bathinda, where pursuit was difficult. Imperial troops again tried to capture him in Kartarpur. There, Bibi Veero's brothers Gurditta and Tyag Mal were old enough to fight alongside him. Tyag Mal fought so valiantly that the Guru renamed him Tegh Bahadur, Sword of Courage.

When Bibi Veero heard of her youngest brother's bravery in battle, she felt pride—and fury. How long was the Empire going to pursue her family? She seized her kirpan and slipped into the forest outside her husband's village, Malla. She closed her eyes. She pictured the imperial soldiers charging at her brother. Rage rose in her like fire in a cage and burned in her throat. She pierced the air with her sword. Another soldier at her back. She spun and lunged. As her rage burned, her swordplay turned into a dance, swift and wild, until before she knew it, she plunged her sword into a tree. She opened her eyes. Tiny beads of sap bled from the tree, like the blood of the imperial soldier writhing in the alley; she heard him moan for his mother. Try as she might, she could not cast the memory of this soldier out of her heart. He was part of her. What did her grandmother teach her? *Don't let your rage blind you to the One. The One who lives in everyone. Ride your rage, harness its energy. The sage must guide the warrior.*

Bibi Veero mounted a horse and went to meet her father. She found his camp in the wilderness, not far from the last battle.

"What was Guru Nanak's wish for the village of good people he met on his travels?" Bibi Veero humbly asked her father.

In that famous story, Guru Nanak blessed the closed-hearted to stay where they were, to confine their cruelty, and the openhearted to disperse compassion throughout the world.

"Ujjarr javo!" replied Guru Hargobind, gazing at the northeastern horizon.

Bibi Veero nodded. *It was time for them to let go.*

A year after the Battle of Amritsar, Guru Hargobind announced to the Sikh realm that it was time for his family to leave their beloved city of Amritsar and set up headquarters in the north. As the Guru's caravan left the city gates, the people of Amritsar chased after them, begging them to stay. They all knew what would happen now: Meharban, Prithi Chand's son, who had long claimed himself Guru, would come and take over the city of Amritsar with his followers. Guru Hargobind comforted them: At least Amritsar would not be the target for any more bloodshed.

As the camels in the caravan kicked up a great cloud of dust, Bibi Veero rode solemnly on horseback alongside her brother Tegh Bahadur. Through the haze, she saw a child crying in the back of a cart. Bibi Veero handed the child a doll. The girl named Gujri clutched the doll to her chest and looked up at her with eyes as bright as the stars.

As Bibi Veero rode on, the girl's eyes stayed with her, and her heart ached. Bibi Veero had grown up in the glory days of the Guru's court; what would become of this child, and all the children? Her beloved grandmother Mata Ganga was gone. The esteemed elder Baba Budda Ji had just passed away. The great Bhai Gurdas Ji had said he would live out his remaining days in his old home in Goindval. All the elders who had known the first five Gurus were gone. Now faced with perpetual war, they were leaving behind their home, the glory of Harmandir Sahib, and the great city their ancestors had built. The cruelty of Guru Arjan's execution was not an aberration; it was just the beginning. The hardship her great-grandmother Bibi Bhani had foretold was now their whole world.

Bibi Veero heard a trumpet-like song and peered up through the clouds of dust. High in the sky, a flock of geese made an arrow pointing in the same direction they were going—northeast to the foothills of the Himalayas, the direction birds fly when the weather changes. Bibi Veero flicked the reins and rode to the head of the caravan, where a gold palanquin carried the Aadi Granth, their sacred poetry. She hummed Sohila. They carried their ancestors' wisdom with them.

GURU HARGOBIND SETTLED HIS FAMILY IN THE NORTH OF PUNJAB, in the foothills of the Himalayas by the River Satluj, on a plot of land that had been gifted by the Raja of Bilaaspur. Surrounded by thick wilderness, the land was difficult for any army to reach. They were left alone by Emperor Shah Jahan and his armies. On this misted northern land, Guru Hargobind built a new city and named it Kiratpur, *the Home of Praise*.

Meanwhile, Bibi Veero lived with her husband in his village, Malla, in Bathinda. She raised five sons as mystics and warriors like her. She taught them the songs of the sages and trained them in the art of defense. She told them stories of the glorious days of her father's court in Amritsar and kept its memory alive.

Three years after the exile, Bibi Veero received news that her eldest brother, Baba Gurditta, was found in the wilderness in Kiratpur, lifeless. No markings on his body. No satisfactory explanation. His heart just stopped. She rode immediately to Kiratpur for the antam sanskar, his final rites.

Bibi Veero walked with her father in a garden in the twilight hour after her brother's ashes were spread. They took their seats beneath a great magnolia tree. She looked into her father's face, marked by battle and age—and heartbreak. The loss of his firstborn, Baba Gurditta—trained for the Guruship since birth, the son who had fought at his father's side—ran deep.

His passing catalyzed more fracture. Baba Gurditta's eldest son, Dheer Mal, stole the original edition of the Aadi Granth, the one that Guru Arjan had prepared with his own hand, and fled to Kartarpur, where he set himself up as a guru to lead a rival community. Two other sons, Ani Rai and Atal Rai, had died early deaths. His two remaining sons, Suraj Mal and Tegh Bahadur, did not want to lead, at least not yet.

Back in Amritsar, his cousin Meharban fortified his hold on the city with conjectures that Guru Arjan's line would soon die out completely.

"Who will lead after you?" Bibi Veero asked her father. It was his grandmother Bibi Bhani's wish for the Guruship to stay in their family, so that any hardship to come would be absorbed by their line.

Her father's eyes rested on a horizon she could not see.

"Dada Ji! Bhua Ji!" called a child's voice. *Grandfather! Auntie!*

Bibi Veero spotted little Har Rai in the distance—her late brother Baba Gurditta's youngest son, only eight years old. Har Rai dismounted a horse and ran toward them. Suddenly, the boy turned around and fell to the ground.

No, no, no. Bibi Veero thought. Was he hurt? Did *his* heart stop? They couldn't bear any more sorrow, not now. She ran to him.

Har Rai was on his knees, sobbing. There was a flash of red in his palms.

"Are you hurt?" asked Bibi Veero, catching her breath.

The boy showed her what he held—red roses broken at the stem. He picked up the fallen roses, one by one, and cried passionately. There was dirt on the hem of the boy's pants. He was wearing a yellow Persian jama with a hundred pleats that must have brushed against the roses and broken them as he ran.

"Koi nahi," cried Bibi Veero, rubbing his back. *It's okay!*

The boy shook his head and sniffled.

"I don't want to harm anything ever!" said Har Rai.

Har Rai buried his face in his arms, waiting for reproach. He was accustomed to grown-ups telling him that if he cried over dead flowers, he would never be able to handle this world. But Bibi Veero studied him closely. Her father joined them.

"This can become your vow," said Guru Hargobind to his grandson. "In a world of violence, to do less harm."

The boy lit up.

"I will lift up my jama wherever I go!" declared Har Rai, wiping his face.

Bibi Veero's heart melted. She returned to the magnolia tree with her father.

"I think you know who to choose," she said to him. The people needed a leader who held fast to the sage in the warrior.

SIX YEARS LATER, GURU HARGOBIND DEPARTED THIS WORLD WITH a warrior's send-off, and his fourteen-year-old grandson became Guru Har Rai, seventh in the House of Nanak. Guru Har Rai made good on his vow to minimize harm. He learned to hunt like his grandfather but did not kill the animals he caught. Instead, he brought them back to Kiratpur, where he built a magnificent zoo for people to meet the creatures who lived among them in the jungle. He studied plants and flowers and their medicinal properties. He built a hospital and research center in the heart of Kiratpur, where he called forth the greatest healers in the land. The institution gained renown as a center for knowledge and healing. And everywhere he went, Guru Har Rai lifted the hem of his jama when he walked on the land.

A year later, when unrest beset the region around Kiratpur, Guru Har Rai did not send his warriors—2,200 Sikhs—into protracted battle. Instead, he took his family and retainers deeper into the foothills of the Himalayas, to a small obscure village in Sirmoor State in the Shivalik Hills. Taking advantage of the Guru's absence from the major cities of the Sikh realm, rival claimants gained ground and the masands began to fracture. So the Guru sent emissaries from city to city to rally the people and hold the Sikh world together. Over the next few years, the manji system that began with twenty-two masands under Guru Amar Das expanded to 360 districts across Punjab. Meanwhile, the Mughal Empire continued to leave the Sikh realm alone.

Until one day, Guru Har Rai received a letter from Emperor Shah Jahan, the same Emperor who had attacked Amritsar and driven them all into exile. The Emperor's eldest son, Dara Shikoh, heir to the throne, was ill. The Emperor's middle son, Aurangzeb, had slipped poisonous tiger whiskers into his eldest brother's dish. Now Dara Shikoh was going to die. They searched the land for plant remedies to save him, but they had no luck. Word of Guru Har Rai's renowned healing center in Kiratpur had reached the royal palace. Out of all the people in the world, it was the Guru of the Sikhs who possessed the rare plants that could save the boy's life. The Emperor asked: *Will you help us?*

Bibi Veero and Guru Har Rai walked together in the great garden in Kiratpur. As she listened to Guru Har Rai deliberate, Bibi Veero fanned her neck. Her mind flashed to her wedding hall smeared with ladoos and dirt and blood and crushed jasmine. The sickening smell of death filled her lungs. She saw her childhood home and the glory of Harmandir Sahib and all that Emperor Shah Jahan had taken from them. She saw her beloved city of Amritsar and the alleyways she knew so well. Her fists clenched, and rage burned her throat. And then—she heard the moan of the soldier, the one who died with his chest spilling blood the color of roses, the one who cried out for his mother. She ran the pearl mala through her hand and paused as her thumb pressed on one creamy gold pearl. *Let the sage guide the warrior.*

"Ohdi madad karo," Bibi Veero finally said to her nephew. *Help him.*

Guru Har Rai lifted the hem of his jama and went to his great storehouse of medicines. He selected jars that contained the rarest flowers.

"Behold, the axe cuts the sandal tree, yet the sandal perfumes the axe," said Guru Har Rai. "And so, we return cruelty with good."

Before the Guru sealed the package, Bibi Veero added a pearl to the medicines. A single creamy white pearl that shone in the twilight. They saved the boy, heir to the Empire that had tormented them, without the expectation of anything in return.

IN TIME, DARA SHIKOH, THE ELDEST SON OF EMPEROR SHAH JAHAN, regained his health and grew into a powerful leader. He stood for an expansive vision of Islam and studied the Sufi mystics who had nourished the vision of Guru Nanak. Dara Shikoh was inspired by his great-grandfather Emperor Akbar, the one who had partaken in langar with the early Sikhs and gifted the land that became Amritsar. Bibi Veero thought: *When this young man becomes the Emperor, he will restore har-*

mony to the land and let us live in peace. This dark age will end and the Guru's family will return to Amritsar and restore its glory, as it was when I was a girl.

They received news that Emperor Shah Jahan had fallen ill and formally nominated his son Dara Shikoh as the next Emperor. But Dara Shikoh's younger brother Aurangzeb launched a rebellion and was backed by the most conservative clerics in the court. Aurangzeb fought his older brother in two battles, defeated him, and drove him northward toward Lahore. There, Aurangzeb's forces captured Dara Shikoh and put him to death. Bibi Veero was enraged. *They killed the boy whose life we saved.*

Aurangzeb took the throne and imprisoned his father. Emperor Shah Jahan was thrown into Agra Fort, which stood across from a marble mausoleum he had built for his wife. The head of his son Dara Shikoh was delivered to him in a box, at the order of Aurangzeb. Emperor Shah Jahan—self-proclaimed King of the World who waged all-out war on the Sikh realm—spent his final days anguished and imprisoned, resting his eyes on his wife's mausoleum, the Taj Mahal.

Emperor Aurangzeb then summoned Guru Har Rai to court to secure the allegiance of the Sikh realm. Guru Har Rai asked his eldest son, Ram Rai, to go on his behalf and represent him. Ram Rai, well trained in the scriptures, vowed that he would. When Ram Rai was asked to recite a shabd of Guru Nanak before the Emperor, he altered a word in the verse in order to make it more palatable to the Emperor.* This was not the way.

"Ram Rai did not keep his promise," Guru Har Rai said quietly to Bibi Veero as they walked together in the garden. "Still, it is time to prepare the Guru Gaddi."

The Guru's hand trembled as he lifted his jama. Bibi Veero realized that Guru Har Rai, at thirty-one years old, was preparing for his succession.

"The rarest plants in my storehouse will not cure me," said Guru

* Guru Granth Sahib, ang 466, Raag Asa, Vaar, Guru Nanak Ji.

Har Rai as he gazed at the horizon. The choice of Guruship was by
virtue but also hereditary: It was Bibi Bhani's wish that any hardship be
absorbed by their family.

"Who will lead?" Bibi Veero wondered once again.

Bibi Veero heard a peal of laughter. Under the great magnolia tree,
Guru Har Rai's five-year-old, Harkrishan, was playing with his mother.
The boy was now climbing into his mother's lap. He carried a cotton
satchel filled with tiny glass bottles from his father's storehouse. He
opened a bottle labeled "Gulab." Rose essence.

Bibi Veero watched as the child slowly rubbed rose oil into his
mother's temples. Krishan, his mother, closed her eyes, the stress of her
husband's illness melting away. Moved, Guru Har Rai went and kissed
his son's forehead.

Bibi Veero remembered the touch of Mata Ganga and how her
grandmother stayed faithful to her people, no matter how dark the future seemed.

She went to the child's mother, Krishan, and whispered:

"I will help prepare the Guru Gaddi ceremony."

Aao chaa peelo . . .
Come, let's have tea . . .

HEADING NORTH

WE DROVE NORTHEAST ACROSS THE PLAINS OF PUNJAB TOWARD the foothills of the Himalayas to Kiratpur. A misty fog enveloped the fields, as if a spell of enchantment had been cast on the earth.

"Bahar dekho!" I begged the children. *Look outside!*

They were busy talking up a storm in the back seat in a make-believe language that sounded like Punjabi but was definitely not, gesturing wildly, making all kinds of expressions. They were in their own world. Which meant that they weren't asking for snacks.

I opened my journal and studied the fog. Through the mist, I caught sight of mustard flowers, sun-yellow as if brushed with gold. As we climbed higher north, the air got colder and crisper, the fog thicker, and I began to see a tangle of wilderness. I imagined our Sikh ancestors traversing this land, making this journey north, pursued by imperial forces. They were refugees dreaming of a future when the world must have felt so dark.

I thought of all the human beings making that same kind of journey now—fleeing missiles and bombs, drought and starvation, fires and floods, vigilante violence and genocidal campaigns—and still singing to their children in the night. They do not know whether life will end beneath a pile of rubble. Or face down in a river they try to cross. Or in a makeshift home in a new land. Soon, there will be more refugees in our lifetime than in any previous era of human history. How do we help one another survive?

The Sikh ancestors chose to *sing*, no matter how dark it got. The song-prayer they sang at night was Sohila. Sikh parents have sung Sohila to their children at night for centuries. I hum Sohila to my children before we drift to sleep. I imagine Mata Ganga singing Sohila to her granddaughter, Bibi Veero; I imagine Bibi Veero carrying Sohila with her in moments when she faced fear and death. In Sohila, death is framed as a wedding day, a return to the Beloved, and the Oneness that always is. A mystical song for practical courage. A way the sage prepares the warrior.

BIBI VEERO'S PLACE

IN KIRATPUR, WE STAYED IN A GUESTHOUSE SURROUNDED BY FARMS and forest. I woke before dawn, slipped out of the bed of sleeping children, and met our driver, Happy, while it was still dark. Happy was in a good mood this morning, as there were no children shouting in the back seat. I gave him directions. We traveled down the main road, turned and went two kilometers, and stopped in front of a small gurdwara tucked between a row of houses across an empty field.

"Ethaay hai?" asked Happy uncertainly. *This is it?* Happy had driven people to all the famous sites in Punjab. But no one had ever asked him to bring them to Gurdwara Manji Sahib in Kiratpur. I was overjoyed: It was said to be the spot where Bibi Veero once lived.

Happy waited in the car to keep it warm as I jumped out and ascended the stairs, hugging my journal to my chest. I entered the humble sanctum, bowed, and went to a big glass case with objects inside.

"Ethay Sikh Ramal Bibi Veero Ji Da," read the sign. *This Is Bibi Veero's Shawl.* Pressed between two panes of glass was a faded embroidered shawl. The faint patterns made flowers. As I thought of the violence she survived, the design of the shawl took on a deeper meaning: *She draped herself in flowers.*

"Ethay Sikh Pakha Bibi Veero Ji Da," read the next sign. *This Is Bibi Veero's Fan.* A large cloth fan was pressed in glass, its pleats frayed at the edges. I thought about the small pleasures of cool air as she walked in the garden.

"Ethay Sikh Manji Sahib Bibi Veero Ji Da," said the next sign. *This Is Bibi Veero's Bed.* It was a low bed with wooden posts. This is where she drifted to sleep after singing Sohila. Seeing these things made her even more real.

Long ago, my Sikh sisters nicknamed me Veero, because it meant warrior. I did not know that Veero was the name of a woman who once lived—the eldest daughter of Guru Hargobind and the first Sikh woman ancestor on record who was trained in both the sacred poetry and the art of defense. She was a true sant sipahi, a sage warrior. Yet I don't remember being told anything about her.

So, I found whatever scraps of history I could: Bibi Veero was born in 1615 and raised in the glory days of the court of Guru Hargobind. As the eldest and only daughter of the Guru, her wedding would have been the most lavish and royal the realm had seen. Yet that was the day when the world she knew ended. In 1634, Emperor Shah Jahan's armies plundered her wedding and waged the Battle of Amritsar. A year later, Guru Hargobind left Amritsar for Kiratpur and Bibi Veero lost her ancestral home. Still, she raised five sons who would go on to become warriors, too, and serve the House of Nanak. She is said to have often visited her family in Kiratpur. I imagine she must have been present when, decades later, according to oral tradition, Emperor Shah Jahan asked for Guru Har Rai's help to save his son.

Bibi Veero witnessed bloodshed, plunder, and exile, yet her family helped the Emperor who had tormented them.

I spotted something on Bibi Veero's bed—a faded brown cap, cream where the cloth was torn, pressed in glass.

"Ethay Sikh Seli Topi Guru Nanak Dev Ji Di," read the next sign. *This Is Guru Nanak's Seli Topi.*

I don't know if this cap really belonged to Guru Nanak. There are many artifacts scattered across Punjab that allegedly belonged to this Guru or that ancestor. What was strange and wonderful was that this particular artifact was on display *here,* in an obscure gurdwara that honored Bibi Veero. It was as if Guru Nanak's energy and hers belonged together. The sage sees humanity in all. The sage sees the One in all. The sage returns to love above all. So that we have the courage to say, even when it's hard: *You are a part of me I do not yet know.*

WHAT IS DIVINE RAGE

RAGE IS A HEALTHY, IMPORTANT RESPONSE TO TRAUMA AND OPPRES-
SION. So many of us have been conditioned to choke down our rage as
a matter of survival. Especially if we are women or people of color or
otherwise marginalized. We have been taught to suppress our rage in
the name of love. But the opposite of love is not rage; it is indifference.
Our fury in response to injustice is a vital source of energy and action.
In order to access our agency, we must let ourselves feel our rage. Let
it burn in you, notice where in your body. The solution is not to suppress our rage, or to let it explode, but to process our rage in safe containers, like many of our ancestors did—singing, drumming, shaking,
sobbing, dancing, running, whirling, wailing. Only when we move
that energy through our body can we then look at it and ask: *What information does my rage carry? What does it say about what's important to
me? How do I wish to harness that energy for what I do in the world?* I call
that harnessed energy *divine rage*.

The aim of divine rage is not vengeance but to reorder the world.

In the Sikh tradition, rage, or krodh, is one of the five thieves, a destructive impulse that can hijack who we want to be. Krodh is often
paired with the word kaam, which refers to unhealthy desire. *Kaam krodh*
suggests that vengeful wrath is tied to desire: When the world denies
what we want, rage rises in us. Guru Nanak calls it a corrosive salt that
destroys the gold in us.* At the same time, Guru Nanak spoke in fiery
language against injustice. Rage, when consciously harnessed, is a force
that connects us with our power to fight for others, and for ourselves.

And so, I choose to imagine Bibi Veero in the clearing among the
trees, dancing with her rage—wielding her sword, piercing the air, bat-
tling her enemies. Only when she moves that fiery energy through her
can she exhale—and begin to wonder about the ones she wants to hate.
Only then can she begin to see their humanity.

---

* "Lust and wrath waste the body, as gold is dissolved by borax." Original: "*Kaam
krodh kaiaa kao gaalai / jiao ka(n)chan sohaagaa dhalai*" —Guru Granth Sahib, ang 932,
Raag Ramkali, Guru Nanak Ji.

SEEING OUR OPPONENT'S
HUMANITY

IN BOTH MY PERSONAL AND ACTIVIST LIFE, I HAVE HAD TO WORK to see the humanity in my opponents—the police officer who injured me at the anti-war protest, the relative who sexually assaulted me, the man who killed a member of my community in hate violence, the correctional officers at the supermax prison my team investigated, the soldiers at Guantanamo where I reported on the hearings of detainees, the elected officials who incite violence and pass policies that continue to hurt our communities. Every time, in the wake of the harm, I feel the fires of rage within me. I used to choke down my rage. I used to think I was only as good or spiritual as my ability to suppress my rage. Now, I understand that my rage is loaded with information and energy. It connects me with my power to fight for others, and for myself. I have to find ways to honor my rage, dance with my rage, and process my rage in safe containers. I walk by the sea, I sing, I dance, I gather with my sisters and vent, I shake, I throw pillows, I breathe. I go to the sovereign space within me and call on the Wise Woman.

Sometimes I need to stay with my rage for a long time. Only when I am safe enough and brave enough, I begin to wonder about my opponents and feel a desire to understand them. Sometimes it's not safe for me to reach out, physically or emotionally. But when I can, I begin with their story. At first, it's very difficult to hear their story. But if I keep asking—*why*—then it happens: I see their wound.

There are no monsters in this world, only human beings who are wounded.

Knowing this frees *me:* My opponents lose their power over me. And I become a smarter activist: *How do I change the systems and cultures that drive that behavior?* If my opponent starts wondering about me in turn, then a portal opens: A process of deep listening begins. Deep listening is an act of surrender: You risk being changed by what you hear. Sometimes this leads to a process of reconciliation. Other times, it does not. The important thing is that you have preserved your opponents' humanity, and your own. You decide *who you are:* You hold fast to the sage in the warrior.

There must have been those in Guru Har Rai's court who did not want him to save the Emperor's son. They must have cried: *They are the enemies! They have traded their humanity for privilege and power!* And yet Guru Har Rai chose to see the pain of his oppressor. He stayed faithful to his great-grandfather Guru Arjan's wisdom: *See no stranger. See no enemy.*

Today, too, there are many who do not want us to see the pain of our opponents. They shout: *Our pain is more real than their pain. Our fear is more justified than their fear, our grief more devastating than theirs ever will be.* But the hierarchy of pain is the old way. If I insist that my pain is worth more than yours, then I can never see your pain, let alone sit with your pain. In seeing the wound in our opponents, we do not relinquish our commitment to justice; we produce the possibility of reconciliation. This does not need to be all of our labor all of the time; but it may be some of our labor, if we are called to play this role.

THE LABOR OF LIFETIMES

IT MUST HAVE TAKEN GREAT COURAGE FOR BIBI VEERO TO CHOOSE to see the humanity of the Emperor and his son; that act of love did not yield reconciliation in her lifetime. But it left a pearl to empower the next generation.

So, too, I may not live to see the results of my labor in this lifetime. I want to see the birth of America as a healthy multiracial democracy where we see no stranger. I want to see our global community embrace coexistence so that war and genocide become relics of the past. I want to see humanity learn how to live sustainably with the earth, so that our future is secured for generations to come. But I also know that I may not live to see those things. That doesn't mean that I give up. Or that I'm not doing enough. It means that I must embrace my particular role in the labor.

Our culture makes us believe that we are inadequate: that anything we do is not enough. We are always comparing ourselves to others and judging ourselves by impossible metrics. It is easy to let the Little Critic dominate: "You are not doing enough. You are not saying enough. You are not enough." But we don't go to battle alone; we don't give birth alone. We need one another. We each have a particular role we are able to play, in this season of our lives, in this brief time on earth. That, too, is sage wisdom: to know that our labors of Revolutionary Love—leading with wonder, harnessing rage, listening with humanity, and reimagining a shared future—are the means *and* the end.

A BOW TO GURU HAR RAI

WHEN I RETURNED TO THE FARM IN KIRATPUR WHERE WE WERE staying, the children were chasing a peacock across the lawn, its feathers open in splendid royal colors. A mist rolled in and wrapped around us, so that the children and the peacock and their delightful squeals all felt enchanted. I sipped my chaa and watched them. This land that Guru Har Rai made home was so beautiful.

There is little in oral tradition about Guru Har Rai, the seventh Sikh Guru. There was no major military action while he was Guru, and therefore, according to most history books, no standout accomplishments. Yet perhaps the greatest deed one can perform is to keep people safe. He communed with animals and plants. He built a world of shelter around his people out of mountains and sky; he encouraged communion with the earth as a way to renew the sage in the warrior. He reminded his people, even in a hostile world, that we must harness our rage and return to humanity: Let the sage guide the warrior.

SAGE WARRIOR,
HARNESS RAGE...

THERE IS NO NEED TO annihilate your rage, or be ashamed of it—or let it consume you. Your rage connects you with your ability to fight for what matters. Where in your body are you carrying rage? Notice its color, shape, and weight. Say: *You are a part of me I do not yet know*. Honor your rage. Your rage shows what matters to you. Ask your rage: *How do you want to move?* Explore a simple gesture: Raise your hand to say stop, pound your fist, shake your head. Go slowly. Then, quickly. See if you want to make a sound with the gesture. What is the fullest expression of this gesture? Perhaps running, drumming, pounding, spinning, dancing, shaking, screaming, venting. Notice what your body wants to do. This is your safe container for rage. Notice the energy coursing through you. Invite the wisest part of you to step forth. Ask: *How do I want to harness this energy?* Listen. Notice what your rage is teaching you.

Think of the source of your rage—a person or group fueling your rage. This is your opponent. Picture their face. Notice what happens in your body. If you feel a lot of activation, release your attention on your opponent and stay with your rage. If you notice some discomfort, but there is still enough spaciousness inside of you to wonder—*Why do they do that? say that?*—then you may be ready to see the wound in your opponent. Invite the wisest part of you to step forth. Ask: *What am I ready for?* Perhaps the labor of understanding, forgiveness, apology, or reconciliation. Perhaps your labor does not require your opponent's participation at all. Let the wisest part of you lead you to the brave next step. The sage prepares the warrior: The sage befriends rage; the warrior harnesses that energy for creative, loving, and courageous action in the world.

ANCESTOR TREE

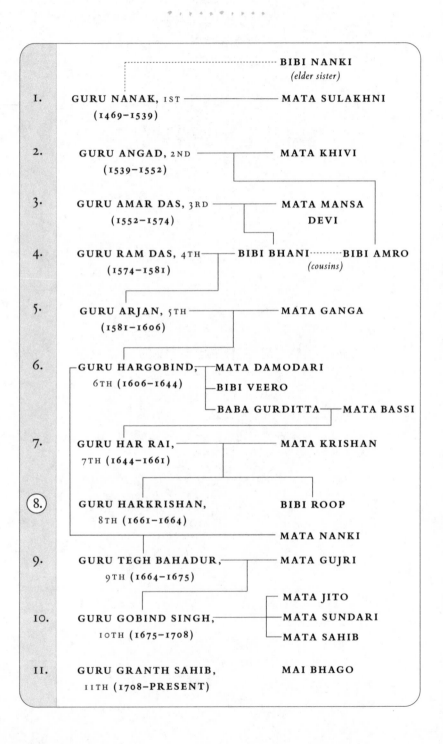

	BIBI NANKI *(elder sister)*		
I.	GURU NANAK, 1ST (1469–1539)	MATA SULAKHNI	
2.	GURU ANGAD, 2ND (1539–1552)	MATA KHIVI	
3.	GURU AMAR DAS, 3RD (1552–1574)	MATA MANSA DEVI	
4.	GURU RAM DAS, 4TH (1574–1581)	BIBI BHANI *(cousins)*	BIBI AMRO
5.	GURU ARJAN, 5TH (1581–1606)	MATA GANGA	
6.	GURU HARGOBIND, 6TH (1606–1644)	MATA DAMODARI / BIBI VEERO / BABA GURDITTA	MATA BASSI
7.	GURU HAR RAI, 7TH (1644–1661)	MATA KRISHAN	
8.	GURU HARKRISHAN, 8TH (1661–1664)	BIBI ROOP	
		MATA NANKI	
9.	GURU TEGH BAHADUR, 9TH (1664–1675)	MATA GUJRI	
10.	GURU GOBIND SINGH, 10TH (1675–1708)	MATA JITO / MATA SUNDARI / MATA SAHIB	
II.	GURU GRANTH SAHIB, 11TH (1708–PRESENT)	MAI BHAGO	

PART 8

GRIEVE
TOGETHER

KRISHAN WAS A SLIGHT WOMAN WITH A STOIC EXPRESSION AND few words. After the cremation of her husband, Guru Har Rai, she comforted the mourners who cried their condolences. When they asked what she needed, she simply replied, "Shanti." *Peace.* And sent them away. She needed to focus on the only task that mattered: to care for her five-year-old son, Guru Harkrishan. The Sikh realm rejoiced at their rare glimpses of the child-Guru and entrusted his mother and the elders to oversee his training.

In the morning, Krishan woke before dawn. She gazed into her son's cherub-like face and watched his eyelids flutter: He was dreaming.

"Guru Harkrishan," she whispered, and rubbed his back. He smiled as he woke. She kissed his neck as he played with the end of her white dupatta.

"Chalo Ji!" called her daughter, Roop. *Let's go!* Thirteen-year-old Roop appeared with a small bucket that carried a wooden comb, a kanga, a bottle of oil, and neem sticks. Krishan walked her children through a thicket to the River Satluj, followed at a distance by retainers carrying spears and swords, guardians of the child-Guru.

Bibi Veero arrived on horseback for Guru Harkrishan's lessons. She picked up a stick and scratched into the sandy bank: IK ONKAR. He followed. Next: SATNAM. Guru Harkrishan hummed as he wrote out the Mool Mantr. During her brother's lesson, Roop wrote stories about her father on banyan leaves. Krishan watched her children as she rubbed oil into her hair.

"He will be a great Guru," said Krishan's mother-in-law, who sat down beside her. Mata Bassi was a stout woman with a strong jaw and matter-of-fact tone. She was dressed in perpetual white—her husband, Baba Gurditta, had passed away as a young man, as had her son, Guru Har Rai.

"Guru Harkrishan has everything he needs," she continued. "His grandfather's warriors, his father's gentleness . . ."

". . . and my hand holding his," finished Krishan.

"Vaisakhi is coming," stated Mata Bassi. "It's time to gather the Sikh world under Guru Harkrishan, eighth in the House of Nanak. We will host them here in Kiratpur."

The young Guru skipped into a joyful run along the river. His face was bright as the sun. Roop chased after her brother, giggling. Their small army of retainers hurried alongside them, forming a protective wall between the child-Guru and the rest of the world. Krishan's eyes still followed his every skip.

When springtime came, the leaders of the masands brought their people to Kiratpur for the first Vaisakhi under Guru Harkrishan. Mata Bassi planned every detail: drumming and dancing, singing and praying, feasting and gift-giving. The harvest festival lasted three days. On the final day, Mata Bassi marched through the crowd to Krishan.

"I have betrothed your daughter, Roop, to this boy!" announced Mata Bassi. "This is Khem Karan of Pasrur."

Krishan looked in shock at the boy and his proud father.

"Vadhayia(n)!" cried her mother-in-law. *Congratulations!* Mata Bassi began talking about the wedding arrangements, but Krishan couldn't breathe. Roop was so young! Her mother-in-law clung to the old ways, and now it was too late. A crowd gathered to congratulate them.

Roop's wedding ceremony took place in the wintertime that same year. Before Roop ascended the palki, the golden palanquin that carried her to her new home, Krishan pressed gifts into her daughter's hands. A pothi, a collection of stories, from her father, Guru Har Rai. It had blank pages at the end. She no longer needed to scratch her stories on leaves! And a dagger that had belonged to her great-grandfather Guru Hargobind. Roop clutched these gifts to her heart and kissed her mother brightly. She ascended the palki, slipped between the purple curtains, and was gone.

As the wedding procession disappeared from sight, Krishan sighed. She wondered at a world that stole daughters from their mothers. Her husband had passed away young. Her eldest son, Ram Rai, went to the Emperor and never returned. Now her daughter was wed and gone. She had only her five-year-old son. In all her quiet sadness, only Guru Harkrishan saw her. She drifted to sleep each night with his little hand on her cheek.

THREE YEARS LATER, AFTER GURU HARKRISHAN TURNED EIGHT, Emperor Aurangzeb summoned him to Delhi to discuss his claim to the Guruship. Krishan recoiled. She had heard that the Emperor gifted her eldest son, Ram Rai, generous land grants in Dehradun in the Himalayas; Ram Rai was now the Emperor's pet. If Ram Rai was seen as the rightful Guru, the Emperor's hold on the Sikh world would be secure. Krishan wondered: *Will the Emperor try to tempt the child-Guru with gifts, or simply exterminate him?*

After her son's morning lesson, Krishan showed Bibi Veero the Emperor's summons. They spoke quietly as Guru Harkrishan climbed a tree on the riverbank.

"The Emperor wants us to come willingly," said Krishan, watching her son in the high branches.

Bibi Veero ran her pearl mala through her hand. When her grandfather Guru Arjan went willingly to Emperor Jahangir, he was tortured and killed. When her father, Guru Hargobind, went willingly, the same Emperor had thrown him into Gwalior prison. She remembered the terror in her body when Emperor Jahangir's son Shah Jahan waged an all-out war on Amritsar and sent her family into exile. Her family helped save Emperor Shah Jahan's son, Dara Shikoh, but he was murdered by the now-Emperor Aurangzeb. What would Emperor Aurangzeb be willing to do to the child-Guru?

"There is hope," said Bibi Veero slowly, her thumb pausing on a bead in the mala. "Before Aurangzeb, Shah Jahan, and Jahangir, there was Akbar. A century ago, Emperor Akbar sat for langar with Guru Amar Das—and gifted land to my great-grandmother Bibi Bhani."

Krishan did not seem to be listening. She was watching her son reach the highest branch of the tree.

Bibi Veero noticed tears in Krishan's eyes and reached for her hand, but Krishan wiped her face and resumed her stoic expression.

"Whatever comes, I will face it with him," Krishan said flatly. She did not think there was time to spend on sorrows.

Bibi Veero sighed. She unwrapped the pearl mala from her wrist.

"You are never alone," said Bibi Veero, and she poured the mala into Krishan's hands.

As she cupped the pearls, Mata Krishan's whole body softened.

"Shakti vastay," said Bibi Veero. *For power.*

Mata Krishan brought the pearls to her forehead in respect.

ON THE DAY OF THEIR DEPARTURE, GURU HARKRISHAN PERCHED at the front of the cart for the best view of the journey. His eyes sparkled, and he waved joyfully at the people of Kiratpur as the caravan lurched forward.

As the procession traveled to Delhi, villagers ran alongside their carts and camels, begging for an audience with the child-Guru. Mata Krishan agreed. They stopped in Roparr, Banurr, and Ambala to hold court.

On their stop in the village Panjokhara, Guru Harkrishan sat on a raised platform to receive a long line of people. His mother stood next to him. A stern man in a crisp dhoti introduced himself as Pandit Lal Chand. He was a Hindu priest who had heard about the child-Guru.

"I notice your name is similar to the name of Lord Krishna," mused Lal Chand.

Guru Harkrishan smiled widely. Krishna, the child-deity of Hindu lore, had radiant blue skin, played a flute, and danced with bells on his ankles on the banks of the River Jamuna.

As a Sikh, he did not worship Krishna, or any deities, but he respected Hindu teachings and adored the stories about Krishna that his mother told him.

"I have come to test your knowledge of the Bhagavad Gita!" declared Pandit Lal Chand. Mata Krishan narrowed her eyes. The pandit rattled off questions about the ancient Hindu text.

"Anyone can answer these questions!" replied Guru Harkrishan. "You don't need to ask me. You can ask anyone in this village!"

"Anyone!" huffed Lal Chand. The child-Guru implied that the knowledge he held as a Brahmin priest, the highest of the high castes, wasn't so exclusive. "We'll see about that!"

A few minutes later, Lal Chand returned with a water carrier, who was introduced as poor and illiterate. The whole village gathered around to watch.

"Tohada naam kee hai?" Guru Harkrishan gently asked. *What's your name?*

"Chhaju Ram," replied the water carrier, and stared at the ground. Told from birth that he was low caste, Chhaju had learned to move through the world without looking anyone of a so-called higher caste in the eye.

Guru Harkrishan gestured for Chhaju to come closer, took his hand, and bowed his head in respect. The people gasped. No one in that village had ever seen an esteemed leader touch the hand of a low-caste person: It broke every rule.

"Pandit Ji, ask your first question!" called out Guru Harkrishan.

"When Lord Krishna reveals his true self to the warrior Arjun, what does he look like?" Lal Chand fired the question like it was an arrow. Chhaju flinched.

Guru Harkrishan gently touched the top of Chhaju's head with a stick as if to shield him, so that Chhaju heard only the question, not the tone.

Chhaju cleared his throat.

"The Beloved looks like . . . a thousand suns rising at once. Unlimited faces. Unlimited eyes. Garlands and fragrances without number. The wonderful and infinite One, whose face is everywhere."

The people whispered to each other in awe. Chhaju's answer was a poetic, mystical description of the Divine that resonated in Hindu tradition, *and* he presented the wisdom in a way that spoke to the heart of the Sikh faith: that the Beloved is everywhere and part of us. The villagers called it a miracle.

Lal Chand pursed his lips and bowed before the Guru.

"We all have wisdom inside," Guru Harkrishan whispered to his mother. "That's the real miracle!"

Mata Krishan kissed her son's forehead.

A FEW DAYS LATER, THE GURU'S PROCESSION ARRIVED IN DELHI. As they rode through the streets, Mata Krishan saw faces stricken with panic. Ash floated in the air and caught in her hair.

"Chhoti mata atay haija," uttered an attendant. *Smallpox and cholera*. The epidemic was spreading fast through Delhi. The funeral pyres smoked day and night. As the cart rumbled on, Mata Krishan gripped her son's hand in hers.

They arrived at the palace of Mirza Raja Jai Singh of Delhi, who had offered to host the Guru. Jai Singh was the most senior general in Emperor Aurangzeb's court. He once supported Dara Shikoh but had shifted his allegiance to Aurangzeb, who awarded him the highest possible rank for any general. He promised the child-Guru safety as he waited for his audience in the Emperor's court. The palace had thick stone walls like a fortress to shield them from the epidemic sweeping the streets of the city. Mata Krishan disembarked with trepidation.

When they entered the palace, the Rani—Jai Singh's wife, who was referred to as a queen—sat among her housemaids in disguise to observe the child-Guru discreetly. Guru Harkrishan skipped over to her lap and asked why she was playing pretend. She was genuinely smitten and promised to make his stay comfortable. Mata Krishan exhaled: *We will be safe here.*

The next morning, a small crowd gathered outside the palace gates. They had heard that the child-Guru was among them and called out for the help of Guru Harkrishan, eighth in the house of Nanak.

"I want to go outside," Guru Harkrishan told his mother.

Mata Krishan went to the Rani, who set up a raised platform in the garden where the young Guru could receive his visitors. The gate opened and people stumbled in, coughing into cloths. Their faces were red with fever. Their skin was covered in blisters. They lined up for an audience with the child-Guru as his mother stood solemnly behind him and watched closely.

Guru Harkrishan smiled and bowed before each person, the way he had bowed before the water carrier. He took their hands, one by one, and said, "Dasso Ji." *I'm here, tell me.*

The people told him of their pain. They were low caste and high, Hindu and Muslim, all genders and ages, and they all suffered in the same ways: On the first day of their illness, they came down with a fever, their bodies grew hot, their breathing rapid. On the second day, sores appeared all over, their skin turned red, and their backs ached. On the third day, the sores turned into blisters filled with pus. At night, they wriggled like fish on hot sand. They feared sleep: If they closed their eyes, they might not awaken.

Guru Harkrishan listened quietly to each person. He opened a wooden chest next to him, selected a bottle from his father's storehouse of medicines, and handed it to them. He then asked them to bathe in the waters that had been drawn from the well on the palace grounds. The people bowed before the Guru in gratitude and went to the small pool. Many wept when they waded in, overcome by relief. They soothed one another's tears. In those cooling waters, they were a sangat, a beloved community: They did not fear one another, just as the child-Guru did not fear them.

"Guru Harkrishan is like the early morning sun!" bards sang in the streets. "Small in size, but his light touches everyone!"

News of the child-Guru who dispelled sorrow spread through the city. Large crowds of sick people flocked to the palace gates for an audience. Mata Krishan spaced out the sessions so that her son could run and play in the garden before he sat very still again, holding people's hands and offering them medicines. Some of them recovered from their illness; some of them died. But none of them suffered alone.

At night, Mata Krishan gazed into her son's face as he slept beside her. She saw the same cherub-like sweetness as when he was five. But his face was growing leaner, his jawline clearer. She imagined him as a grown man with a black beard like his father's, his gaze tender, his voice kind. She marveled at the power in his simple words to the people: *I'm here. Tell me. I understand. You are not alone.* She smiled as she imagined his legacy: the sage warrior who healed people with his hands.

Emperor Aurangzeb still had not sent for them. The Emperor was locking himself inside his palace walls until the epidemic was over. But he must have heard about the songs in the streets: Muslims in the city called Guru Harkrishan "Baal Pir," the child saint. Perhaps the Emperor realized that Guru Harkrishan was indeed the leader of the Sikh world, and celebrated as such, and would leave them alone. Perhaps it was time to prepare for the journey home.

Mata Krishan rested her head on her son's chest and closed her eyes. She felt the rise and fall of his breathing, like waves on an ocean. Softly, she sang her child the shabd for protection, the song of his great-great grandfather Guru Arjan:

taati vao na lagayee paarbrahm sarnaaee
chaugird hamarai raam kaar dukh lagai na bhaee
satgur poora bheytiaa jin banat banaaee
raam naam aukhadh deeyaa ekaa liv laaee
raakh leeay tin rakhanhaar sabh biyaadh mitaee
kaho nanak kirpaa bhayee prabh bhaye sahaee

Hot winds cannot touch me, I am shielded by the Infinite
Our Beloved on all four sides, pain cannot strike me, oh brother
Meeting the true One who composed all of this

I was given the medicine of the mystical name, I immersed in
    the One
The Keeper safekept me, took away all my ailments
Nanak says, blessings fell upon me, the Beloved has come to my
    side*

THE NEXT MORNING, MATA KRISHAN AWOKE TO THE TOUCH OF HER
son's hands rubbing her back. It was not yet dawn.

"Mai(n) bahar jaana aaj," said Guru Harkrishan. *I want to go outside
today.*

"Kithay?" she asked, sleepily. *Where?* Maybe she could take him to
the riverbank.

"Galiyaa(n) vich," he said. *Into the streets.*

Mata Krishan sat up. Her son was dressed in a royal blue robe and
matching turban. He wore a cotton satchel across his chest, filled with
bottles of oils and herbs. He wanted to go to the people who needed
these medicines the most, the ones who were too sick to come to him.

Mata Krishan gazed out the window. High above the walls of the
palace garden, long gray coils of smoke from all the funeral pyres
wound up into the sky.

She shook her head no.

"Close your eyes, please," he said as he shuffled through his satchel.

Mata Krishan closed her eyes and felt her son's touch on her forehead. The fragrance of crushed roses filled her lungs. *Gulab.* Her son
was rubbing rose essence into her temples. Her husband's storehouse
of medicines and potions always smelled of roses. She thought of how
her husband lifted up their son to look at all the little bottles and learn
the names of their contents. How he taught their son to rub oil into his
mother's skin. How her son's touch dispelled her sorrows, again and
again.

---

*   Guru Granth Sahib, ang 819, Raag Bilaval, Guru Arjan Ji.

Mata Krishan sighed and nodded without opening her eyes.

Guru Harkrishan and his attendants filled wooden carts with medicines and food. He planned to take the practice of langar out into the streets where it was most needed. He led them all to the outer gate of the palace.

As the palace gate rumbled open, Mata Krishan smelled blood and manure from the streets. Smoke filled the air. She tasted ash in her mouth.

"Guru Ji!" Mata Krishan called.

Her son paused and turned around, beaming. Mata Krishan asked him to wait a moment. She ran back to her chambers, returned with a wrapped blue cloth, and handed it to her son. He opened it curiously. It was a kirpan, small enough to fit in his hand. The dagger sparkled in the sunlight.

"This was your father's," she said. "Use it to seal wounds."

Guru Harkrishan nodded solemnly. He knew how to heat a piece of metal over fire and use it to seal open sores to stop an infection from spreading. He slid the kirpan into his kamarkassa waist belt and stood a little taller. He then double-checked the contents of his satchel; his potions were in order. He touched his mother's feet in respect and said he would be back before sundown.

Guru Harkrishan entered the noise and dust of the streets of Delhi, followed by his retainers and provisions. Mata Krishan stood for a long time under the smoky orange sky and watched her son until he disappeared from sight: He was a sage who saw no stranger; he was a warrior stepping into the battlefield of the world.

IN THE MORNING, MATA KRISHAN AWOKE TO THE TOUCH OF HER son's hand resting on her cheek. She did not stir. Let the moment stretch: Before they had to rise and dress and tend to the day's labors, before anyone called him Guru, let them just be mother and son. She rested in his embrace. Then, she noticed that his hand was hot.

Mata Krishan sat up and felt her son's forehead. He was burning.

She shook him gently. He did not open his eyes. She kissed his neck. He moaned. She called out to the guard posted at her door. A doctor came and examined him. The child-Guru was stricken by the epidemic that ailed the city. The protocol was containment.

Mata Krishan held her voice steady as she sent the Guru's attendants to make a camp along the River Jamuna, not far from the palace. They would wait out the illness there. The Rani promised to send provisions daily. When the camp was ready, Mata Krishan carried her son out of the palace. At eight years old, he was heavy in her arms, but she was strong. She glanced back one last time at the fortress that had protected them, stepped through the gates, and carried her son all the way to the riverbank.

The River Jamuna was serene and surrounded by trees that swayed in the breeze, so like the River Satluj, where her children loved to play and run. She entered a tent that was pitched beneath the shade of a great tree. Outside the tent, the Guru's attendants unpacked their musical instruments—rabab, saranda, taus, tanpura, mridang, and jori. As the sacred music filled the air, Mata Krishan thought of the Hindu legends of the radiant boy-deity Krishna who played his flute by this very river and awoke the forest to joy.

Mata Krishan took her son's hand and hummed along to the music of kirtan. She pressed a cold washcloth to his forehead, which warmed instantly, and so she squeezed another. She cleaned his nostrils so that he could breathe. She rubbed rose essence into his temples. She poured saro(n) da tel into her palms and rubbed the mustard oil into his belly. The smell of herbs and oils filled the tent. She sat at his bedside and ran her pearl mala through her hand. She watched his eyelids flutter; he was dreaming. That was good. She did not know when she slept or ate. She was only aware of her son's eyelids, and her hands in motion, and the music of the kirtan merging with the roar of the river.

In the dead of night, Mata Krishan awoke to the sound of wind howling over the river. The tent shook, and her son shivered in her arms.

"Mata Ji," he whispered.

"Mai(n) ethay haa(n)," she said, holding him tight. *I'm here.*

"Bakala," said Guru Harkrishan.

She did not know what that meant.

"Baba Bakala!" he said again, and circled his finger in the air.

Mata Krishan reached for the bottle of rose essence on the table. Her mind filled with regret and anguish: She wondered why she had ever let her son out of her sight. A hard gust of wind rattled the tent, and the bottle fell to the floor. She reached down for it, but her son pulled her to him and cradled her face on his chest. As the fragrance of the spilled rose essence filled her lungs, he rested his hand on her cheek. She closed her eyes and listened to his slow, labored breathing. She felt his chest rise, and hummed:

taati vao na lagayee paarbrahm sarnaaee
Hot winds cannot touch me, I am shielded by the Infinite[*]

A deafening roar ripped through the night. A great wind gathered speed across the river. The wind tore a hole in the tent and rushed in. The torch went out. The winds roared all around them. Mata Krishan held on to her son with all her might. She squeezed her eyes shut and kept singing. She felt her son's chest rise and fall, rise and—he sighed long and deep, and the sound was like a string that, once plucked, resounds until there is no sound left.

She pressed her ear to his heart.

Mata Krishan heard a wail. It was a primal and guttural wail, a birthing wail that was coming from her womb, but that could not be, because her body was not there anymore. Her chest had torn into a thousand pieces, and time was folding in on itself: She was chasing her son as he ran down the riverbank. Now he was a toddler, and she was holding his little hands as he took his first steps. Now he was a newborn, and she was cupping his tiny soft feet in her hands. Her son was inside her body now, tucked safely in her womb, and Mata Krishan was flying—soaring with him on the winds roaring over the river, and they

---

[*]   Guru Granth Sahib, ang 819, Raag Bilaval, Guru Arjan Ji.

were following the path of the river up north, into the mountains of the Himalayas, higher and higher, all the way to the source.

WHEN THE GURU'S ATTENDANTS FOUND MATA KRISHAN HOLDING her son's body in the morning, they realized that the wail in the night was not the wind; it was her. They quietly wept, and sang the ancestors' songs as they built a pile of wood on the riverbank. They pulled the Guru's small body from his mother's arms and lit the funeral pyre. Mata Krishan watched silently from the tent until every bit of flesh was consumed and the smoke burned her eyes. Then she went to sleep in the bed where her son had lain.

Mata Krishan awoke to her mother-in-law's voice.

"Kot Kalyani," Mata Bassi called her tenderly. It was a name that her mother-in-law had never used for her before; there was sweetness in it. *The girl from Kot Kalyan.*

"I have instructed the Sahaj Path," she said. *The continuous reading of the Aadi Granth.* Mata Krishan wondered why. Then she realized that the nightmare she had had was real.

"I have sent messengers to deliver the news to Kiratpur," Mata Bassi continued quietly. "They are waiting for us. It's time to return home."

Mata Bassi lifted her up and led her to the river. She washed her daughter-in-law's face, cleaned her teeth, brushed her hair, and presented her with a new set of white salvaar kameez. Finally, Mata Bassi pressed a small wooden box into her hands.

When the Guru's caravan returned to Kiratpur, the people waited eagerly, looking both heartbroken and confused: Guru Harkrishan, eighth in the House of Nanak, the one whose sight dispelled all sorrow, had departed this world at eight years old. *Who was the Guru now?*

Mata Krishan descended from the cart, expressionless, the small wooden box pressed to her chest. Mata Bassi steered her toward the house as though her body was lifeless. Mata Krishan paused, spun around, and entered the thicket, as if in a dream. The crowd followed her at a distance.

When Mata Krishan reached the bank of the River Satluj, her jaw clenched. There was nowhere she could not see her son: He was running down the riverbank, climbing trees, scratching letters in the sand, laughing as she kissed his face. Mata Krishan waded into the cold water where she used to bathe him. The cold stung. Only when the river reached her breasts did she stop. She pressed her forehead to the wooden box, opened it, and poured its contents into the river. Ashes fluttered down to the water, rested for a moment, and merged into the river.

Mata Bassi's voice rose powerfully behind her: "Sat Kartar!" The people responded in unison: "Sat Kartar!" *True is the Great Doer; I honor the truth that is.*

Mata Bassi instructed everyone to return to the house for kirtan and prashaad. She said that they would still distribute prashaad even for a child's death: *The return to the Beloved, in whatever circumstance, is still sweet.* As everyone left, Mata Krishan stayed in the icy river, holding the empty wooden box. The cold numbed her until she no longer felt her body, or her pain at all. She thought: *I could just stay here with him.* The water kissed her neck. She closed her eyes and let out a long deep sigh—

Someone seized her hand. The wooden box fell from her grasp. Bibi Veero was inside the icy river with her. Her aunt's eyes were ablaze and she gripped Mata Krishan's hand tightly. Bibi Veero was not going to let her go. Pain rushed back into Mata Krishan's body—all the grief she had pushed down since her husband's passing. She had built a fortress around her heart to survive, but now her grief was a torrent, and she thought it would drown her, but she was still breathing, and now she was sobbing. Mata Krishan wept in her Bhua Ji's arms, and her aunt held her for a long time. They were two women, dressed in white, barely above water; the river parted around them, honoring their embrace.

When they climbed back onto the bank, Bibi Veero squeezed the water out of Mata Krishan's hair.

"You are never alone," Bibi Veero murmured, and she touched the mala resting on Mata Krishan's wrist. The white pearls were lit by the warm setting sun. Mata Krishan slipped off the mala and ran her thumb over the worn beads as they watched the sunset.

"His last word was Bakala," she said finally.

Bibi Veero furrowed her brow. Bakala was a small village near the River Beas on the plains of Punjab.

"Baba Bakala," said Mata Krishan. "That's what he said."

Bibi Veero rose to her feet. There was only one sage warrior in Bakala who the child-Guru could have known. Only one Baba Bakala. And his name was Tegh Bahadur, Bibi Veero's youngest brother.

Bibi Veero kissed Mata Krishan's forehead and readied her horse. A long journey lay before her. In order to reach Tegh Bahadur, she would need to speak to his wife—the child she had handed a doll to on a cart thirty years ago, the girl with stars in her eyes, her brother's companion and closest confidante, the one who held more power than anyone knew: Her name was Gujri.

Aao chaa peelo . . .
Come, let's have tea . . .

MY GRANDFATHER'S PROMISE

THE RIVER SATLUJ IN THE NORTHERN CITY OF KIRATPUR IS WHERE
Sikhs pour the ashes of loved ones. The ashes of Guru Hargobind and
Guru Har Rai, the sixth and seventh Gurus, were spread here. In 1664,
Mata Krishan brought her eight-year-old son Guru Harkrishan's ashes
from faraway Delhi, so that he could return to *this* river. Ever since
then, Sikhs from across Punjab and around the globe have made the
same journey to this place in the foothills of the Himalayas. It is a site
of pilgrimage, a place of return.

I visited this place for the first time with my grandfather, Papa Ji,
when I was eleven years old. We stood on the bank of the Satluj and
looked into the serene waters. "This is where I will return to my Master," Papa Ji said. I gripped his chocolate-brown sweater and sobbed
until it was soaking wet. I could not bear the thought of my grandfather's death; I wanted him never to leave me. Startled, he patted my
back.

"Listen to Gurbani, my dear," he said gently. He was asking me to
listen to our sacred musical poetry, to rest in our ancestors' wisdom.
The Sikh Gurus give a similar instruction in all the stories. Before they
breathe their last, they tell the people who cling to them: *Don't mourn
me. Listen to our ancestors' songs. Death is a return. Death is union with the
Beloved. Death is a wedding day.*

Papa Ji saw that I needed more.

"If you summon me, I will come," Papa Ji whispered.

"Promise?" I asked.

"Promise."

THE ONENESS THAT ALWAYS IS

I AWOKE BEFORE DAWN IN KIRATPUR TO GO FOR A MORNING WALK. I kissed my sleeping children on my way out. *Why do my children always look the sweetest when they are sleeping?* I shook off their seduction, wrapped myself in a thick dupatta, and went outside. Happy drove me to the River Satluj.

I wanted to be with my grandfather.

I walked slowly along the river, taking in the trees and mist and morning light. Birdsong filled the air: starlings, crows, and parakeets. A buffalo huffed in the distance. A woman in a maroon sari swept the ghats, the steps that lead down to the water. The music of kirtan drifted from Gurdwara Patal Puri behind us. Longing filled my heart. *Papa Ji, I miss you so much.* Fifteen years had passed since he died, and I am a mother with children of my own. But I was still that eleven-year-old child, longing for him. I held on to the words: "If you summon me, I will come."

I wiped my tears with my dupatta and slowly looked around. Papa Ji became fire and ash and entered the river. Now he was the sun-yellow leaves of the trees that draped over the river, and the buffalo who drank from it. He was the starling who splashed its wings in the water before taking flight. He was the mist that enveloped us. I took a deep breath. Even as I longed for him, I was in his embrace.

There is no afterlife in the Sikh tradition. No heaven and hell. Those realms come from a theology of good versus evil. There is only One. We are part of Oneness, ever-unfolding, and so is everyone we have ever known and loved. Death is a return to the Oneness that always is. A return to the energy and matter and mystery of the universe. We are part of that universe. And so, after a loved one dies, they can return to you in a different form. Their love can occur within you: Love outlasts life.

Grieving is a kind of transition: a process of drawing the one we love within us, until there comes a moment when we can hear their voice or feel their touch or access their love inside us. The transition is long and painful and nonlinear. We cannot survive the throes of grief alone. We need people to hold on to us, the way I imagine Bibi Veero held Mata Krishan in those icy waters. The wisdom of ancestors, across time and tradition, is that grieving must not be done in isolation. To bear the unbearable, we must grieve *together*.

This is especially true when we lose someone suddenly, violently, or unjustly.

BEARING THE UNBEARABLE

IN 2022, A SIKH FAMILY WAS MURDERED IN THE FARMLANDS OF California where I grew up. The Dheri family was kidnapped, shot, and left to die in an orchard. Their eight-month-old baby was found next to the bodies of her parents and uncle. Her name was Aroohi Kaur. The motive was unknown, but the assault took place amid a climate of racial violence, and the Sikh American community was shaken. The family asked me to come and speak at their vigil.

I drove through the farmlands to the family's house, trying to think of what to say. When I stepped through the door, the aunties, all dressed in white, held one another on the couch. They wept together as one body. When they saw me, they handed me a cup of chaa. I sat with them and thought of Aroohi's sweet, small face. She was every child who died with the music still inside them. Every child lost in violence or war or genocide. I had no words. I unwrapped a cloth from my bag and handed the family a tiny karra, a steel bracelet, a Sikh article of faith. They said they would cremate Baby Aroohi with it, and we embraced and cried again.

This is how my community grieves: We weep together. Even if we do not know each other, we show up to each other's doorstep and sit together. We drink tea together. We share langar together. We sing and pray together.

There is no fixing grief, only bearing it—and only in bearing it *together* can we survive it, even if we can't make sense of it.

In oral history, Guru Harkrishan is said to have told his mother on his deathbed: "The Beloved is the reaper of the crop, and reaps when the crop is ripe and half-green, and sometimes when it is still green!"

Even in the most unbearable circumstances, Sikh wisdom asks us to accept death as *a return*, whenever it comes, for whomever it comes, however senseless it might seem.

And so, even as I vow to fight the forces that took her life, I choose to believe that Baby Aroohi will return to the earth and trees, seas and stars. She will return to the Beloved. Our ancestors distributed prashaad after the child-Guru's passing. So too, we let the sweet taste linger on our tongue, along with the salt of our tears. We taste *both*. We are allowed both—agony and acceptance.

At her vigil, I closed my remarks with my grandfather's favorite shabd, the one he sang to us every day, the one I sang to him on his deathbed, the one I sing to my children:

taati vao na lagayee paarbrahm sarnaaee
Hot winds cannot touch me, I am shielded by the Infinite*

TOGETHER IN THE DARK

IN THE WAKE OF HORROR AND ATROCITY, PEOPLE OFTEN ASK: WHY would a good God allow such suffering?

I have never heard a satisfying answer. Perhaps the problem is with the question. Perhaps we need to release the notion of a "good" God. In Sikh wisdom, the Divine is not any one thing. The One is *everything*. The Beloved is the sun and stars and earth and rivers. The Beloved is the mud and the lotus that blossoms from the mud. The Beloved is the creatures and their sweat and blood and dreams, and the tissue that connects all human beings on earth, and the galaxies spinning in the universes. The Beloved is past and future and present ever-unfolding. As with a prism, there are many ways to experience the mystery. Sometimes the Beloved is a bearer of gifts, sometimes a trickster who takes what you hold dear. I was never comforted by the belief that "everything happens for a reason." The universe is filled with wonder and

---

* Guru Granth Sahib, ang 819, Raag Bilaval, Guru Arjan Ji.

terror and beauty beyond our senses. The only part we control is what we do next. Perhaps our task is not to find the reason. Perhaps our task is to reach for one another in the dark. To hold fast to one another. To grieve together and give each other strength to shape the inevitable changes we face.

In Sikh oral histories, Mata Krishan's mother-in-law, Mata Bassi, was practical: She oversaw the festivals and weddings and even her grandson's final rites. That kind of help is indispensable when you are grieving. *And* you also need someone who will plunge into the waters and take your hand and keep you from drowning. Sometimes it is the same person. More often, you need a community. In the Sikh tradition, it's called sangat, beloved community.

In an era of relentless crisis, I find "self-care" to be inadequate. No body can bear this much pain alone. I need *community* care: a sangat of sisters and brothers and kin willing to hold the grief together. We gather in living rooms and around kitchen tables. We weep and lament. Eat and pour tea. Tell stories and share wisdom. Inevitably, a child bolts through the room in a silly dance. And we laugh. We sing. We go outside to look at the trees and the sky. We breathe. We make a plan. Only *together* can we alchemize this much pain into energy and action.

You might say: But it's not my place to grieve with this family, or that community. I don't know them.

Here's what I learned after witnessing many communities reeling from violence and calamity: You don't have to know people in order to grieve with them; you grieve with them in order to know them. Just show up. Showing up to the vigil or march or memorial gives you information for what to do next, for how to fight for them. You do not have to speak at all. You have only to say with your presence: *You are grieving, but you are not grieving alone.* Whenever people who have no obvious reason to love one another come together to grieve, they give rise to new relationships, and new bodies of solidarity.

You might say: It's too much. I can't look into the faces of all the children dying on my screen.

I can't either. When I stare into the abyss too long, I risk falling in. I need to go outside and look at the trees and water to remember there is still beauty in the world, and that we are held by the great mother. Then, I look again at the faces of the children. And I see my children. I let my body respond.

When Ananda was a few months old, I was invited to a funeral for an infant who died of a rare illness. I did not know the family well, but it felt important to go. I was nursing my daughter every three hours, so we left her with a sitter and went between feeds. The funeral was held inside a grand church amid rolling green hills. The parents stood bravely next to a tiny white coffin. My husband and I followed a line of people down the aisle to pay our respects. Above us, there was a gigantic screen that played videos of the baby. The baby laughed as his mother sang the alphabet—a gorgeous sunlit laughter that echoed off the stained glass. Suddenly, my chest tingled. My milk let down. And the milk leaked right through my black dress. *My body is making milk for a baby who is dead.* It didn't matter that I was staring at his coffin. Or that he did not look like me. Or that he was dead. I heard an echo, a need, a hunger, and my body answered.

Our bodies were *made* to care.

THE COURAGE TO REMEMBER

IN THE CITY OF DELHI, ONE CAN VISIT THE PLACE WHERE GURU Harkrishan tended to the ill during the outbreak of cholera and smallpox that plagued India. It is called Gurdwara Bangla Sahib—"Bangla" meaning "bungalow," another name for the Raja's palace that once stood here. Outside the gold sanctum, there is a great sarovar, a vast pool of sacred water where the waters from the well were drawn. This place has taken on new significance since the Covid-19 pandemic. To date, Covid-19 has taken six million lives and is still ongoing in some form. Like Guru Harkrishan, many brave doctors and nurses, who risked their lives to save people they did not know, succumbed to the disease, too.

How did Mata Krishan survive her grief? How do any of us? The world feels like it has ended. And in a way it has; the world we knew no longer is. A part of us has died, too. We die to who we once were. We are remade in the grief, rebirthed into something new. The sovereign space within me, my Throne Room, is where I practice summoning loved ones—elders like Papa Ji who have wisdom still to give me, and the child-ancestors whose sweetness lingers, when I have the courage to remember them.

In the Ardaas, the Sikh prayer at the end of every service, Sikhs recite:

> *sri harkrisan dhiaaieai jis ditthe sabh dukh jaie*
> Let us remember blessed Harkrishan whose sight dispels all
>   sorrow[*]

We can remember Guru Harkrishan and his mother, Mata Krishan, together—his courage to grieve with others, and her courage to grieve *him*.

WHEN I RETURNED FROM THE RIVER TO THE FARM STAY IN KIRAT-pur, Kavi and Ananda were enjoying a cookie party in the room, supervised by my husband. My daughter was almost the same age Guru Harkrishan had been when he became Guru, and my son almost the same age as the Guru when he treated the ill. As I looked at them both, their mouths covered in crumbs as they giggled uncontrollably, I wondered: Does wisdom really have no age? Then I thought of when Kavi recites the Mool Mantr and rests his hand on my cheek, or when Ananda connects my heart to hers with an invisible string. In those moments, their touch is deeply healing. Perhaps it is because children are already fully present.

We don't need the perfect words to show up for one another. We just need to be willing to be fully present. That is how grieving together turns into healing together.

[*]   Dasam Granth, ang 119, Chandi Di Vaar, Guru Gobind Singh Ji.

SAGE WARRIOR,
GRIEVE TOGETHER . . .

WHERE IN YOUR BODY ARE you carrying your grief? No-
tice color, shape, and weight. Say: *You are a part of me I do not yet
know*. Ask your grief: *What do you need me to know?* Your grief is
not a sign of your weakness. It's a sign of how deeply you love.
Ask your grief: *What form do you want to go into?* Think of water
or air or earth or fire. You can pour your grief into water, rest it
in the earth, let flames transport it up to the heavens. Some of
your grief may want to stay in your body; some may want to
transmute into new forms of energy and insight. Now, think of
people in your life who can accompany you in this grief. Think
of those who need *your* accompaniment. How do you want to
gather? Candles, song, prayer, food, stories. A sage befriends
grief; a warrior has the courage to grieve *together*.

When you lose someone very close to you, remember: Love
outlasts life. Picture standing on the bank of a great river. Across
the river, you see someone you long for. They are smiling at
you. Reach out your arms to them. Wade into the river. They
are wading in, too, coming toward you. You are meeting in the
middle. They smile before you. Gaze into their face. You can
touch their hand. You can embrace them. Notice what it feels
like in your body. Ask: *Is there something you need me to know?*
Listen. See if they would like to visit your sovereign space. Perhaps they want to rest by a pool of water, or under a tree, or at
the foot of the throne. Or perhaps they wish to be free. If so, let
them dissolve before your eyes. They become sparkles: They
swirl in the air and go into clouds and trees and stones and rivers. Let some sparkles fall on you and become part of your body.
The sage embraces love in all forms; the warrior lets that love
make them brave.

ANCESTOR TREE

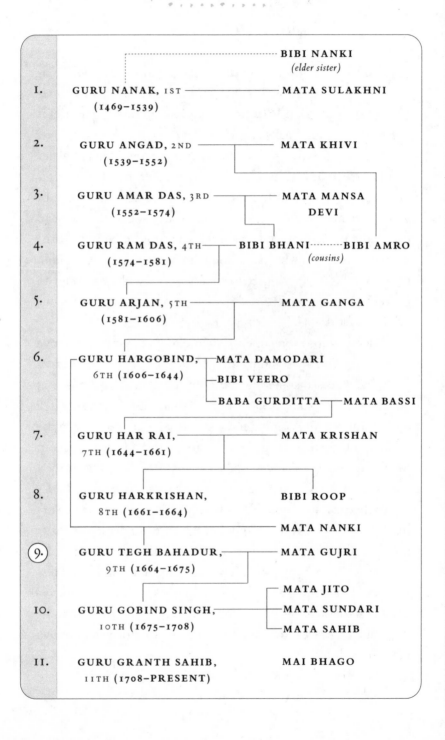

		BIBI NANKI *(elder sister)*	
I.	**GURU NANAK, 1ST** (1469–1539)	**MATA SULAKHNI**	
2.	**GURU ANGAD, 2ND** (1539–1552)	**MATA KHIVI**	
3.	**GURU AMAR DAS, 3RD** (1552–1574)	**MATA MANSA DEVI**	
4.	**GURU RAM DAS, 4TH** (1574–1581)	**BIBI BHANI**	**BIBI AMRO** *(cousins)*
5.	**GURU ARJAN, 5TH** (1581–1606)	**MATA GANGA**	
6.	**GURU HARGOBIND, 6TH (1606–1644)**	**MATA DAMODARI** / **BIBI VEERO** / **BABA GURDITTA**	**MATA BASSI**
7.	**GURU HAR RAI, 7TH (1644–1661)**	**MATA KRISHAN**	
8.	**GURU HARKRISHAN, 8TH (1661–1664)**	**BIBI ROOP**	
		MATA NANKI	
9.	**GURU TEGH BAHADUR, 9TH (1664–1675)**	**MATA GUJRI**	
10.	**GURU GOBIND SINGH, 10TH (1675–1708)**	**MATA JITO** / **MATA SUNDARI** / **MATA SAHIB**	
11.	**GURU GRANTH SAHIB, 11TH (1708–PRESENT)**	**MAI BHAGO**	

PART 9

CHOOSE
COURAGE

I. THE SACRIFICE:
THE STORY OF MATA GUJRI AND
GURU TEGH BAHADUR

. . .

AS FAR BACK AS SHE COULD REMEMBER, GUJRI LOVED THE STARS.
She lay on her back in her family's courtyard in Kartarpur and counted
the stars as they pierced the twilight. She smiled so brightly, people said
she carried the stars in her eyes.

When she was five years old, Gujri skipped into the mela, the festival, that had come to their village. Her parents pointed out Guru Hargobind, sixth in the House of Nanak, holding court in the distance; he
looked like a king to her. Then they gestured to the Guru's youngest
son, Tyag Mal, a sweet-faced boy of eight, kicking a ball with his brothers. "He will be your husband one day," her parents told her. She did
not know what that meant, but they fed her ladoos, and she beamed.

After Gujri turned nine, her parents took her to the great city of
Amritsar for the first time. She was dazzled by how Harmandir Sahib
floated on water. Her mother dressed her in red and painted mehndi
on her hands; her father tied one end of her garment to the boy's and
told her she was married now. She still did not know what that meant.
Then her parents left. She was alone with a family she did not know.
The boy they called her husband was off in the distance, playing with
his brothers, and she was glad of it. Her mother-in-law, Mata Nanki,
gave Gujri warm milk with cardamom, but she still cried herself to
sleep. She peered at the stars outside her window and made out new
shapes—the tiger, the rabab, the hawk—and they became her friends.

A year later, war drums pounded in the night and she was evacuated
with the Guru's family. Her young husband went away to fight and
came back with a new name: Tegh Bahadur, the Sword of Courage.
Then, a great lady with a swan neck and fierce eyes said it was time to
leave Amritsar. Bibi Veero was her husband's elder sister, and every-

one did what she said. Gujri climbed onto a cart headed north. When the camels kicked up a great cloud of dust, she sobbed. She was eleven years old, and they were taking her even farther away from her parents. That's when the great lady Bibi Veero rode up on horseback and gave her a doll and galloped away. She lifted the doll up high so that her star friends could see.

When they arrived in Kiratpur, Gujri lived in the house of Guru Hargobind near the River Satluj. She learned how to sing, play rabab, weave, and cook. One day, she noticed her husband, Tegh Bahadur, under a tree with a great drum, a pakhavaj. The earth shook beneath her as he drummed. This pakhavaj drum was a gift from his elder sister, Bibi Veero. When he was a child, Tegh Bahadur trained with Babak Rababi, a great warrior and rababi, in his father's court in Amritsar. As they walked in the garden, she told him about her stars. They fell in love. Gujri was content to make the Shivalik Hills their home forever. Then, after nine years in Kiratpur, her father-in-law, Guru Hargobind, passed away. Gujri was twenty, and Tegh Bahadur twenty-three. The couple had no clear role in the new court. So, Tegh Bahadur's mother, Mata Nanki, took them both to live with her in her family village, Bakala, and Gujri found herself on a cart once again.

In her new home in Bakala, Gujri hoped to raise a family, but a baby never came. When her husband awoke in a sweat in the night from flashes of the battlefield of his youth, she pressed a washcloth to his forehead and retrieved their musical instruments—the pakhavaj and rabab. They gathered around the fire in the courtyard under the stars, drumming and singing; their sorrows quieted. As the seasons turned, Gujri found peace, content to live out her life in the quiet music of Bakala.

BIBI VEERO FLEW ACROSS THE PLAINS ON HORSEBACK AS HER GOLD dupatta rippled behind her like a flag. Her eyes still burned from the sorrow of losing the child-Guru, her great-nephew Guru Harkrishan. She had heard that the plague in Delhi was subsiding, and Emperor

Aurangzeb planned to emerge from his isolation with edicts to punish subjects who did not conform to his narrow brand of religion. His agenda was more extreme than that of his father, Shah Jahan, or his grandfather, Jahangir. He assumed no one would resist him. Bibi Veero rode from Kiratpur to Bakala alongside a contingent led by the elder Durga Mal to install the next leader of the Sikh world.

The torches of the village Bakala came into sight. Tegh Bahadur, a tall man with a black beard and serene gaze, waited for them in the doorway. Bibi Veero rushed into her brother's arms and told him that they would hold the ceremony in the morning.

"Nahi," said Tegh Bahadur. *No.*

"Nahi?" said Bibi Veero, incredulous. She never expected no for an answer.

He gestured to the saintly men outside who flocked around the elder Durga Mal for an audience. A great many men in the village were claiming that they were the "Baba Bakala" named by the child-Guru.

"They seem to want it," said Tegh Bahadur quietly.

Bibi Veero studied her brother's face. They had grown up together in the glorious court of their father, Guru Hargobind, when Amritsar was still theirs. Their grandmother Mata Ganga had passed away just after he was born, so Bibi Veero poured the old stories, songs, and music into her little brother, and Tegh Bahadur became a courageous warrior who fought alongside their father in battle. What had happened to her brother in these twenty years in Bakala?

A woman with bright eyes appeared with tumblers of warm milk. Bibi Veero's mind flashed to the little girl on the back of a cart, wide-eyed and terrified, when they were all exiled from Amritsar. Gujri was forty years old now and radiated serenity; her eyes sparkled in the night. Bibi Veero looked around at their humble home: The couple had spent two decades here together, childless, living a quiet, contemplative life. The outer courage of Tegh Bahadur's youth was now tempered by the inner spiritual life he led with Gujri. He was like a sword sharpened on both sides. Only such a Sword of Courage could stop Emperor Aurangzeb.

"We need *you*," Bibi Veero said finally.

"Why?" asked her brother as he took Gujri's hand.

"Because you don't want it," she said to both of them. "The House of Nanak needs those who serve with their head on their palm."

AFTER EVERYONE WENT TO SLEEP, GUJRI AND TEGH BAHADUR GAZED wordlessly into the fire. The mantle of the Sikh world was the last thing Gujri ever imagined at their doorstep. Bibi Veero rushed into their lives with her fiery will and asked them to choose between quiet comfort and a world of uncertainty. What was the courageous answer: To stay in the freedom she had worked so hard to find, or risk it all to stand up to an empire?

Emperor Aurangzeb's reign of terror was coming. Would it reach their small remote village? That was uncertain. Would it send a new generation of children into exile, or worse? Certainly, yes.

Gujri looked up at the night sky. It was a new moon, and a cloud of stars ribboned across the heavens from one side to the other—the tiger, the rabab, the hawk. The dark patches in the milky cloud were just as defined as the points of light. She focused on one bright star, and more came into view, like rubies and sapphires circling a diamond. She had not exhausted the wonders of this world.

"Vah," she breathed in awe. *Wow.*

Tegh Bahadur, who was staring into the flames, followed his wife's gaze to the sky.

"What does your heart say?" her husband asked.

"We have been happy in Bakala for many years," she said.

He murmured in agreement.

She recited:

aap karaae aap karei
The Beloved acts, and inspires us to act[*]

---

[*]   Guru Granth Sahib, ang 349, Raag Asa, Guru Nanak Ji.

"Sat Kartar," he breathed in agreement.

In the morning, under the shade of a great banyan tree, the village of Bakala gathered for the ceremony, including the scowling would-be Gurus. Bibi Veero watched proudly as the elder Durga Mal presented a coconut, panj paisay, swords, and a royal turban to her youngest brother. Tegh Bahadur—the youngest child of Guru Hargobind, grandson of Guru Arjan and Mata Ganga, great-grandson of Guru Ram Das and Bibi Bhani, celebrated early in life as the Sword of Courage and later in life as the Baba of Bakala, whose lifetime with Mata Gujri had developed the sage in the warrior—became the ninth Guru in the house of Nanak.

AFTER THE CEREMONY, GURU TEGH BAHADUR AND HIS FAMILY traveled, looking for a place to establish the new center of the Sikh world. First they went to Kiratpur to offer their condolences to Mata Krishan upon the passing of her son, the child-Guru. Then they went to Amritsar to pay their respects at Harmandir Sahib, but they were shut out by Prithi Chand's son Meharban and his followers, who now controlled the city. They returned to Kiratpur in the fall to find Mata Krishan in new mourning clothes for her mother-in-law, Mata Bassi. Soon after, Guru Tegh Bahadur was driven out of Kiratpur by his own brother Suraj Mal, who seized control of the city after the child-Guru's passing. So, they purchased land farther north in the Shivalik Hills for five hundred rupees from the Dowager Rani Chamba of Bilaaspur and called it Chak Nanki after the Guru's mother. Shortly after, they received an invitation from eastern congregations to visit, and the Guru's procession was on foot again.

On their way east, imperial soldiers stopped their caravan on the outskirts of Delhi and arrested Guru Tegh Bahadur. Ram Rai had him arrested for claiming to be the rightful heir to the Guruship after the child-Guru passed. He was released after a few days. They decided to travel far away to consolidate the Sikh world from the outside in. The Guru taught in far-flung congregations, engaging Brahmin priests in

Allahabad, Buddhist pilgrims in Gaya, Sufis in Malda, and Ahom tribes in Assam. They built new langar halls and baolis, stepwells, to bring food and water to poor communities. Everywhere they went, Guru Tegh Bahadur gathered people in large numbers, energized their hearts, and called them to courage in the face of repression. Emperor Aurangzeb's reign of terror was under way—demolitions of temples, taxation of those who did not follow imperial order, detentions and interrogations and executions of anyone who resisted the regime.

One warm spring evening on their travels, Gujri tucked jasmine flowers into her hair as she sat down to dinner with her husband. She lifted the roti to her mouth, paused, put her hands on her knees, and vomited. Guru Tegh Bahadur rubbed her back; Mata Nanki held her hair. She closed her eyes and moaned. *Was this the deadly illness that plagued Delhi?*

Mata Nanki felt her pulse.

"She's not sick," she announced. "She is with child."

Gujri was forty-two years old; the impossible had found her. As she wept joyfully, her husband took her hand with delight, and Mata Nanki hurried to fetch the village vaid for medicines and herbs.

The family continued on to the ancient city of Patna along the sacred River Ganga.

"Tusee(n) jaavo Ji," Gujri told her husband as she rubbed her melon-like belly. *You go on without me.* The Guru was a beacon of resistance, and the people needed him. He kissed her hand tenderly and went on to Bengal.

Shortly after, Gujri birthed her son in the wintertime and named him Gobind Rai. She nursed him in the safety of Patna, under the care and patronage of a prosperous Jain community whose ancestor Salis Rai Johri had once housed Guru Nanak on his udasis, his great travels. The Jains were a spiritual community committed to ahimsa, non-harm, and were drawn to the Sikh Gurus' teachings on Oneness and care for all.

When Gobind Rai turned three, Guru Tegh Bahadur was able to return and meet his son for the first time. He brought news: Their rivals in Punjab were retreating in fear of Emperor Aurangzeb. It was time to return to Punjab and settle on their land in the Shivalik Hills. Gujri bundled up her son and made the long journey. Gobind Rai was four years old by the time they arrived.

As they descended from the cart, Gujri breathed in the cold misty air and her eyes watered. After all the years of travel and displacement, all those shut doors, she returned to the land where she had first found a sense of home. She was tired, her bones ready to rest in these foothills of the Himalayas, where the stars were closer than she had ever seen them. She gazed up at the Shivalik Hills as the evening stars appeared over their peaks. Her heart filled with hope: *This is the place we will raise our son and lead our people.*

"Anandpur," she breathed. *The City of Joy.*

SHORTLY AFTER THE GURU'S FAMILY SETTLED IN ANANDPUR, MATA Krishan, the mother of the late child-Guru, came up north to visit. Gujri received her joyfully, and the two women chatted over warm milk. Mata Krishan was dressed in white, the color of mourning. As she watched young Gobind Rai climb a tree, she rested her hand on her heart. His smile was radiant, so like the son she had lost.

"Taati vao na lagayee," she murmured the song-prayer. *The hot winds cannot touch him.*

Mata Krishan unwrapped the white pearl mala on her wrist, and poured the pearls into Gujri's hands as though they were water.

"Paarbrahm sarnaaee," she finished. *He is shielded by the Infinite.*

The pearls rested heavy in Mata Gujri's palms. She felt energy ripple through her body.

"Shakti vastay," whispered Mata Krishan. *For power.*

As Mata Gujri draped the mala over her neck, she thought of all the women of the House of Nanak; their power was in their love, and their love was protection. She watched as Mata Krishan kissed her son's forehead and left for home.

SIX YEARS WENT BY IN PEACE IN ANANDPUR. GURU TEGH BAHADUR
and Mata Gujri raised young Gobind Rai under the stars of their mountain city, and the city grew strong. No one came for them, neither rival
claimants, nor the Emperor.

One night, Mata Gujri was awakened by hushed voices. She
wrapped her shoulders in a dupatta and went to the rooftop to join
Guru Tegh Bahadur. Guards pointed to shadows on the horizon heading toward the Guru's residence. Mata Gujri flashed to Bibi Veero's
story of the Battle of Amritsar—how the Emperor's men came in the
dead of the night. Her eyes adjusted to the dark.

A full moon lit the mountainside and cast a shadow over the mass of
people that moved toward them. The Guru's guards were stationed in
front of the house with torches and swords ready. The shadows grew
larger and larger, hundreds of them, until they entered a patch of
moonlight. Mata Gujri saw bald and bare-chested men, draped in yellow and white lungis, beads wrapped around their arms, and barefoot.
These were not soldiers. They were pandits, Hindu priests, and they
looked like they were about to collapse.

"Do we lift the gates?" a warrior asked.

Guru Tegh Bahadur nodded.

Mata Gujri prepared tumblers of warm milk for their guests. The
pandits bowed and drank deeply. One stepped forward and introduced
himself as Kirpa Ram. He had led five hundred Hindu Brahmins here
from Kashmir Valley. The Mughal governor of Kashmir, Iftikhar Khan,
was carrying out Emperor Aurangzeb's edicts with horrific zeal. The
people were given a choice: convert to Islam or die. Kirpa Ram and his
priests went to the Amarnath Cave to pray for deliverance. They saw
Lord Shiva in one of their dreams; he instructed them to seek support
from Guru Tegh Bahadur, the Sword of Courage. The Sikh Guru
would be the one to save the Hindu people. They had heard of the courageous Guru, a principled warrior and sage-poet who spoke against
the Empire. So, they came a great distance on foot to ask for his help.

"Your very name brings comfort," said Kirpa Ram, hands folded.
"Will you protect us?"

Mata Gujri invited their guests to stay overnight. They would resume their meeting in the morning. She returned to her chambers with her husband. Nine-year-old Gobind Rai was awake. He looked up at his parents with big, searching eyes.

"Will their suffering end?" asked Gobind Rai. He had heard every word.

"Jeh koi vaddee kurbani devay," replied Guru Tegh Bahadur gently. *Only if someone makes a great sacrifice.*

"Who else could do that but you, Pita Ji?" said Gobind Rai.

Mata Gujri wrapped her arms around her son. *Did he understand what sacrifice really meant?*

"Sau(n) jaavo," she said. *Go to sleep.* She sang him Sohila until his eyes closed.

"Let's go sit by the fire," Mata Gujri said to her husband. They went out into the moonlit night, canopied by the stars. She ran the pearl mala through her hand. All she could think of was the children of Kashmir and their wide-eyed terror. So far, they had been left alone by imperial armies, but if they chose to help these people, they would surely provoke the wrath of the Empire.

"What does your heart say?" Guru Tegh Bahadur asked her. It was a choice to make together.

Mata Gujri sighed, unable to speak. She retrieved his drum and her rabab. Guru Tegh Bahadur began to drum the pakhavaj: *Dha dha doon ta! Tita kata ghadi ginu!* As the rhythms reverberated in her chest, Mata Gujri's fingers danced on the rabab. She kept her eyes on the stars.

Only the boldest stars were visible, but she felt the multitudes in the darkness, watching her. The stars had witnessed it all: the rise and fall of empires, the birth and death of civilizations, the prayers of people whose dreams were lost to time. Emperor Aurangzeb was one of a thousand faces of terror; his destruction had played out many times before. So, too, their visitors had made a journey that countless others had made before, traversing distances to call for help. In every cycle, there were those who pretended not to hear, and those who answered the call. The question in her heart was one that echoed through time: *Who do I want to be?*

Mata Gujri began to hum a shabd of Guru Nanak:

je dar maa(n)gat kook kare mahlee khasm(u) sune
bhaavai dheerak bhaavai dhakay ek vaddaiee dei
jaanh(u) jot na poochhah(u) jaatee aagai jaat na he

If a beggar cries out at the door, the owner hears it in the
    palace
and gives the gift: to receive them or push them away
Know the light within all, ask not of caste:
There are no hierarchies in the world beyond*

The next morning, Kirpa Ram and the pandits waited in the Guru's
court.

Guru Tegh Bahadur stepped forth in a royal turban and blue warrior's dress. Mata Gujri stood tall by his side, draped in a blue dupatta
studded with jewels; her eyes sparkled.

"Next time the imperial armies come for you," announced the Guru
for all to hear, "tell them they have to come for me first."

Guru Tegh Bahadur turned his body into a shield.

Kirpa Ram nodded solemnly and sent the message to the Emperor
by way of the Governor of Lahore. The Guru did not wait for the Emperor to come for him. He gathered his most trusted companions—
Bhai Mati Das, Dayal Das, and Sati Das—to set out for Delhi himself.
Before leaving, he placed a coconut and five paisay before his nine-
year-old son and bowed.

On the morning of the Guru's departure, a thick wall of fog encircled the mountain city of Anandpur. The Guru bid farewell to his people, who tried to mask their confusion. Mata Gujri took hold of her
husband's broad shoulders and gently kissed his eyelids.

Guru Tegh Bahadur kneeled down and said to his son:

bhay kahoo kou det neh
neh bhay maanat aan

---

* Guru Granth Sahib, ang 349, Raag Asa, Guru Nanak Ji.

Do not incite fear in others
and do not let anyone incite fear in you*

The words echoed in their ears as Guru Tegh Bahadur mounted his horse, flanked by three faithful companions, and entered the mist that wrapped the mountain city, ready to confront the world that waited on the other side.

AS THE DAYS WENT ON, MATA GUJRI SLEPT ONLY A FEW HOURS EACH night. She tended to her son, ran the affairs of the city, prayed under her stars, and waited for word. She heard that her husband had stayed a night with Mata Krishan and her daughter, Roop, in Kiratpur on his journey to Delhi. Roop, now a brilliant writer, grieved when he told them where he was going. That was all the news Mata Gujri had for a long time. Summer turned into fall, and fall into winter. Then, a man named Jaita arrived at dawn with an urgent message from Delhi.

Mata Gujri stood tall with her son, Gobind Rai, as the court filled with people eager to hear news of their Guru. All eyes fell on Jaita, the young, weathered man who stood before them. He held a small bundle in his arms. Jaita looked uncertainly from the boy to his mother. Mata Gujri implored him with her eyes. Jaita pulled back the end of the shawl, revealing strands of coarse black hair.

Mata Gujri was looking at the top of her husband's head. She shielded her son's eyes, then slowly peeled back her fingers for him to see.

"Bolo," she commanded, and Jaita told them what happened.

Guru Tegh Bahadur was arrested on the way to Delhi. The Emperor's armies forced him into an iron cage and took him the rest of the way. They imprisoned him in Delhi and tortured him for five days. They demanded allegiance to the Emperor and to his brand of Islam,

---

*   Guru Granth Sahib, ang 1427, Salok Mahla Nauvaa(n), Guru Tegh Bahadur Ji.

but he refused. The Guru's three companions—Bhai Mati Das, Dayal Das, and Sati Das—were killed in front of him: The first was sawn in two, the second boiled alive, the third burnt alive.

Then, Guru Tegh Bahadur was dragged to a market square near the Red Fort called Chandni Chowk, where a crowd of people gathered upon the Emperor's instruction. He lay his head down. The executioner raised his sword. Guru Tegh Bahadur was beheaded in one blow. His lips recited praise of the Beloved even as his head rolled onto the earth. They were the words of his grandfather Guru Arjan:

tera keeya meetha lagai
Your will is sweet to me*

The people stifled their cries. Mata Gujri felt her son grow still under her hands.

"Agay dasso." She told Jaita to go on.

Imperial soldiers drew their swords and descended on the Guru's body. They planned to quarter the body and hang it for display on the gates of Delhi, as per the Emperor's order. Suddenly, a great dust storm overcame the square and enveloped the people in a fiery cloud that blinded their eyes. A man named Lakhi Shah Vanjara, a devotee of the Guru, had been unloading lime from his cart for the royal forces at the fort. He ran into the dust and lifted the Guru's body onto his bullock cart. He smuggled it past the guards out of the walled city that night. He placed the Guru's body in his house in Rakabganj and set his own house on fire—the only cremation that would not be detected. Meanwhile, Jaita leapt into the cloud of dust to retrieve the Guru's head. He wrapped it in cotton sheets and traveled by night to Anandpur to deliver the head of the Guru to his wife and son.

Silence.

Mata Gujri heard wailing, but the sound did not come from her or her court, where the people held one another in shock. It came from a distant recess in her mind. Bibi Veero had once told her the story about

---

* Guru Granth Sahib, ang 394, Raag Asa, Guru Arjan Ji.

her grandmother: Mata Ganga, too, sent her beloved Guru Arjan into the arms of the Empire. Mata Ganga, too, waited for word of his return. Mata Ganga, too, was given an account of his courage—how he sat upon a burning cauldron, how they poured hot sand over him, how the river took his blistered body. Mata Ganga, too, had a son she had to shield. A son who would go on to don two swords and grow up to fight an empire and name his only daughter Veero, warrior, and his youngest Tegh Bahadur, the Sword of Courage.

Now the Sword of Courage was gone. Her husband was gone. And it was Mata Ganga's wail she heard. His grandmother's wail. Mata Gujri did not need to make a sound at all. She only needed to focus on what needed to be done.

"Marigolds," said Mata Gujri.

"Mata Ji?" Jaita was confused.

"Rest Guru Ji's head on a bed of marigolds," she said.

Jaita bowed.

Mata Gujri returned to her chambers with Gobind Rai, who was still as a stone. He slowly bowed before the coconut and paisay his father had presented him.

"Let go," Gujri said as she embraced him. "If you don't break down, you won't rise up."

Gobind Rai turned in to his mother's shawl and dissolved into grief.

As news of Guru Tegh Bahadur's execution spread, people came to Anandpur in caravans from across the land of Punjab—the followers of Guru Nanak's son the Udasis, the descendants of Guru Angad from Khadoor, the descendants of Guru Amar Das from Goindval, and the remaining family of Guru Hargobind from Kiratpur. They gathered on a hilltop around Mata Gujri and her nine-year-old son, Gobind Rai. In the clearing, Guru Tegh Bahadur's head rested on a bed of bright marigolds on a golden palanquin. The Guru's eyes were closed, and his hair was carefully tucked into a cream-gold turban. The blood at the base of his neck had been cleaned, and his torn skin merged into flower petals. Mata Gujri gazed at the eyelids that she had kissed. Her beloved looked beautiful somehow.

The people stepped forth, one by one, and bowed before the Guru.

As the drums pounded, a rababi sang that Guru Tegh Bahadur was the martyr who gave his life for people who weren't his own, and, in doing so, made all people his people! Together, the people sang a shabd of Guru Nanak:

> *jao tao prem khelan kaa chaao*
> *sir(u) dhar talee galee meree aao*

> If you desire to play the game of love
> place your head on your palm and come my way*

The procession marched down from the hilltop to the Guru's house in the heart of Anandpur, where a sandalwood pyre awaited them. The sound of conches filled the air. They planned to conduct this cremation out in the open, in direct defiance of the Emperor. Gobind Rai solemnly lifted his father's head onto the sandalwood, lit a torch, and set the pyre on fire. The people sang until the ashes were collected. Then, Gobind Rai mounted a horse and led the procession five kilometers south to Kiratpur, where he poured his father's ashes into the River Satluj.

Mata Gujri found two women waiting for her on the riverbank in Kiratpur. Mata Krishan, draped in her forever-white dupatta, stood in the same spot where she had poured her son's ashes into the river. Guru Harkrishan would have been nineteen by now. Mata Krishan's expression was tender. She steadied a woman whose face was contorted in grief. Mata Gujri barely recognized her elder sister-in-law.

"Bibi Veero," breathed Mata Gujri.

"Bhain Ji, mainu maaf karna," said Bibi Veero, unable to meet her eyes. *Sister, forgive me.*

"It's all my fault." Bibi Veero wept. "I asked you to take on the Guruship when you did not seek it. He is gone because of me. You suffer because of me . . ."

---

* Guru Granth Sahib, ang 1412, Salok Vaara(n) te Vadheek, Guru Nanak Ji.

"Stop." Gujri raised her hand, a flash of rage in her eyes. *How dare she?*

Bibi Veero looked at her, startled.

"*I* chose this," said Mata Gujri. "This was *my* choice. No matter what came. Don't take that away from me."

Mata Krishan took both of their hands, brought them together, and whispered a verse of Guru Nanak:

hukam rajai chalna
nanak likhyea naal

Go with the order ever-unfolding
Oh Nanak, it is written and we are writing it*

Mata Gujri felt an iron resolve within her. She thought: *The Guru made his body a shield. I will make my body a shield around my son.*

Jaikaras filled the air as people shouted praise.

The three women looked on, their faces lit by the setting sun as Gobind Rai prepared to be anointed before all the people: Guru Gobind, tenth in the House of Nanak.

Aao chaa peelo . . .
Come, let's have tea . . .

---

*   Guru Granth Sahib, ang 1, Jap, Guru Nanak Ji.

BENEATH THE NIGHT SKY

WE WOVE OUR WAY UP TO THE MOUNTAIN CITY ANANDPUR SAHIB, the second-holiest city in the Sikh world after Amritsar, high in the foothills of the Himalayas, founded by Guru Tegh Bahadur in 1665. A thick mist enveloped the enchanted city. As we stepped out of the car into the cold, Sharat and I rubbed coconut oil onto the children's chapped lips.

"Anandpur is named after joy!" I said.

"Like me!" exclaimed Ananda. "I'm made of joy!"

I laughed and scooped her up and carried her on my hip as we wandered the old narrow streets of the city. Everywhere we turned, we could see the misty mountains called the Shivalik Hills in the distance, shrouded in bronze and indigos, keeping their ancient watch. We entered a great clearing where Guru Tegh Bahadur received the five hundred Hindu Brahmins of Kashmir. On that spot stood Gurdwara Thara Sahib, a pearly-white structure a few steps away from where the Guru had lived, Gurdwara Bhora Sahib. As night fell, we could no longer see the mountains, only the stars that peered through the charcoal clouds. I imagined Guru Tegh Bahadur and Mata Gujri deliberating together under these stars before he left for Delhi.

"Mommy, I'm cold."

I buttoned my coat around Ananda and carried her back to the car, wondering how she had gotten heavier in an hour. Jasso guided me past the carts of sugarcane juice and trinkets. Kavi skipped ahead with Sharat, who brought out the snacks. As the children happily ate granola bars in the car, I told them about how the people of Kashmir came to Anandpur to ask Guru Tegh Bahadur for help. Their eyes grew wide listening to the story.

"Did he help them?"

"Yes." I nodded. "He made his body a shield."

"What happened to him?"

"Um." I looked into their sweet small faces. "I'll tell you when you're a little older."

"I'm older now!" Kavi said. "I'm older than I was a second ago!"

"Um, look! Popcorn!" I pointed to the man with the cart outside. We scrambled out for popcorn sprinkled with black salt.

WHAT IS SACRIFICE

THE NEXT MORNING, I AWOKE EARLY AND SLIPPED OUT OF THE room for another predawn sojourn. Happy drove me to Qila Anandgarh, a great redbrick fort on a misted hilltop. Rubbing his hands together for warmth, he said that he would wait for me in the car. I held my journal to my chest, stepped into the darkness, and ascended the stairs. My feet immediately turned to ice on the cold marble. "Vaheguru, Vaheguru," I breathed. I reached the top and looked out over a vista. My eyes grew wide. The city of Anandpur spread before me: The small bright domes of gurdwaras dotted the mountain slopes like gold stars under the dark sky. The city was silent, enveloped in a thin mist, suspended in time. A conch sounded in the darkness. Then another, and another. A trumpeting of conches! And voices on loudspeakers reciting the Mool Mantr: "Ik Onkar, Satnam." My heart ached as I watched the city of joy awaken to conches and song-prayers.

I wandered the grounds of Qila Anandgarh, the old fort, as if in a dream. Down a long set of narrow steps, I found the gurdwara built where the head of Guru Tegh Bahadur was displayed after his execution. A Sikh elder was seated inside next to the open door, behind a great bowl of warm prashaad. He wore a large white turban and long silver beard, eyes half closed in meditation. To his left was a large painting on the wall.

In the painting, nine-year-old Gobind Rai wept as he beheld his father's head on a bed of flowers. Mata Gujri stood stoically nearby; the Kashmiri Pandit Kirpa Ram folded his hands in tribute, surrounded by hundreds of Sikhs who watched mournfully. Among them was Bhai Jaita, the one who had leapt into a firestorm to retrieve the Guru's head, a Hindu who later became a Sikh. This scene took place here, in this very spot, a few hundred years ago. I opened my journal and began to sketch.

"Beti!" the elder called out. *Daughter!* I nearly dropped my pen. Did I do something wrong?

"Havva aundiya!" he said. *The wind is blowing!* He gestured for me to move to the wall, so that the stinging wind blowing through the door wouldn't touch me. I thanked him. The elder resumed his inward meditation. He was like an ancient guardian of this place, and of the memories it holds. I breathed on my fingers as I sketched the marigolds under the Guru's head.

Guru Tegh Bahadur was executed on November 11, 1675, recent enough for the places in his story to be well preserved. I once visited the place in Delhi where he was imprisoned and killed, Gurdwara Sees Ganj. I saw where he and his companions were tortured, the well where he bathed, and the trunk of the tree where the executioner's sword fell. But I had never been here: the spot where the people beheld the Guru's sacrifice and made meaning of his choice.

Today Sikhs remember Guru Tegh Bahadur as the second Guru martyred in Sikh history.* The first was his grandfather Guru Arjan, whose serenity under torture came to embody spiritual defiance and nonviolent resistance. Seventy years later, Guru Tegh Bahadur made a similar sacrifice, but for people who were not his own. To this day, he is known as "Srishti di Chadar!" *Shield of Humanity!* It was an act of *deep* solidarity. His sacrifice came from Guru Nanak's call to see all people as One. Not *my* people versus *your* people. Not *chosen people*

---

* "He protected their forehead mark and sacred thread / marking a great deed in the age of darkness / For the sake of the sages / he gave his head but did not flinch." Original: "*tilak janju rakhaa prabh taa kaa / keeno baddo kaloo meh saakaa / saadhan het itee jin karee / sees deeyaa par see na ucharee.*" —Dasam Granth, ang 54, Bachitar Natak, Guru Gobind Singh Ji.

versus the rest. One people. One family. If I see you as kin, then I must answer the call to stand for you when you are in harm's way. And that means being willing to risk myself for you.

Shallow solidarity is rooted in the logic of exchange: *I show up for you, so you show up for me.* It is transactional, useful in the short term but inadequate for transformation in the long term. Deep solidarity is rooted in love. *I show up for you because I choose to see you as my sister, my brother, my kin.* Deep solidarity is durable, powerful, and magical: It is both a means and an end. When I am in deep solidarity with people, we grieve together. Then we sit and eat together. Soon we are laughing, even singing together. As we face the darkness, we keep each other in the light. Our bonds last beyond any news cycle. We practice the world as it could be in the space between us, and in those spaces, we are free.

I grew up with the story of Guru Tegh Bahadur's sacrifice. But standing here, I felt the very real choice that he and Mata Gujri made, and I wondered: Is courage a practice?

CULTIVATING COURAGE

I BECAME AN ACTIVIST SO YOUNG, BEFORE I REALLY KNEW WHAT sacrifice was. A Sikh man from my community was the first person murdered in the racial violence that exploded across the United States after the terrorist attacks on September 11, 2001. I did not know what to do with the distress in my body except to be in motion. I took a leave of absence from college, drove across the country, and documented my people's stories. Along the way, I met my husband, Sharat, who is a filmmaker, and together we eventually turned the stories into a documentary. As I began to speak on our work and meet more people, I learned that my people's struggle was bound up in a larger movement for liberation in the United States, and in the world: None of us are free until all of us are free. For the next twenty years, I found myself constantly on the road, lifting up stories in order to shift culture, change policy, and inspire solidarity.

When I first started out, people called me brave. In truth, I was also naïve. I did not know what it meant to dedicate my life to the work of justice. I did not know what it would cost: financial instability, arrests, detention, police brutality, chronic pain, death threats, and personal attacks. Perhaps it means more for me to choose courage now, in my forties, because I understand the risk. It is not popular to speak truth to power—to call for ceasefire when so many want vengeance, to organize around love instead of hate, to bring people together when powerful forces benefit from keeping us apart. Every day, I lose something: allies, funding, forms of safety. When I read the hate directed at me online, it feels like drinking a thimble of poison. In order to neutralize this much hate, I need to build up the antidote in my body.

Amrit vela is the Sikh name for the ambrosial hours in the morning before the sun rises and the world awakes. In those predawn hours, Sikhs are called to meditate. It feels impossible to wake that early consistently with small children on top of me. But when Sharat can look after them, I rise early in the morning, meet my parents outside, and we walk through the wetlands together, the stars spread over us. As I walk, I scan my body, notice sensations, and address the parts of me in pain: "I'm here. What do you need me to know?" It is a practice to befriend the body. I go through each of my senses and notice what I can see, hear, smell, taste, touch. Like opening the aperture and letting more beauty in. We arrive at the ocean just as the sun rises and we walk along the water, listening and reciting Jap Ji Sahib, Guru Nanak's song of love.

One morning as we walked, the full moon hovered above the sea, and its light made a golden path on the water from the moon to us, just as the sun rose behind us. We stood between these two gorgeous orbs, held together in their embrace. Jap Ji Sahib ends with:

pavan guru paani pita
maata dharat mahat
divas raat due daaee dayaa
khelai sagal jagat

Air our teacher, water our father
Mother Earth, the great womb

Day and night are both midwife and caregiver
The whole world plays in their embrace*

Drinking in the beauty and wonder of the earth, our mother, is *how*
I build the antidote to hate and despair in my body. She is nursing me.
If I can walk with the earth in the morning, I can sustain whatever the
day brings. On our way back home, I think of the challenges and
choices facing me and listen to the Wise Woman in me. She asks: *What
does love demand?*

Inevitably, there will be days or months at a time when I do not have
that kind of morning quiet or stillness. But if I can go outside for just a
few seconds and look at the sky, I can touch the sage in me. Tending to
beauty is not escape: It is how we create the conditions within us to
choose courage. The sage prepares the warrior; the warrior fortifies the
sage.

WHAT COURAGE LOOKS LIKE

WHEN I SPEAK ABOUT FIGHTING FOR JUSTICE, PEOPLE ASK, "WHAT
should I do?" I offer ideas, but then I need to say: "Only *you* know, deep
inside, what it means for you to be brave with your life in this moment."

Sikh wisdom teaches that courageous action looks infinitely diverse.
For Mata Krishan, choosing courage looked like sending her eight-
year-old son into the world to serve the diseased and dying of Delhi.
For Mata Gujri, it looked like taking her nine-year-old son out of dan-
ger deep into the Himalayas to raise him. For Guru Tegh Bahadur,
courage looked like offering his life to save many lives. For his son, it
looked like charging into battle to defend his people.

What does courage look like for you? In one season of my life,
courage looked like putting my body in the street to get arrested in
protest. In another, it looked like taking my children out of the country
to write and think in the refuge of a rainforest. There are many ways to
make your body the shield. If you wish to be brave with your life, you

* Guru Granth Sahib, ang 8, Jap, Guru Nanak Ji.

have only to ask: *What does love demand of me?* And keep choosing that, even when it's hard.

There is no prescription in Sikh ethics. No rigid set of rules. No commandments. The sage warrior is one whose deepest wisdom is aligned with their words and actions. It is a way of being: The sage sees the world through the eyes of wonder; the warrior acts on that inner wisdom.

Everywhere I go, as I travel the country, I meet people who risk themselves to help people they do not know—nurses and doctors, teachers and healers, firefighters and first responders, faith leaders and community leaders, organizers and artists, caregivers and parents. In big, public ways and most often in the quiet spaces no one sees, we sacrifice for each other.

Sometimes, sacrifice leads to triumph. Sometimes, it leads to loss and disappointment. Most often, it leads to both. The key is not to measure sacrifice by outcomes but by our faithfulness to the labor. Every day, we can ask: *Are my words and actions aligned with my deepest wisdom?* And do our best so that they are. When we choose courage as a way of being, we know what freedom is, even if we do not live to see it in the world, because we know it within ourselves.

I am grateful for what choosing courage has given me—a community of people I trust, a heart that can contain multitudes, a sense of purpose and belonging, a profound gratitude for all that is good and beautiful and wondrous about being alive. Perhaps the greatest thing I have received is the capacity to feel the depth of my joy. For allowing myself to feel the depth of my grief and pain means that I have not exited my body: I can feel all parts of myself. And that means that when joy comes, I feel *all* of it. Choosing courage is the most pleasurable way to be on this earth—alive, awake, and true to our heart.

Choose courage, every time.

Could you lose your head? Yes. Is victory still possible? Yes.

EVERY DAY, A CHOICE

A VISITOR KNOCKS ON YOUR DOOR. DO YOU KEEP THEM OUT IN the cold, or let them in? You are a good person, so you build the fire and serve them milk. They tell you their story: Their lands are on fire, and armies pursue them in the night. At first, you are relieved you are not them. You nod politely from a safe distance. But the borders of your heart are porous. As you listen, their pain enters your body. It is terrible. Your chest aches, and it is hard to breathe. You want to flee, but where would you go? You are already home. The separation between you and the visitor is illusion. Their children carry different names but have the faces of your children. The fires in their lands are blowing into your fields. You feel the breath of the armies that pursue them on your back. The body of the land is one body, and the body of the people is one, and no one is outside your circle of care. Not the earth nor its rivers nor its forests nor its people. You are given this night to choose a response. When morning comes, will you have an answer?

You step outside to breathe fresh air. Of course, you don't want anyone to suffer. You are a good person. But this moment is asking more of you than ever before. Violence never happens in a vacuum. Violence is reinforced by institutions that drive it, justify it, or otherwise profit from it. To undo the injustice, you must confront institutions of power. An industry. A regime. An empire. A system. This has always been dangerous.

You start to pace and weigh the risks and benefits. Ultimately, courage is not a calculation of the mind: It is a choice of the heart. You must go to the sovereign space inside you and ask: *What does love want me to do?*

Perhaps in the final hour before dawn, you feel a tug on your sleeve. You look down and see a child, gazing at you with wide eyes. The child will inherit the story of what you do in this moment. They ask: *Who else but you?* They believe in you. Can you see yourself through their eyes?

You give your reply in the morning.

And you will give your reply, again and again, every morning of your life. Every day is a choice.

Until one day, you might be the one who must make the journey and knock on doors. Your fields are the ones on fire, the torches stalk your town, and it's your children who are afraid. You must traverse the borders of comfort and pride and ride until dawn, looking for the door of those who will answer. That, too, is warrior courage. To seek help until you find those who will answer the call.

Today you may be the one to receive the visitor. Tomorrow you may be the one to seek help. There is no true hierarchy between you. It is circumstance and not disposition that determines who gets to be whom on any given day. So greet the visitor with humility, just as you knock on the door with dignity.

HONORING HER

I FINISHED MY SKETCH OF THE PAINTING IN THE GURDWARA, tucked away my journal, and thanked the elder, who handed me warm, sweet prashaad with a grandfatherly smile. Before I left the gurdwara, I glanced back at the painting of Mata Gujri. She stood in the background, behind the palanquin that carried her husband's head. Her expression was inscrutable, her inner world hidden from us. There were always two sage warriors in this story: Guru Tegh Bahadur *and* Mata Gujri. From the moment the sangat appeared at her doorstep, she chose to leave behind a world of comfort to answer the call—to accept the mantle of leadership, to birth her baby alone, to confront the Empire, and to take her son deep into the Himalayas to raise him without fear. All this would be only the beginning of her sacrifice.

It was time to tell my children the whole story.

SAGE WARRIOR,
CHOOSE COURAGE . . .

THINK OF A COMMUNITY THAT is suffering, your own or another. Picture yourself responding in the most courageous way possible. Notice what happens in your body. Where is the fear in your body? Say: *You are a part of me I do not yet know*. Ask what makes this part of you afraid. Your fear carries information. Picture the worst thing that could happen if you responded with courage. What could you lose? Imagine that has already happened. Notice what you feel in your body. Now, picture the most beautiful thing that could happen. What impact could you make? Whose life would change? Imagine that has already happened. Notice what you feel in your body. Courage is not a calculation of the mind but a choice of the heart. Invite the wisest part of you to step forward and ask: *What does love demand?* Listen.

The Little Critic within will want you to believe it's dangerous to choose courage. He might be right about the risk. He's just wrong about the solution. The solution is not silence; it's more solidarity. Who can stand with you? Sometimes courageous action will be in the quiet contours of your life and relationships. Other times, it will be loud and public. Both matter. The key is to make courage a practice. Choose courage every day. Daily acts of courage prepare you for when the stakes are high. Measure your success not by the outcome of your choice, but by whether your choice is aligned with your deepest wisdom. The sage warrior chooses courage as a way of being.

What are the sage practices that allow you to be a warrior in the world? The deeper your internal practices—to wake to Oneness, to befriend the body, to practice pleasure, to build sovereign space, to rest in wisdom—the more you are able to answer the call to courage.

ANCESTOR TREE

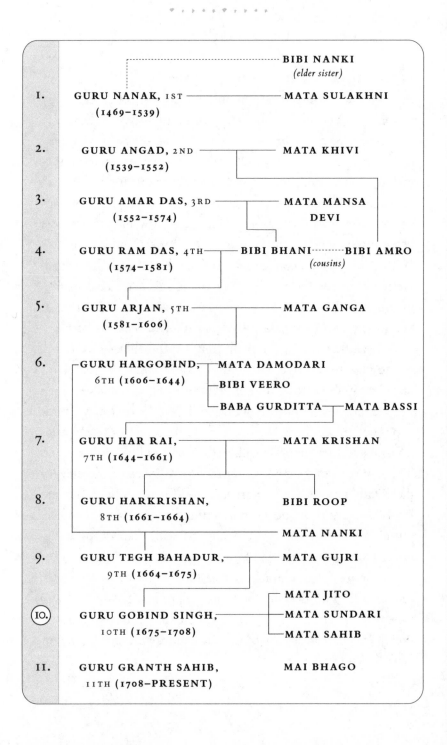

BIBI NANKI
(elder sister)

1. GURU NANAK, 1ST ——————— MATA SULAKHNI
   (1469–1539)

2. GURU ANGAD, 2ND ——————— MATA KHIVI
   (1539–1552)

3. GURU AMAR DAS, 3RD ——————— MATA MANSA
   (1552–1574)   DEVI

4. GURU RAM DAS, 4TH —— BIBI BHANI········BIBI AMRO
   (1574–1581)   *(cousins)*

5. GURU ARJAN, 5TH ——————— MATA GANGA
   (1581–1606)

6. GURU HARGOBIND, —— MATA DAMODARI
   6TH (1606–1644)   BIBI VEERO
                        BABA GURDITTA —— MATA BASSI

7. GURU HAR RAI, ——————— MATA KRISHAN
   7TH (1644–1661)

8. GURU HARKRISHAN, ——————— BIBI ROOP
   8TH (1661–1664)
                        MATA NANKI

9. GURU TEGH BAHADUR, ——— MATA GUJRI
   9TH (1664–1675)

10. GURU GOBIND SINGH, —— MATA JITO
    10TH (1675–1708)   MATA SUNDARI
                          MATA SAHIB

11. GURU GRANTH SAHIB,   MAI BHAGO
    11TH (1708–PRESENT)

PART 10

BECOME
VICTORY

I. THE SURRENDER:
THE STORY OF MATA GUJRI
AND GURU GOBIND SINGH

...

AFTER GURU TEGH BAHADUR'S MARTYRDOM, MATA GUJRI RAISED
their son, Guru Gobind, in the protection of the Himalayan refuge Pa-
onta, where she ran the affairs of the Sikh world with her brother Kirpal. She trained Guru Gobind in the music and poetry of the sages, and
his own poems reflected his fluency in Persian, Arabic, Sanskrit, Braj,
Avadhi, and the ancient classics. She filled his childhood with the warrior arts of horse racing, musket shooting, and archery; Bibi Veero's
own son trained him in swordsmanship. When local hill chiefs at-
tempted to drive the Sikhs out of the mountains, the young Guru
fought in the Battle of Bhangani along with Bibi Veero's five sons, who
were great warriors. Two of Bibi Veero's sons, Sango Shah and Jit
Mall, were killed in combat. But the Sikhs prevailed. A few years later,
the same hill chiefs requested their help to fight the Mughals, and they
won the Battle of Nadaun.

Shortly after, Guru Gobind returned to Anandpur, and the mountain city flourished as a cultural center for poets, musicians, warriors,
and sages. The Guru fortified the city with a chain of fortresses like a
necklace around them: Kesgarh, Lohgarh, Fatehgarh, Holgarh, and
Anandgarh. He created alliances, marrying three times, and his part-
ners were revered by the people: Sundari for her fiery brilliance, Jito
for her quiet fortitude, and Sahib for her wise insight. They had four
sons: Sundari gave birth to Ajit, the eldest child; Jito gave birth to Jujhar, Zoraver, and Fateh. Mata Gujri adored her grandchildren and
oversaw their training.

Every day, Mata Gujri walked the children to the Guru's court.
Guru Gobind was seated on the throne in a warrior's dress and royal
turban. The rababis readied their musical instruments—rabab, saranda,

jori, taus, and tanpura. At his signal, the court filled with music—the sacred kirtan of the sages, the ballads of warriors. The court of Guru Gobind, tenth in the House of Nanak, was glorious.

One afternoon Bibi Veero entered the court, walking slowly with a long wooden staff. She was in her eighties now, and her hair was pure white, tied in a bun above her long swan neck. Her face held an ancient beauty, and the lines etched around her eyes spoke to the grief she had survived. She bowed to Guru Gobind, who touched his Bhua Ji's feet in respect.

In honor of her visit, Mata Gujri signaled her grandsons to sing a composition by their father. The boys nodded and tuned the taus, a peacock-hooded bowed stringed instrument, and the jori, the drums. As the strings and drums began to play, they lifted their small voices and, in full-throated abandon, sang the warrior's song for courage:

deh siva bar mohe ihai
subh karman te kabhoo(n) naa ttaro
na ddaro ar so jab jae laro nischai kar(i) apnee jeet karo
ar(u) sikh hou aapne hee man ko eh(i) laalach hou gun tau ucharo
jab aav kee aoudh nidaan banai at(i) hee ran mai tab joojh maro

Oh Beloved, give me this one gift:
May I never hold back from doing good
May I not be afraid when I go into battle;
    resolved, I become victory
May I teach my heart this desire alone: to utter your praises
When my life nears the end, may I embrace the battlefield and die
    fighting*

Their voices filled the court alongside the galloping rhythms of the jori and the wailing cries of the peacock-hooded taus. Mata Gujri looked over at Bibi Veero, who was weeping.

Bibi Veero had not believed she would live to see the court of the

---

*   Dasam Granth, ang 98, Chandi Charitar Ukat Bilas, Guru Gobind Singh Ji.

Guru as glorious as it was in her father Guru Hargobind's time, in the great city of Amritsar. When they fled north pursued by the Empire, she worried that her people would be forever lost in exile. But here they were, in the misty mountains of Anandpur, the city of joy, and it was as though all the music, poetry, stories, training, and wisdom of their ancestors converged in this court and poured into these children. Their bodies were as strong as their voices, their minds as sharp as their swords.

Afterward, Guru Gobind requested a private audience with his aunt, Bibi Veero, and his mother, Mata Gujri. He confided in them: They led a glorious court in Anandpur, but the rest of the Sikh realm was fracturing. The leaders of the masands, the Sikh districts, withheld offerings and built alliances with the Empire. Rival factions led people astray—Prithi Chand's son Meharban and his followers still held control of Amritsar, Dheer Mal claimed his own guruship in Kartarpur, and Ram Rai built his own following in Dehradun. Meanwhile, Emperor Aurangzeb and his armies continued their reign of terror across Punjab.

"How do we turn sparrows into hawks?" Guru Gobind uttered.

"Without losing their memory of how to sing," added Bibi Veero.

A great white hawk circled above them.

"When your father was executed," Mata Gujri began, "a large crowd watched in Chandni Chowk. No one stepped forth when the executioner raised his sword."

"Sikhs do not hide," finished Bibi Veero.

Guru Gobind kissed his mother's hand and touched his aunt's feet in respect. He whistled for his hawk, who alighted on his forearm and accompanied him on a long walk in the mountains. When he returned, he dispatched messengers throughout Punjab and called on the Sikh realm to gather in Anandpur on Vaisakhi Day.

THE SPRINGTIME SUN LIT THE MOUNTAINS OF ANANDPUR, AND THE city of joy shimmered gold and green. Mata Gujri stepped into the morning light and surveyed the hillside. Before her spread thousands of people, more than she had ever seen in one place in her life—warriors and farmers, merchants and musicians, and families with children on their laps. They had all come, on camel and cart and oxen and horse and on foot, from across the land of Punjab, climbing the mountain paths at the call of Guru Gobind, tenth in the House of Nanak, on this Vaisakhi Day.

The great war drum nagara sounded, and the people sang out praises of Guru Gobind: "Kalgi-dhar Patshaah! Neelay ghorray da svaar! Chittiyan baaja(n) vaala! Guru Ji!" *Wearer of royal plumes! Rider of the blue horse! King of the white hawks! Our beloved teacher!*

Guru Gobind stepped out from the tent pitched on the mountaintop, and the crowd fell silent. He was dressed in a royal blue warrior's dress and a turban adorned with pearls. The arrows at his back were dipped in gold. There was fire in his eyes. His great white hawk perched on his left forearm.

The Guru drew his sword, and sunlight struck the tip of the blade.

"Kaun sees bhet karoo?" he called out. *Who among you will give your head for the Guru?*

Mata Gujri held her breath. The wind rustled the trees, and no one breathed. The question was repeated among the crowd and whispered until it rippled through the rest of the hillside and reached every ear in the clearing. She heard murmurs: "Has he lost his mind?"

Guru Gobind was still as stone, sword lifted, hawk poised on his forearm, waiting for an answer.

Slowly, a figure in the heart of the crowd rose to his feet. All eyes turned to him.

"Mera naam Daya Ram hai," he said. *My name is Daya Ram.*

Guru Gobind gestured for Daya to step forth. Whispers flew that Daya was a simple merchant from Lahore. The crowd cleared a path for him as if he were otherworldly. Guru Gobind launched his hawk into the air, pulled back the flap of the tent, and nodded for Daya to step inside. Daya took one last look back at the crowd, who stared at him in shock. He let out a deep breath and disappeared into the tent.

THUD!

People cried out. Some fainted. Mata Gujri covered the ears of her youngest grandchildren, Fateh and Zoraver, who were sleeping soundly next to her. Her eldest grandsons, Ajit and Jujhar, watched wide-eyed. Their mothers, Sundari, Sahib, and Jito, kept their gaze on the tent.

Guru Gobind emerged from the tent a moment later, his sword stained with blood.

"Kaun sees bhet karoo?" the Guru bellowed. His voice echoed against the mountains. *Who is ready to give your head for the Guru?*

The wind rustled the trees, and the people did not move. A lone figure at the front of the crowd stood.

"Dharam Das," he announced himself.

Guru Gobind nodded for Dharam Das to step forth. People whispered that he was a farmer from near Delhi. Guru Gobind swept him inside the tent.

THUD!

Guru Gobind reemerged, his sword dripping with blood, and the drops stained the earth where he stood.

"Kaun sees bhet karoo?" he bellowed out again. *Who is ready to give your head for the Guru?*

The air filled with cries that the Guru had lost his mind. A crowd of men got to their feet to persuade everyone to leave. Others hushed them to quiet. In the midst of the chaos, one person made his way close enough to the Guru to be heard.

"Mohkam Chand," he presented himself. A washerman from Dwarka. He bowed and Guru Gobind swept him inside. The crowd fell silent. Once more, a dull thud shook the earth. When the Guru emerged with a bloody sword, he was out of breath.

"Kaun sees bhet karoo?" the Guru called out again. *Who is ready to give your head for the Guru?*

Another stood and introduced himself as Himmat Rai. A cook from Jagganathpuri. As Himmat Rai stepped toward the Guru, a little girl hung on his leg and would not let go until he leaned down and kissed her. She cried in her mother's arms as her father disappeared into the tent with the Guru.

Four had been taken.

This time, Guru Gobind called out so loudly that the mountains seemed to bow down:

"Kaun sees bhet karoo?" *Who is ready to give your head for the Guru?* Sundari, the Guru's wife and partner, leaned over and recited to Mata Gujri a verse from Guru Nanak:

jao tao prem khelan kaa chaao
sir(u) dhar talee galee meree aao

If you desire to play the game of love
place your head on your palm and come my way[*]

Her eyes were serene. Sundari rose to her feet and smiled warmly at her eldest child, Ajit, who looked back at his mother astonished. Mata Gujri grabbed her daughter-in-law's wrist and pulled her down with all her might.

"You have already given your head," she whispered hoarsely.

As Sundari was held back, another man stepped forward. His name was Sahib Chand, a barber from Bidar. He followed Guru Gobind inside. The thud was deafening, followed by silence.

Stunned, Sundari rubbed her wrist. Mata Gujri soothed Baby Fateh, who stirred in the blanket beside her. If there was anything she had learned from her husband's sacrifice, it was that there was more than one way to give one's head.

Guru Gobind emerged from the tent. He set his sword down on the earth and looked out at the crowd tenderly. For a moment, no one moved, transfixed in fear and awe. *Was he going to call for another head? Would he keep going until there was no one left?*

Time stood still. Then, Guru Gobind took a deep breath and, with one mighty swoop, tore away the door of the tent. The cloth fluttered to the earth. Standing before the people were all five Sikhs. They were alive. But they had changed. They were dressed in deep-blue robes with saffron sashes, and their faces were glowing, lit by the sun.

---

[*]   Guru Granth Sahib, ang 1412, Salok Vaara(n) te Vadheek, Guru Nanak Ji.

"These are my Panj Pyare," Guru Gobind announced. *My five be-loved ones.*

The crowd gazed up in awe at the scene. This was not annihilation; it was rebirth.

Guru Gobind called for water. An iron cauldron was set before him. He lifted a khanda, a double-edged sword, and stirred the cauldron as he recited Jap. Mata Gujri began to recite with him, and the people followed. He continued to sing Vaar Asa, and the rababis added their voices.

As they sang, a black crow swooped down from the sky and perched on the edge of the iron cauldron. The crow began to drink the water. Another crow came to join it, and the crows started to fight each other.

Sahib rose to her feet. Mata Gujri was about to pull her other daughter-in-law back, too, when she noticed patasay in her shawl, white sugary discs that she had brought for the children. She stepped forth and poured the patasay into the cauldron. Sahib stirred in the sugar, and the sweetness spread throughout the water. The crows stopped fighting and took flight.

The people watched in awe: Sahib was turning the water into amrit, sacred nectar infused with the sweetness of love *and* the strength of steel. As Sahib stirred, Mata Gujri, Jito, and Sundari raised their voices higher and sang with her.

"From here on, we will become Khalsa," announced Guru Gobind. *Khalsa. Beloved community, strength of steel, pure of heart.* "Mata Sahib, who sweetened the amrit, will be known as the Mother of the Khalsa."

Mata Sahib bowed.

Guru Gobind then turned to the five men who had spontaneously offered their lives, the Panj Pyare. He reached into the cauldron and sprinkled the sacred water on their heads and into their eyes. They recited after him:

Vaheguru Ji Ka Khalsa
Vaheguru Ji Ki Fateh

The beloved community (Khalsa) belongs to Divine Oneness
  (Vaheguru)
In that Oneness, all become victory (Fateh)

The five kneeled, cupped their hands, and drank from the same iron vessel as the first members of the Khalsa. They were rebirthed, and the people along with them. As they drank, Guru Gobind asked the people to shed their old names that signaled caste and clan, and take on new royal names. They would henceforth be known as *Singh* and *Kaur:* Singh means lion or warrior; Kaur means lioness, princess, or sovereign woman warrior. The Guru presented five articles of faith, five Kakkars, to wear on their body and show the world their commitment to embody the sage and the warrior.

"Because Sikhs never hide," he said, and looked at his mother, Mata Gujri, who gazed back with watery eyes.

The crowd studied the articles worn by the Panj Pyare. On their wrists, they each wore an iron bracelet, a *karra,* to remind them of their commitment every time they acted. Beneath their clothes, they wore a *kachhera,* a white undergarment, to remind them to make mindful and conscious choices with their body. Beneath their turbans, they kept their *kes,* long, uncut hair, to embrace the body as whole and sacred, just as it was. Tucked in their hair was a *kanga,* a wooden comb to remind them to be self-sufficient and care for their body. And each wore a *kirpan* at their side, a miniature sword that showed the world their commitment to stand for justice and protect those in need.

"Embrace one creed and leave behind the hierarchies between you and mix freely with one another," Guru Gobind declared. "Drink from the same cup. Eat from the same vessel. Feel no contempt for one another."

The Guru lifted his voice:

maanas kee jaat sabai ekai pahchaanbo
All of humankind is one caste, recognize each other as one[*]

***

[*] Dasam Granth, ang 17–20, Akaal Ustat, Guru Gobind Singh Ji.

Then, Guru Gobind folded his hands and kneeled before the Panj Pyare. They looked stunned. They had never seen their Guru surrender to anyone. Guru Gobind washed their feet, the way Guru Nanak had washed Guru Angad's feet. He transmitted his sovereignty not to any one person but to the body of the people. The five beloved ones lifted the iron vessel for the Guru to drink, and anointed him. Now there was no hierarchy among them, not even between them and their Guru.

The Guru stood and introduced himself no longer as Guru Gobind; he was Guru Gobind Singh.

"Who will become Khalsa today?" called out Guru Gobind Singh.

All across the mountainside, people stepped forth to be anointed. Hundreds of others picked up their belongings quietly and set out to leave. The rest stayed seated and watched. Those ready to become Khalsa formed one grand procession to take amrit from the Guru.

Mata Gujri watched as a young woman in two long braids appeared before the Guru. She was the first woman in the line.

"Tohada kee naam hai?" Guru Gobind Singh asked. *What is your name?*

The young woman's face shone with hope.

"Bhagbhari," she said. "My family calls me Bhago."

Bhago kneeled, and the Guru anointed her. The young woman ran back to her family and asked her father if she could stay in Anandpur. She wanted to train with the sword and become a warrior. As her father led her away, Mata Gujri heard the girl persist.

Mata Gujri looked back at her daughter-in-law Sundari, the one who was willing to offer her life. Sundari was breaking off the rest of the patasay to give to the children when they awoke. Mata Gujri kneeled by her side and reached for her wrist, gently this time, and placed a set of bright pearls threaded with gold in Sundari's palm.

"Mata Ji," implored Sundari, as if asking, "Why me?"

Mata Gujri hummed a shabd as she wrapped the pearl mala around Sundari's wrist:

jao tao prem khelan kaa chaao
sir(u) dhar talee galee meree aao

If you desire to play the game of love,
place your head on your palm and come my way *

Mata Sundari pressed the glittering pearls to her heart, her face wet with tears.

"Shakti vastay," said Mata Gujri. *For power.*

The drums pounded, and Baby Fateh awoke. His little cries awoke Zoraver, who was hungry. As she fed the children patasay, Mata Sundari felt a light sweetness throughout her whole body.

"Chalo chaliye," said Mata Gujri to the family. *Let's go.* It was time to oversee the langar. They would have many mouths to feed today.

NEWS OF THE SPECTACULAR SCENE IN ANANDPUR ON VAISAKHI DAY spread across Punjab. The birth of the Khalsa took hold as a powerful idea in people's hearts, and people of all castes and classes chose to take amrit. The neighboring hill chiefs grew threatened by the rise of a new power among them and attacked Guru Gobind Singh, bringing on the Battles of Nirmoh and Basoli. The hill chiefs were defeated. So they petitioned Emperor Aurangzeb, who sent his subedars, district governors of Sarhind and Lahore. The combined forces of the hill chiefs and the Mughal Empire waged all-out war on Anandpur.

Guru Gobind Singh defended Anandpur valiantly, but the hillmen and the armies of the Mughal Empire eventually encircled the mountain city. Anandpur was under siege. They stopped all food grains from coming in. Guru Gobind Singh evacuated most of the city to safety. Only his most loyal Sikhs remained, along with family, including his four sons. They stayed within the protection of the Red Fort, Qila Anandgarh.

Guru Gobind Singh's eldest sons, Ajit and Jujhar, seventeen and thirteen, joined the warriors in lightning forays across battle lines to find provisions. His youngest children, Fateh and Zoraver, five and

* Guru Granth Sahib, ang 1412, Salok Vaara(n) te Vadheek, Guru Nanak.

eight, clung to their grandmother Mata Gujri. The mother who birthed them, Mata Jito, had died shortly after Vaisakhi Day four years back. Mata Gujri was their world.

Every day, the children helped Mata Gujri distribute rations to the family and warriors, a quarter pound of corn each day. They steadied her as she descended the steps of the baoli, the underground stepwell, to retrieve water. They continued their daily lessons with her in music, poetry, and stories. And they played.

"Mainu labho!" called Fateh. *Come find me!* Zoraver ran around the fort looking for his little brother and found him hiding under Mata Gujri's long dupatta. Fateh rolled on the floor laughing; his musical voice filled the air. Mata Gujri gathered up the children and kissed their faces.

As the siege went on, the food stores diminished. Mata Gujri sent soldiers out to strip bark off the trees, and she baked it into bread. Soon they ate all the leaves and flowers within the city walls. Fateh's and Zoraver's bellies grew hollow, and their eyes sunken. When the children stopped playing, Mata Gujri grew worried.

Then, nearly a year into the siege, the warrior Maha Singh presented Guru Gobind Singh with a scroll. Mata Gujri watched hopefully. *Was it news from the world outside? Was it a letter promising reinforcements?* Guru Gobind Singh signed the paper and handed it back to the soldier, who scurried away like a mouse.

"What does it say?" she asked.

"Bedava," he replied. A document that renounced allegiance. The warrior Maha Singh had renounced his loyalty to the Guru; he was no longer a Sikh. If he successfully presented the signed document at enemy lines without being killed, he would be allowed safe passage out of the city.

"How hard to lose one," sighed Mata Gujri.

"Forty," he said. He was losing forty. The bedava was on behalf of forty Sikh warriors from the village Jhabal. They had all taken amrit and vowed to become Khalsa on Vaisakhi Day. But that was five years ago. Before the battles and bloodshed. Before their bellies were starved and death was all but assured.

Morale in the fort plummeted in the days that followed. Mata Gujri felt herself grow weak from starvation. She gave whatever roti she had to the children, who cried themselves to sleep. Soon the children were too weak to cry.

Shortly after the desertion of the forty warriors, a message arrived from Emperor Aurangzeb.

"Aurangzeb offers us safe passage out," Mata Gujri told the children, "if we leave the city forever."

"Can we trust it?" asked Zoraver hopefully.

"He says he vowed on the Quran," replied Mata Gujri. She showed them the Emperor's letter, along with a Quran that bore his signature.

The children helped Mata Gujri pack all their possessions onto carts, including a great wooden box that carried the Aadi Granth. When his family and warriors were ready, Guru Gobind Singh set fire to his stores and led the procession out of the fort, flanked by his eldest sons, Ajit and Jujhar. Mata Gujri mounted a horse with Fateh and Zoraver. Mata Sundari and Mata Sahib followed behind them. Together, they set out into the dark, moonless night.

An hour into the journey, her grandsons nodded off. Mata Gujri gripped the reins and made her arms stiff as guardrails to keep the boys from slipping. They passed the village Roparr and arrived at a mighty river. The River Sarsa was flooded from the winter rains.

The procession came to a halt. The night was still except for an owl screeching in the darkness. Guru Gobind Singh gave the signal to cross the river. The warrior in front of Mata Gujri steered his horse into the water. Her horse followed. As they slowly waded in, her feet touched the cold, stinging water.

Mata Gujri took a deep breath and looked at the stars above her. Her star friends. She made out the tiger, the rabab, the hawk. Her first companions, watching her, always watching.

A dark flash zoomed across the sky, and then another. *Bats? Bats don't whistle as they fly past.* The warrior on the horse in front of her slumped over. *Was he asleep?* His body slid into the water.

There was a deafening roar—the cry of a thousand men—and a rain of arrows fell around her. Conches bellowed. Her horse lunged; the children awoke and screamed. No one could hear their screams above the battle cries of the soldiers, the rain of arrows, and the roar of the river.

Guru Gobind Singh called out a battle cry and swung his sword at the dark mass charging at him across the river. Ajit and Jujhar were by their father's side. The soldiers descending on them wore imperial garb. It was an ambush.

The great wooden box that carried the Aadi Granth plunged into the river. Mata Gujri cried out as the manuscript that carried all their sacred wisdom disappeared in the depths.

An arrow flew over her, missed Fateh, and pierced her horse's head. The horse heaved. Mata Gujri plunged into the icy river. The waters closed over her. She reached for the surface and gasped for air. *Are they drowning?* She searched for her grandsons and spotted them in shallow water. Fateh and Zoraver cried out to her. She pulled the children to their feet and ran—away from the screams and arrows, through the icy water, until the chaos faded behind them. When she could not hear the roar of the battle anymore, they climbed onto the bank and lay on the sand, out of breath.

Cold and weak, Mata Gujri looked up at the night sky, stunned they were still alive. Suddenly, a shadow blocked the stars.

"Mata Ji."

She knew the voice.

"Gangu?"

Gangu had served their family in Anandpur, brought them meals, and helped her put the children to sleep. He had somehow escaped.

"The Guru charged me with your safety," he said. "Follow me."

Mata Gujri gripped her boys, who were shivering, and they followed Gangu into the deep night. She put one foot in front of the other, her mind set on one objective: to keep these children alive and moving. At the break of dawn, they arrived at a village.

"Mai(n) aaiya," said Gangu. *I'll be right back*. He disappeared into a large house. They waited outside, cold and hungry. When Gangu emerged, he stayed back and stared at the ground. Something was wrong. Suddenly, someone grabbed her arms from behind. Soldiers wrestled the children into chains.

"Gangu!"

Gangu did not look at her. He fidgeted with a money pouch in his hands.

The soldiers shackled Mata Gujri and the boys at the ankles and dragged them into a tall, cold, stone tower. The soldiers chained them and left. Mata Gujri crawled on her knees to Fateh and Zoraver, who cried into her chest. The three of them made one sobbing body against the wall. The children's clothes were ragged from thrashing through the forest, their faces hollow from starvation, their eyes wide with shock. Mata Gujri took a deep breath. She recited their father's epic battle cry of a poem, Deh Siva. As the children sang with her, their bodies calmed.

deh siva bar mohe ihai
subh karman te kabhoo(n) naa ttaro

Oh Beloved, give me this one gift:
May I never hold back from doing good[*]

When the children were too tired and cold to sing, Mata Gujri hummed Sohila, the nightly prayer, until they drifted to sleep. She shivered, even as she tried to keep them warm. It was the dead of winter, and cold north winds blew down from the Himalayan mountains and whipped through the tower. She gazed up through the open arches of the cold tower, this Thanda Burj. She saw the night sky, the whirling stars she knew so well. If her son survived the ambush, he would come for them.

MATA GUJRI AWOKE WITH HER ARMS WRAPPED AROUND FATEH AND Zoraver. Someone was watching them. He wore an imperial uniform. The soldier unshackled the boys and told them to follow him. The chil-

---

[*]   Dasam Granth, ang 98, Chandi Charitar Ukat Bilas, Guru Gobind Singh Ji.

dren looked back at her longingly. She nodded at them and pulled herself to the window. The soldier led the boys into another building. She waited and watched. After an hour, the children were led back up the tower.

"It was a court," said Zoraver.

"But the door was so small!" cried Fateh, jumping up and down.

"They wanted us to bow down low to go through the door," said Zoraver. "They were tricking us to bow to them!"

"But we didn't bow, Dadi Ji!" exclaimed little Fateh. "We went in feet first!"

"When we got inside, we folded our hands like this," said Zoraver. "And we said, 'Vaheguru Ji Ka Khalsa, Vaheguru Ji Ki Fateh!'"

It was the greeting their father had taught them, the words that bound them to their ancestors and way of being. A declaration of victory.

"Shaabash!" Mata Gujri praised her grandsons. "Then what happened?"

"They wanted us to renounce our father," said Zoraver. "They offered us riches."

"But we said no, Dadi Ji!" cried little Fateh.

"They got angry and said they will . . ." Zoraver glanced at his little brother, ". . . not let us leave."

Mata Gujri drew her boys to her and kissed them. They had done well. If the officials had set up a court, then they were at least making a show of the rule of law. And no law condoned harm to small children: Fateh was five years old; Zoraver was eight.

"Chalo, let's sing your father's shabd," she said. They sang Deh Siva together and drifted to sleep to the song of courage.

A few hours later, Mata Gujri awoke in the dead of night to the sound of a hoarse whisper.

"Mata Ji!" someone called out.

She peered out of the tower. A tree below her swayed.

"Ji?" she called out. *Was it Guru Gobind Singh? Was it her son?*

"Dudh," cried the man. He tossed up a tumbler of milk and two cups.

"Shukar hai," said Mata Gujri as she caught them. *Thank you.*

"Keep faith!" cried the man. His name was Moti Ram Mehra. "We are working for your release!"

Days passed and hours blurred together. The boys were taken away from time to time into the court, tested, and returned. Their visitor brought milk in the dead of night. She sang to the children and told them stories. Someone was always stirring her awake.

"Guru Gobind Singh?" she said. "Puttar?"

A soldier was unshackling the chains and leading the children to the door. Mata Gujri reached out to them as they disappeared. She looked down from the tower. The imperial soldier pushed the children into a clearing where a large crowd had gathered.

Zoraver folded his hands, and Fateh followed. They called out:

Vaheguru Ji Ka Khalsa
Vaheguru Ji Ki Fateh

The beloved community belongs to Divine Oneness
In that Oneness, all become victory

"Renounce!" a voice bellowed.

A man emerged from the shadows in an adorned imperial dress: the Nawab Wazir Khan, one of the most loyal and zealous officials of the Emperor. The boys looked at each other. They had done this before. They shook their heads no.

"Renounce," the Nawab yelled again, "and you will receive riches and honors and anything your heart desires."

Mata Gujri watched as the children were once again asked to renounce their allegiance to their father and ancestors, to swear they were not Sikh anymore, and to bow down to the Emperor as their only chance for freedom.

Zoraver took his little brother's hand in his and they both shook their heads.

"Renounce or you will die!" shouted the Nawab.

This time, Fateh recited a shabd of the sage-poet Bhagat Kabir:

kabir jis marnae te jag ddarai mere man aanand
marnae hee te paaeeai pooran parmaanand

Oh Kabir, the world fears death, yet ecstasy fills my mind
Only in death do we merge completely in eternal ecstasy*

Nawab Wazir Khan curled his lip in fury and nodded to a shadow in the crowd. A large man charged at the children with a brick. Mata Gujri cried out.

THUD!

The man threw the brick down in front of the children in a cloud of dust. He then returned with another brick and another. Others joined him. One by one, the men lay down bricks until the boys were encircled. Fateh and Zoraver stood tall and held each other as the bricks grew higher, front and back. They recited "Vaheguru."

When the bricks reached their eyes, the sneering faces in the crowd disappeared. Fateh and Zoraver looked up. Above them was the pale morning sky and the stone tower, and within the tower, they saw their grandmother. And she saw them. Her face was contorted in grief, but when their eyes met hers, her expression went soft, and she began to recite Jap, Guru Nanak's song of Oneness.

Mata Gujri smiled and nodded and recited. The children recited with her and lifted their voices louder and louder. The crowd stirred uncomfortably. The Nawab grew angry and called for his soldiers to move faster. But the children's sweet voices reached the ears of everyone there, and filled their grandmother's chest.

Mata Gujri kept her gaze on them as they sang. Fateh's eyes were wide, and his little face shone with sweat and light; Zoraver's jaw trembled but his voice was loud and strong. They rested their eyes on their grandmother as the bricks grew higher, and their song grew louder. The bricks started to close over them, until only one small gap was left—one final brick. Mata Gujri fixed her eyes on the children and they recited together the final line of Jap:

* Guru Granth Sahib, ang 1365, Salok, Bhagat Kabir Ji.

nanak te mukh ujalay
ketee chhuttee naal

Oh Nanak! Their faces are radiant
And many more are freed with them!*

Fateh stood on his toes to see his grandmother one last time, and
Zoraver hugged his brother and began to close his eyes. The last brick
slid into the gap—and they were gone.

Mata Gujri let herself fall to the ground. Her body convulsed and
shivered. The air was running out of the brick tomb below her, and the
air was running out of her lungs, and all she could feel was the hard
stone floor. She lay there for hours in a half-death.

The sky went dark. Mata Gujri awoke from the sound of bricks top-
pling to the earth. She pulled herself up and peered into the night.
There was a hole in the brick tomb. Someone was dragging the children out. Their eyes were closed. Fateh's sweet round face still seemed
to radiate light; Zoraver looked noble even in his sleep. The man who
pulled them out rested his fingers on their pulses. Mata Gujri gripped
the stone ledge.

The man gently cupped Fateh's round face. A cloud shifted. The
light of the moon fell on a dagger in the man's hand. He slit Fateh's
throat. Fateh's body dropped with a sickening thud. Then the man slit
Zoraver's throat, too. His body fell atop his brother's.

The Nawab stepped out from the shadows, arms folded, and nodded at his executioner.

Mata Gujri fell back onto the stone floor and stared at the sky. The
moon looked back at her, round as Fateh's face when he was singing.
They used to sing in the Guru's court together. She used to sing under
the stars with her husband as he drummed, before he rode into the fog
to make his body a shield, before his eyelids melted in the fire. The
same stars were watching her now. The constellations that kept her

---

* Guru Granth Sahib, ang 8, Jap, Guru Nanak Ji.

company when she was a girl. There was the tiger, the rabab, the hawk. *How do you turn sparrows into hawks?*

She gazed into the cloud of stars and saw the shape of Bibi Veero, the great lady with the swan neck riding toward her on horseback, her gold dupatta rippling behind her like a banner. She would have died a comfortable death in Bakala if she had just sent Bibi Veero on her way. But Bibi Veero was reaching out to her now, offering her a bright pearl mala, and the pearls shone in the starlight. Would she accept the gift? Mata Gujri reached out to accept. And she would accept again and again, in every eternity. Bibi Veero dissolved into a milky cloud of stars, and Mata Gujri breathed *Vah* in awe.

In that cold, desolate tower, as her grandchildren's bodies lay below, Mata Gujri closed her eyes and her body lifted into the air. The wind rushed past her as she fell into the heavens and into the stars.

Aao chaa peelo . . .
Come, let's have tea . . .

. . .

REDEFINING VICTORY

SOME SAY MATA GUJRI WAS THROWN OUT OF THE TOWER WHERE SHE was imprisoned, others that she fell. All agree that she died of grief after watching her grandchildren executed. When Guru Gobind Singh learned what had happened to them, he wrote a famous letter to Emperor Aurangzeb, 111 poetic verses in Persian, called the Zafarnama. It means the Epistle of Victory. The Emperor broke his promise of safe passage, ambushed the Guru's family at the River Sarsa, executed the Guru's youngest sons, and imprisoned his mother, who passed away in custody. Yet Guru Gobind declared victory to the Emperor: *You killed my family, you lay ruin to my city, you pursue me in the night. But you broke your oath to Allah. So, who does victory belong to?**

"Fateh," the word for victory, was also the name of the Guru's five-year-old son. In his response, Guru Gobind Singh redefined victory—not what we produce but *who we are*. I wondered: When the world feels like it is ending, what is victory?

On our travels, we decided to retrace the steps of Guru Gobind Singh's youngest sons—from the clearing in Anandpur where Sikhs became the Khalsa on Vaisakhi Day, to the fort where they lived under siege, to the River Sarsa where they were ambushed and betrayed, to the tower where they were imprisoned with Mata Gujri. We began in Anandpur and ended in Fatehgarh—from "the city of joy" to "the home of victory."

---

*   Dasam Granth, Zafarnama, Guru Gobind Singh Ji.

INVITATION TO REBIRTH

OUR FIRST STOP WAS THE PLACE IN ANANDPUR WHERE GURU Gobind Singh birthed the Khalsa. It is the second most revered site in the Sikh world, after the Golden Temple in Amritsar. On this spot, Guru Gobind Singh established the Khalsa on Vaisakhi Day on March 30, 1699. The day is emblazoned in Sikh consciousness, the story told and retold as the essence of who Sikhs are today. While scholars debate exactly what took place that Vaisakhi Day of 1699, what is certain is that Guru Gobind Singh established the Khalsa as a spiritual community and concretized the sage warrior path. Eighty thousand Sikhs gathered to listen to the Guru, twenty thousand took amrit that day, and sixty thousand took amrit over the next few days. Inside Gurdwara Takht Kesgarh Sahib, there are swords that belonged to Guru Gobind Singh, including a khanda, the kind of double-edged sword that he used to prepare amrit in the iron cauldron.

As we explored the grounds, Ananda plopped down between marigolds in the marble courtyard of the gurdwara. Just behind her was a splendid vista that overlooked Anandpur. The sun was a bloodred orb sinking into the mist over the city and the Shivalik Hills. I wanted to show her the spectacular view, but she was asking for snacks, and we had eaten them all. She began to cry. I carried her in my arms as she pulled on my neck.

In the Vaisakhi story, the five beloved ones who volunteered that day, the Panj Pyare, were all men. *Why weren't any of them women?* I always wondered. *Where were they?* As I bounced my daughter on my hip, I imagined all the women who gathered on this hillside that Vaisakhi Day of 1699: They were nursing babies. They were chasing toddlers who ran after butterflies. They were soothing children with fevers. They were preparing the massive langar and rolling atta for thousands of rotis. They were ensuring everyone was fed, warm, and safe. The mothers and grandmothers and sisters and elders were already doing what the Guru was asking of us: offering up their lives for love.

I like to imagine that Mata Sundari wanted to volunteer that Vaisakhi Day, but Mata Gujri held her back. Why? She had already given her head. They all had. Bibi Nanki cared for Guru Nanak's children as her own; Mata Khivi devoted forty years of her life to langar; Bibi Bhani held the realm together even as her children fractured; Mata Ganga led the resistance after her husband, Guru Arjan, was executed; Bibi Veero steered her family through decades of loss; Mata Krishan held her small child through life and death; Mata Gujri sacrificed her beloved Guru Tegh Bahadur and raised her son and grandchildren as sage warriors. The women ancestors in these stories gave their heads without title or recognition. The bards did not compose elaborate ballads praising their names; historians did not devote reams of parchment to their labors. Any poems they composed were not preserved. Only Mata Khivi is mentioned in scripture, for her rice pudding. As I hugged my daughter, I wondered: *Could they have imagined us?* These women gave their life and labor for a future they would not live to see.

Spiritual leaders in history often talk about annihilating their egos. I think that's because most of them never birthed or mothered or engaged in constant caregiving, day after day. The choice to love that deeply is not experienced as annihilation but transition—a surrender of one's old identity and an embrace of a new way of being, where you are no longer singular but multiple. When my first child was born and landed in my arms, one of my first thoughts was: *I would give my life for you.* It was spontaneous. Not annihilation. To love with your whole heart is an act of surrender. I raised my hand to volunteer, and my Beloved took me into the tent, and it was a birthing tent. In the dark of the tent, I was rebirthed into a new way of being.

The Vaisakhi story is particular to the Sikh tradition—it is the birth of a specific community, the moment many of our ancestors committed to the Khalsa path and set forth a lineage and set of practices that continue today. The Vaisakhi story is also universal: It is a way to think about what it means for *all* of us to love and serve as sage warriors.

No matter who we are, what body we are in, or whether we birth or parent, the sage warrior path invites us to love with our head in our palm. The Guru's tent is a birthing tent. *Not the darkness of the tomb; the darkness of the womb.* It is an invitation to rebirth.

Every springtime, my Sikh sisters and I gather our children on the grass to hear the Vaisakhi story. When I tell the story, the children are the ones in the clearing who hear the Guru's call. Instead of: *Who among you will give your head for the Guru?* I say: *Who among you will give your whole life to love and serve others?* I shift the focus from death to life. It is an appropriate edit for small children, and perhaps the rest of us, too. The deeper teaching in the story is to surrender to love *all* the days of your life, rather than just one. The children raise their hands eagerly to volunteer, and one by one, they disappear behind my grandmother's phulkari, which is the Guru's tent. At the end of the story, I drop the phulkari and the children reappear, delighted to surprise the audience. "Here they are!" I announce. "But they are changed." The children fold their hands together and sing Guru Gobind Singh's song of victory as Kavi plays the tabla:

deh siva bar mohe ihai
subh karman te kabhoo(n) naa ttaro

Oh Beloved, give me this one gift:
May I never hold back from doing good*

"What do you feel in your body?" I ask the children after they sing. "Joy!" They beam.

If they know what victory feels like in their bodies, perhaps they will be able to find it inside them, even when the world becomes terrifying.

RETRACING STEPS

AFTER WE VISITED THE BIRTHPLACE OF THE KHALSA, OUR NEXT STOP was the fort where Guru Gobind Singh's family lived during the year-long siege of Anandpur in 1704. The fort Qila Anandgarh had been rebuilt, but the original baoli is preserved—the same underground

---

*   Dasam Granth, ang 98, Chandi Charitar Ukat Bilas, Guru Gobind Singh Ji.

stepwell the Guru's family used for water. My grandfather Papa Ji once brought me here when I was a girl. He was frail, but he insisted on going down all 135 steps of the baoli to touch the sacred water; I held him steady as he went down. I imagined Mata Gujri descending these very steps in her old age, steadied by her grandchildren Baba Fateh and Baba Zoraver. I explained to the children that it was from this fort that the Guru's family journeyed into the night on the promise of safe passage.

The children nodded cheerfully. So far, the story wasn't too scary.

Our next stop was the River Sarsa, where the Guru's family and warriors were ambushed the night of December 20, 1704. We drove the same distance the Guru's family had traveled on horseback and arrived at the place they were attacked. Here stands Gurdwara Parivar Vichhora, which honors all who were killed in the icy waters that night. We walked onto a bridge.

"This is the River of Betrayal," I said. "Here is where the Guru's youngest sons were separated from their parents." The sky was gray, and we were chilled to the bone. Below us, a trickle of water wound through a riverbed filled with bramble and bush; after decades of water pollution and climate change, the river is just a fraction of what it once was. The children waited in the car as I finished my sketch.

We had one last stop of the day.

"Do you think he can handle it?" I asked my husband.

"I do," he said.

We reached the town of Sarhind, the place where Mata Gujri and her grandchildren were imprisoned in a cold tower. Baba Zoraver and Baba Fateh were bricked alive here on December 26, 1704. After their execution, the town was renamed after Fateh and became Fatehgarh, the Place of Victory.

Happy pulled the car into the parking lot. Sharat played with Ananda in the car, where they had a snack party of Indian potato chips. As Kavi and I walked up to Gurdwara Fatehgarh Sahib, I realized that my children were almost the same age as Baba Fateh and Baba Zoraver had been when they were executed. I held Kavi's hand tight.

We had visited so many gurdwaras across Punjab, we called Kavi a gurdwara expert. He washed his hands and feet before entering, folded his hands before the Guru Granth Sahib, offered rupees, and bowed. He circumambulated the Guru Granth Sahib clockwise, paused halfway to bow again, and cupped his hands to receive prashaad. Kavi made his round and looked around: The prashaad was not in the usual place.

I spotted a doorway in the inner sanctum that led downstairs. We went down to an underground level where crowds of people bowed before the Guru Granth Sahib under a gold dome, Gurdwara Bhora Sahib. On either side of the dome was a preserved brick wall, literally the same brick wall that had suffocated the children.

"This is where the children were executed," I said to Kavi quietly.

I was about to say something more. But nothing came.

"It's sad," I finally said.

"Yeah," Kavi said. And we just let ourselves be sad together.

As we stepped outside, he whispered: "Mommy, we didn't get prashaad!"

We went back inside the gurdwara, bowed and retraced our steps, and still could not find the prashaad. We found ourselves outside again.

"Mommy, look!" Kavi pointed to a tall structure topped by a gold dome in the shape of a lotus. It was a tower—the same tower Mata Gujri and the children had been trapped in, Thanda Burj. It had been turned into a gurdwara in her memory: Gurdwara Burj Mata Gujri.

"That's where their Dadi Ji died," I said.

"So close!" he said as he looked back at where the brick wall stood.

"Yeah," I said. "She must have watched it happen."

"What happened to her?" asked Kavi.

"Well, she was so sad, she died right then, too."

"But that doesn't make sense," Kavi said. "How, Mommy? How can someone die like that?"

We walked to the tower, pulled by the music drifting toward us. As we bowed, I imagined Mata Gujri's final moments here. Mata Gujri spent a lifetime cultivating the sage within her and exhibited warrior-courage in the face of life and death. I imagined the stars through the open archways. Victory is to live and die resting in one's deepest wisdom, the portal to the infinite. In those final moments, I'm convinced that Mata Gujri was sovereign. She was victory.

As we exited, Kavi spotted a little stall in the courtyard.

"I knew we would have prashaad!" he said.

As we took the warm, sweet prashaad in our hands, Kavi beamed like the sun. He finished every morsel. Even here, on this site of so much sadness, there was still music all around us, and the taste of sweetness.

As we walked back to the car, I knew that we would be back here in a few years to tell Ananda the story, too.

WHAT IS VICTORY

TODAY BABA FATEH AND BABA ZORAVER ARE KNOWN AS THE *CHHOTE Sahibzaade,* the Little Princes. Every year on December 26, Sikhs honor the anniversary of the children's shaheedi, martyrdom. The boys filled the tomb of bricks with song and prayer, held each other, and became indomitable, unbroken, even when their throats were slashed. So that hundreds of years later, we still hear their song.

The visitor who served them milk in the tower was Moti Ram Mehra, a servant in the kitchen. When imperial soldiers found out what he had done, they sentenced Moti Ram Mehra—along with his mother, his wife, and his young son—to death. Their bodies were smashed through an oil press, a kohlu. There is a gurdwara in Fatehgarh on the place where they died. It displays the two large cups he used to serve the milk. An embodiment of mercy and courage.

This story has happened many times before. It's happening now. Every day, we see promises of safe passage broken. Every day, we watch children killed in a rubble of bricks. Every day, we die of a broken heart. A thousand Fatehs and Zoravers. And every day, we have a choice: Who do we wish to be in the story? Do we follow orders and pass along the bricks? Do we stand back and watch from the crowd? Do we offer milk in the dead of night? Do we dare to sing from the cold tower, so that our song can be heard generations from now?

Victory is in the song.

MY GRANDFATHER'S FINAL LESSON

WHEN I THINK OF WHAT VICTORY LOOKS LIKE, I SEE MY GRANDFA-
ther Papa Ji on his deathbed. He gazed at each of his children around
him, sighed, and died. I thought he left me without teaching me the
secret to his fearlessness, but his final lesson was his example. "Be like
me; be better than me!" Papa Ji used to say. If I wanted to die like him,
I had to practice. So I developed a nighttime meditation.

Every night, when I rest my head on the pillow, the Wise Woman in
me says: *Think of today as an entire lifetime. What was the most joyful
part? What was the hardest part? What are you grateful for in this lifetime?*
Finally, she asks: *Are you ready to let go of this lifetime?* Each night, I
practice dying. Each morning, when I wake up, it is a gift. A rebirth. I
wake with my children and we say to each other:

I get to be *alive.*
I get to be alive *today.*
I get to be alive today *with you.*

I don't tell them that they will be safe today. Or that everything will
be okay today. I tell them that *we get to be alive* today. And that alone is
wondrous and good. We get to decide how we experience life today, no
matter what comes. We get to decide *who we will be* today.

Just recently, after sixteen years of this practice, I realized that my
personal nightly meditation mirrors the meaning of the song-prayer
Sohila, what Papa Ji listened to every night. In Sohila, death is a wedding day, a return to the Oneness that always is. It is ancestral wisdom
for how to become victory: Every night, practice dying. Every morning, embrace the gift of a new lifetime.

LAST STOP IN ANANDPUR

ON OUR LAST NIGHT IN THE MOUNTAIN CITY OF ANANDPUR, WE
wandered the marketplaces around Gurdwara Kesgarh Sahib, the place
where the Khalsa was born.

"Mommy, kirpans!" Since Kavi was four, he has been asking me for a kirpan, a sacred miniature sword, one of the articles of faith.

Sharat nodded. Jasso talked to the storekeeper, who presented a hundred varieties.

"How do I choose?" Kavi asked me brightly.

"It will choose you," I said.

Kavi carefully studied dozens of tiny ornate kirpans. They were all engraved with animals or stars or diamonds. Finally, he held up a beautiful black kirpan with a leopard on the hilt, emblazoned with silver. The body strap he chose was marigold with gold flowers. Kavi slipped it on and smiled.

"What about you, Mommy?"

"Me?" I wore a karra, a steel bracelet, and had kept my hair long my whole life, but I had never owned a kirpan. I never knew how to reclaim my warrior heritage. But our sojourn across Punjab was changing that.

I chose a kirpan that matched Kavi's. Ananda tugged on my sleeve and held up a tiny mala. Not for herself, but for me. We walked out of the marketplace of Anandpur with the kirpan and the mala—the sage in the warrior, the warrior in the sage.

SAGE WARRIOR,
BECOME VICTORY . . .

BEYOND THE ENDLESS CYCLE OF winning and losing, there is field of being. This is where the sage warrior resides.

Who you are—not what you do—defines victory. You become victory when you boldly walk into the hot winds of the world with the eyes of a sage and the heart of a warrior. Every night offers a chance for renewal. Before you go to sleep, invite the wisest part of you to step forward and say:

Think of today as an entire lifetime,
with a beginning, middle, and end.
Let the day flash before your eyes and imagine
that it's a lifetime in itself.

What was the hardest part of this lifetime?
Notice how you overcame that hardship to get
to the end of the day.

What was the most joyful part of this lifetime?
Notice what joy feels like in your body.

What are you grateful for in this lifetime?
Notice what gratitude feels like in your body.

Are you willing to let go of this lifetime?
Are you willing to embrace what you did in
this life as enough?
Are you willing to die a kind of death?
If you want to think a few more thoughts, go ahead.
When you are ready, take a deep breath in
and consciously let go.

ANCESTOR TREE

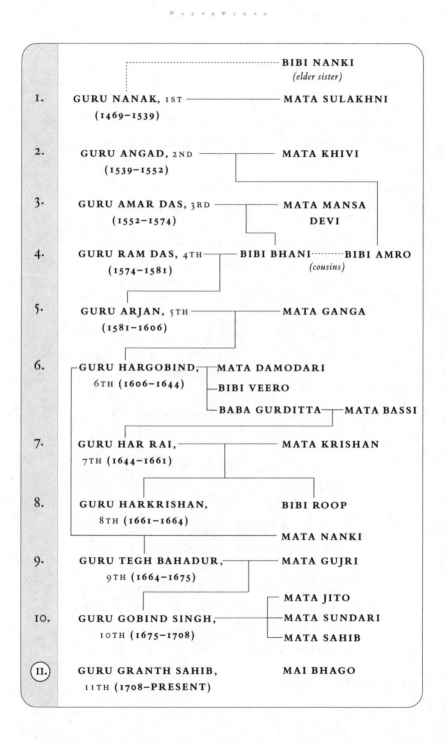

BIBI NANKI
(elder sister)

1. GURU NANAK, 1ST ———— MATA SULAKHNI
   (1469–1539)

2. GURU ANGAD, 2ND ———— MATA KHIVI
   (1539–1552)

3. GURU AMAR DAS, 3RD ———— MATA MANSA
   (1552–1574)   DEVI

4. GURU RAM DAS, 4TH —— BIBI BHANI ········ BIBI AMRO
   (1574–1581)   *(cousins)*

5. GURU ARJAN, 5TH ———— MATA GANGA
   (1581–1606)

6. GURU HARGOBIND, — MATA DAMODARI
   6TH (1606–1644) — BIBI VEERO
                    — BABA GURDITTA — MATA BASSI

7. GURU HAR RAI, ———— MATA KRISHAN
   7TH (1644–1661)

8. GURU HARKRISHAN, ———— BIBI ROOP
   8TH (1661–1664)
                    ———— MATA NANKI

9. GURU TEGH BAHADUR, — MATA GUJRI
   9TH (1664–1675)

                    — MATA JITO
10. GURU GOBIND SINGH, — MATA SUNDARI
    10TH (1675–1708)   — MATA SAHIB

11. GURU GRANTH SAHIB,   MAI BHAGO
    11TH (1708–PRESENT)

PART II

EMBRACE
REBIRTH

I. THE NEW:

THE STORY OF MAI BHAGO,

MATA SUNDARI, AND THE

GURU GRANTH SAHIB

. . .

ON THE WINTER NIGHT EMPEROR AURANGZEB BROKE HIS PROMISE
and ambushed Guru Gobind Singh's family at the River Sarsa, the
family was split into three. Mata Gujri and her youngest grandsons
were delivered into the hands of the Empire, and perished. The Guru's
wives Mata Sundari and Mata Sahib escaped and found the trusted
scholar-warrior Bhai Mani Sahib, and the three of them traveled to safe
harbor in Delhi. Guru Gobind Singh was driven into the wilderness,
along with his two eldest sons, Ajit and Jujhar, the Panj Pyare, and a
band of warriors who had survived the ambush. They came upon the
village Chamkaur, and took up defense in a mud fortress, Budhi Chand
Ravat.

Shortly after, ten thousand imperial soldiers appeared in Chamkaur
and surrounded the fort. Ten thousand against four dozen Sikh warriors. The Guru's warriors quickly exhausted their meager stock of
arrows and ammunition. The air was still for a moment. Suddenly, five
Sikh warriors emerged from the fort with their swords and spears and
charged into the mass of ten thousand imperial soldiers. They were immediately cut down. A moment later, another batch of five Sikh warriors appeared and charged the soldiers, and were struck down. Each
new batch of five warriors charged to their deaths, until there were
only a handful left inside the fort.

Ajit and Jujhar turned to their father and urged him to flee. *Our
people need you alive.* The remaining warriors agreed. The Guru had
transferred his sovereignty into the body of his people on Vaisakhi
Day; he was required to honor their will. They had him exchange
clothes with the loyal warrior Sant Singh, who put on the Guru's garb.

Ajit and Jujhar touched their father's feet in respect and asked him for permission to fight. The Guru drew them close and kissed them on their foreheads. The boys, along with Sant Singh and two of the Panj Pyare, formed the final batch of five warriors. They exited the fort and charged onto the battlefield. All five were struck down. Jujhar was thirteen; Ajit was seventeen. When the imperial soldiers killed the warrior who was disguised as the Guru, they gave a full-throated cry of victory: "We killed the Guru of the Sikhs! The Sikh realm is ours!"

As they shouted in glee, Guru Gobind Singh slipped out of the fortress and followed the North Star into the wilderness; the diamond-star was his guide. He wandered the Machhivara jungle alone. He avoided the rivers and took cover in thick jungle. The forest was filled with leopards, wild boar, antelope, and snakes. He sheltered in bushes. He ate berries. His shoes tore in the thick bramble, and his feet bled as he stumbled forth barefoot through the forest. In that dark wilderness, he raised his eyes to the moon and composed a song of divine love for the Beloved.

> *mitr pyare noo(n) haal mureedaa(n) da kehna*
> *tudh bin rog, rajaiyaa da oddan naag nivaasaa de rehna*
> *sool surahee khanjar piyalaa bing kasaiyaa de sehna*
> *yaararre da sanoo(n) sathar changa*
> *bhatth kherriyaa da rehna*

Tell our Beloved Friend the plight of the devoted!
Without You:
the comforter is diseased
the house, infested with cobras
the pitcher, a spike
the cup, a dagger
like bearing the butcher's blows
Resting on the ground of my dearest Friend is good
the mansion, a furnace[*]

---

[*]   Dasam Granth, ang 709, Shabd Hajaray Patsahi 10—Khyaal, Guru Gobind Singh Ji.

Guru Gobind Singh emerged from the forest into the village Lamma-Jatpura. He drank from a well using a tind, a clay pot, and slept under a great jand tree with the pot as his pillow. His three remaining Panj Pyare—Mani Singh, Daya Singh, and Dharam Singh—found him under the tree, having journeyed through the jungle and survived. Reunited, they traveled on to the village Dina with the help of two Muslims who disguised the Guru as their sage. In Dina, the Guru wrote a letter to Emperor Aurangzeb, a Zafarnama declaring spiritual victory. Shortly after, imperial forces deciphered his location and the Guru was on the move again.

As the imperial army pursued Guru Gobind Singh across Punjab, the song of divine love he sang in the dark wilderness spread from village to village, as one candle lights another.

A YOUNG WOMAN WITH BRONZE SKIN AND A THICK BRAID PACED THE fields outside the village Jhabal, her fingers calloused from swordplay. She carried a long spear, a sangh, on her back. Listless, she gazed at the horizon. It had been a year since her father, her husband, and her two brothers had left home to fight in Guru Gobind Singh's army. She had heard about the siege of Anandpur, the ambush at the River Sarsa, the Battle of Chamkaur, and the Guru's escape out of the wilderness. But she did not know what had become of her family.

As the sun set over the fields, Bhago saw soldiers on horseback riding toward her. *The Emperor's men?* She looked again and recognized their faces. She ran to her father, husband, and brothers and embraced them. They tumbled off their horses, exhausted and sallow-faced. She asked how they had prevailed. Maha Singh, the one who led them, did not look her in the eye. Only her husband, Nidhan Singh, whispered to her as she held him upright. They were starving under siege in Anandpur and could not go on. They found a way to come home.

"When will you return?" she breathed.

"Bedava," whispered her husband, and he signed the air with a quill. Forty of them had signed a document that renounced their allegiance to Guru Gobind Singh. There was no going back.

They entered a clearing in the village, and all the women and children of Jhabal rushed out to embrace the men they had sent to war. Her mother cupped her sons' faces and kissed them.

Bhago left to bring them water from the well. Her jaw was clenched. She thought of Guru Gobind Singh alone in the wilderness, his children martyred, his warriors gone, his city lost, yet he lifted his face to the moon and sang.

Bhago slipped into her family's hut. Her heart beat in her ears like a drum; she unlocked a chest.

A few moments later, the people of Jhabal heard the sound of galloping. They peered through the great cloud of dust. *Who is coming for us—the Emperor's men? The Guru's men?* As the dust settled, a figure rose before them on horseback. A woman held the reins of a great bronze horse. She was dressed in a blue warrior's dress with a saffron sash, her long hair tied in a turban. She held a sword in her hand. There was fire in her eyes.

"Bhago?" her mother whispered.

"I am going to the Guru," declared Bhago for all to hear.

The people were frozen on the spot. Her brothers sighed. Her husband looked at his hands. Only her father held her gaze.

"You will return to the battlefield." Bhago addressed the men. "I will lead you."

The wind rustled in the trees, and the men did not move. Bhago locked eyes with her father. Malo Shah did not let his daughter stay in Anandpur after she took amrit on Vaisakhi Day, but he trained her in the art of Shastar Vidya and taught her how to wield a sword. Now, she was the warrior who was fighting him. No, leading him. *Why wasn't he saying anything?*

Slowly, a grandmother in the clearing stepped forward and hung her bangles on the door of her mud hut. Bhago's mother followed, and another woman. Some threw their bangles to the ground. Others returned wearing their brothers' warrior dresses. All the women and girls made a circle behind Bhago, who kept her eyes on her father.

Malo Shah shook as if waking from a great slumber, called out a jaikara, a shout of praise, and stepped forth to stand with his daughter. Bhago's husband, Nidhan Singh, followed, along with her brothers, Dilbagh Singh and Bhag Singh. In a few moments, the rest of the men stepped forward, and the air filled with jaikaras. The forty men who had abandoned the Guru vowed to ride with the woman warrior, and follow her into battle.

Bhago rode with the forty warriors toward Khidrana, where the imperial army was likely to stop for water in their pursuit of the Guru. They sent messengers ahead to coordinate with the Guru's forces. When they arrived at Lake Khidrana, they covered the bushes with white sheets, to give the impression of a large contingent, and waited in the fog.

Through the mist, Bhago spotted Guru Gobind Singh on horseback on a mound that overlooked the lake. He wore gold-tipped arrows at his back. The Guru was still as stone. Bhago thought back to the misted Shivalik Hills on Vaisakhi Day, the day she took her vow by the Guru's hand. She met the eyes of her father and brothers, who bowed to her. She glanced at her husband, who nodded back at her. A vast serenity overtook her.

Suddenly, Guru Gobind Singh raised his arm and gave the signal. The sky filled with a thousand arrows raining down on a mass of imperial soldiers that appeared in the fog. Bhago heard a roar and saw bloodthirsty faces rushing toward her. She took a breath, raised her sword, and cried a jaikara. As the forty warriors met her battle cry, Bhago charged and led them onto the battlefield.

The wind roared past her as she swung her sword. She dodged an arrow; she drove her spear. Imperial soldiers charged at her; she cut them down. She did not think, she only moved. The clangs of swords, screams, and moans filled the air. In the cloud of dirt and fog, she watched an arrow pierce her father's heart. She leapt off her horse to catch him, but a soldier tackled her, his dagger inches from her neck, and she wrestled him off. She caught sight of her brother Dilbagh as a sword sliced through him. His body fell atop her other brother, Bhag, who was bleeding from his neck. All around her, Sikh warriors were dead or dying. An imperial soldier knocked her sword out of her hand; she whipped out her kirpan. She cried out as he drove his spear into her left leg. She cut him down and stumbled toward her husband, Nidhan, just as a soldier stabbed his ribs. Her husband's eyes rolled back as he fell. Bhago cried out and crawled on the earth toward him as shadows closed over her. The stench of blood and dirt filled her lungs. Her husband, her brothers, her father were dead. The forty warriors she had led into battle were all dead. The Guru would soon be killed, too. It was over. She closed her eyes and heard a single songbird.

tera keeya meetha lagai
Your will is sweet to me *

A conch blew. *The Khalsa's conch.* They had won. Bhago was stunned. Her forty warriors had inflicted so much damage that the imperial army retreated. Guru Gobind Singh was safe.

Guru Gobind Singh rode onto the battlefield and spotted the Sikh warrior Maha Singh in a pool of blood. The Guru kneeled down and cradled his head. With great effort, Maha Singh handed the Guru a scroll. It was the Bedava, the document in which he and the forty warriors had renounced their allegiance. The Guru tore the bedava into pieces and scattered it to the wind. The Guru blessed Maha Singh as he died in his arms.

"They are the Chalee Muktay," Guru Gobind Singh announced. *The forty liberated ones.* Not because they were liberated in death, but because they were liberated in life.

Guru Gobind Singh was at Bhago's side now.

"Puttar," he whispered. *My daughter.*

The Guru took her back to camp and dressed her wounds. Bhago was the lone survivor of the Battle of Muktsar. Guru Gobind Singh told the people her story: the woman warrior who turned deserters into fighters, who saved the life of the Guru and the life of the Khalsa. From then on, she was honored by the name Mai Bhago.

* Guru Granth Sahib, ang 394, Raag Asa, Guru Arjan Ji.

After she healed, Mai Bhago did not return to her village, Jhabal. She donned her warrior's dress and asked to become the Guru's body-guard. She accompanied the Guru to Talvandi Sabo, a forest refuge where he planned to regroup the Khalsa and reunite with his family, at last.

A YEAR AFTER THEY WERE SEPARATED AT THE RIVER SARSA, MATA Sundari and Mata Sahib received word that their husband was alive. The women immediately prepared to travel from Delhi to Talvandi Sabo. On the journey, they ground flour, butter, and sugarcane—roti, ghee, and gurr—and made choori, their children's favorite sweet dish.

When they arrived, Guru Gobind Singh was holding court in a great clearing in Talvandi Sabo. He was seated gloriously on a throne, his white hawk on his arm, the radiance in his eyes undimmed. Hundreds of people lined up to take amrit by his hand. The spirit of the Khalsa was alive. Mata Sundari searched the crowd for their children.

"Where are my beloved sons?" Mata Sundari called out to her husband. The court grew silent as all eyes fell on the women.

Mata Sundari was dressed in a deep-green salvaar kameez, a gold ornament pinned on her dupatta, a pearl mala wrapped around her wrist. Her eyes shone wet with hope. Mata Sahib stood quietly next to her, dressed in sky blue. In her hands was a platter of choori, the sweet dish they had prepared for their children.

Whispers flew: *The women did not know.*

Guru Gobind Singh gazed at them tenderly. The people watched and waited. He cleared his throat.

"All the Khalsa are your sons," said Guru Gobind Singh, gesturing to the people. "Chaar mooay to kya hoa, jeevat kaee hazaar?" *Even if four sons are gone, thousands more live.*

Mata Sundari bowed her head stoically and disappeared into her chambers, followed by Mata Sahib. When the door was closed, Mata Sundari fell on her knees and sobbed. Mata Sahib wept quietly, even as she offered words of comfort: *The Khalsa will remember them as our*

Chaar Sahibzaade, our four princes. They will live on through their sha-heedi, their martyrdom. But all Mata Sundari wanted to do was cup their faces and kiss their eyes. Rage burned in her throat. Mata Sahib left to retrieve water.

A warrior entered the chambers. Mata Sundari was about to hide her face when she realized that the Nihang warrior before her, wearing a royal blue turban and holding a long spear, was a woman.

"I remember you," said Mata Sundari. "You took amrit on Vaisakhi Day."

Mai Bhago nodded. "I was rebirthed."

Mata Sundari looked in her eyes. This was the woman warrior who had saved the Guru's life at the Battle of Muktsar.

"You lost your father . . ." said Mata Sundari.

"I lost my husband, my brothers, *and* my father," said Mai Bhago softly. "Forty men in my village perished when they followed me into battle."

"And?" prodded Mata Sundari.

"I mourn them."

"And?"

"I live."

Mata Sundari studied this woman warrior. A broad face, flashing eyes, stillness in her presence. An aching tenderness in her voice when she spoke of her family. Mata Sundari had never seen anyone like her. A woman who understood the birthing table *and* the battlefield. A woman who knew how to sing and fight, mourn and live, weep and lead. A woman who imagined herself anew in a world on fire and rose from the ash. No one knew what to make of her, yet here she was.

"How?" asked Mata Sundari.

"Chardi Kala," replied Mai Bhago. *Ever-rising spirit—even in dark-ness, ever-rising joy.*

The next day, Mata Sundari prepared to return to Delhi. She asked Mata Sahib to stay with the Guru in Talvandi Sabo. The Guru set out to produce from memory the Aadi Granth that was lost in the river, with the help of Bhai Mani Singh. He needed her help, too. In all her quiet fortitude, Mata Sahib nodded and let her go.

Mata Sundari distributed the sweet choori they had prepared for their sons to all the people in the court, and departed.

UPON HER RETURN TO DELHI, MATA SUNDARI WALKED THE STREETS every day. She watched children at play. She wept and smiled at the same time. She came across a small orphan boy in a goldsmith and was struck by his resemblance to her eldest son. She adopted him and named him Ajit after the son she lost. As she nurtured this child, Mata Sundari felt life rushing back into her.

Two years went by. Mata Sundari received word that Guru Gobind Singh was on his way to the Deccan to meet with Emperor Aurangzeb. The Emperor had been surprisingly moved by the Guru's Zafarnama, his epistle of victory, and asked to meet him. Mata Sundari prepared to see her husband, but before the Guru arrived, the Emperor died.

At nearly ninety, Emperor Aurangzeb confessed to his son Bahadur Shah on his deathbed: "I came alone, and I go as a stranger. I do not know who I am, nor what I have been doing." Bahadur Shah became the new Emperor.

Shortly after, Emperor Bahadur Shah met with Guru Gobind Singh in Agra, bearing gifts. Negotiations began. Mata Sundari waited for word. A year went by and then—

A messenger arrived in the night, sent by Mata Sahib.

"The Guru has ascended," said the messenger.

"How?" breathed Mata Sundari as she reached for the pearl mala on her wrist.

Guru Gobind Singh had retired to his chambers after leading the evening service in Nanderr. An assassin sent by the Nawab Wazir Khan, the same man who had executed her youngest children, entered his tent and stabbed him. The Guru's stitches burst a few days later, and he breathed his last.

Mata Sundari ran the mala through her hands.

"Who did he appoint to succeed him?" She kept her voice steady.

"He placed a coconut and five paisay before the Aadi Granth and bowed. Then, he left this earth."

"The Aadi Granth," she whispered. *The sacred canon of musical poetry.*

"He gave the Aadi Granth a new name—the Guru Granth Sahib."

Mata Sundari nodded in understanding. *No more living Gurus.* It was the solution to their internal strife: A call to end the schisms and struggle for power and needless destruction. *Our ancestors' wisdom will be our lasting teacher.* When Guru Gobind Singh created the Khalsa, he transmitted his sovereignty into the people. Now he transferred authority into the Guru Granth Sahib, the music and poetry that returned people to the wisdom of Oneness.

"Mata Ji," started the messenger, "we still need someone to lead us."

"Please ask Mata Sahib to return to me," she said.

Mata Sahib arrived in Delhi, dressed in the white of widows. The two women made Delhi their home together and listened as news poured in from the heartland of Punjab—

One of the Guru's commanders, Banda Bahadur, launched a campaign to seek justice for the execution of their children, Fateh and Zoraver. After the Guru's assassination, Banda and his men swept Punjab in pursuit of imperial troops and their allies. Banda carried with him five gold-tipped arrows and swords the Guru had gifted him, and a nagara war drum. His troops lay waste to villages that had conspired with the Empire, including Sarhind, where the Guru's children were bricked alive. There, Banda's men cut down the Nawab Wazir Khan. People rejoiced to see them:

"Banda Singh Bahadar ne Sarhind dee itt de naal itt kharrkaa ditee!" *Banda smashed his brick against the brick of Sarhind.* He shook the very foundations of the Empire.

Banda inspired Sikh and Hindu peasants alike to rebel against the Empire's feudal order. He successfully abolished the zameendaar system, granting farmers ownership over their own land. Banda was now seen as the new leader of the Sikh world.

But then, Banda's followers kept going, carried away by their conquests. They swept the countryside—plundering, burning, killing, forcing conversions, digging up graves and burning the corpses. They struck terror in people's hearts. *No, no, no,* thought Mata Sundari. Endless vengeance was not the Guru's wish.

Mata Sundari knew who she had to see. She draped her green and gold dupatta over her head and readied her horse. Mata Sahib looked after her son, Ajit, as Mata Sundari made the long journey to the misted foothills of the Himalayas. As she rode, she could not stop thinking of the woman warrior Mai Bhago. *If there could be a woman warrior, could there be a woman-king? And a woman-king would not be a king at all—she would be something new. But what would that look like?*

Mata Sundari arrived in Kiratpur and found the home of the elder Bibi Veero—only daughter of Guru Hargobind, granddaughter of Mata Ganga, trained in the poetry of the sages *and* the art of defense, who saw the glory days of Amritsar *and* Anandpur, and guided her family through cataclysm into rebirth.

Bibi Veero craned her swan neck to see who had come to visit her. She was now in her nineties. Even on her deathbed, she retained her elegant beauty.

"Bhua Ji," said Mata Sundari, and bowed her head before her aunt.

"Puttar." Bibi Veero rested her hand on Mata Sundari's head to bless her.

"Banda Bahadur . . ." Mata Sundari started.

"Mainu pata," sighed Bibi Veero. *I know.* It was an old pattern repeated through time: justice morphed into vengeance, survivors of violence gaining power to inflict it. Whenever people wield force to strike down another, the cut takes part of their own soul, too.

Bibi Veero hummed:

khaniah(u) tikhee vaalah(u) nikee aet maarag jaanaa
Tread with care: This path is sharper than a double-edged sword
　　and finer than a hair*

---

* Guru Granth Sahib, ang 918, Raag Ramkali, Guru Amar Das Ji.

The setting sun flooded the room with light. Something sparkled on Mata Sundari's wrist. Bibi Veero reached for her niece's hand.

A long mala of shining white pearls, strung with gold thread, hanging on a gold tassel.

The last time Bibi Veero had seen the pearl mala was in the hand of her beloved sister-in-law, Mata Gujri, in the glorious court in Anandpur where sacred music swirled all around them. That was before the terror of the siege and the ambush, before the betrayal and the cold tower . . .

"When did she give it you?" asked Bibi Veero quietly.

"On the day I was willing to offer my head . . ." Mata Sundari recalled the Vaisakhi Day that Mata Gujri wrapped the pearl mala around her wrist. It was the day the Khalsa was born.

"Shakti vastay," the women said in unison. *For power.*

With all her strength, Bibi Veero lifted herself up and cupped Mata Sundari's face in her hands. Her old eyes had gone dim, but she concentrated until Mata Sundari came into focus. Then, she held up the pearl mala between them. The pearls hung from her fingers and swayed gently in the light.

"Look closely," whispered Bibi Veero. She slowly ran each pearl through her hand.

Mata Sundari looked with her heart.

Each pearl in the mala held a story. In them, she saw all the women she had loved: Bibi Nanki singing songs of love; Mata Sulakhni watering the soil of a new community; Mata Khivi stirring the kheer; Bibi Amro writing with her ink pen; Bibi Bhani keeping the stool from breaking; Mata Ganga raising two swords; Mata Krishan rising from the river of ashes; Mata Gujri singing in the cold tower. She saw Bibi Veero on her wedding day, dressed in red and gold, a dagger in her hands, red roses blossoming from her chest. And then she saw the face of the woman warrior Mai Bhago, her flashing eyes and tall spear, her regal turban and steady gaze, and she was riding into the moon. And the moon was her own heart. Mata Sundari wept. All the stories of the ancestors she loved were part of her, and she was part of them: *To be multiple is to know the heart of things.*

Bibi Veero rested her thumb on one pearl.

"Tat Khalsa," she said finally.

"Ji?" asked Mata Sundari.

"You must be the Tat Khalsa." *The true and ready Khalsa.*

Mata Sundari nodded. She was being asked to lead, to become more than she was, and to trust that she could. She bowed before Bibi Veero and kissed her hand.

In the morning, Mata Sundari went to the River Satluj, the river that carried the ashes of the ancestors. The song of wild green parakeets filled the trees. She bathed in the sacred waters of the rivers of Punjab and made the journey back to Delhi to begin her work.

MATA SUNDARI LED THE SIKH WORLD FOR THE NEXT FORTY YEARS. She formed the Tat Khalsa, the group that ultimately prevailed over those who followed Banda, the Bandai Khalsa. She used tools of peace and persuasion. She issued hukamnamas, edicts that carried the highest authority in the Sikh realm, that embodied the core values of the Khalsa. She sent the elder scholar-warrior Bhai Mani Singh to take his seat at Harmandir Sahib in Amritsar and restored the golden city of their ancestors to its former glory. And when her adopted son, Ajit, claimed himself as heir, the next Sikh Guru, she disowned him. She maintained that the everlasting Guru was not to be a person, but the Guru Granth Sahib, the fount of ancestral wisdom that lives in all of us. After Emperor Bahadur Shah died, a new reign of terror began, and Sikhs were hunted like animals in the jungles for decades, yet Mata Sundari still managed to grow their numbers, and the songs of the Gurus rose on the lips of new generations. Her beloved Mata Sahib managed the affairs of the Sikh realm with her, and the two women lived together as sisters until their deaths. Mata Sundari served longer than any Sikh Guru.

Aao chaa peelo . . .

Come, let's have tea . . .

BECOMING NEW

IN MY ROOM AT HOME, THERE IS A PAINTING THAT HANGS ON THE WALL.
My Sikh sister Nirinjan, whom I call Baaj, gifted me a print of Mai
Bhago leading warriors back into battle. She is wearing a blue warrior's
dress, and a saffron dupatta drapes her turban and billows around her
body. She holds a shield with one hand, and points the way forward
with a long sword.

I have always loved the story of Mai Bhago. She was the first Sikh
woman ancestor who was not defined in tradition by her relationship to
the men in her life. She was not the mother of, or daughter of, or wife
of the Guru. She was just Mai Bhago. A woman who devoted her life to
the path. When she led the forty deserters back into battle, she became
the one she was waiting for.

I always wanted to be the warrior in the story. But I am the deserter,
too. I am the one who wants to give up when the fight beats me down.
The Wise Woman in me allows me to rest, to breathe for a night, and
then takes my hand in the morning and leads me back into the battlefield of the world. We can choose to be reborn each night, as Mai Bhago
was reborn.

We can become new.

When Guru Nanak was rebirthed in the river, he set out into the
world with songs of love, wearing Hindu and Muslim garb. People did
not know what to make of him. He made himself new in order to
awaken the world. When Mai Bhago mounted her horse as a woman
warrior, people did not know what to make of her, either. She imagined
herself anew in order to ignite resistance to oppression. And when

Mata Sundari chose to lead, she became the woman-king who bowed before the Guru Granth Sahib and ensured that this canon of musical wisdom was upheld as the everlasting teacher. People did not know what to make of that, either. They were so accustomed to rallying behind a single leader, a man. Her own son claimed himself the next Guru. Yet Mata Sundari insisted that the greatest authority on earth was not a person outside us, but the wisdom embodied within us. She and Mata Sahib *both* issued edicts, hukamnamas: They modeled a way of leading *together*.

A few years ago, I started to gather Sikh women leaders in Mai Bhago Retreat Circles. I saw the courageous Sikh American women fighting for dignity and justice around me as modern-day Mai Bhagos, wielding voices and pens as swords and shields. I became very close with two of those women, Jasvir and Nirinjan. (I call them Jasso and Baaj; they call me Veero.) We come together to renew, fortify, and nourish one another. We light incense and sing kirtan. We let our Wise Women call forth what we are ready to live into. As we talk in a circle, my daughter lies on my lap and plays with my dupatta, listening. This is the way the women ancestors gathered as they strung flower garlands and passed on stories and shared dukh-sukh, their joys and sorrows and dreams. I want to carry that generative, life-giving energy into all my sisterhoods, friendships, and collaborations. It's a model of leadership that Mata Sundari, Mata Sahib, and all the women ancestors embodied: to love one another into rebirth.

A BEACON IN THE BATTLEFIELD

DEEP IN THE MISTED MOUNTAIN SLOPES OF ANANDPUR, AT THE end of a long dirt path, on land that was once a battlefield, we came upon a humble gurdwara. Inside, there was a painting of a Sikh elder serving water to fallen soldiers under a battleworn sky. His name was Bhai Ghanaiya.

As the story goes, during one of the battles at Anandpur, Sikh warriors spotted a man running into the battlefield with a white flag and a goatskin water pouch. Bhai Ghanaiya knelt down beside fallen soldiers, cradled their heads, and helped them drink. He went from one fallen soldier to another, tending Sikhs, Mughals, and Hindu hillmen alike. He was brought before Guru Gobind Singh.

"This man gives water to the enemy!" the warriors yelled.

"Is what they say true?" asked Guru Gobind Singh.

"Yes," replied Bhai Ghanaiya. "Wherever I looked, I only saw your face."

The court fell silent.

"Bhai Ghanaiya is a true Sikh, for he sees the Light within all," declared Guru Gobind Singh. He called forth his warriors to bring medicines and give them to Bhai Ghanaiya.

"Naal malham patti vee karya karo," instructed the Guru. *Take these ointments and bandages to tend their wounds, too.*

In that humble gurdwara named after Bhai Ghanaiya, I studied the objects in the display case: a simple iron bowl and a large water pouch. Bhai Ghanaiya used these to tend to the fallen. My heart soared. In an era of history when Sikhs charged into war to fight soldiers of the Empire, here was a lone water bearer. He chose to *see no stranger, no enemy*. In the thick of war, Bhai Ghanaiya held fast to the core of the *sage* inside the warrior. And Guru Gobind Singh saw that, and blessed him.

I finished my sketch, overjoyed.

YOUR MALA

SO MANY OF US DON'T KNOW WHAT TO DO WITH OUR HISTORIES because they are problematic. We grow up in faith traditions that have caused great harm; scriptures we were taught to revere have also been used to justify all kinds of atrocities. We wrestle with family lineages when we realize that our ancestors participated in other people's oppression, or abused the women around them, or passed on their dysfunctions to us. We identify with liberation movements in history only to discover shades of racism or sexism, or covered-up abuses, or errors and misallocations. We put our heroes on pedestals, and when they do not live up to our hopes, we are left adrift. What do we do with all our messy, complicated histories?

Here's what I have learned: You will be tempted to throw up your hands and walk away. But look back. Look closely. Find the one moment, the one choice, the one example, that strikes you as good and beautiful and wise. It might be as simple as the image of a water bearer in a field of death. Or two women penning edicts side by side. Cup the story in your hands and bring it forward. Hold it up for all to see. You don't need to bring forth all of your history, just what you think will help us all love more and become more.

Before you know it, you will have a string of pearls.

COME, LET'S HAVE TEA

AS I HEADED TO THE CAR, A WOMAN APPEARED IN THE DOORWAY of a small hut. She was one of the guardians and caretakers of the gurdwara that honored Bhai Ghanaiya.

"Chaa peeni?" she smiled. A cup of hot tea on this chilly morning sounded perfect.

"Driver vastay?" I asked, gesturing to Happy, who was waiting in the car.

"Haa(n)," she said and disappeared inside to prepare two cups.

Happy came out, and the two of us sat side by side on the ground, warming our hands around the steaming cups of chaa. We watched the sun rise over the trees, and the birdsong filled the silences. My Punjabi was simple, and so our conversation was simple.

"The morning is beautiful," I said.

"Haa(n)," he agreed.

"It is cold," he said.

"Haa(n)," I agreed.

"The chaa is good," I said.

"When it's sweet, it's always good," he quipped.

I laughed.

I thought of what it might be like for him to be driving us all across Punjab, our family from California with two children who were wild but also sweet. At least I hoped he thought they were sweet.

"Did you have a good night?" I asked.

Happy frowned. He spoke in Punjabi so quickly that I had to focus to keep up. The manager at the hostel where we were staying kicked him out of his room last night. Said that drivers were not allowed in guest rooms. Even after we had paid for it. Forced him out. Showed him the drivers' quarters, which were dank and cold and dirty. He slept in the car all night.

"Veer Ji, I'm so sorry," I said. "I'll talk to them."

"What good will it do?" he said. "Some people think they are better than others."

In all this time since Guru Nanak sang songs of Oneness on the soil of Punjab, the land is still plagued. Caste hierarchy and poverty. Drug addiction and suicide. Female infanticide and gender oppression. Farmland poisoned by insecticides. Economies wrecked by decades of state policy that drained the people of their agency. Torture, detentions, and disappearances from police crackdowns. Relentless human rights abuses. And a litany of daily injustices—like a driver thrown out of a hostel because he was not deemed worthy of a warm room.

I don't know how much longer it will take to birth the world Guru Nanak called us to. But looking into Happy's worn face, and thinking of *his* children, I knew that I do not have the option of giving up.

OUR ANCESTRAL VILLAGE

WE HAD ONE FINAL PLACE TO SEE BEFORE WE LEFT PUNJAB. IT WAS the culmination of our trip: my family's ancestral village. My paternal grandfather, Kehar Singh, was born in the village Chand Navan, near Moga, in 1892. At nineteen, he left his village to begin a journey to the United States. He traveled by train to Calcutta, then took a steamship to the Philippines, where he earned enough money to board the *Nippon Maru*, a Japanese steamship headed for San Francisco. In 1913, he arrived and settled in California's Central Valley, where the soil and air felt like home. He worked as a Punjabi Sikh farmer for the rest of his life; I was raised on the land he farmed. My grandfather's generation endured racial violence and state violence, but they stayed in the labor, for us. On this family pilgrimage, 110 years later, we brought his great-grandchildren to his ancestral land—and to his home village.

We drove through endless fields down dirt paths to the village Chand Navan, *New Moon*. The winter mist hugged the earth. We reached a brick house where a man who resembled my father waved us in. We parked in the family's courtyard. Buffalos and cows grazed along the wall, a green tractor rolled in, and a worker washed his face in the water pump. Chacha Ji and Chachi Ji, my father's cousin and his wife, greeted us kindly. Chachi Ji served us cups of chaa and platters of ladoos and barfee she had made from the milk of their cows. The sweets were sublime. As the children ate and listened politely, I updated them with news from our family in California. Chachi Ji told me about how they marched to Delhi in the Farmers' Protest. I beamed. While I was organizing in solidarity with those farmers back in the United States, she was courageously on the front lines in Punjab.

"Tere kheta(n) noo(n) chaliye," said Chacha Ji as we finished our tea. *Come see your fields.*

We walked into misty green fields—seven acres of wheat fields that belong to my family. The children skipped joyfully ahead while Sharat filmed them. Chacha Ji told us that children of the village flew their kites into our fields and trampled the potatoes, which are fickle. So he planted wheat on our seven acres. He pulled out a sturdy green shoot and handed it to me. I pressed it in my journal.

I knelt down and dug my hands into the earth, and the children excitedly followed. Together we ran our fingers through the cool, damp soil. I pictured my grandfather running through these fields as a child, flying a kite. I thought about *all* the ancestors this soil has witnessed, going back to the Sikh Gurus, and long before. Wherever we travel, we teach our children the names of the peoples indigenous to the land and say their names together.

"Children," I realized. "You can say your own names."

They laughed and said their names. We gathered a little soil to take home to the rest of our family, so that they could touch it, too. The children's clothes got muddy, and their sweet laughter filled the air.

They were so free. I wondered how much of this trip they would re-member. Perhaps these stories and songs will offer them refuge when they are older. Or they will forget for many years and remember all of a sudden, in a time of need. Maybe they will be drawn to come back here. Like I was.

I felt so despondent about the world before we made our trip. When the ancient trees we loved so much were killed en masse in the wildfires in California, it represented to me all the beauty and life that was being destroyed before our eyes. By capitalism, militarism, racism, sexism, and campaigns of violence. I wrote in my journal: "The world we have known is ending . . ." Then we came to Punjab and bowed before all the sacred sites and immersed ourselves in the stories of the ancestors, and where did it leave me? I could still taste the ash in my mouth. But holding that ancient soil in my hands, I realized: *The world has ended many times before, and the world will be rebirthed many times.* The ques-tion is: *What will I do with my turn in the cycle?*

I want to meet apocalyptic times in the spirit of Chardi Kala, ever-rising joy even in darkness. I want to walk the path of a sage warrior—awake to Oneness, committed to love, ready to serve. The wheat from our seven acres in Punjab will be made into roti that will nourish people near and far: The land belongs to my family, but its fruits belong to the world. So, too, the stories of our ancestors belong to the world. As does their wisdom. Like pearls on a mala. I want to pass them along. "Shakti vastay." *For power.*

When we finished gathering the soil, Kavi and Ananda grinned widely and showed us their hands, stained with dirt. Sharat took pho-tos. I smiled at him in gratitude—our pilgrimage was complete; it was time to go home. I carried Ananda on my hip and walked slowly back through the fields, drinking it in. We thanked Chacha Ji and Chachi Ji and prepared to head to Delhi with Happy and Jasso, and then fly back to Los Angeles. As we got into the car, Chacha Ji and Chachi Ji handed us an enormous platter of sweet barfee and ladoos and gave the chil-dren an envelope full of rupees. We tried to intervene, but they hushed us as elders do. We made a plan to buy a beautiful set of tabla drums in

Delhi, so that the children could learn to play at home the music that was all around us in Punjab.

As the village receded, we waved at my aunt and uncle until they were tiny dots. Happy grinned as the children thanked him. The green fields of Punjab stretched on all sides of us. The sun touched down on the horizon, and the mustard flowers in the fields shone gold. As we picked up speed, the flowers became a gold ribbon that followed us home.

"Vah," I breathed. *Wow*.

SAGE WARRIOR,
EMBRACE REBIRTH . . .

HOLD THE WISDOM OF THE ancestors in my hand like a mala.
Each wisdom practice is a pearl. One is not higher than another.
I can rest my attention on the one I need in this moment. Any
one of them can lead to rebirth, here and now, starting within.

The mala of wisdom is on my wrist—and yours.

When you feel isolated and disconnected, *wake to Oneness*.
   Drop into the present moment, look around, and let in wonder. Say: "You are a part of me I do not yet know."
When confronted with pain, *befriend the body*. Listen to parts of
   yourself, or parts of the world, that are hurting. Ask what
   they need.
When numb and defeated, *practice pleasure*. Turn to music and
   movement and breath and taste and touch and bring your
   senses back to life. Make this a sacred practice, without
   guilt.
When the world feels like it's closing in, *build sovereign space*.
   Use your splendid imagination and go to a place of beauty
   and wonder and safety. Be with the ancestors and the Beloved, and with yourself.
When you need guidance, *rest in wisdom*. Get quiet and let your
   deepest wisdom speak to you with compassion and care. Let
   it mother you. And do the next right thing.
When you feel helpless, *activate power*. Remember who benefits
   from your inaction. Go to the people, places, and stories
   that revive your sense of agency.
When you are enraged, *harness rage* as a source of energy and
   information. Move that energy through your body and decide
   how to direct it. Refuse to surrender your humanity.

When overwhelmed by grief, remember that we can bear the
unbearable when we *grieve together*. Reach out to people and
be with them. Trust the power this holds.

When you witness suffering, *choose courage*. Go outside and let
the beauty of the earth breathe into you, and ask: "Who do
I want to be?" Do what love demands.

When you wonder what all your work is for, *become victory*.
Measure success not by outcomes but by your faithfulness
to the labor of love.

And when the world feels like it's ending, *embrace rebirth*.

LEFT TO RIGHT:
*Ananda, Valarie, Kavi, and "Chacha Ji" collecting soil
on their ancestral land, Chand Navan, Punjab*

BEGAMPURA

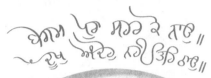

A YEAR AFTER OUR TRIP TO PUNJAB, I SIGNED UP TO GO ON Kavi's third-grade field trip to the Los Angeles River. I lived in LA for the better part of twenty years and never knew the LA River was a place anyone could visit. We drove to a park in Glendale. All the children gathered on the grass.

"When you think of the LA River, what do you think of?" the tour guide asked the children.

"Dirty!" "Concrete!" "A trickle!" "Is it even a river?"

The tour guide nodded, then he walked us all to the riverbank. We sat along the rim and looked down. It was indeed dirty—there was a red shopping cart stuck in the mud, and concrete all along the sides, and the water was little more than a trickle.

"The LA River is thousands of years old," explained the tour guide. It was called Paayme Paxaayt by the Tongva people who have lived on this land for thousands of years. The first accounts we have of the river describe it as a lush paradise filled with wildlife. The river was ancient and sacred, and the source of all life. But it was also wild and temperamental. It would meander widely, sometimes miles away from its earlier bed. Every few years, the river flooded, leaving wide swaths of destruction in its path. It turned the land into marshes and swamps for miles. The Tongva people used the tule grass to craft boats to navigate the swamps. In the early 1900s, settlers who built up the town had had enough of the sudden floods. In 1938, they began to pour concrete on the river. Literally fifty-one miles of concrete all up and down the river. Everything around the river began to die—the trees, and wildlife, and earth.

"Who thinks it was a good idea to pour concrete on the river?" asked the tour guide.

None of the children raised their hands.

"Yeah, we don't think it's a good idea now," he said. "A group of people formed Friends of the LA River to try to bring the wildlife back. And now engineers are trying to figure out how to restore the river. The engineers have determined that they can't pull out all of the concrete, otherwise Los Angeles would flood again. But they *can* pull out small sections of the concrete, and nourish the land in those parts."

The section of the river at Glendale where we were seated was one of the special sections where the river had a natural soft bottom.

"Look closely," said the tour guide. "What do you see?"

Kavi took out his packet and studied the chart of the wildlife.

"Mommy! Look! A snowy egret!" he said. A single snowy egret stretched its neck out of the grass. And floating behind it was a flock of American coot. The more we looked, the more we saw: willow trees, tule grass, mugwort, and a hint of an osprey nest.

I couldn't believe it. I had spent all year since our trip to Punjab thinking about ancient sacred rivers, immersing myself in all the stories that took place on the riverbanks of my ancestors. And all this time, there was an ancient sacred river just a few miles away from me.

We don't have to go to other lands to reconnect with the ancestors and currents of wisdom. The land is ancient right where we are. There are sacred rivers right where we are. The sacred is all around us. And even when we think we have destroyed it all, we haven't. Today there are sections of the LA River where life is growing back: There is re-birth. Just like how, amid the thousands of ancient sequoia trees felled in California's wildfires, the Great-Grandfather Tree still stands. A symbol of rebirth.

In a time when we taste ash every day, we can focus only on the destruction, or we can choose to participate in rebirth.

ALL THE STORIES OF THE ANCESTORS IN THIS BOOK TAKE PLACE
among the five rivers of Punjab. The rivers stretch northeast across
the land like a hand reaching for the Himalayan mountains; their veins
shimmer blue. The rivers feed into each other—Jhelum and Raavi
join Chenab, Beas joins Satluj, and the Satluj and Chenab join together
to form one mighty river called Panjnad. And the Panjnad becomes
the Indus, which spills into the Arabian Sea—and connects to all the
waters of the earth. The water connects us all. As do the stories. The
stories of these ancestors did not just happen once. They have happened many times before. They will happen many times again. It is
humanity's play. Countless sages, countless warriors. And a shared
dream—

In Sikh imagination, there is a place called Begampura, sings the
sage-poet Ravidas. He was born an "untouchable," yet he imagined a
world beyond the one he knew. Begampura means city without sorrow.
It is a place without caste, poverty, or injustice. The sage Kabir called
it Premnagar, city of love. Dr. Martin Luther King, Jr., called it the
Promised Land. It's a place our hearts long for.

Ravidas sings of Begampura:

begam puraa sahar ko naao
dookh a(n)doh(u) nahee teh tthaao
naa tasvees khiraaj na maal
khauf na khataa na taras javaal
ab moh(i) khoob vatan geh paaee
ooha(n) khair sadaa mere bhaee
kaaim daaim sadaa paatsaahee
dom na sem ek so aahee
aabaadaan sadaa masahoor
ooha(n) ganee baseh maamoor
tiou tiou sail kareh jiou bhaavai
mahram mahal na ko attkaavai
keh ravidaas khalaas chamaaraa
jo ham saharee s(u) meet hamaaraa

A place without despair, Begampura, the name of the city
Agony and anxiety are not in that refuge
No stress or taxation, no property
No fear of fault, no denial of mercy
Now I have found my splendid homeland and abode
There, peace is always, my brother
Secure and lasting, always sovereign
None are second or third, all are one
Fully inhabited and eternally famous
Those who dwell there are rich and content
They stroll freely, wherever they wish
They know the inner-palace, no one blocks their way
Says Ravidas, a shoemaker set free
Those who live there with me are my friends*

We can birth Begampura right here and now, starting within us.
Begampura is a place where we are as sovereign as the rivers.

WE ARE THE RIVERS, STRONG AND POWERFUL. WE LOVE THE EARTH
as we move against her. We hit a rock. Later, it's sand. It's effortless.
People drink from us, play in us, pray with us. We carry their ashes. We
bless their babies. Civilizations rise and fall; empires are fleeting. We
have no beginning and no end. We are always now. Here comes a beloved one to our shores, full of longing. Let her come to our waters.
We embrace her: We flow into her eyes and throat and womb. We make
ribbons through her. She is a pearl on a gold thread. We whisper: *You
are beloved in this form. You don't have to hold back any longer. Seize this
brief moment, while you are in this body. Sing your song of love.*

You are the body in the river. You are the river. And you are the
song.

---

*   Guru Granth Sahib, ang 345, Raag Gauri, Bhagat Ravidas Ji.

GLOSSARY

amrit	sacred nectar; water sweetened and made sacred
amrit sanchar	initiation ceremony for taking Sikh vows and becoming Khalsa
amrit vela	the predawn hour, the ambrosial hour; ideal for meditation
anand	ecstatic joy; ecstasy embodied
Anand Karaj	the Sikh wedding ceremony; literally means *transport to ecstatic joy*
antam sanskar	final rites upon death
Ardaas	prayer of supplication
baaj	hawk
Baba	wise man; a respected term for an elder—"Baba Ji"
badam	almonds
Bandi Chhorr	one who liberates; name given to Guru Hargobind when he released the prisoners in Gwalior Fort
Bandi Chhorr Divas	day of liberation, when Guru Hargobind and the prisoners of Gwalior found freedom; celebrated by Sikhs every year around Divali season
baoli	stepwell; stairs down to an underground well; a place of prayer
Begampura	land without despair
Bhagats	Hindu mystics; practitioners of the Bhakti liberation movement rooted in loving devotion of the Divine

Bhua Ji	aunt; father's sister
Bibi	elder sister; a respected term for an elder woman; an honorific for the Sikh women ancestors—"Bibi Ji"
Brahmin	Hindu priest; highest caste
chaa	black tea with milk and spices ("chai" in Hindi)
Chalee Muktay	the forty liberated ones; refers to the forty soldiers led into battle by the woman warrior Mai Bhago
Chardi Kala	ever-rising spirits; ever-rising joy (even in darkness)
chaunki	a stool; a four-footed wooden platform
chaur	a whisk of yak hair or horsehair
daal	lentils
Darbar Sahib	inner sanctum of a gurdwara
Dasvandh	the practice of donating one-tenth of one's earnings and time to the community; initiated by Guru Arjan; an ongoing Sikh practice
dharamsala	an abode of the Divine; a house of gathering; initial name for a Sikh house of worship (called "gurdwara" after Guru Hargobind's time)
doli	a palanquin for the bride after the wedding ceremony; also refers to the moment when the bride departs her family's home to live with her new partner
dudh	milk
dukh-sukh	sorrows and joys, both as part of life; sharing dukh-sukh means having a heart-to-heart conversation
dupatta	a long scarf worn by women and girls
granthi	a reader of the Guru Granth Sahib who leads services in a gurdwara
gurdwara	a Sikh house of worship, traditionally pronounced "gur-dvara"; a place that ushers you into light

Gurmukhi	script in which the sacred poetry in the Guru Granth Sahib is written; created by Guru Angad
gurr	jaggery; coarse brown sugar made from sugar cane juice
guru	teacher and wisdom-keeper
Guru	one who leads you to the light; honorific of the ten Sikh Gurus; also refers to the Divine; comes from Sanskrit: "gu," darkness; "ru," light
Guru Gaddi	succession ceremony for the Sikh Gurus
Gurpurab	birthday of the Sikh Gurus; celebrated annually today
Guru Granth Sahib	eternal teacher; living teacher; everlasting source of wisdom; compilation of sacred poetry from the Sikh Gurus and sages of Hindu and Muslim traditions; often given the honorific *Sri* Guru Granth Sahib
hukamnama	command or order from a source of spiritual authority
Ik Onkar	Oneness, ever-unfolding; the heart of Sikh wisdom; a declaration of our Oneness as the source of all love
jaikara	a cry of victory to rally spirits; a jubilant call and response. In the most common jaikara today, a speaker calls out: "Jo Bolay So Nihaal!" *Those who speak will be liberated!* The community responds: "Sat Sri Akaal!" *True is the Timeless One (I honor the truth that is).*
Jap	the name of Guru Nanak's first epic sacred poem; also means *to contemplate*
Ji	an honorific after a name to convey respect
jori	a two-set percussion drum created in the court of the Sikh Gurus; predecessor to the tabla; the musician applies fresh dough on the larger drum to create resonance

kakkar	five articles of faith in the Sikh tradition: kes (uncut hair), kanga (a wooden comb), karra (a bracelet made of iron or steel), kachhera (a cotton undergarment), kirpan (a miniature sword); also known as "the five Ks"
kaleeray	ornaments attached to the bride's bangles during the wedding ceremony; originally dried coconuts, now gold or silver umbrella-shaped ornaments
Kaur	lioness; princess; sovereign woman warrior; the royal surname given to women and girls by Guru Gobind Singh to abolish caste hierarchies and patriarchy; a declaration of sovereignty today
khanda	double-edged sword; used in Sikh ceremonies; also refers to the modern symbol of Sikhs
kheer	sweet rice pudding
kirpan	sword; dagger; miniature sword; represents the commitment to fight for justice
kirtan	singing of the sacred poetry in the Guru Granth Sahib
langar	a free and open community kitchen; a meal where everyone is served as equals; a core liberation practice in all gurdwaras
lavaa(n)	the sacred poem of four verses in the Guru Granth Sahib that is sung in the Sikh wedding ceremony (Anand Karaj) to marry a couple
mala	beads for meditation or prayer
Mata	mother; a respected term for an elder woman; a wisdom-keeper; an honorific for the Sikh women ancestors—"Mata Ji"
mehndi	henna
Miri Piri	inner and outer sovereignty; a declaration of spiritual and temporal power; the energies that ignite the path of the *sant sipahi,* sage warrior
mridang	a percussion drum; a single-barreled two-headed wooden drum (also known as a pakhavaj)

Nanke	maternal family
Nawab	ruler; administrator in the Mughal Empire
pakhavaj	a percussion drum; a single-barreled two-headed wooden drum (also known as a mridang)
palki	palanquin, a carriage on two horizontal poles, carried by four or more people; also refers to the adorned structure where the Guru Granth Sahib is seated in the gurdwara
pangat	the practice of sitting together side by side, on the floor, in unbroken rows, to eat together and share langar; an embodiment of equality
panj	five
panj paisay	five coins
Panj Pyare	five beloved ones; the five who volunteered their lives on Vaisakhi Day 1699; the first members of the Khalsa
patka	a head covering for a young Sikh boy
phulkari	Punjabi folk embroidery, known for its bright colors, flower motifs, and geometric patterns
Pita Ji	father
pothi	a book of sacred poems; today called a "gutka"
prashaad	blessing in the form of a sweetened confection, usually flour, ghee, and gurr (jaggery)
Punjab	land of five rivers, ancestral home of Sikhs; also spelled "Panjab"
put, puttar	dear child; a term of endearment
raag	a mood derived through musical melodies that correlate to emotions; a structure of melody and rhythm for classical music
Raag Vidya	the knowledge and learning of sacred music in raag
raagis	musicians of the court of the Sikh Gurus who sing in gurdwaras today

rabab	a plucked stringed musical instrument; a sacred Sikh instrument played by Bhai Mardana as he accompanied Guru Nanak
rababis	musicians of the court of the Sikh Gurus who played stringed instruments and traditionally sang the sacred poetry in raag
Sach khand	realm of truth
sant	a sage
sant sipahi	sage warrior
saranda	a bowed-string musical instrument similar to a lute or fiddle with a hollow sound box; a sacred Sikh instrument
sarovar	a sacred pool of water where people bathe in meditation; often part of a gurdwara
Sat Kartar	traditional greeting used in the time of the Sikh Gurus: *True is the Great Doer (I honor the truth that is)*
Sat Sri Akaal	traditional greeting of Sikhs today: *True is the Timeless One (I honor the truth that is)*
seva	sacred service, selfless and spiritually inspired
sevadaar	one who performs seva
shabd	a sacred poem from the Guru Granth Sahib
shaheedi	martyrdom
Shastar Vidya	the knowledge and art of weapons
Sikh	one who learns and is always learning; a practitioner of the Sikh faith
Sikhi	the term Sikhs use to refer to the Sikh tradition
Singh	lion or warrior; the royal surname given to men and boys by Guru Gobind Singh to abolish caste hierarchies; a declaration of sovereignty today
sipahi	warrior
slok	a couplet
Sohila	the nightly song-prayer in the Sikh tradition

Sufis	Muslim mystics; practitioners of an Islamic liberation movement rooted in loving devotion of the Divine
tanpura	a long-necked four-stringed drone musical instrument
taus	a bowed-string musical instrument in the shape of a peacock; a sacred Sikh instrument
tilak	crushed red powder used to mark the forehead in rites of passage or sacred ceremonies; a gesture of blessing
Udasi(s)	a sacred journey; the name for Guru Nanak's four epic travels across South Asia and beyond; also refers to the ascetic followers of Guru Nanak's son Sri Chand
Vaheguru	the name for the Divine in Sikh practice; literally, "vahe," in wonder of; "guru," the one who ushers us into light
vaid	a healer in ayurvedic medicine
Vaisakhi	the spring harvest festival; the birth of the Khalsa in the Sikh tradition; celebrated annually in April
vismaad	ecstatic wonderment

SIKHS 101

THE SIKH FAITH IS AMONG THE WORLD'S LARGEST FAITH TRADI-
tions. It originated 550 years ago in Punjab, which spans present-day
India and Pakistan, as a devotional liberation movement. There are
twenty-six million Sikhs worldwide, and more than half a million in the
United States. "Sikh" is pronounced "Sik-h" with an aspirated "h"
sound. Sikh wisdom is grounded in Oneness, love, and service. The
three pillars of the faith are: Naam Japo, Kirat Karo, and Vand Chhako.
Recite the mystical name, live honestly, and share resources. The most
common last names for Sikhs are Kaur and Singh—Kaur means sovereign woman warrior, princess, or lioness; Singh means warrior or lion.
These last names are meant to embody radical equality and abolish
caste hierarchies. Many Sikhs wear articles of faith, the five kakkars
(the five Ks): a wooden comb (kanga), a steel or iron bracelet (karra),
a cotton undergarment (kachhera), a miniature sword (kirpan), and
long, uncut hair (kes), which men and some women wrap in a turban.
Most people you see in the United States who wear turbans daily are
Sikh.

A Sikh house of worship is called a gurdwara. You can go to any
gurdwara near you to partake in langar, a free communal meal, and
listen to the sacred musical poetry. The canon of Sikh scripture is called
Sri Guru Granth Sahib. It is composed of sacred poems from the Sikh
Gurus and sages from Hindu and Islamic traditions. Sikhs listen to,
recite, and sing this sacred poetry. At the end of every service, Sikhs
open the canon and take a hukam, an edict, and apply it to their lives.
Sikhs revere the canon as the living Guru.

Sikhs do not proselytize: All paths are seen as paths to the One.
Prayers are for all of humanity. In the Ardaas, the daily supplication,

the community sings: "Nanak Naam Chardi Kala / Tere Bhaanay Sarbat Da Bhala." *Oh Nanak, we sing the mystical name in ever-rising spirits / Within Your will, blessings for all of humanity.* In Sikh wisdom, all people can transform from *manmukh*—one who is oriented to their own desires and fears—to *gurmukh,* one who is centered on the Beloved and therefore the Beloved in all.

The largest annual Sikh celebrations are Vaisakhi, the springtime harvest festival in April where Sikhs commemorate the birth of the Khalsa (beloved sovereign community), and Gurpurab, the birthday of Guru Nanak, commonly honored in November.

The traditional Sikh greeting is "Vaheguru Ji Ka Khalsa, Vaheguru Ji Ki Fateh!" *The beloved community belongs to Divine Oneness / In that Oneness, all become victory.* A simple traditional greeting is: "Sat Sri Akaal!" *True is the Timeless One (I honor the truth that is).* You are welcome to use these greetings when you meet Sikh people.

This book chronicles the era of the Sikh Gurus, which spans about 250 years, from 1469 to 1708. Mata Sundari led the Sikh world for forty more years after that, until she and Mata Sahib died in 1747. Shortly after, the realm broke into factions called misls, and one eventually rose to become the Sikh Empire led by Maharaja Ranjit Singh. In the mid-1800s, the British colonized India and conquered the Sikhs. British colonial rule relied on political, social, and economic oppression. Sikhs led armed resistance to the British; many gave their lives. Others enlisted with the British to fight in World Wars I and II. After the Second World War, the British prepared to withdraw from India.

In 1947, the British left India and severed the subcontinent in two: Muslims to the newly formed Pakistan, Hindus and Sikhs to India. The Partition of India was the largest, most violent forced migration in history. Millions died. Punjab was fractured and bleeding for decades, subject to oppressive policies by the new Indian government. A separatist movement emerged to demand a sovereign state. In 1984, the Indian government sent tanks into the Golden Temple complex to crush the movement; the government chose a day of gathering (the martyrdom of Guru Arjan) and massacred thousands of innocent people. In retaliation, the prime minister was assassinated by two Sikh body-guards, and genocidal violence swept India. More than three thousand Sikhs were killed in New Delhi alone.

Since the 1980s, thousands of Sikhs have been detained, tortured, or disappeared by the government in a long chain of human rights abuses. The Farmers' Protest that caught global attention in 2020 was led by Punjabi Sikh farmers fighting for their dignity and livelihood. Today, a far-right Hindu nationalist government continues to oppress minorities in India. In the last few years, the government escalated transnational repression and ordered the assassinations of Sikh leaders in the United States and Canada. Some Sikhs believe that the only way to a just future is to create the separate nation-state Khalistan, a sovereign state where all belong. Others invoke Khalistan as a way of being together that honors sovereignty where we are—a call to fight for multicultural democracies rather than cut new borders. The Sikh community is profoundly diverse in worldviews, geographies, and aspirations, but tied together by a shared honoring of the Sikh Gurus and ancestral wisdom.

Sikh history in the United States begins more than a century ago. The first migrants from South Asia to North America were Punjabi Sikh farmers who sailed by steamship in the early 1900s. Sikhs who arrived in San Francisco were processed through Angel Island, a detention center designed to detain, interrogate, and deport as many Asian immigrants as possible. Others survived white nationalist mobs. Sikhs went on to build the first gurdwara in the United States in Stockton, California, where many organized to overcome laws that denied them citizenship. After U.S. immigration laws shifted in the 1960s, Sikhs built communities across the country and entered every kind of profession. Marked by their turbans, Sikhs continue to be on the forefront of racial violence in the United States. A turbaned Sikh father, Balbir Singh Sodhi, was the first person to be murdered in hate violence after the terrorist attacks on September 11, 2001. The largest massacre of Sikh Americans was the 2012 mass shooting by a white nationalist inside a gurdwara in Oak Creek, Wisconsin. Sikhs often respond to hate with the call to live in Chardi Kala—ever-rising spirits or ever-rising joy. Every generation of Sikh Americans has created new organizations, educational campaigns, artwork, music, scholarship, and networks of solidarity to advocate for the rights of all. Today, a new generation of Sikhs are reclaiming ancestral wisdom to inspire courageous action for a new time.

RESOURCES TO LEARN MORE

Ensaaf: ensaaf.org

Jakara Movement: jakara.org

The Sikh Coalition: sikhcoalition.org

Sikh Research Institute: Sikhri.org

Sikh American Legal Defense and Education Fund (SALDEF): saldef.org

United Sikhs: unitedsikhs.org

SUGGESTED INTRODUCTORY READINGS

Kaur, Keerat. *Panjabi Garden: Nature's Wonders, Through the Gurmukhi Script*. Tellwell, 2022.

Mandair, Arvind-pal Singh. *Sikhism: A Guide for the Perplexed*. Bloomsbury Academic, 2013.

Mandair, Arvind-pal Singh, and Christopher Shackle, editors and translators. *Teachings of the Sikh Gurus*. Routledge, 2005.

Singh, Nikky-Guninder Kaur. *Guru Nanak Poems from the Guru Granth Sahib*. Harvard University Press, 2022.

Singh, Nikky-Guninder Kaur. *Sikhism: An Introduction*. Bloomsbury Publishing, 2011.

Singh, Nikky-Guninder Kaur. *The First Sikh: The Life and Legacy of Guru Nanak*. Viking India, 2019.

Singh, Pashuara, and Arvind-pal Singh Mandair. *The Sikh World*. Routledge, 2023.

Singh, Pashaura, and Louis E. Fenech, editors. *The Oxford Handbook of Sikh Studies*. Oxford University Press, 2014.

Singh, Simran Jeet. *The Light We Give: How Sikh Wisdom Can Transform Your Life*. Riverhead Books, 2022.

STORY NOTES

PART ONE: WAKE TO ONENESS

ABOUT BIBI NANKI AND GURU NANAK, THE FIRST GURU

MY TELLING OF GURU NANAK'S COMING-OF-AGE AND REVELATION is anchored in the four written collections of life stories of Guru Nanak, known as the Janamsakhis. The four Janamsakhi traditions are *Bala*, *Miharban*, *Adi*, and *Puratan*. All the main events in my rendition are taken from these collections: Guru Nanak's birth and thread ceremony, his conduct of "true business" and his father's rage, Bibi Nanki's love and protection for her brother, his disappearance and revelation at the River Kali Bein, and his great travels, udasis. Bibi Nanki is often referred to as *Bebe* Nanki in Sikh tradition, another honorific term for "elder sister." I imagined scenes of Bibi Nanki's life before her brother was born. I also created a story of how she might have inspired Guru Nanak's verse *Pavan Guru*, which concludes Jap Ji Sahib. In oral tradition, Guru Nanak recited Jap Ji Sahib to Bibi Nanki on her deathbed.

TIMELINE

- **1464:** Bibi Nanki is born
- **1469:** Guru Nanak is born
- **1475:** Bibi Nanki marries Jai Ram
- **1485:** Guru Nanak moves to Sultanpur Lodhi to live with Bibi Nanki
- **1487:** Guru Nanak marries Mata Sulakhni
- **1494:** Mata Sulakhni gives birth to Sri Chand

1497:   Mata Sulakhni gives birth to Lakhmi Das

1499:   Guru Nanak disappears in the River Kali Bein and
emerges with a revelation
    Guru Nanak departs on his legendary udasis for
    twenty-four years

1518:   Bibi Nanki passes away

PART TWO: BEFRIEND THE BODY

ABOUT MATA KHIVI AND GURU ANGAD, THE SECOND GURU

IN THE JANAMSAKHIS, THE LIFE STORIES OF GURU NANAK, HIS
wife, Mata Sulakhni, is often depicted as sullen and dissatisfied. In my
retelling, I imagined her at the riverbank, finding the courage to lead
Kartarpur after so many years of separation. The scenes of Guru
Nanak testing Bhai Lehna and anointing him as Guru Angad are taken
from oral tradition, as is Guru Angad's grief after Guru Nanak departed. Mata Sulakhni likely met Guru Angad's wife, Mata Khivi, in
Kartarpur, and so I imagined their meeting and exchange.

In oral tradition, Mata Khivi is the one to establish langar as an institution in Khadoor, a direct defiance of caste and social hierarchy. I
created a scene to display the caste frictions that catalyzed her first langar. Her daughter, Bibi Amro, is the first Sikh woman on record to
read, write, and lead. She introduced Guru Amar Das to her parents'
community. In a patriarchal culture, Bibi Amro must have found a way
to embrace all the parts of herself. So, I imagined the scene of Bibi
Amro starting her cycle, and her parents' response. Sikh wisdom rejects customs that view women's bodies as polluted—wisdom we are
still working to put into practice today.

TIMELINE

1521:   Guru Nanak arrives in Kartarpur with Mata Sulakhni
and their children

1532:   Bhai Lehna becomes a disciple of Guru Nanak

1539:   Guru Nanak appoints Bhai Lehna as Guru Angad,
        his successor, and passes away

1539:   Guru Angad joins Mata Khivi in Khadoor
          Mata Khivi establishes langar

PART THREE: PRACTICE PLEASURE

ABOUT BIBI BHANI AND GURU AMAR DAS, THE THIRD GURU

BIBI BHANI'S DEVOTION TO HER FATHER, GURU AMAR DAS, IS widely celebrated in Sikh memory. I added the detail that she accompanied her father on his first visit to Khadoor and encouraged him to stay. The story of Bibi Bhani holding fast to the breaking stool is beloved: It is the moment when Guru Amar Das gave her a vision of the hardships to come and, upon her request, blessed Bibi Bhani's lineage with the Guruship. Bhai Jetha was known to work in the langar hall in Goindval. It is possible that Mata Khivi visited Goindval to help run that langar hall. So, I chose the langar hall as the setting for how Bhai Jetha and Bibi Bhani met and fell in love; I also wove Mata Khivi into their love story. Guru Amar Das composed the Anand Sahib, the song of ecstatic joy, and sang it at weddings; I imagined that he sang it at his daughter Bibi Bhani's wedding. According to oral histories, around this time, Emperor Akbar visited Goindval and gifted land to Bibi Bhani on the occasion of her wedding as a powerful gesture of respect.

TIMELINE

1535:   Bibi Bhani is born to Guru Amar Das and Mata
        Mansa Devi

1539:   Guru Amar Das visits Khadoor at the age of sixty
        and stays to serve Guru Angad
          Guru Amar Das moves to Goindval with his
          family and walks to Khadoor daily to serve

1552:   Guru Amar Das is anointed as the third Guru
         Guru Angad passes away

1554:   Bibi Bhani and Bhai Jetha are married; they choose
         to live in Goindval to serve the Guru

PART FOUR: BUILD SOVEREIGN SPACE

ABOUT BIBI BHANI AND GURU RAM DAS,
THE FOURTH GURU

THE WELL-PRESERVED HOUSE OF GURU AMAR DAS IN GOINDVAL IS
the setting for the scenes of Bibi Bhani's early life in my retelling. There
is no account of Bibi Bhani's birthing labor, but visiting the room where
she birthed Guru Arjan inspired me to imagine her labor. Guru Arjan
was born during Vaisakhi time, so I set the great harvest festival as
backdrop for Bibi Bhani's labor. I also imagined that Bibi Bhani found
a sovereign space within her that resembled the land she was gifted
from Emperor Akbar, present-day Amritsar. Finally, Bibi Bhani is
known to have served in a leper colony later in life; I imagined that her
decision was preceded by her final visit to Mata Khivi, who spent her
life in service.

The details of all other major events in my rendition are taken from
oral tradition and historical record—how Guru Amar Das tested and
appointed Guru Ram Das; how Guru Ram Das chose Guru Arjan to
succeed him after receiving his son's letters of sacred poetry; how
Prithi Chand betrayed his family; how Guru Arjan constructed Harmandir Sahib. According to oral tradition, Guru Arjan composed his
cherished shabd *Poota Mata Kee Asees* based on his mother's blessing.
In my imagination, Bibi Bhani sang the first lines to him as a lullaby. It
was a delight to picture Bibi Bhani singing to him, and he to her.

TIMELINE

1563:   Bibi Bhani births her son, Arjan, in Goindval

1563:   Bibi Bhani's cousin Bhai Gurdas is adopted by Guru
         Amar Das

1574:   Guru Amar Das tests Bhai Jetha and anoints him as
        Guru Ram Das
            Guru Amar Das passes away

1574:   Guru Ram Das and Bibi Bhani move to present-day
        Amritsar

1577:   Guru Ram Das builds up Amritsar and expands the
        pool of water into a sarovar

1580:   Guru Ram Das sends his son, Arjan, to represent him
        at a wedding in Lahore

1581:   Guru Ram Das appoints his son as Guru Arjan and
        passes away

1581:   Guru Arjan begins to build Harmandir Sahib, known
        today as the Golden Temple

1582:   Mata Khivi passes away

1589:   Guru Arjan completes Harmandir Sahib and leaves
        for his travels

PART FIVE: REST IN WISDOM

ABOUT MATA GANGA AND GURU ARJAN, THE FIFTH GURU

THE MAIN EVENTS IN MY TELLING ARE TAKEN FROM ORAL TRADITIONS—
Bibi Bhani's leadership as she led the realm with the elders while Guru
Arjan traveled, Prithi Chand's assassination attempts on his nephew
Hargobind, and Guru Arjan's compilation and installation of the Aadi
Granth. Bibi Bhani passed away in Goindval around the same time that
Guru Arjan retrieved the remaining shabds from his uncle in Goind-
val, so I wove the two events together in my retelling. Guru Arjan's
trial and torture in Lahore by order of Emperor Jahangir for sheltering
Prince Khusrau is well-documented in historical records. I imagined
into Mata Ganga's experience through all of these events, including a
possible early miscarriage that brought her close to Bibi Bhani. In oral

tradition, a young Mata Ganga longs for a child and visits the elder Baba Budda Ji; she goes to great lengths to ask for his blessing. This story inspired me to imagine Mata Ganga's inner journey from a young uncertain wife to a wise woman elder.

TIMELINE

1589: Mata Ganga marries Guru Arjan

1590: Guru Arjan travels and founds Tarn Taran, Kartarpur, and Sri Hargobindpur

1595: Mata Ganga births Guru Hargobind; Guru Arjan returns to Amritsar

1598: Bibi Bhani passes away in Goindval

1604: Guru Arjan installs the Aadi Granth on the throne in Harmandir Sahib

1605: Mata Ganga and Guru Arjan arrange their son Hargobind's marriage to Damodari

1605: Emperor Akbar passes away; his son Jahangir crushes Prince Khusrau's rebellion

1606: Emperor Jahangir summons Guru Arjan to Lahore to stand trial for treason

       Guru Arjan is tortured and martyred

PART SIX: ACTIVATE POWER

ABOUT MATA GANGA AND GURU HARGOBIND, THE SIXTH GURU

GURU HARGOBIND'S CHOICE TO DON TWO SWORDS, MIRI AND PIRI, is emblazoned in Sikh consciousness. The scenes of his succession ceremony, his call to arms, and his imprisonment in Gwalior Fort are drawn from oral traditions and the epic hagiographic text *Suraj Prakash*

(1843). The length of the Guru's imprisonment in Gwalior is disputed: Some sources say six months, some twelve years, others two years. I chose two years. New historical research from the *Bhatt Vahi* text suggests that Guru Hargobind was five years older than commonly believed, so he would have been nineteen instead of fourteen when imprisoned. I chose fourteen, the age that is most common in Sikh tradition. The Guru's journey out of Gwalior has been told and retold every Divali season on Bandi Chhor Divas. His original legendary cloak (chola) is preserved and displayed at Ghudani Kalan village near Amritsar in Punjab. I imagined into his mother Mata Ganga's experience through all of these events, including her grief after her husband's martyrdom, her role in preparing her son for the ceremony, and how she made the choice to defy a patriarchal culture and name her only granddaughter Veero.

TIMELINE

1606:   Guru Hargobind is officially anointed the sixth Guru in his succession ceremony

1606:   Guru Hargobind builds the Akaal Takht

1609:   Emperor Jahangir imprisons Guru Hargobind in Gwalior Fort

1611:   Guru Hargobind is released, as are fifty-two Hindu kings, the origin of Bandi Chhor Divas
            Guru Hargobind reunites with his first wife, Mata Damodari

1613:   Guru Hargobind marries Mata Nanki, his second wife

1613:   Mata Damodari births Baba Gurditta, their eldest son

1615:   Guru Hargobind marries Mata Mahadevi, his third wife

1615:   Mata Damodari births her daughter Bibi Veero, named by her grandmother Mata Ganga

PART SEVEN: HARNESS RAGE

ABOUT BIBI VEERO AND GURU HAR RAI, THE SEVENTH GURU

THE SCENE OF BIBI VEERO'S WEDDING IN MY RENDITION WAS IN-
spired by the account that appears in the text *Suraj Prakash* (1843). I
imagined into Bibi Veero's experience of the Battle of Amritsar on
her wedding day—her heartache and rage and humanity. In a scene
in *Suraj Prakash*, Bibi Veero is trapped in the Guru's house during
the battle, and two Sikh warriors toss her father Guru Hargobind's
mala to her to prove who they are. That scene inspired me to imagine
an entire history around the pearl mala. In written accounts, Bibi
Veero was devoted to her family of origin and visited Kiratpur often,
so I imagined her conversations with her father and nephew through
the major events of their lives. The scene of young Guru Har Rai
trampling on flowers and vowing not to harm is strong in oral tradition, as is his decision to save the life of Emperor Shah Jahan's son.
Oral tradition holds that he included a single pearl with the medicine
sent to the Emperor.

TIMELINE

1621:	Bibi Veero's youngest brother, Tyag Mal, is born
1621:	Mata Ganga passes away
1627:	Emperor Jahangir dies, succeeded by his son Emperor Shah Jahan
1630:	Har Rai is born to Guru Hargobind's eldest son, Baba Guditta, and Mata Bassi
1631:	Baba Budda Ji passes away at 124
1634:	Bibi Veero's wedding takes place; Emperor Shah Jahan wages the Battle of Amritsar

1635:   Guru Hargobind and his family leave Amritsar for Kiratpur

1636:   Bhai Gurdas Ji passes away in Goindval

1638:   Guru Hargobind's eldest son, Baba Gurditta, passes away

1644:   Guru Hargobind appoints his nephew Guru Har Rai as the seventh Guru
        Guru Hargobind passes away

1645:   Guru Har Rai retires briefly to a village in Sirmoor State in the Shivalik Hills

1658:   Emperor Shah Jahan appoints his eldest son, Dara Shikoh, to succeed him; a battle for succession ensues

1659:   Dara Shikoh is murdered by his brother Aurangzeb, who takes the throne

1660:   Emperor Aurangzeb summons Guru Har Rai, who sends his eldest son, Ram Rai

1661:   Guru Har Rai appoints his five-year-old son, Guru Harkrishan, to succeed him
        Guru Har Rai passes away at thirty-one

PART EIGHT: GRIEVE TOGETHER

ABOUT MATA KRISHAN AND GURU HARKRISHAN, THE EIGHTH GURU

THE CHILD-GURU IS CHERISHED IN THE SIKH TRADITION. I WOVE in the traditional stories about him: He inspires the water carrier's wisdom and charms the Rani of the house; he tends the ill in the streets of Delhi and succumbs to their illness; he passes away by the river, just after declaring "Baba Bakala." I chose to imagine all these events through the eyes of his mother, Mata Krishan. Mata Krishan is also referred to as Mata Sulakhni in Sikh records; I went with Mata Krishan to distinguish her from Guru Nanak's wife. Since Bibi Veero supported her family for generations, I imagined that Bibi Veero assisted Mata Krishan with her son's education and helped her survive her grief.

It was important for me to mention Roop, daughter of Guru Har Rai and Mata Krishan. Roop is known as the first woman-editor in the Sikh tradition: She compiles her father's stories and preserves his memory for future generations. I included her early life with her brother as the foundation for her life's work.

TIMELINE

1656: Mata Krishan births her youngest son, Harkrishan

1661: Guru Harkrishan becomes the eighth Guru after his father's passing

1662: Mata Krishan's daughter Roop marries Khem Karan

1664: Emperor Aurangzeb summons Guru Harkrishan to Delhi to discuss his claim to Guruship

1664: Guru Harkrishan tends the ill of Delhi
Guru Harkrishan falls ill, names "Baba Bakala" as successor, and passes away

PART NINE: CHOOSE COURAGE

ABOUT MATA GUJRI AND GURU TEGH BAHADUR, THE NINTH GURU

I PIECED TOGETHER MATA GUJRI'S EARLY LIFE FROM THE SCRAPS of information we have about her birth, her marriage, and her life in Bakala with her husband before he became Guru. I imagined her inner journey from a young girl separated from her family to becoming a beacon of courage and strength for her people. The story of

Guru Tegh Bahadur's decision to protect the Kashmiri Pandits, his execution, and his cremation is embedded in Sikh consciousness. Sikhs believe the Guru sacrificed himself to protect the Hindu people. Some historians assert that Emperor Aurangzeb executed the Guru in order to squash an armed rebellion; I retold the story according to Sikh tradition. I focused on the role of Mata Gujri in the story and imagined her visits with Mata Krishan and Bibi Veero as events unfolded.

TIMELINE

1624: Mata Gujri is born

1633: Mata Gujri marries Tyag Mal (Guru Tegh Bahadur)

1635: Mata Gujri is exiled along with the Guru's family from Amritsar to Kiratpur

1644: Mata Gujri lives in the village Bakala with her husband and mother-in-law, Mata Nanki

1664: Guru Tegh Bahadur is anointed as the ninth Guru in Bakala

1665: Guru Tegh Bahadur founds the city of Anandpur and embarks on travels

1666: Mata Gujri births her son, Gobind Rai, in Patna

1669: Guru Tegh Bahadur meets his son, Gobind Rai, for the first time in Patna

Mata Gujri and Gobind Rai return to Anandpur

1675: Kashmiri Pandits ask Guru Tegh Bahadur for protection

Guru Tegh Bahadur is arrested, imprisoned, and executed in Delhi

Mata Gujri and Gobind Rai cremate Guru Tegh Bahadur's head in Anandpur

PART TEN: BECOME VICTORY

ABOUT MATA GUJRI AND GURU GOBIND SINGH, THE TENTH GURU

THE STORY OF THE BIRTH OF THE KHALSA ON VAISAKHI DAY 1699 is central in the Sikh tradition. It is retold every springtime on Vaisakhi. Some historians believe that the story as we know it developed a century later; I told the story according to oral tradition. I included the popular detail of Mata Sahib sweetening the amrit. The scene where Mata Sundari wants to volunteer her life is my own addition. I also imagined the scene of how Bibi Veero and Mata Gujri might have met with the Guru and inspired the creation of the Khalsa. It is important to note that Sikhs took on the last names "Kaur" and "Singh" as an explicit rejection of caste. Today, caste prejudices continue to persist in Sikh communities; new generations are reviving the Guru's call to radical equality.

I drew on historical records to tell the story of Emperor Aurangzeb's siege of Anandpur, his promise to offer safe passage to Guru Gobind Singh, his betrayal at the River Sarsa, and his imprisonment of Mata Gujri and her grandchildren. The Sikh tradition celebrates Mata Gujri's strength in the cold tower, and how she fortified the children Baba Fateh and Baba Zoraver to face execution with courage. My retelling embraces the humanity of the children, along with their bravery. I imagined into the sovereign space within Mata Gujri, including during her last breaths.

TIMELINE

> **1687:** Mata Sundari births Baba Ajit, eldest grandson of Mata Gujri
>
> **1691:** Mata Jito births Baba Jujhar, second grandson of Mata Gujri
>
> **1696:** Mata Jito births Baba Zoraver, third grandson of Mata Gujri

1699:　　Mata Jito births Baba Fateh, youngest grandson of
　　　　　Mata Gujri

1699:　　The Khalsa is born on Vaisakhi Day in Anandpur

1700:　　Mata Jito passes away

1704:　　Emperor Aurangzeb lays siege to the city of
　　　　　Anandpur
　　　　　　　Emperor Aurangzeb vows safe passage to Guru
　　　　　　　Gobind Singh and his family;
　　　　　　　Guru Gobind Singh is ambushed by the Emperor
　　　　　　　at the River Sarsa in the Battle of Sarsa

1704:　　Mata Gujri is imprisoned with her youngest grand-
　　　　　children, Baba Fateh and Baba Zoraver
　　　　　　　Baba Fateh and Baba Zoraver are executed;
　　　　　　　Mata Gujri passes away in custody

PART ELEVEN: EMBRACE REBIRTH

ABOUT MAI BHAGO, MATA SUNDARI,
AND THE GURU GRANTH SAHIB,
THE EVERLASTING GURU

THE BATTLES OF GURU GOBIND SINGH ARE WELL-DOCUMENTED IN
Sikh history, including the Battle of Chamkaur, where his eldest sons,
Baba Ajit and Baba Jujhar, perished. The story of the Sikh woman warrior Mai Bhago, who led forty soldiers into the Battle of Muktsar, is
widely celebrated in Sikh tradition; her portrait hangs in gurdwaras
around the world. In my retelling, the women of the village rise to
stand behind her. I imagined her inner world as she made herself anew.
The records show that both Mai Bhago and Mata Sundari were with the
Guru when he held court at Talvandi Sabo. So, I imagined their encounter. Historical records show the emergence of the Tat Khalsa, led
by Mata Sundari after the Guru's passing, in response to the Bandai
Khalsa, those who followed Banda Bahadur. I explored how Mata Sun-

dari found the inner resolve to take the reins of leadership in the Sikh world; I imagined her visit to Bibi Veero as a way she found the power of all the women ancestors inside her.

TIMELINE

1704: Guru Gobind Singh's sons Baba Ajit and Baba Jujhar perish in the Battle of Chamkaur

1705: Mai Bhago leads forty Sikh warriors in the Battle of Muktsar

1705: Mata Sundari and Mata Sahib reunite with Guru Gobind Singh in Talvandi Sabo

1707: Emperor Aurangzeb dies, succeeded by his son Emperor Bahadur Shah

1708: Guru Gobind Singh is stabbed by an assassin
Guru Gobind Singh anoints the sacred canon Sri Guru Granth Sahib as the lasting Guru;
Guru Gobind Singh passes away;
Banda Bahadur leads a campaign for justice (he is executed by imperial forces in 1716)

1708: Mata Sundari leads the Sikh world for the next forty years

GENERAL

ABOUT THE PEARL MALA

THE SIKH GURUS ARE CONSIDERED ONE LIGHT IN TEN BODIES: The light of Guru Nanak passes to each successive Guru. The gifting of the pearl mala is a way to imagine the energy and wisdom passing between the woman ancestors. Every time a Sikh Guru is anointed, he receives the honorific "Guru." So too, in the book, every time a woman ancestor is given the mala, I add the honorific "Bibi," which means elder sister, or "Mata," mother. In their time, these women were called Bibi or Mata by all people, not just their families. They were respected as sisters and mothers to all. These honorifics capture a form of leadership rooted in kinship, care, and love.

ABOUT THE PORTRAITS

"THE PORTRAITS IN THIS BOOK CAPTURE POIGNANT MOMENTS from the lives of the Sikh Gurus and women ancestors. Just as Guru Nanak spent his later years harvesting crops, these illustrations harvest symbols from Sikh poetics to converse with the author's words. Inspired by the orthogonal perspectives and stoic facial expressions in Indian-miniature paintings, the artwork employs artful composition and subtle body language to animate the characters and evoke the emotions of the story. Elements rooted in agrarian life—stones, flowers, herbs, celestial bodies, and human-made sacred objects—are interwoven into the visual tapestry. Traditionally depicted with divine halos, the Sikh Gurus are presented with luminous orbs that extend the enchantment of the narrative. The women ancestors are accorded similar honor, adorned with sacred orbs that capture their powerful wisdom." —KEERAT KAUR

ABOUT LANGUAGE AND TRANSLITERATION

PUNJABI IS THE NAME OF THE LANGUAGE OF THE REGION OF PUNjab in South Asia. Gurmukhi is the name of the script created by the Sikh Gurus for the Punjabi language. My team and I used a transliteration rubric, and we departed from that rubric in instances to help readers approximate the original sounds. We retained standard English spelling for common words like *Punjab* and *gurdwara*. The Sikh ancestors spoke dialects of the fifteenth to seventeenth centuries; I wove in colloquial Punjabi to give us not an exact rendering but a flavor of what they sounded like. I also imagined ways Sikh scripture might have emerged and been recited, shared, and embodied by them. In translating those scriptures, we decided to render most of the names of the Divine or God as "the Beloved," even when it did not match the original. The word best captures the sense of sacred intimacy in Sikh devotional poetry, a way of reimagining God.

ERRORS AND OMISSIONS

I BRING DEEP RESPECT FOR SIKHI AND LOVE FOR THE ANCESTORS to this work. While I have done my best to do right by them, I am certain there are errors and omissions in this book. I ask for forgiveness. These stories, people, and places are dear to millions who walk in the Sikh tradition. This book does not claim to be a definitive interpretation, only how these stories and wisdom come alive in me. To be a Sikh is to learn: This book is my effort to learn, and to share with integrity. May this book inspire us all to reconnect with ancestors and explore how their wisdom lives within us.

Explore the artwork, music, and study guide that
accompany this book at sagewarrior.us

BIBLIOGRAPHY

PRIMARY SOURCES

Sri Guru Granth Sahib Ji
Dasam Granth
Vaara(n) Bhai Gurdas Ji
Janamsakhi Collections: *Bala, Miharban, Adi,* and *Puratan*

SECONDARY SOURCES

Arshi, Pradeep S. *The Golden Temple: History, Art & Architecture*. Harman Publishing House, New Delhi, 1989.

Aulakh, Ajit Singh. *Illustrated Life Stories of Baba Buddha Sahib Ji*. B. Chattar Singh Jiwan Singh, 2008.

Axel, Brian. *The Nation's Tortured Body*. Duke University Press, 2001.

Bhogal, Balbinder Singh. "Text as Sword: Sikh Religious Violence Taken for Wonder." *Religion and Violence in South Asia: Theory and Practice*. Edited by John R. Hinnells and Richard King. Routledge, 2007, pp. 101–31.

Chauhan, G. S., and Meenakshi Rajan. *Shri Guru Nanak Dev: Life, Travels, and Teachings*. All India Pingalwara Charitable Society (Regd.), March 2012.

Dhavan, Purnima. *When Sparrows Become Hawks: The Making of the Sikh Warrior Tradition, 1699–1799*. Oxford University Press, 2011.

Dhillon, Harish. *Janamsakhis: Ageless Stories, Timeless Values*. Hay House India, 2015.

Dhillon, Harish. *The Sikh Curse*. Hay House India, 2018.

Fenech, Louis E. *The Cherished Five in Sikh History*. Oxford University Press, 2021.

Fenech, Louis E., and W. H. McLeod. *Historical Dictionary of Sikhism*. Historical Dictionaries of Religions, Philosophies, and Movements Series. 3rd ed., Rowman & Littlefield Publishers, 2014.

Gill, M. K., editor. *Eminent Sikh Women*. 1st ed., South Asia Books, 1996.

Gill, M. K. *The Role and Status of Women in Sikhism*. National Book Shop, 1998.

Gommans, J. J. L. *Mughal Warfare: Indian Frontiers and Highroads to Empire 1500–1700*. 1st ed., Routledge, 2002.

Grewal, J. S. *History, Literature, and Identity: Four Centuries of Sikh Tradition*. Oxford University Press, 2011.

Grewal, J. S. *The Sikhs of the Punjab*. Cambridge University Press, 1991.

Gupta, Manik Lal. *Sources of Mughal History*. Atlantic Publishers & Distributors, New Delhi, 1989.

Gupta, Shabnam. *Guru Angad Dev: His Life and Teachings*. 2nd ed., Singh Brothers, 2012.

Hess, Linda. *Bodies of Song: Kabir Oral Traditions and Performative Worlds in North America*. Oxford University Press, 2015.

Hess, Linda, and Sukhdev Singh. *The Bijak of Kabir*. Oxford University Press, 2002.

Hundle, Anneeth Kaur. "Sikh Diasporic Feminisms: Provocation 1." *Sikh Formations*, vol. 13, no. 4, 2017, pp. 237–40.

Jain, Harish, editor. *The Making of Punjab*. Unistar Books, 2003.

Kaur, Mallika. *Faith, Gender, Activism in the Punjab Conflict: The Wheat Fields Still Whisper*. Palgrave Macmillan, 2019.

Khalsa-Baker, Nirinjan Kaur. "Engendering the Female Voice in Sikh Devotional Music: Locating Equality in Pedagogy and Praxis." *Sikh Formations Religion Culture Theory*, vol. 15, no. 4, May 2019, pp. 1–41.

Macauliffe, Max Arthur. *The Sikh Religion: Its Gurus, Sacred Writings and Authors: Vol. 1–4*. Oxford at the Clarendon Press, 1909.

Mandair, Arvind-pal Singh, and Christopher Shackle, editors and translators. *Teachings of the Sikh Gurus*. Routledge, 2005.

McLeod, W. H. *The A to Z of Sikhism (Volume 45)* (The A to Z Guide Series, 45). Scarecrow Press, 2009.

Patnaik, Saanika, and Nehal Agarwalla. *Sikhs: The Story of a People, Their Faith and Culture*. DK Publishing, 2023.

Sidhu, G. S. *Sikh Religion and Women*. 1st ed., Guru Nanak Charitable Trust, 2006.

Singh, Bhai Baldeep. "Memory and Pedagogy of Gurbani Sangita: An Auto-ethnographic Udasi." *Sikh Formations*, vol. 15, no. 1–2, 2019, pp. 14–141.

Singh, Jagraj. *A Complete Guide to Sikhism*. Unistar, 2011.

Singh, Jvala. *The Suraj Podcast*. Manglacharan, 2020–Present, https://podcasts.apple.com/us/podcast/suraj-podcast/id1502884205.

Singh, Khushwant. *A History of the Sikhs: Volume 1: 1469–1839*. Princeton University Press, 1963.

Singh, Khushwant. *A History of the Sikhs: Volume 2: 1839–1988*. Princeton University Press, 1966.

Singh, Kirpal. *Janamsakhi Tradition: An Analytical Study*. Singh Brothers, 2004.

Singh, Nikky-Guninder Kaur. *The Birth of the Khalsa: A Feminist Re-Memory of Sikh Identity*. State University of New York Press, 2005.

Singh, Nikky-Guninder Kaur. *Sikhism: An Introduction*. Bloomsbury Publishing, 2011.

Singh, Nikky-Guninder Kaur. *The First Sikh: The Life and Legacy of Guru Nanak*. Viking India, 2019.

Singh, Pashaura. *The Routledge Companion to the Life and Legacy of Guru Hargobind*. Routledge, 2024.

Singh, Sardar Harjeet. *Faith & Philosophy of Sikhism*. Kalpaz Publications, 2009.

Singh, Trilochan. *Guru Tegh Bahadur, Prophet and Martyr*. Gurdwara Parbandhak Committee Sis Ganj, Delhi, Calcutta, 1967.

Singh, Trilochan. *The Turban and Sword of the Sikhs: Essence of Sikhism*. 2nd ed., Bhai Chattar Singh Jiwan Singh, Amritsar, 2001.

Singh, Trilochan, and Anurag Singh. *Nanak Naam Chardi Kala: Celebrating the Life and Legacy of Guru Nanak Dev Ji*. Times Group Books, 2019.

Singha, H. S. *The Encyclopedia of Sikhism (over 1000 Entries)*. 1st ed., Hemkunt Press, 2000.

Tuzuk-i-Jahangiri (Memoirs of Jahangir). Translated by Alexander Rogers. Edited by Henry Beveridge. London Royal Asiatic Society, 1909, pp. 72–73.

Xavier, Jerome Francis. "Letter from Lahore" (1609). Relação Anual das Coisas que Fizeram os Padres da Compenhia de Jesus Nassuas Missõs. Edited by Father Fernão Guerreiro, 1609. Reprint, Coimbre Impresnsa da Universidade, 1931, pp. 369–70.

PUNJABI LANGUAGE SOURCES

Aulakh, Ajit Singh. *Sri Gur Pratap Suraj Granth Steek*. Bhai Chattar Singh Jiwan Singh, 2010.

Kaur, Preetam. *Guru Tegh Bahadur, Rachna te Rehas*. Manjit Printing and Publication Company, Chandigarh, 1976.

Kaur, Simran. *Parsidh Sikh Bibiyan*. Singh Brothers, 2002.

Nabha, Bhai Kahan Singh. *Gurshabd Ratanakar Mahan Kosh*. Lahore Books Ludhiana, 2017.

Seetal, Sohan S. *Gur-Itihaas Das Patshaheea(n)*. Lahore Book Shop, Ludhiana, 2011.

Singh, Bhagat. *Gurbilas Patshahi 6*. Edited by Gurmukh Singh. Publication Bureau Punjabi University, Patiala, 1997.

Singh, Bhai S. *Sri Gur Pratap Suraj Granth*. Edited by Kirpal Singh. Dharam Parchar Committee, Amritsar, 2008.

Singh, Bhai V. *Vaara(n) Bhai Gurdas Ji, Steek*. Bhai Vir Singh Sahit Sadan, 2011.

Singh, Giani H. *Vaara(n) Bhai Gurdas Ji, Steek*. Khalsa Sahit Sadan, Amritsar, 2008.

Singh, Giani Jujhar "Azaad." *Mata Sahib Kaur, Khalsay Di Mata*. Bhai Chattar Singh Jiwan Singh, 2008.

Singh, Paramveer. *Mata Sundri Ji, Sangarsh ate Shakhsiyat*. Singh Brothers, Amritsar, 2012.

Singh, Professor Sahib. *Gur Itihaas Patshahi 2 to 9*. Singh Brothers, Amritsar, 2006.

Singh, Sangat. *Itihaas'ch Sikh*. Vishesh Pustaka(n), New Delhi, 1996.

Singh, Shaheed Bhai Mani. *Sikhan di Bhagat Mala*. Edited by Bhai Vir Singh. Bhai Vir Singh Sahit Sadan, 2011.

Talvarra, Bhai Joginder Singh. *Jeevan Katha Sri Guru Amardass Ji*. Singh Brothers, Amritsar, 2004.

ACKNOWLEDGMENTS

This book was written in community—in quiet communion with ancestors, in rich conversations with Sikh elders, sisters, brothers, and peers, and in joyful storytelling circles with our children. To all who joined me in this journey: This book is infused with your energies and insights—and love.

Chris Jackson, my editor at One World, made our journey possible. He saw the medicine that Sikh wisdom holds for our time and gave me the freedom to retrieve and reimagine these stories. Our working relationship is like none other in my life, anchored in profound trust, mutual learning, and deep inspiration. I am grateful to him and the entire One World team for believing in this book. To my literary agent, Margaret Riley-King, thank you for finding a home for my work, and for blessing this book with your early notes.

Dr. Nirinjan Kaur Khalsa was my senior collaborator. She heard this book into being from the beginning, listened to my first renderings of these stories, reviewed every draft, and labored with me over every choice. As a professor of Sikh studies, she taught early drafts of this book at Loyola Marymount University: I sent her a chapter, she taught it the next day, and we integrated what we learned into the next draft. I am so grateful to her students. Nirinjan authored the study guide that accompanies this book. Her scholarly rigor, tender witness, and sisterly love were daily gifts.

Jasvir Kaur Rababan was our senior co-conspirator. She gathered with my family in the rainforest as I read aloud the first complete draft. After every chapter, my mother made chaa and we all talked for hours. Jasvir's notes were brilliant, culturally sensitive, and spiritually grounded. She researched, transliterated, and translated alongside me with tireless dedication. She crafted raag-based compositions of the sacred poems in the book. She was our amazing guide on our family trip to Punjab. To Jasso and Baaj: Our sisterhood is a powerful wellspring of wonder, creativity, and courage.

Sonny Singh created the official musical album *Sage Warrior* that accompanies this book. He composed new renditions of the shabds, the sacred poems, that appear in each story. It was an electrifying process: He sent me music tracks as I wrote; I sent him chapters as he composed. The book and album were birthed together. It was a joy to collaborate with my longtime brother.

Keerat Kaur created the beautiful portraits of the Sikh Gurus and women ancestors that open each part of the book, along with the map of Punjab. She wove vivid story elements into each original artwork, which in turn inspired my retelling. In our collaboration, I found a new sister. In her portraits, our ancestors come to life.

Nimarta Narang served as dedicated researcher and lead consultant, building a strong foundation for the project. She pored through countless books, surfaced historical details, edited drafts, and compiled our bibliography. Nimarta, thank you for helping me center Bibi Nanki from the start.

My mother, Dolly Kaur Brar, was our guardian on this journey. In this book, she saw a tapestry of all the stories she loved; she infused the text with her childhood memories of these stories and poured hours into research and transliteration. We translated the sacred poems in the book together with Jasvir and Nirinjan. Only when my mother gave her blessing was the translated verse complete. And we celebrated with her kheer. My mother was our Mata Khivi, bringing out the best in us. This book was born of her radiant care.

As the project unfolded, we began to gather people in our living room to hear the stories in this book. I told the stories (katha) alongside sacred music (kirtan). My Sikh sisters performed traditional raag-based kirtan—Jasvir on the rabab and dilruba, Nirinjan on the jori drum— and we were all transported to the riverbanks of our ancestors. Then, our brother Sonny Singh sang his bold new renditions with his trumpet, ushering us into new experiences of the sacred. My children joined in: Kavi on the tabla, Ananda singing on my lap. After the story was done, we gathered in conversation as my mother fed us all. Thank you to all who joined us: Your input at our "samagams" shaped the final text of this book.

I honor the great Sikh scholars and storytellers who came before us. Dr. Nikky-Guninder Kaur Singh paved the way for our generation of Sikh feminist thought. Her body of work—translations and stories, essays and histories—instructed and inspired us. The scholarship of Dr. Arvind-pal Mandair and Dr. Balbinder Bhogal profoundly shaped my approach to Sikh ethics. Dr. Pashaura Singh, prolific Sikh historian, carefully read early drafts and helped us align the text with historical record and collective memory. Bhai Baldeep Singh, revivalist of Sikh musical and wisdom traditions, ensured that we rendered the ancestors with integrity. Dr. Brian Axel wielded his pen like a sword, cutting excess and sharpening my first draft. Dr. Linda Hess, scholar of the sage-poet Kabir and my lifelong teacher, masterfully reviewed every line of the final proof. Mirabai Starr, author and translator of mystical texts, was the godmother of this book with her beautiful encouragement.

Thank you to the many Sikh readers—scholars, artists, activists, and educators—who read drafts and contributed to retelling our ancestors' stories, including: Aasees Kaur, Amandeep Singh, Gurmeet Kaur, Harleen Kaur, Inni Kaur, Preeti Kaur, Anusha Mehar, Tejpreet Kaur Saini, Neetu Kaur Sandhu, Angad Singh, Dr. Anurag Singh, Deeptej Singh, Gurmustuk Singh, and T. Sher Singh. This project was fueled by the support of Nitasha Kaur Sawhney, community leader and my elder sister. I am grateful to all my elders, especially Dr. Jaswant Singh Sachdev, for their blessings.

I am lucky to have deep friendships with women who are also powerful writers. Brynn Saito, poet and professor, heard my first rendering of these stories and reflected back the gold. She helped me see how Sikh ancestors could speak to all of us. Jessica Chen Weiss counseled me nearly every day and read my drafts. With deep love, she reconnected me to the joy of choosing courage as daily practice.

I am indebted to all my early readers for your caring notes: Rupa Balasubramaniam, Sharon Groves, Dr. Hille Haker, Jessica Jenkins, Dr. John Paul Lederach, Amy Olrick, Faizah Malik, Rev. Brian McLaren, Rev. Scotty McLennan, Rev. Tracy Wells Miller, Dr. Deonnie Moodie-King, Eric Parrie, Prachi Patankar, Elizabeth and Tom Rand, and Ryan Piers-Williams. Julianna Piazolla encouraged me to go deeper into the inner worlds of the women ancestors. My cousin Sharmila Kaur Singh listened as I read her the final manuscript, and sealed it with her love.

The meditations in the book were inspired by my teachers and master practitioners: Kim Gillingham and her transformative instruction in Creative Dreamwork, Richard Schwartz and his groundbreaking work Internal Family Systems, and Tommy Woon and his lifelong mentorship in somatic literacy and Breaths Together for a Change. I am grateful to Naomi Aeon for her wise coaching; she empowered me to live into Oneness without fear.

To my team at the Revolutionary Love Project, thank you for building the channels for people to apply the wisdom in this book: Melissa Canlas, Sharon Groves, Annette Luba-Lucas, Leo Martinez, Anusha Mehar, Amy Olrick, Harini Padmanaban, and Ashley Torres. I am grateful to our phenomenal collaborators, including Michael Skolnik and his team at Soze, Cleo Barnett and her team at Amplifier, Cara Tripicchio and Marla Farrell at Shelter PR, and Connor Buss at Forward Films. Thank you to our whole team at One World—including Avideh Bashirrad, Elizabeth Mendez-Berry, Nicole Counts, Hiab Debessai, Carla Bruce-Eddings, Lulu Martinez, and Sun Robinson-Smith. I am indebted to Rupa Balasubramaniam for her brilliant guidance as we build the Revolutionary Love movement.

As I wrote this book, I found encouragement in my conversations with friends and colleagues, including: Ari Afsar, Michelle Alexander, Natalie Antoci, Rabbi Sharon Brous, Tommy Clancy, Arelis Diaz, Ani DiFranco, Shepard and Amanda Fairey, America Ferrera, Michelle

Goldhaber, Rev. Victor Kazanjian, Kalia Lydgate, Rev. Michael-Ray Matthews, Shannon Moore-Langston, Rev. Jacqui Lewis, Mark Nepo, Maren Nielsen, Parker Palmer, Brandon Piper, john powell, Lauren Oleykowski, Layla Saad, Reva Siegel, Joey Soloway, Baratunde Thurston, Jeremy Wallace, Zach Warren, and Rainn Wilson. I was enriched by my exchanges with visionary thinkers brought together by Auburn Seminary, the Fetzer Institute, Harness, W. K. Kellogg Foundation, One World, and Pop Culture Collaborative.

Thank you to the caregivers who supported me as I worked on this book: Delia Soza for loving daily care for our family, Roxana Rodriguez and William Barrondo for helping keep our house in order, and Jamie Brewster for healing bodywork. I am grateful to my parents and my husband's parents, Vidya and Tonse Raju, for meals and playdates with the children. I was uplifted time and again by my cousin-sisters, Andrea (Simran), Anika, Ginny, Neena, Neetu, Serena, and Sharmila. My cousin Jyoti Didi took care of us in India, and my aunt and uncle in our ancestral village, Chand Navan. To Happy, thank you for your skillful driving (and equally skilled patience).

This book originated in a deep conversation about Sikh history with my brother, Sanjeev Brar. He urged me to write the story of the Sikh Gurus through my eyes. As always, my brother opened my heart to new possibilities. Sanjeev, this book would not be without you.

During my summers of writing in the rainforest, my father, Judge Singh Brar, drove me down the mountain every day to write in a little café by the river, and took me back up before the afternoon rains. He listened to these stories with tears in his eyes. He and my mother made this journey joyful and sacred.

I found my greatest support in my partner, Sharat Raju. He organized our trip to India, listened to me distill the stories when we got home, protected space for me to write, and poured his brilliance as a storyteller and writer into this text. Every day, he counseled me, helped me hear the wisdom within me, *and* made me laugh. As he has for twenty years. Because of him, this beautiful life.

Kavi and Ananda: You listened to these stories many times and brought out their magic. You colored the chart on our wall after every completed chapter, popped popcorn, and danced with me. I love when you sing me the sacred songs. Your great-grandfather, Captain Gurdial Singh Gill, transmitted the spirit of the sage warrior to me; it is alive in you. Papa Ji would be so proud of you. May the ancestors accompany you all the days of your life.

ABOUT THE AUTHOR

VALARIE KAUR is a visionary civil rights leader, lawyer, award-winning filmmaker, educator, innovator, and bestselling author of *See No Stranger* and *World of Wonder*. Her work has reached millions worldwide and inspired a movement to reclaim love as a force for justice. She now leads the Revolutionary Love Project, where she equips communities to answer the call to love and courage. A daughter of Punjabi Sikh farmers in California, Kaur earned degrees at Stanford University, Harvard Divinity School, and Yale Law School, and holds several honorary doctorates. In 2022, Kaur was honored at the White House in the first-ever Uniters Ceremony, recognizing her as a prophetic leader whose work is healing America. She lives with her family in a multigenerational home in Los Angeles.